Macromedia
Dreamweaver
Introductory Concepts and Techniques

Gary B. Shelly
Thomas J. Cashman
Dolores J. Wells

THOMSON

COURSE TECHNOLOGY

COURSE TECHNOLOGY
25 THOMSON PLACE
BOSTON MA 02210

SHELLY
CASHMAN
SERIES®

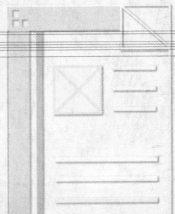

Australia • Canada • Denmark • Japan • Mexico • New Zealand • Philippines • Puerto Rico • Singapore
South Africa • Spain • United Kingdom • United States

Macromedia Dreamweaver MX
Introductory Concepts and Techniques
Gary B. Shelly
Thomas J. Cashman
Dolores J. Wells

Managing Editor:
Cheryl Ouellette

Marketing Manager:
Katie McAllister

Senior Product Manager:
Alexandra Arnold

Product Manager:
Erin Runyon

Associate Product Manager:
Reed Cotter

Editorial Assistant:
Emilie Perreault

Print Buyer:
Denise Powers

Director of Production:
Becky Herrington

Production Manager:
Doug Cowley

Developmental/Copy Editor:
Ginny Harvey

Proofreader:
Lori Silfen

Illustrators:
Michelle French
Andrew Bartel

Cover Design:
Kenny Tran
Michelle French

Signing Representative:
Cheryl Ouellette

Compositor:
Jeanne Black

Printer:
Banta Company

Dreamweaver MX
Introductory Concepts and Techniques

Contents

Preface

The Shelly Cashman Series® offers the finest textbooks in computer education. We are proud of the fact that our textbook series has been the most widely used series in educational instruction. We are pleased to announce the addition of the Macromedia® Dreamweaver® MX textbooks to the series with *Macromedia Dreamweaver MX: Introductory Concepts and Techniques*. This book continues with the innovation, quality, and reliability that you have come to expect from the Shelly Cashman Series.

Macromedia Dreamweaver is known as the standard in visual authoring. Macromedia Dreamweaver MX is a significant upgrade to previous editions and enhances the work experience for users in the following ways: (1) an intuitive new workspace that uses panels and views; (2) templates designed for customized layout control; (3) prebuilt code libraries; (4) increased server support for ASP, JSP, and ColdFusion® applications; (5) XML and Web Standards support; (6) improved cascading style sheet support; and (7) new coding and accessibility features.

In this *Macromedia Dreamweaver MX* book, you will find an educationally sound and easy-to-follow pedagogy that combines a step-by-step approach with corresponding screens. All projects and exercises in this book are designed to take full advantage of the Dreamweaver MX enhancements. The popular Other Ways and More About features offer in-depth knowledge of Dreamweaver MX. The project material is developed carefully to ensure that students will see the importance of learning Dreamweaver for future coursework.

Objectives of This Textbook

Macromedia Dreamweaver MX: Introductory Concepts and Techniques is intended for a course that covers a brief introduction to Dreamweaver MX. No experience with a computer is assumed, and no mathematics beyond the high school freshman level is required. The objectives of this book are:

- To teach students how to use Dreamweaver MX
- To expose students to proper Web site design and management techniques
- To acquaint students with the proper procedures to create Web sites suitable for coursework, professional purposes, and personal use
- To develop an exercise-oriented approach that allows learning by doing
- To encourage independent study, and help those who are working alone

The Shelly Cashman Approach

Features of the Shelly Cashman Series *Macromedia Dreamweaver MX* books include:

- **Project Orientation:** Each project in the book presents a practical problem and complete solution in an easy-to-understand approach.
- **Step-by-Step, Screen-by-Screen Instructions:** Each of the tasks required to complete a project is identified throughout the project. Full-color screens accompany the steps.
- **Thoroughly Tested Projects:** Every screen in the book is correct because it is produced by the author only after performing a step, resulting in unprecedented quality.
- **Other Ways Boxes:** The Other Ways boxes displayed at the end of many of the step-by-step sequences specify the other ways to do the task completed in the steps. Thus, the steps and the Other Ways box make a comprehensive reference unit.
- **More About Feature:** These marginal annotations provide background information and tips that complement the topics covered, adding depth and perspective.

■ Integration of the World Wide Web: The World Wide Web is integrated into the Dreamweaver MX learning experience by (1) More About annotations that send students to Web sites for up-to-date information and alternative approaches to tasks; and (2) the Dreamweaver companion Web site, scsite.com/dreamweavermx.

Organization of This Textbook

Macromedia Dreamweaver MX: Introductory Concepts and Techniques provides detailed instruction on how to use Dreamweaver MX. The material is divided into an introduction chapter, three projects, four appendices, and a quick reference summary.

Introduction – Introduction to Web Development and Macromedia Dreamweaver In the Introduction, students are presented with the basics of the Internet and World Wide Web and their associated terms. Topics include differentiating between Web pages and Web sites and types of Web pages; identifying Web browser features; an overview of planning, designing, developing, testing, publishing, and maintaining a Web site; a discussion of HTML; various methods and tools used in Web site creation; and a brief description of the new features in Dreamweaver MX.

Project 1 – Creating a Dreamweaver Web Page and Local Site In Project 1, students are introduced to the Dreamweaver environment. Students create a local site and the home page for the Web site that they develop throughout the projects in the book. Topics include starting and quitting Dreamweaver; an introduction to the Dreamweaver workspace; creating a local site; creating a Web page and applying a color scheme and formatting properties to the Web page; inserting line breaks and special characters; inserting a horizontal rule and an absolute link; using the Check Spelling feature; previewing and printing a page in a Web browser; and an overview of Dreamweaver Help.

Project 2 – Adding Web Pages, Links, and Images In Project 2, students learn how to add new pages to an existing Web site and then how to add links and images. Topics include using Dreamweaver's integrated file browser feature; understanding and modifying image file formats; adding background and page images to a Web page; creating relative, absolute, and e-mail links; changing the color of links and editing and deleting links; using the site map and Link Checker; showing the page in Code view; and using Code view to modify HTML code.

Project 3 – Tables and Page Layout In Project 3, students are introduced to techniques for using tables in Web site design. Topics include an introduction to page layout using Standard view and Layout view to design a Web page; modifying a table structure; understanding HTML table tags; adding content to a table and formatting the content; formatting the table; and creating head content.

Appendices The book includes four appendices. Appendix A presents an introduction to the Macromedia Dreamweaver Help system. Appendix B describes Dreamweaver Authoring for Accessibility features; and Appendix C explains how to use Fireworks for image modification within Dreamweaver. Appendix D illustrates how to define and publish a Web site to a remote server.

Quick Reference Summary In Dreamweaver, you can accomplish a task in a number of ways, such as using the mouse, menu, context menu, and keyboard. The Quick Reference Summary provides a quick reference to common keyboard shortcuts.

End-of-Project Student Activities

A notable strength of the Shelly Cashman Series *Macromedia Dreamweaver MX* books is the extensive student activities at the end of each project. Well-structured student activities can make the difference between students merely participating in a class and students retaining the information they learn. The activities in the Shelly Cashman Series *Dreamweaver MX* books include the following:

- **What You Should Know** A listing of the tasks completed within a project together with the pages on which the step-by-step, screen-by-screen explanations appear.
- **Apply Your Knowledge** This exercise usually requires students to open and manipulate a file on the Data Disk. To obtain a copy of the Data Disk, follow the instructions on the inside back cover of this textbook.
- **In the Lab** Three in-depth assignments per project require students to apply the knowledge gained in the project to solve problems on a computer.
- **Cases and Places** Five unique real-world case-study situations.

Shelly Cashman Series Instructor Resources

The ancillaries that accompany this textbook are Instructor Resources (ISBN 0-7895-6555-2) and Online Content. These ancillaries are available to adopters through your Course Technology representative or by calling one of the following telephone numbers: Colleges and Universities, 1-800-648-7450; High Schools, 1-800-824-5179; Private Career Colleges, 1-800-347-7707; Canada, 1-800-268-2222; Corporations with IT Training Centers, 1-800-648-7450; and Government Agencies, Health-Care Organizations, and Correctional Facilities, 1-800-477-3692.

Instructor Resources

The contents of the Instructor Resources CD-ROM are listed below.

- **Instructor's Manual (Lesson Plan and Teaching Tips)** The Instructor's Manual includes the following for each project: project objectives; a file listing table with all files from the data disk and created from scratch; and detailed lecture notes that include teacher notes with page number and figure references, classroom activities, and projects to assign.
- **Syllabus** Any instructor who has been assigned a course at the last minute knows how difficult it is to come up with a course syllabus. For this reason, sample syllabi are included that can be customized easily to a course.
- **PowerPoint Presentation** This lecture ancillary contains a PowerPoint presentation for each project in the textbook. You also may make these PowerPoint presentations available to students on a network for project review, or to be printed for distribution.
- **Figures Files (Illustrations from the Text)** Illustrations for every screen and table in the textbook are available in electronic form.
- **Solutions to Exercises** Solutions to the end-of-project exercises including required files for all the In the Lab assignments and sample answers for any Cases and Places assignment that supplies data at the end of each project are available.
- **Test Bank and Test Engine** ExamView is a state-of-the-art test builder that is easy to use. With ExamView, you quickly can create printed tests, Internet tests, and computer (LAN-based) tests. You can enter your own test questions or use the test bank that accompanies ExamView. A Word document version of the test bank containing 110 questions for every project (25 multiple-choice, 50 true/false, and 35 fill-in-the-blank) with page number references and transparency references also is available.

■ **Data Files for Students** All files required by students to complete the Apply Your Knowledge exercises are included.

Online Content

If you use Blackboard or WebCT, a free test bank for this textbook is available in a simple, ready-to-use format. Visit the Instructor Resource Center for this textbook at course.com to download the test bank, or contact your local sales representative for details.

Acknowledgments

The Shelly Cashman Series would not be the leading computer education series without the contributions of outstanding publishing professionals. First, and foremost, among them is Becky Herrington, director of production and designer. She is the heart and soul of the Shelly Cashman Series, and it is only through her leadership, dedication, and tireless efforts that superior products are made possible.

Under Becky's direction, the following individuals made significant contributions to these books: Doug Cowley, production manager; Ginny Harvey, series specialist and developmental editor; Ken Russo, senior Web and graphic designer; Michelle French, graphic artist and cover designer; Jeanne Black, Betty Hopkins, and Kellee LaVars, QuarkXPress compositors; Lori Silfen and Richard Hansberger, proofreaders; and Cristina Haley, indexer.

Finally, we would like to thank Richard Keaveny, associate publisher; Cheryl Ouellette, managing editor; Jim Quasney, series consulting editor; Alexandra Arnold, senior product manager; Erin Runyon, product manager; Reed Cotter, associate product manager; Emilie Perreault, editorial assistant; and Katie McAllister, marketing manager.

Gary B. Shelly
Thomas J. Cashman
Dolores J. Wells

Macromedia Dreamweaver MX 30-Day Trial Edition

A copy of the Dreamweaver MX 30-Day trial edition can be found on the Macromedia Web site (www.macromedia.com). Click DOWNLOADS in the left pane and follow the on-screen instructions. When you activate the software, you will receive a license that allows you to use the software for 30 days. Course Technology and Macromedia provide no product support for this trial edition. When the trial period ends, you can purchase a copy of Macromedia Dreamweaver MX, or uninstall the trial edition and reinstall your previous version.

The minimum system requirements for the 30-day trial edition is a Pentium II-class processor, 300+ MHz; Windows XP, 2000, NT, ME, or 98 (160 MB RAM); Netscape Navigator or Internet Explorer 4.0 or higher; 96 MB of available RAM (128 MB recommended); 275 MB available disk space; and a 256-color monitor capable of 800 × 600 resolution (1024 × 768, millions of colors recommended).

Macromedia Dreamweaver MX

Introduction to Web Development and Macromedia Dreamweaver

You will have mastered the material in this project when you can:

OBJECTIVES

- Describe the significance of the Internet and its associated terms
- Describe the World Wide Web and its associated terms
- Identify the difference between the Internet and the World Wide Web
- Specify the difference between a Web page and a Web site
- Define Web browsers and identify their main features
- Identify the six types of Web pages
- Discuss how to plan, design, develop, test, publish, and maintain a Web site
- Identify the various methods and tools used to create a Web page and Web site
- Recognize the basic tags within HTML
- Discuss the advantages of using Web page authoring programs such as Dreamweaver
- Describe the new features of Dreamweaver MX

Macromedia Dreamweaver MX

Introduction to Web Development and Macromedia Dreamweaver

The Internet

The **Internet**, sometimes simply called the **Net**, is a global network, connecting millions of computers. Within this global network, a user who has permission at any one computer can access and obtain information from any other computer within the network. A **network** is a group of computers and associated devices that are connected by communications facilities. A network can span a global area and involve permanent connections, such as cables, or temporary connections made through telephone or other communications links. Within this global network are local, regional, national, and international networks. Each of these networks provides communications, services, and access to information.

The Internet has had a relatively brief, but explosive history. This network grew out of an experiment begun in the 1960s by the U.S. Department of Defense (DOD). Today, the Internet is a public, cooperative, and self-sustaining facility that is accessible to hundreds of millions of people worldwide.

The World Wide Web and Web Browsers

The **World Wide Web** (**WWW**), also called the **Web**, is the most popular service on the Internet. The Web consists of a system of global **network servers** that supports specially formatted documents and provides a means for sharing these resources with many people at the same time. A network server is known as the **host computer**, and your computer, from which you access the information, is called the **client**. The protocol that enables the transfer of data from the host computer to the client is the **Hypertext Transfer Protocol** (**HTTP**).

Accessing the Web

Users access Web resources, such as text, graphics, sound, video, and multimedia, through a **Web page**. Every Web page is identified by a unique address, or Uniform Resource Locator (URL). The URL provides the global address of the location of the Web page. URLs are discussed later in this Introduction. To view data contained on a Web page requires a Web browser. A **Web browser** is a software program that requests a Web page, interprets the code contained within the page, and then displays the contents of the Web page on your computer display device.

Web Browsers

Web browsers contain special buttons and other features to help you navigate through Web sites. The more popular Web browser software programs are **Microsoft Internet Explorer** and **Netscape Navigator**. This book uses Internet Explorer. When you start Internet Explorer, it opens to a Web page that has been set as the start, or home, page (Figure I-1). The home page can be any page on the Web and can be designated by the user through the browser Tools menu. Important features of Internet Explorer are summarized in Table I-1 on the next page.

More About

Protocols

Another widely used protocol is File Transfer Protocol (FTP), which is a protocol used on the Internet for uploading files. To learn more about protocols, visit the Dreamweaver MX More About Web page (scsite.com/dreamweavermx/more.htm) and then click Protocols.

FIGURE I-1

Table I-1	Internet Explorer Features
FEATURE	**DEFINITION**
Title bar	Displays the name of the program and the name of the Web page you are viewing
Menu bar	Displays the name of the menus; each menu contains a list of commands you can use to perform tasks such as printing, saving, editing, and so on
Standard Buttons toolbar	Contains buttons, boxes, and menus that allow you to perform tasks more quickly than using the menu bar and related menus
Address bar	Displays the Web site address, or URL, of the Web page you are viewing
Document window	Contains the Web page content

Nearly all Web pages have unique characteristics, but almost every Web page contains the same basic elements. Common elements you find on most Web pages are headings or titles, text, pictures or images, background enhancements, and hyperlinks. A **hyperlink**, or **link**, can link to another place in the same Web page or to an entirely different Web page. Normally, you click the hyperlink to follow the link pathway. Figure I-2 illustrates navigating a Web site using different types of links.

Most Web pages are part of a Web site. A **Web site** contains a home page, which generally is the first Web page visitors see when they enter the site. A **home page** provides information about the Web site's purpose and content. Most Web sites also contain additional content and pages. Each Web site is owned and managed by an individual, company, or organization.

NAVIGATING USING A VARIETY OF LINKS

FIGURE 1-2a Link Displays in Different Color

FIGURE 1-2b   Link Underlined

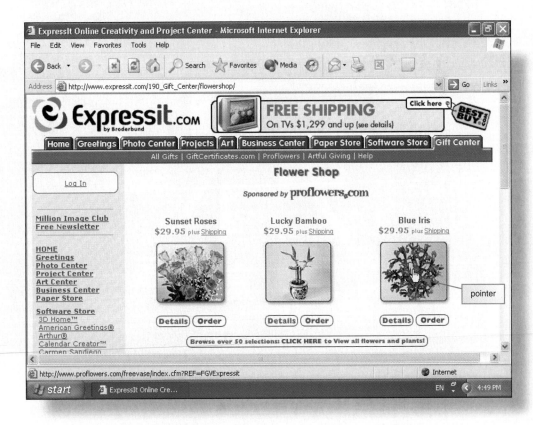

FIGURE 1-2c   Graphical Image Used as Link

More *About*

Wireless Service Providers

Wireless service providers (WSPs) offer a broad range of plans and may include features such as no roaming charges or unlimited minutes. To learn more about WSPs, visit the Dreamweaver MX More About Web page (scsite.com/dreamweavermx/more.htm) and then click Service Providers.

Accessing the Web requires a connection through a regional or national Internet service provider (ISP), an online service provider (OSP), or a wireless service provider (WSP). An **Internet service provider** (**ISP**) is a business that has a permanent Internet connection and provides temporary connections to individuals, companies, or other organizations. An **online service provider** (**OSP**) is similar to an ISP, but provides additional member-only services, such as financial data, travel information, and so on. America Online is an example of an OSP. A **wireless service provider** (**WSP**) provides Internet access to users with Web-enabled devices or wireless modems. Generally, all of these services charge a fee.

Figure I-3 below illustrates ways to access the Internet using these service providers. **Point of presence** (**POP**) is a telephone number that gives you dial up access.

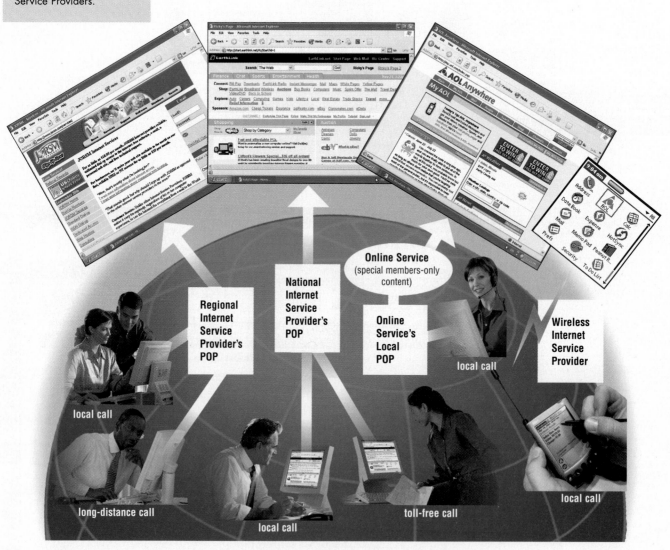

FIGURE I-3

Types of Web Pages

The six basic types of Web pages are portal, news, business/marketing, advocacy, informational, and personal. A **portal Web page** (Figure I-4a) provides a variety of Internet services from a single, convenient location. Most portals offer free services such as search engines, local, national, and worldwide news, sports and weather, reference tools, maps, stock quotes, newsgroups, chat rooms, calendars, and so on. A **news Web page** (Figure I-4b) contains news articles relating to current events. A **business/marketing Web page** (Figure I-4c) contains content that promotes or sells products or services. Within an **advocacy Web page** (Figure I-4d), you will find content that describes a cause, question, or idea. An **informational Web page** (Figure I-4e on the next page) contains factual information, such as research, statistics, sports scores, and so on. Governmental agencies and nonprofit organizations are the primary providers of informational Web pages. A **personal Web page** (Figure I-4f on the next page) is published by an individual. As you progress through this book, you will have an opportunity to develop these types of Web pages.

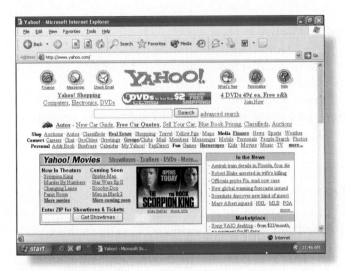

(a) Portal Web Page

(b) News Web Page

(c) Business/Marketing Web Page

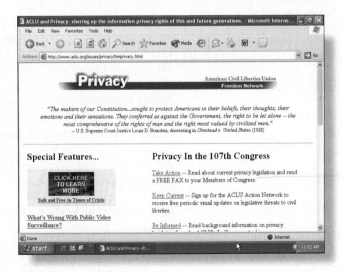

(d) Advocacy Web Page

FIGURE I-4

(e) Informational Web Page

(f) Personal Web Page

FIGURE I-4 (continued)

Planning a Web site

Although it is easy to publish a Web page, advanced planning is paramount in ensuring a successful Web site. Publishing a Web site, which makes it available on the Internet, is discussed later in this Introduction. Thousands of individuals create and publish Web pages every day, some using word processing software or markup languages to create their pages. Others use professional HTML editors such as Dreamweaver.

Planning Basics - Purpose

Those who rush into the publishing process without the proper planning tend to design Web sites that are unorganized and difficult to navigate. Visitors to this type of Web site will lose interest quickly and will not return. As you begin planning your Web site, consider the following guidelines to ensure you set realistic goals and attain them.

PURPOSE AND GOAL Determine the purpose and goal of your Web site. Create a focus by developing a **purpose statement**, which communicates the intention of the Web site. Consider the six basic types of Web pages previously mentioned. Will your Web site consist of just one basic type or a combination of two or more types?

TARGET AUDIENCE Identify your audience. The people who visit your Web site will determine whether your Web site is a success. Although you welcome all visitors, you need to know as much as possible about your target audience. To learn more about the visitors to your Web site, determine whether you want to attract people with similar interests, and consider gender, education, age range, income, profession/job field, and computer proficiency.

NEW WEB TECHNOLOGIES Evaluate whether your potential visitors have access to high-speed broadband media or baseband media, and use this information to determine what elements to include within your Web site. **Broadband** transmits multiple signals simultaneously and includes media and hardware such as **T1 lines, DSL**

More About

Web Site Planning

The first step in creating your Web site is to define the purpose. Consider what you want to accomplish and then list your objectives. To learn more about Web site planning, visit the Dreamweaver MX More About Web page (scsite.com/dreamweavermx/more.htm) and then click Web Site Planning.

(**digital subscriber lines**), or **cable modems. Baseband** transmits one signal at a time and includes media and hardware such as 28K to 56K modems. Baseband works well with a Web site composed mostly of text and small images. Web sites that contain many images or **multimedia,** such as video and animations, generally require that the visitor has a broadband connection.

WEB SITE COMPARISON   Visit other Web sites that are similar to your proposed site. What do you like about these sites? What do you dislike? Look for inspirational ideas. How can you make your Web site better?

Planning Basics – Content

An informative, well-planned Web site is not difficult to create. To ensure a successful Web experience for your visitors, consider the following guidelines to provide appropriate content and other valuable Web page elements.

VALUE-ADDED CONTENT   Consider the different types of content to include within your Web site. Use the following as guidelines:

- What topics do you want to cover?
- How much information will you present about each topic?
- What will attract your target audience to your Web site?
- What methods will you use to keep your audience returning to your site?
- What changes will you have to make to keep your site updated?

TEXT   Because text is the primary component of most Web pages, be brief and incorporate lists whenever possible. Use common words and simple language, and check your spelling and grammar. Create your textual content to accomplish your goals effectively.

IMAGES   After text, images are the most commonly included content. Ask yourself these questions with respect to your use of images:

- Will you have a common logo and/or theme on all Web pages?
- Are these images readily available?
- What will you have to locate?
- What will you have to create?
- How many images per page?

MULTIMEDIA   Multimedia adds interactivity and action to your Web pages. Animation, audio, and video are types of multimedia. If you plan to add multimedia, determine whether the visitor will require plug-ins. A **plug-in** extends the capability of a Web browser. Some of the more commonly used plug-ins are Shockwave™ Player, Macromedia Flash™, and RealNetworks® RealPlayer®. Most plug-ins are free and can be downloaded from the Web.

COLOR PALETTE   The color palette you select for your Web site can enhance or detract from your message or goal. Do not think in terms of your favorite colors, but consider how color can support your goal. Ask yourself the following questions:

- Do your selected colors work well with your goal?
- Are the colors part of the universal 216 browser-safe color palette?
- Did you limit the number of colors to a selected few?

More *About*

DSL

DSL technology uses existing 2-wire copper telephone wiring to deliver high-speed data services to homes and businesses. DSL provides almost instant access to bandwidth-intensive applications such as streaming audio/video, online games, application programs, video conferencing, and other high-bandwidth services. To learn more about DSL, visit the Dreamweaver MX More About Web page (scsite.com/ dreamweavermx/ more.htm) and then click DSL.

Designing a Web Site

It is not possible to predict how a visitor will access a Web site or at what point the visitor will enter within the Web site structure. Visitors can arrive at any page within a Web site by a variety of ways: a hyperlink, a search engine, a directory, typing a Web address directly, and so on. On every page of your Web site, you must provide clear answers to the two basic questions your visitors will ask, Where am I? and Where do I go from here? A well-organized Web site provides the answers to these questions. Once the visitor is at a Web site, **navigation**, which is the pathway through your site, must be obvious and intuitive. Individual Web pages cannot be isolated from the rest of the site if the site is to be successful. Most Web designers use a navigation map to visualize the navigation pathway.

Design Basics – Navigation Map

A **navigation map** outlines the structure of the entire Web project, showing all of the pages within the site and the connections from one page to others. The navigation map provides the structure, or road map, through the Web site, but does not provide detail as to the content of the individual pages. Consider the following for site navigation.

STRUCTURE The goal and the type of a Web site is a major determinant in the type of structure selected for a specific Web site. The navigation map serves as a blueprint for your navigational structure. Consider the following navigational structure types and determine which one best meets your needs:

▶ In a **linear structure**, (Figure I-5a) the user navigates sequentially, moving from one page to the next. This is the simplest way to organize a Web site. Information that flows as a narrative, timeline, or in logical order is ideal for sequential treatment. Simple sequential organization, however, usually works only for smaller sites. Many online tutorials use a linear structure.

▶ A **hierarchical structure** (Figure I-5b) is one of the better ways to organize complex bodies of information. This type of structure is well-suited for Web sites because most visitors are familiar with hierarchical charts. For a hierarchical structure to be effective requires thorough organization of content.

▶ A **web structure** (Figure I-5c), which also is called a **random structure**, poses few restrictions on organizational patterns. This type of structure is associated with the free flow of ideas and can be confusing to a user. Random structure is better suited for experienced users looking for further education or enrichment and is not recommended if your goal is a basic understanding of a particular topic. If a Web site is relatively small, however, a random structure could work well.

▶ If a Web site consists of a number of topics of equal importance, a **grid structure** (Figure I-5d) could be the best navigational choice. Procedural manuals, events, and item lists are examples of content suited for this type of structure.

▶ Large Web sites frequently use a **hybrid structure**, which is a combination of the above listed structures, to organize information (Figure I-6).

More About

Design

Poor site design will discourage Web site visitors. To learn more about good Web site design, visit the Dreamweaver MX More About Web page (scsite.com/ dreamweavermx/ more.htm) and then click Web Site Design.

(a) Linear Structure

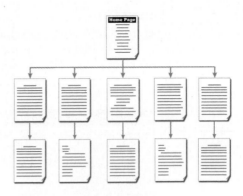

(b) Hierarchical Structure

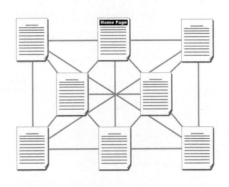

(c) Web Structure   **(d) Grid Structure**

FIGURE I-5

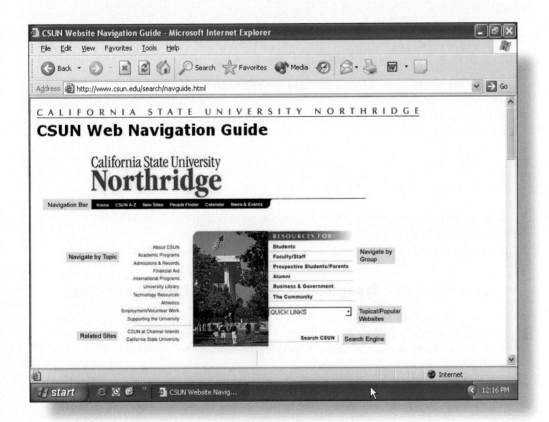

FIGURE I-6

TOOLS Determine the tool to be used to create the navigation map. If your Web site is small, the organizational chart included in the Microsoft Office applications, shown in Figure I-7 using PowerPoint, is an easy-to-use tool. For larger, more diverse Web sites, Visio Professional, Flow Charting PDQ, FlowCharter Professional, and OrgPlus are programs you can use to chart and organize your Web site.

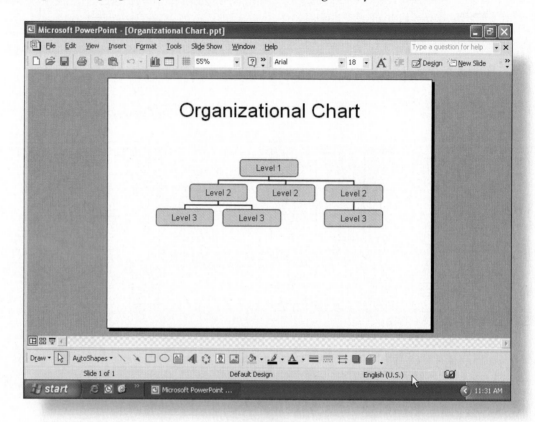

FIGURE I-7

NAVIGATION ELEMENTS The more common types of navigation elements include text, buttons, other images, image maps, a site index, menu, search feature, and frames. Depending on the complexity of your Web site, you may want to include some or all of these elements.

Developing a Web Site

Once the structure is complete, the next step is to develop the Web site. Because text and images are a Web site's more common elements, make them your main focus. Then consider page layout and color.

Development Basics – Typography, Images, Page Layout, and Color

The combination of typography, images, page layout, and color comprise the elements of your finished Web page. Correct use of these elements plays an important part in the development process. Consider the following guidelines.

TYPOGRAPHY Good **typography**, which is the appearance and arrangement of characters that make up your text, is just as important for a Web page as it is in any other medium. A **font** consists of all the characters available in a particular style and weight for a specific design. Selecting fonts for display on a computer screen, however, is different from selecting fonts for a magazine, a book, or other printed medium. Although the text displays on a computer screen and not on a piece of paper, it still should be easy to read. As a viewer of a Web page, you may consciously never notice the **typeface**, which is the design of the text characters, but the typeface subconsciously affects your reaction to the page.

When selecting the font, determine its purpose. Is it to be used for a title? For onscreen reading? Is it likely to be printed? Will the font fit in with the theme of the Web site? Is it a Web-safe font, such as Times New Roman, Courier, or Arial? **Web-safe fonts** are the more popular fonts and ones that most visitors are likely to have installed on their computers.

IMAGES Using images can enhance almost any Web page if used appropriately. Without the visual impact of shape, color, and contrast, Web pages can be uninteresting graphically and will not motivate the visitor to investigate their contents. Images and page performance are issues for many visitors. When adding images, consider your potential audience and the technology they have available. Also remember that a background image or a graphical menu increases visitor download time. You may lose visitors who do not have broadband access if your Web page contains an excessive number of graphical items.

PAGE LAYOUT The importance of proper page layout cannot be overemphasized. A suitable design draws visitors to your Web site. Although no single design is appropriate for all Web pages, a consistent, logical layout allows you easily to add text and images. The Web page layouts shown in Figure I-8 illustrate two different layouts. The layout on the left (Figure I-8a) illustrates a plain page without text or images. The page layout on the right (Figure I-8b) presents strong visual contrast by using a variety of layout elements. In laying out your Web pages, consider the following guidelines to ensure visitors have the best viewing experience.

- Include only one topic per page
- Control the vertical and horizontal size of the page
- Start text on the left to accommodate the majority of individuals who read from left to right
- Use concise statements to get your point across; studies indicate most people scan the text

More About

Web-Safe Fonts

When creating your Web site, the best approach is to specify your favorite common font and include alternate choices for those users who do not have that font installed. To learn more about fonts, visit the Dreamweaver MX More About Web page (scsite.com/ dreamweavermx/ more.htm) and then click Fonts.

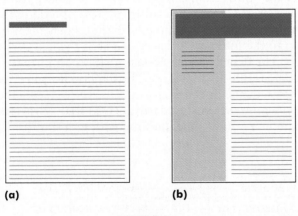

(a)   (b)

FIGURE I-8

COLOR When creating a Web page, use color to add interest and vitality to your site. Color can be used in tables, as backgrounds, and with fonts. Use the right combination of colors to decorate the layout and to tie the Web site pages together.

Reviewing and Testing a Web Site

Some Web site developers argue that reviewing and testing should take place throughout the developmental process. While this may be true, it also is important to review and test the final product. This ongoing process ensures that you identify and correct any problems before publishing to the Web. When reviewing and testing your Web site, ask the following questions.

- Is the Web site free of spelling and/or grammatical errors?
- Is the page layout consistent and does it generate a sense of balance and order?
- Are any links broken?
- Do multimedia interactivity and forms function correctly?
- Does the Web site display properly in the most widely used browsers?
- Does the Web site function in different browsers, including older browser versions?
- Have you initiated a **group test** in which you have asked other individuals to test your Web site and provide feedback?

Publishing a Web Site

After thoroughly testing your Web site, it can be published. **Publishing** a Web site is the process of making it available to your visitors. This step involves the actual uploading of the Web site to a server. After the uploading process is completed, all pages within the Web site should be tested again.

Publishing Basics — Domain Name, Server Space, and Uploading

With a Web site thoroughly tested and problems corrected, you must make the site available to your audience by obtaining a domain name, acquiring server space, and uploading your Web site. Consider the following to ensure site availability.

OBTAIN A DOMAIN NAME So visitors can access your Web site, you must obtain a domain name. Web sites are accessed by an IP address or a domain name. An **IP address** (**Internet Protocol address**) is a number that uniquely identifies each computer or device connected to the Internet. A **domain name** is the text version of an IP address (Figure I-9). The **Domain Name System** (**DNS**) is an Internet service that translates domain names into IP addresses. The **Uniform Resource Locator** (**URL**), also called a **Web address**, tells the browser on which server to locate the Web page. A URL consists of a communications standard, such as **HTTP** (**Hypertext Transfer Protocol**), the domain name, and sometimes the path to a specific Web page.

| IP address ———————→ | 199.95.72.10 |
| Domain name ———————→ | www.scsite.com |

FIGURE I-9

More *About*

Reviewing and Testing Your Web Site

A Web site should be tested at various stages of the development process. A compatibility test verifies that the Web site works with a variety of browser versions. To learn more about Web site testing, visit the Dreamweaver MX More About Web page (scsite.com/ dreamweavermx/ more.htm) and then click Testing Your Web Site.

More *About*

Domain Names

It is not unusual to read news articles describing where domain name owners fail to pay their registration fees and then lose their domain names. To learn more about domain name registration, visit the Dreamweaver MX More About Web page (scsite.com/ dreamweavermx/ more.htm) and then click Domain Names.

Domain names are unique and must be registered. The **Accredited Registrar Directory** provides a listing of **Internet Corporation for Assigned Names and Numbers** (**ICANN**) accredited domain name registrars. Your most difficult task likely will be to find a name that is not already registered. Use a specialized search engine at one of the many accredited domain name registrars you will find listed on the ICANN Web site (icann.org) to locate a name. In addition to registering your business name as a domain name, you may want to register the names of your products, services, and/or other related names. Expect to pay approximately $20 to $35 per year for a domain name.

Consider the following guidelines when selecting a domain name.

▶ Select a name that is easy to pronounce, spell, and remember.
▶ Select a name that relates to the Web site content and suggests the nature of your product or service.
▶ If the Web site is a business, use the business name.
▶ Select a name that is free and clear of trademark issues.

Some ISPs will obtain a domain name for you if you use their service to host your Web site.

ACQUIRE SERVER SPACE Locate an ISP that will host your Web site. Recall that an ISP is a business that has a permanent Internet connection. These providers offer temporary connections to individuals and companies free or for a fee.

If you select an ISP that provides free server space, most likely your visitors will be subjected to advertisements and pop-up windows. Other options to explore for free server space include the provider from which you obtain your Internet connection; **online communities,** such as Yahoo! GeoCities (geocities.yahoo.com), Tripod (tripod.com), and MSN Web Communities (communities.msn.com); and your educational institution's Web server.

If the purpose of your Web site is to sell a product or service or to promote a professional organization, you should consider a fee-based ISP. Use a search engine such as Google (google.com) and search for Website hosting, or visit Hosting Repository (hostingrepository.com) where you will find thousands of Web hosting plans and reviews and ratings of Web hosting providers. Selecting a reliable provider requires investigation on your part. Many providers provide multiple hosting plans. Consider the following questions and how they apply to your particular situation and Web site when selecting an ISP:

1. What is the monthly fee? Is a discount available if you sign up for a year? Are setup fees charged?
2. How much server space is provided for the monthly fee? Can you purchase additional space? If so, how much does it cost?
3. What is the average uptime on a monthly basis? What is the average downtime?
4. What are the server specifications? Can they handle many users? Do they have battery backup power?
5. Are **server logs**, which keep track of the number of accesses, available?
6. What is their connectivity – how do they connect to the Internet: OC3, T1, T3, or other?
7. Is a money-back guarantee offered?
8. What technical support do they provide and when is it available? Do they have an online knowledge base?
9. Does the server on which the Web site will reside have CGI capabilities and Active Server Page (ASP) support?
10. Does the server on which the Web site will reside support e-commerce, multimedia, and **Secure Sockets Layer** (**SSL**) for encrypting confidential data such as credit card numbers? Are additional fees required for these capabilities?

More *About*

Selecting a Domain Name

When selecting a domain name, keep it simple. If possible, it is best to avoid hyphens. To learn more about domain name selection, visit the Dreamweaver MX More About Web page (scsite.com/ dreamweavermx/ more.htm) and then click Domain Name Selection.

UPLOAD THE WEB SITE Copy, or upload, the files from your computer to the server where your Web site will be accessible to anyone on the Internet. **Uploading** is the process of transmitting from your computer all the files that comprise your Web site to the selected server or host computer. Files that make up your Web site can include Web pages, images, audio, video, and animation.

A variety of tools and methods exist to manage the upload task. Some of the more popular of these are FTP applications, Windows Web Publishing Wizard, Web Folders, and Web authoring programs such as Dreamweaver. These tools allow you to link to a remote server, enter a password, and then upload your files. An FTP program, such as WS_FTP, is the most widely used method to upload files. Dreamweaver contains a built-in function similar to independent FTP programs. The Dreamweaver FTP function to upload your Web site is covered in Project 3.

Maintaining a Web Site

Most Web sites require maintenance and updating. Some types of ongoing Web maintenance include the following:

> Changing content, either adding new or deleting obsolete text and images
> Checking for broken links and adding new links
> Documenting the last change date (even when no revisions have been made)

Use the information from the server logs provided by your ISP to determine what needs to be updated or changed. Statistics contained within these logs generally include the number of visitors trying to access your site at one time, what resources they request, how long they stay on the site, at what point they enter the site, pages they view, and what errors they encounter. Learning to use and apply the information contained within the server log will help you to make your Web site successful.

After updates and/or changes are made to the site, notify your viewers with a What's New announcement.

Methods and Tools Used to Create Web Pages

Web developers have several options for creating Web pages: a text editor, an HTML editor, software applications, or a WYSIWYG editor. Microsoft Notepad and WordPad are examples of a **text editor**. These simple, easy-to-use programs allow the user to enter, edit, save, and print text. An **HTML editor** is a more sophisticated version of a text editor. In addition to basic text-editing functions, more advanced features, such as syntax highlighting, color-coding, and spell checking are available. **Software applications**, such as Microsoft Word, Excel, and Publisher, provide a Save as Web Page command on the File menu. This feature converts the application document into an HTML file. Examples of a **WYSIWYG editor** are programs such as Microsoft FrontPage and Macromedia Dreamweaver. These programs provide an integrated text editor with a graphical user interface that allows the user to view both the code and the document as it is being created.

A Web developer can use any of these options to create Web pages. Regardless of the option selected, however, it still is important to understand the specifics of HTML.

HTML

Web pages are written in plain text and saved in the American Standard Code for Information Interchange format. The **American Standard Code for Information Interchange**, or **ASCII** (pronounced ASK-ee), is the most widely used coding system to represent data. Using the ASCII format makes Web pages universally readable by different Web browsers regardless of the computer platform on which they reside.

Hypertext Markup Language (**HTML**) is an authoring language that defines the structure and layout of a document so that it displays as a Web page in a Web browser, such as Microsoft Internet Explorer or Netscape Navigator. A Web page has two components: source code and document content. The **source code**, which contains tags, is program instructions. The **tags** within the source code control the appearance of the document content. **Document content** is the text and images that the browser displays. The browser interprets the tags contained within the code. The code instructs the browser how to display the Web page. For instance, if you define a line of text on your Web page as a heading, the browser knows to display this line as a heading.

All HTML tag formats are the same. They start with a left angle bracket (< or less than symbol) followed by the name of the tag and end with a right angle bracket (> or greater than symbol). Most tags have a start and an end tag and are called **two-sided tags**. The end tags are the same as the start tags except they are preceded by a forward slash (/). Some HTML tags, such as the one used to indicate a line break <BR>, do not have an end tag. These are known as **one-sided tags**. Other tags, such as the one to indicate a new paragraph <P>, have an end tag, but the end tag can be omitted. For consistency with this type of tag, it is better to include both the start and end tags.

Some tags can contain an **attribute**, or **property**, which is additional information placed within the angle brackets. Attributes are not repeated or contained in the end tag. Some attributes are used individually and other attributes can include a value modifier. A **value modifier** specifies conditions within the tag. For example, you can use a value modifier to specify the font type or size or the placement of text on the page. To create and display a centered heading, for instance, you would use the following code:

```
<H1 ALIGN="CENTER">This is the largest header tag and the text will be centered</H1>
```

In this example, H1 is the HTML tag, ALIGN is the attribute, and CENTER is the value modifier. Notice that the attribute does not appear as part of the end tag.

You can use Microsoft Notepad or WordPad (which are text editors) to create HTML documents. You place each tag in a pair around the text or section that you want to define (**mark up**) with that tag. HTML tags are not case sensitive; therefore, you can enter HTML tags in uppercase or lowercase or a combination of both. To be consistent, however, you should adopt a standard practice when typing tags. Examples in this book use uppercase.

HTML tags also are used to format the hyperlinks that connect information on the World Wide Web. HTML tags number in the hundreds, but some are used more than others. All documents, however, require four basic tags. Figure I-10 on the next page illustrates the basic tags required for all HTML documents. Table I-2 on the next page summarizes the most commonly used HTML tags.

More *About*

HTML

The World Wide Web Consortium (W3C) develops and updates Web protocols. To learn more about the most recent changes to HTML, visit the Dreamweaver MX More About Web page (scsite.com/ dreamweavermx/ more.htm) and then click W3C.

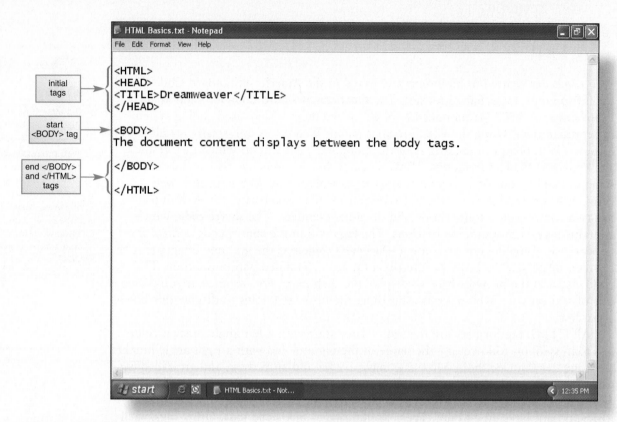

FIGURE I-10

Table I-2 Commonly Used HTML Tags

TAG	STRUCTURE
<HTML>...</HTML>	Encloses the entire HTML document
<HEAD>...</HEAD>	Encloses the head of the HTML document
<BODY>...</BODY>	Encloses the body of the HTML document

TAG	TITLE AND HEADINGS
<TITLE>...</TITLE>	Indicates the title of the document
<H1>...</H1>	Heading level 1
<H2>...</H2>	Heading level 2
<H3>...</H3>	Heading level 3
<H4>...</H4>	Heading level 4
<H5>...</H5>	Heading level 5
<H6>...</H6>	Heading level 6

TAG	PARAGRAPHS, BREAKS, AND SEPARATORS
<P>...</P>	Plain paragraph; end tag optional
 	Line break
<HR>	Horizontal rule line

TAG	LISTS
<OL>...</OL>	Ordered, numbered list
<UL>...</UL>	Unordered, bulleted list
<MENU>...</MENU>	Menu list of items
<DIR>...</DIR>	Directory listing
<LI>...</LI>	List item, used with <OL>,<UL>,<MENU>,<DIR>
<DL>...</DL>	Definition of glossary list
<DT>...</DT>	Definition term; part of a definition list
<DD>...</DD>	Corresponding definition to a definition term

TAG	CHARACTER FORMATTING
<B>...</B>	Bold text
<U>...</U>	Underline text
<I>...</I>	Italic text

TAG	LINKS
<A>...</A>	Combined with the HREF attribute, creates a link to another document or anchor
<A>...</A>	Combined with the NAME attribute, creates an anchor which can be linked to

TAG	IMAGE
<IMG>...</IMG>	Inserts an image into the document

Web Page Authoring Programs

Many of today's Web page authoring programs, including Dreamweaver, are a What You See Is What You Get (WYSIWYG) HTML text editor. A **WYSIWYG text editor** allows a user to view a document as it will appear in the final product and to edit the text, images, or other elements directly within that view. Before programs such as Dreamweaver existed, Web page designers were required to type, or hand-code, Web pages. Educators and Web designers still debate the issue surrounding the necessity of knowing HTML. You do not need to know HTML to create Web pages in Dreamweaver, but an understanding of HTML will help you if you need to alter Dreamweaver-generated code. If you know HTML, then you can make changes to code and Dreamweaver will accept the changes.

Macromedia Dreamweaver® MX

Dreamweaver is the standard in visual authoring. Macromedia Dreamweaver MX is part of the new MX product family that includes Macromedia Flash™ MX, ColdFusion® MX and Fireworks® MX. Dreamweaver includes features that access these separate products. Some of the new features of Dreamweaver MX include the following:

- An intuitive new workspace
- Templates designed for customized layout control
- Prebuilt code libraries
- Server technology to support ColdFusion MX, ASP.NET, and PHP websites
- Increased server support for ASP, JSP and ColdFusion applications
- XML and Web Standards Support
- Improved cascading style sheet support
- New coding features
- New accessibility features

Dreamweaver makes it easy to get started and provides you with helpful tools to enhance your Web design experience. Working in a single environment, you create, build, and manage Web sites and Internet applications. The workspace environment is customizable to fit your particular needs.

Coding tools and features included within Dreamweaver are references for HTML, cascading style sheets (CSS), and JavaScript and code editors that allow you to edit the code directly. **Macromedia Roundtrip® HTML technology** imports HTML documents without reformatting the code. Downloadable extensions from the Macromedia Web site make it easy to add functionality to any Web site. Examples of some of these extensions include shopping carts and online payment features.

Instead of writing individual HTML files for every page, use a database to store content and then retrieve the content dynamically in response to a user's request. Implementing and using this feature, you can update the information one time instead of manually editing many pages.

Dreamweaver allows you to publish Web sites with relative ease to a local area network that connects computers in a limited geographical area or on the Web for anyone with Internet access. The concepts and techniques presented in this book provide the tools you need to plan, develop, and publish professional Web sites, such as Web sites shown in Figures I-11 and I-12 on the next page.

> More *About*
>
> **Macromedia**
>
> Evaluation copies of Dreamweaver MX and other Macromedia products are available on the Macromedia Web site. To learn more about Macromedia products, visit the Dreamweaver MX More About Web page (scsite.com/dreamweavermx/more.htm) and then click Macromedia.

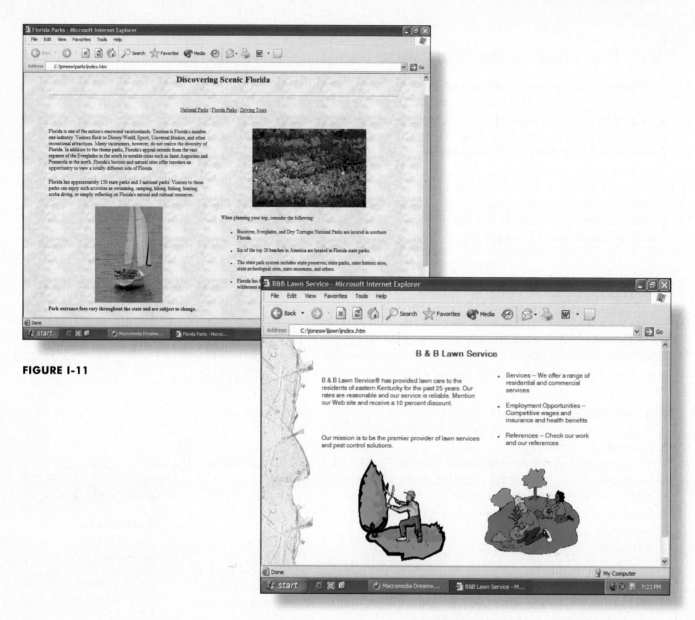

FIGURE I-11

FIGURE I-12

Summary

The Introduction to Web Development and Macromedia Dreamweaver provided an overview of the Internet and the World Wide Web and the key terms associated with those technologies. An overview of the six basic types of Web pages was presented. The Introduction presented information on developing a Web site, including planning basics. Designing a Web site and each phase within this process was discussed. Testing, publishing, and maintaining a Web site was also presented, including an overview of obtaining a domain name, acquiring server space, and uploading a Web site. Methods and tools used to create Web pages were introduced. A short overview of HTML and some of the more commonly used HTML tags were presented. Finally, the advantages of using Dreamweaver in Web development were discussed. These advantages include a WYSIWYG editor; a visual, customizable development environment; accessibility compliance; downloadable extensions; database access capabilities; and in-product reference sources.

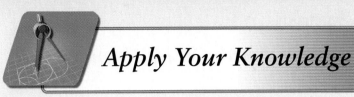

Apply Your Knowledge

1 Web Page Creation

Instructions: As discussed in this chapter, creating a Web site involves planning, designing, developing, reviewing and testing, publishing, and maintaining. Open the applyI.doc file on the Dreamweaver Data Disk. See the inside back cover of this book for instructions for downloading the Data Disk or see your instructor for information on accessing the files required for this book. As shown in Table I-3, the applyI.doc file contains information about the Web site creation process. Enter your answer to the questions in this table to develop a plan for creating a Web site.

Table I-3 Creating a Web Site		
PLANNING		
Web site name:	What is your Web site name?	
Web site type:	What is the Web site type: portal, news, business/ marketing, advocacy, informational, personal?	
Web site purpose:	What is the purpose of your Web site?	
Target Audience:	How can you identify your target audience?	
Web Technologies to be used:	Will you design for broadband or baseband? Explain your selection.	
Content:	What topics will you cover? How much information will you present on each topic? How will you attract your audience? What will you do to entice your audience to return to your Web site? How will you keep the Web site updated?	
Text, images, and multimedia:	Will your site contain text only? What type of images will you include? Where will you obtain your images? Will you have a common logo? Will plug-ins be required?	
DESIGNING		
Navigation map:	What type of structure will you use? What tools will you use to design your navigation map?	
Navigational elements:	What navigational elements will you include?	
DEVELOPING		
Typography:	What font will you use? How many different fonts will you use on your site?	
Images:	How will you use images to enhance your site? Will you use a background image?	

(continued)

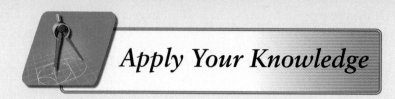

Apply Your Knowledge

Web Page Creation *(continued)*

Table I-3 Creating a Web Site		
DEVELOPING *(continued)*		
Page Layout:	What type of layout will you use? How many topics per page? How will text be presented: bulleted or paragraph style? Will the audience need to scroll the page?	
Color:	What color combinations will you use for your site? To what elements will you apply the color(s) — fonts, background, tables, other elements?	
REVIEWING AND TESTING		
Review:	What elements will you review? Will you use a group review?	
Testing:	What elements will you test? Will you use self-testing? Will you use group testing?	
PUBLISHING		
Domain name:	What is your domain name? Have you registered your domain name? What ISP will host your Web site? What criteria did you use to select the ISP?	
MAINTAINING		
Ongoing maintenance:	How often will you update your Web site? What elements will you update? Will you add additional features? Does your ISP provide server logs? Will you use the server logs for maintenance purposes?	

Perform the following steps using your word processing program and browser.

1. With the file applyI.doc open in your word processing program, select a name for your Web site.
2. Use a specialized search engine at one of the many accredited domain name registrars to verify that your selected Web site name is available.
3. Answer each question in the table. Type your answers in column 3.
4. Save the document with the file name, knowI-1.doc. Print a copy of the document and hand it in or e-mail it to your instructor.

In the Lab

1 Using Internet Explorer

Problem: Internet Explorer (IE) 6 is Microsoft's latest Web browser. IE has many new features that can make your work on the Internet more efficient. Using the Media bar, for example, you can play music, video, or multimedia files, listen to your favorite Internet radio station, and enhance your browsing experience. You can customize the image toolbar that displays when you point to an image on a Web page. IE also includes other enhancements. Visit the Microsoft Internet Explorer How-to Articles Web page (Figure I-13) and select three articles containing topics with which you are not familiar. Read the articles and then create a word processing document detailing what you learned.

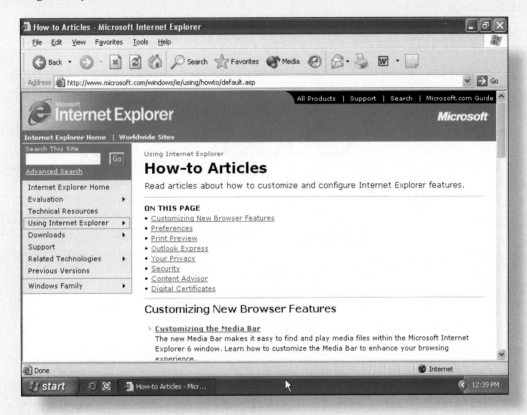

FIGURE I-13

Instructions: Perform the following tasks.

1. Start your browser. Open the Microsoft Internet Explorer How-to Articles Web page (microsoft.com/windows/ie/using/howto/default.asp).
2. Select three articles that contain information with which you are not familiar.
3. Click the link for each article and read the article.
4. Start your word processing program.
5. List three important points that you learned from this Web site.
6. Write a summary of what you learned from each article. Include within your summary your opinion of the article and if you will apply what you learned or use it with your Web browser.
7. Save the document with the file name, labI-1.doc. Print a copy of the document and hand it in or e-mail it to your instructor.

In the Lab

2 Types of Web Pages

Problem: A Web designer is familiar with different types of Web pages and the type of information displayed on these types of Web pages. The Introduction describes six types of Web pages. Search the Internet and locate at least one example of each type of Web page.

Instructions: Perform the following tasks.

1. Start your browser. Open the Google (google.com) search engine Web page (Figure I-14) and search for an example of the following types of Web pages: portal, news, business/marketing, advocacy, informational, and personal.

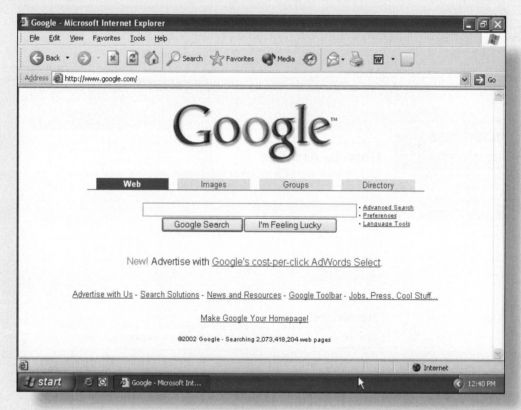

FIGURE I-14

2. Start your word processing program.
3. Copy and paste the link from each of these Web page types into your word processing document.
4. Identify the type of Web page for each link.
5. Explain why you selected this Web page and how it fits the definition of the specific type.
6. Save the document with the file name, labI-2.doc. Print a copy of the document and hand it in or e-mail it to your instructor.

In the Lab

3 Web Site Hosting

Problem: Selecting the correct host or ISP for your Web site can be a confusing process. Many Web sites offer this service, but determining which one is best for your particular needs can be somewhat complicated. Assume your Web site will sell a product. Compare several ISPs and select one that will best meet your needs.

Instructions: Perform the following tasks.

1. Review the information and questions on page DW I.15 discussing guidelines for acquiring active service space to host your Web site.
2. Start your browser. Open the Hosting Repository Web page shown in Figure I-15.

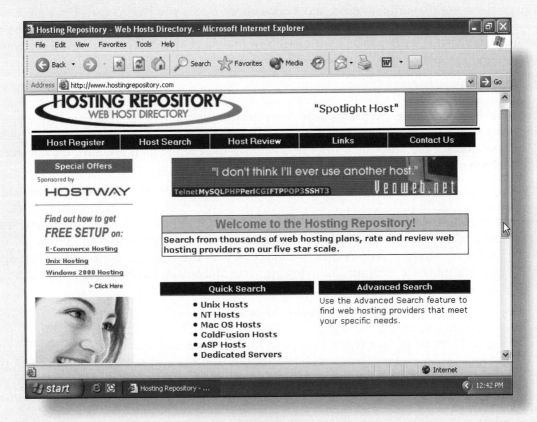

FIGURE I-15

3. Click the Dedicated Servers link.
4. Click one of the host server links and review the information relating to the services offered by your selected ISP.
5. Start your word processing program.
6. Read and answer the ten questions on page DW I.15. Use the information provided in the services offered by your selected ISP.
7. Write a short summary explaining why you would or would not select this ISP to host your Web site.
8. Save the document with the file name, labI-3.doc. Print a copy of the document and hand it in or e-mail it to your instructor.

Cases and Places

The difficulty of these case studies varies:
▶ are the least difficult; ▶▶ are more difficult; and ▶▶▶ are the most difficult.

1 ▶ Use a search engine such as Google (google.com) and research information about planning a Web site. Use your word processing program and write a two-page summary of what you learned. Save the document as caseI-1.doc. Print a copy and hand it in or e-mail a copy to your instructor.

2 ▶ Your goal is to create a personal Web site navigation map that contains three pages – the home page, a page about your favorite hobbies, and a page about places you like to visit. On a piece of paper, draw a navigation map for your proposed Web site. Write a sentence or two describing the type of structure you used and why you selected that structure. Save the document as caseI-2.doc. Print a copy of the document and hand it in or e-mail it to your instructor.

3 ▶▶ Plug-ins are used on many Web sites. Start your browser and search for plug-ins. Prepare a list of the plug-ins you found. Create a summary statement describing how and why you could use each plug-in in a Web site. Include the link where you can download each of the plug-ins. Save the document as caseI-3.doc. Print a copy of the document and hand it in or e-mail it to your instructor.

4 ▶▶ Typography within a Web page is one of its more important elements. Start your browser and search for examples of Web sites that include what you consider appropriate typography and Web sites with inappropriate typography. Write a short summary of why you consider these appropriate and inappropriate. Copy and paste the Web site addresses into your document. Save the document as caseI-4.doc. Print a copy of the document and hand it in or e-mail it to your instructor.

5 ▶▶▶ Web site structures are of four types: linear, hierarchical, grid, and random. Search the Internet for Web sites illustrating each of these structures. Describe the Web site and explain why you think this is an appropriate or inappropriate structure for that particular Web site. Include the Web site addresses for each site. Save the document as caseI-5.doc. Print a copy of the document and hand it in or e-mail it to your instructor

Macromedia Dreamweaver MX

PROJECT

Creating a Dreamweaver Web Page and Local Site

You will have mastered the material in this project when you can:

O B J E C T I V E S

- Describe Dreamweaver and identify its key features
- Start Dreamweaver
- Describe the Dreamweaver window and workspace
- Open and close panels
- Create a local site using the Site Definition Wizard
- Create a Web page
- Apply a color scheme
- Display and describe the Property inspector
- Format and modify text elements on a Web page
- Insert a horizontal rule
- Define and display the Insert bar
- Define and insert a line break and special characters
- Change a Web page title
- Check spelling
- Insert an absolute link
- Save a Web page
- Preview a Web page in a Web browser
- Print a Web page
- Define Dreamweaver Help
- Quit Dreamweaver
- Open a Web page

Macromedia Dreamweaver MX

Creating a Dreamweaver Web Page and Local Site

CASE PERSPECTIVE

Florida native Will Jones worked with you last summer at a state environmental agency. Your job at the agency included Internet communications. Because you both love the outdoors, particularly Florida's state and national parks, you became good friends. Will visits several parks every year. During each visit, he discovers something new and exciting. Will wants to share his knowledge and provide a way to make Florida residents and visitors aware of the uniqueness, beauty, and wildlife of the parks.

Will knows the far-reaching capabilities of the Internet. He wants to use the Web to communicate to the public about Florida's parks, but he has limited knowledge about Web design and development. Will knows that your interest and experience with the Internet could assist him in this endeavor, and he asks for your help. You like the idea and tell him that you can create a Web site using Dreamweaver. You get together to plan the index page. When you are finished creating the Discovering Scenic Florida Web page, you will show it to Will for his feedback.

What Is Macromedia Dreamweaver® MX?

Macromedia Dreamweaver® MX is a powerful Web page authoring and Web site management software program and HTML editor used to design, code, and create professional-looking Web pages. The visual editing features of Dreamweaver allow you to create pages without writing a line of code. Dreamweaver provides many tools and features, including the following:

▶ **Automatic Web Page Creation** – Dreamweaver provides the tools you can use to develop your Web pages without having to spend hours writing HTML code. Dreamweaver automatically generates the HTML code necessary to publish your Web pages.

▶ **Web Site Management** – Dreamweaver enables you to view a site, including all local and remote files associated with the selected site. Using Dreamweaver, you can perform standard maintenance operations such as viewing, opening, and moving files; transferring files between local and remote sites; designing your site navigation with the Site Map; and more.

▶ **Standard Macromedia Web Authoring Tools** – Dreamweaver includes a user interface that is consistent across all Macromedia authoring tools. This consistency enables easy integration with other Macromedia Web-related programs, such as Macromedia Flash™, Director® Shockwave® Studio, ColdFusion®, and others.

Other key features include the integrated user interface, the integrated file explorer, panel management, database integration, and standards and accessibility support. Dreamweaver MX is customizable and can run in operating systems such as Windows XP, Windows 2000, Windows NT, and Mac OS X.

Project One — Florida Parks

To create documents similar to those you will encounter on the Web and in academic, business, and personal environments, you can use Dreamweaver to produce Web pages such as the Discovering Scenic Florida Web page shown in Figure 1-1. The Web page shown in Figure 1-1 is the index page for the Florida Parks Web site. This informational page provides interesting facts about Florida's state and national parks. The page begins with a centered main heading, followed by a horizontal rule. Following the rule are two short informational paragraphs. The first paragraph contains two occurrences of the registered trademark symbol. Following the second paragraph is an introductory sentence for a bulleted list. The list contains four bulleted items. A concluding sentence, the author's name, and current date end the page. A Dreamweaver color scheme is applied to the page.

More About

Dreamweaver Features

For more information about Dreamweaver MX features, visit the Dreamweaver MX More About Web page (scsite.com/ dreamweavermx/ more.htm) and then click Dreamweaver MX Features.

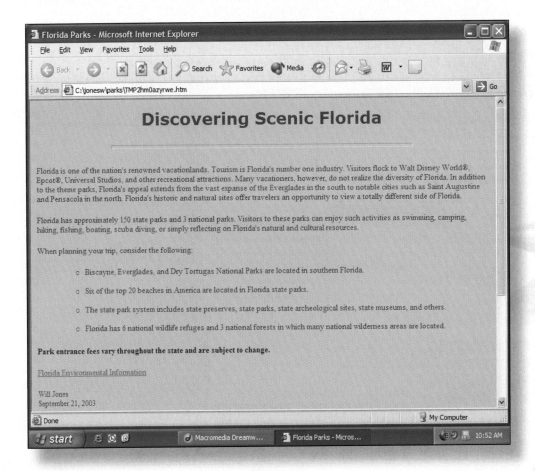

FIGURE 1-1

Starting Dreamweaver

Getting started in Dreamweaver is as easy as opening an existing HTML document or creating a new document. The Dreamweaver environment consists of toolbars, windows, objects, panels, inspectors, and tools you use to create your Web pages and to manage your Web site, which is a collection of Web pages. It is important to understand the basic concepts behind the Dreamweaver workspace and how to choose options, use inspectors and panels, and set preferences that best fit your work style.

The first time Dreamweaver is launched after the initial installation, a Workspace Setup dialog box is displayed with two options: Dreamweaver MX Workspace or Dreamweaver 4 Workspace. If you are installing the program on your own computer, select Dreamweaver MX Workspace. The Dreamweaver program starts and the Welcome window is displayed. If you choose to do so, select a tutorial category or categories to review and then close the Welcome window. This startup screen is a one-time event. The tutorials, however, are still accessible through Dreamweaver Help. If you are opening Dreamweaver from a computer at your school, most likely the program is set up and ready to use.

To start Dreamweaver, Windows must be running. Perform the following steps or ask your instructor how to start Dreamweaver.

Steps To Start Dreamweaver

1 **Click the Start button on the Windows taskbar, point to All Programs on the Start menu, point to Macromedia on the All Programs submenu, and then point to Macromedia Dreamweaver MX on the Macromedia submenu.**

The Start menu, All Programs submenu, and Macromedia submenu are displayed (Figure 1-2).

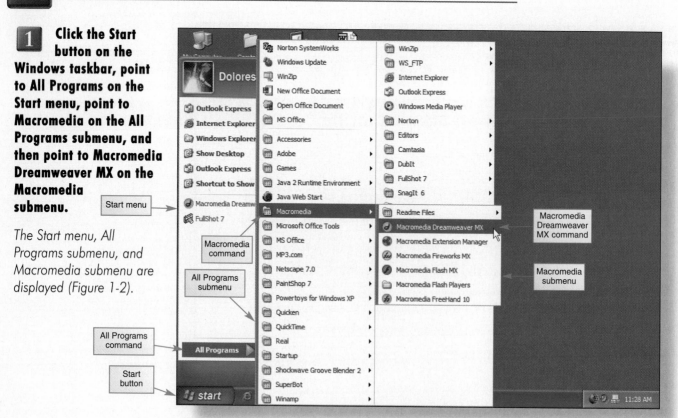

FIGURE 1-2

2 **Click Macromedia Dreamweaver MX. If necessary, maximize the Dreamweaver window and the Document window by clicking the Maximize button in the upper-right corner of the windows.**

The Macromedia splash screen is displayed instantaneously and then Dreamweaver displays an untitled Document window (Figure 1-3). The Dreamweaver window contains menu names, tool-bars, and panel groups. The Windows taskbar displays the Macromedia Dreamweaver MX button, indicating Dreamweaver is running. Dreamweaver retains the settings last used when the program was closed, so your window may look different.

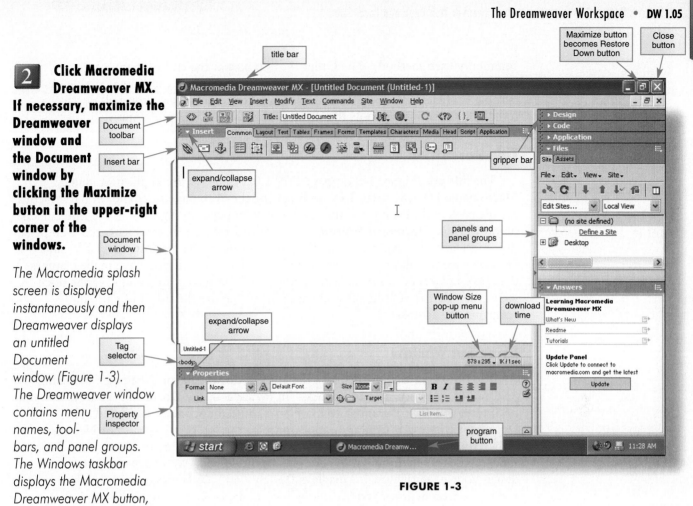

FIGURE 1-3

Other Ways

1. Double-click Dreamweaver icon on desktop

The screen in Figure 1-3 shows how the Dreamweaver window looks the first time you start Dreamweaver after installation on most computers. The **workspace** is an integrated environment in which the Document window and panels are incorporated into one larger application window. The panel groups are docked, or attached, on the right. The Insert bar is located at the top of the Document window and the Property inspector is located at the bottom of the Document window. Panels can be moved, resized, and/or collapsed to accommodate individual preferences.

The Dreamweaver Workspace

The **Dreamweaver workspace** consists of a variety of components to make your work more efficient and Web pages appear more professional. This section discusses the following components of the Dreamweaver window: title bar, Document window, panels and panel groups, status bar, menu bar, and toolbars.

As you learn to use each of these tools, you will discover some redundancy among these elements. To apply a Font tag, for instance, you can access the command through the Property inspector or on the Text menu. The different options are available for various user preferences. The projects in this book present the more commonly used methods. The Other Ways boxes at the end of many of the step-by-step sequences give other ways to accomplish a task when they are available. As you become proficient working in the Dreamweaver environment, you will develop a technique for using the tools that best suits your personal preferences.

Title Bar

The **title bar** (Figure 1-3 on page DW 1.05) displays the application name, Macromedia Dreamweaver MX; in brackets, the Web page title; and, in parentheses, the file path and file name of the displayed Web page. In Figure 1-3, the title bar displays [Untitled Document (Untitled-1)]. Untitled Document represents the Web page title and Untitled-1 represents the file path and file name. Following the file name, Dreamweaver displays an asterisk (shown in Figure 1-4) if you have made changes that have not yet been saved. After you give a Web page a title and save the document, the title bar reflects these changes by displaying the title and path and removing the asterisk.

Document Window

The **Document window** displays the current document, or Web page, including text, tables, graphics, and other items. In Figure 1-3, the Document window is blank. Each time you start Dreamweaver, a blank untitled document is created. The Document window is similar in appearance to the Internet Explorer or Netscape browser window. You work in the Document window in one of three views: **Design view**, the design environment where you assemble your Web page elements and design your page (Figure 1-3 displays Design view); **Code view**, which is a hand-coding environment for writing and editing code; or **Code view and Design view**, which allows you to see both Code view and Design view for the same document in a single window. When you start Dreamweaver, the default is Design view. These views are discussed in Project 2.

Panels and Panel Groups

Panel groups are sets of related panels docked together below one heading. Panels provide control over a wide range of Dreamweaver commands and functions. Each panel group can be expanded or collapsed, and can be docked or undocked with other panel groups. Panel groups also can be docked to the integrated application window. This makes it easy to access the panels you need without cluttering your workspace. Panels within a panel group appear as tabs.

To expand a panel group, click the expand/collapse arrow to the left of the group's name; to undock and move a panel group, drag the gripper bar at the left edge of the group's title bar (Figure 1-3). To open panels, use the Window menu. Each panel is explained in detail as it is used in the projects throughout the book.

Some panels, such as the Property inspector and the Insert bar, are stand-alone panels. The **Insert bar** allows quick access to objects and behaviors. It contains buttons for creating various types of objects, such as images, tables, layers, frames, and tags, and inserting them into a document. The buttons are organized into tabs. Each object on a tab is a piece of HTML code that allows you to set various attributes as you insert it. For example, you can insert an image by clicking the Image button on the Insert bar and then set the alignment attribute through the Property inspector. The default position for the Insert bar is at the top of the Document window.

More About

Panel Groups

Panel groups are sets of related panels grouped together below one heading. To expand a panel group, click the expand/collapse arrow to the left of the panel group's name. To undock a panel group, drag the gripper at the left edge of the panel group's title bar.

The **Property inspector** displays settings for the selected element's properties, or attributes. This panel is **context sensitive** because it changes based on the selected element, which can include text, tables, images, and other elements. When Dreamweaver starts, the Property inspector is positioned at the bottom of the Document window and displays text properties. Clicking the expand/collapse arrow of the Insert bar or Property inspector expands or collapses these panels (Figure 1-3 on page DW 1.05). To move the Insert bar or Property inspector, drag the gripper at the left edge of the title bar (Figure 1-4).

Status Bar

The **status bar** at the bottom of the Document window (Figure 1-3) provides additional information about the document you are creating. The status bar presents the following information.

▶ **Tag selector:** Displays the hierarchy of tags surrounding the current selection. Click any tag in the hierarchy to select that tag and all its contents.

▶ **Window Size pop-up menu button:** Displays the Window Size pop-up menu, which includes the window's current dimensions (in pixels).

▶ **Estimated document size and download time:** Displays the size and estimated download time of the current page. Dreamweaver MX calculates size based on the entire contents of the page, including all linked objects such as images and plug-ins.

Menu Bar

The **menu bar** displays the Dreamweaver menu names (Figure 1-4). Each menu contains a list of commands you can use to perform tasks such as retrieving, storing, printing, previewing, and exporting data in your Web page. When you point to a menu name on the menu bar, the area of the menu bar containing the name is highlighted.

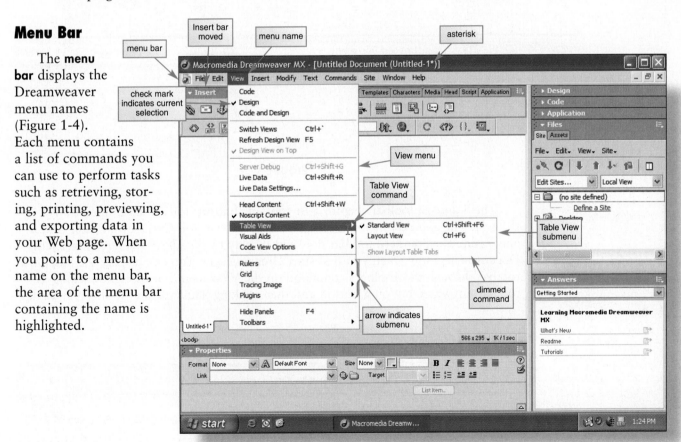

FIGURE 1-4

To display a menu, such as the View menu (Figure 1-4 on page DW 1.07), click the View menu name on the menu bar. If you point to a command on a menu that has an arrow to its right edge, a submenu displays another list of commands. Most menus display some commands that appear gray, or dimmed, instead of black, which indicates they are not available for the current selection.

Toolbars

Dreamweaver contains two toolbars: the Document toolbar and the Standard toolbar. You can choose to display or hide the toolbars by clicking View on the menu bar and then clicking Toolbars. If a toolbar name has a check mark next to it, it is displayed in the window. To hide the toolbar, you click the name of the toolbar with the check mark, and it no longer is displayed.

The **Document toolbar** (Figure 1-5) is the default toolbar that displays in the Document window. It contains buttons that provide different views of the Document window (e.g., Show Code View, Show Code and Design Views, Show Design View, and Live Data View); access to the Reference panel; and some common operations such as file management, browser preview, Code Navigation, and the Title text box through which you name your Web page. All View option commands also are available through the View menu.

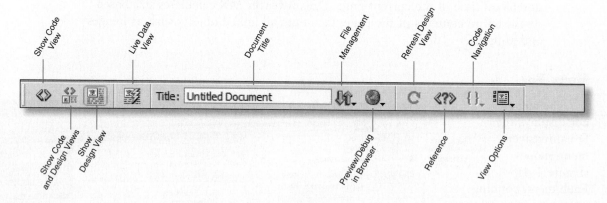

FIGURE 1-5

The Standard toolbar (Figure 1-6) contains buttons for common operations from the File and Edit menus: New, Open, Save, Save All, Cut, Copy, Paste, Undo, and Redo. The Standard toolbar does not display by default in the Dreamweaver Document window when you first start Dreamweaver. You can display the Standard toolbar through the Toolbars command on the View menu, or by right-clicking a toolbar anywhere but on a button and then clicking Standard on the shortcut menu.

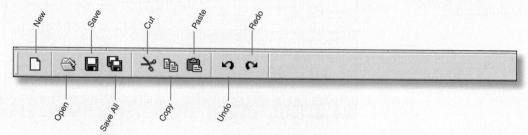

FIGURE 1-6

Opening and Closing Panels in the Workspace

The Dreamweaver workspace accommodates different styles of working and levels of expertise. Through the workspace, you can open and close the panel groups and other Dreamweaver features as needed. To open a panel group, select and then click the name of a panel on the Window menu. Closing unused panels provides uncluttered workspace in the Document window. To close an individual panel group, click Close Panel Group on the Options menu accessed through the panel group's title bar (Figure 1-7). To expand/collapse a panel, click the panel's expand/collapse arrow.

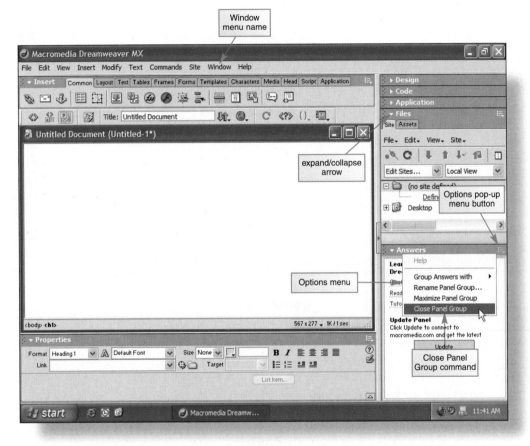

FIGURE 1-7

Opening and closing each panel individually is a time-consuming task. Dreamweaver provides a shortcut to accomplish this job quickly. The **F4 key** is a toggle key that opens and/or closes all panels and toolbars, except the Document toolbar and menu bar, at one time. The following step closes all open panels.

To Close All Open Panels

1 **Press the F4 key.**

All the open panels and inspectors close and maximum workspace is available within the Document window (Figure 1-8).

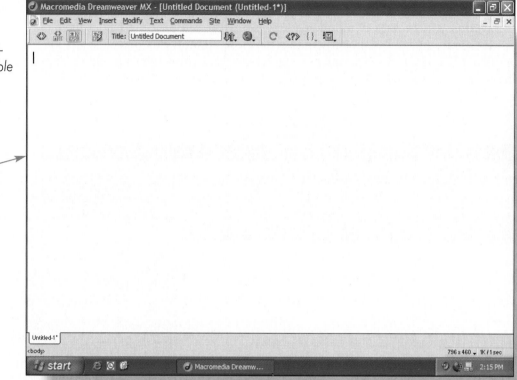

Document window maximized

FIGURE 1-8

Creating a Local Site

Web design and Web site management are two important skills that a builder of Web sites must understand and apply. Dreamweaver MX is a site creation and management tool. To use Dreamweaver efficiently, you first must develop the local site. After defining the local site, you then publish to a remote site. Publishing to a remote site is covered in Project 3.

The general definition of a **site**, or Web site, is a set of linked documents with shared attributes, such as related topics, a similar design, or a shared purpose. In Dreamweaver, however, site can refer to any of the following:

- A **Web site**, which is a set of pages on a server that are viewed through a Web browser by a visitor to the site.

- A **remote site**, which are files on the server that make up a Web site, from the author's point of view rather than a visitor's point of view.

- A **local site**, which are files on your local disk that correspond to the files on the remote site. You edit the files on your local disk, and then upload them to the remote site.

- A Dreamweaver **site definition**, which is a set of defining characteristics for a local site, plus information on how the local site corresponds to a remote site.

As a builder and designer of Web sites, you will find that the site structure feature provides a way to maintain and organize your files.

All Dreamweaver Web sites begin with a local root folder. As you become familiar with Dreamweaver and complete the projects in this book, you will find references to a **local root folder**, a **root folder**, and **root**. These terms are interchangeable. This folder is no different from any other folder on your hard drive, except for the way in which Dreamweaver views it. When Dreamweaver looks for Web pages, links, images, and other media, the program defaults to the designated root folder. Any media within the Web site that are outside of the root folder will not display when the Web site is previewed in a Web browser. Within the root folder, you can create additional folders or subfolders to organize graphics and other elements. A **subfolder** (also called a **nested folder**) is a folder inside another folder.

Dreamweaver provides two options to create a site: create the root folder and any subfolders; or, create the pages and then create the folders when saving the files. In this project, you create the root folder and then create the Web page.

One of Dreamweaver's more prominent organizational tools is its Site panel. Use the **Site panel** for standard file maintenance operations, such as the following:

- Creating files
- Viewing, opening, and moving files
- Creating folders
- Deleting items

The Site panel enables you to view a site, including all local, remote, and testing server files associated with a selected site. In this project you view only the local site.

Using Site Definition to Create a Local Site

Because many files are required for a Dreamweaver Web site, it is advisable to create the projects using another location rather than the floppy disk drive (A:). Steps in this project instruct you to create the local site at the C:\ on the computer's hard drive. It is suggested, however, that you check with your instructor to verify the location and path you will use to create and save your local Web site. Other options may include a Zip® drive or a network drive. You first will create a folder using your last name and first initial. Examples in this book use Will Jones as the Web site author. Thus, the Will Jones folder is jonesw. Next, you will create a subfolder and name it parks. All Florida Parks-related files and subfolders are stored within the parks folder. When you navigate through this folder hierarchy, you are navigating along the path.

When creating a Web site, it is important to understand paths. The term, path, is sometimes confusing for new users of the Web. It is, however, a simple concept: A **path** is the succession of folders that must be navigated to get from one folder to another. In the DOS world, folders are referred to as **directories**. These two terms often are used interchangeably. To organize a Web site and understand how Web documents are accessed, it is important to understand paths and folders.

A typical path structure has a **master folder**, usually called the root and designated by the backslash (\) symbol. This folder contains within it all other nested folders or subfolders. Further, each folder may contain additional nested folders or subfolders. The Web site files are contained in these folders. The path and folder within the Florida Parks Web site are C:\jonesw\parks\. In Project 2, you will add an images folder to the site, and the path to that folder will be C:\jonesw\parks\Images\. When you create the site, you will use your last name and first initial for the root folder (the your name folder). In all references to jonesw, substitute your last name and first initial.

More About

Site Definition

For more advanced users, the Site Definition dialog box includes an Advanced tab based on the Dreamweaver 4 interface.

You create a site using the Site Definition dialog box. Two approaches are available: Basic or Advanced. The Basic approach, or **Site Definition Wizard**, guides you through site setup step by step. As you become more proficient in Dreamweaver, you can switch to the Advanced method.

Use the Site Definition Wizard and perform the following steps to create a local Web site.

Steps **To Use the Site Definition Wizard to Create a Local Web Site**

1 **Click Site on the menu bar and then point to New Site (Figure 1-9).**

Dreamweaver displays the Site menu and the New Site command is highlighted (Figure 1-9).

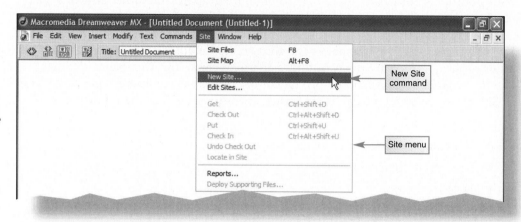

FIGURE 1-9

2 **Click New Site. If necessary, click the Basic tab.**

Dreamweaver displays the Site Definition dialog box with the Editing Files options (Figure 1-10)

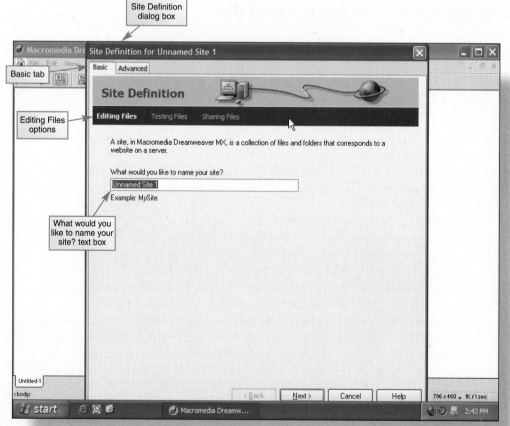

FIGURE 1-10

3 **Type** Florida Parks **in the What would you like to name your site? text box. Point to the Next button.**

Florida Parks is displayed in the What would you like to name your site? text box (Figure 1-11). This name is for reference only. It is not part of the path.

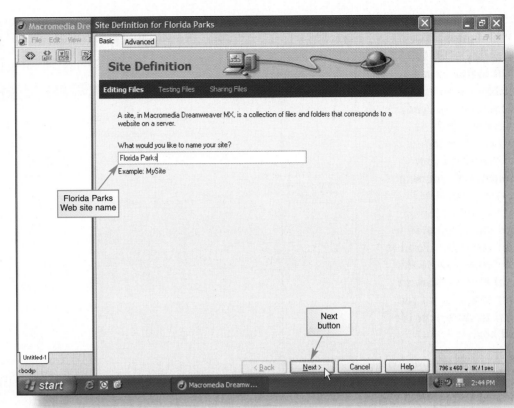

FIGURE 1-11

4 **Click the Next button. If necessary, click No, I do not want to use a server technology. Point to the Next button.**

The Site Definition dialog box displays the Editing Files, Part 2 options (Figure 1-12).

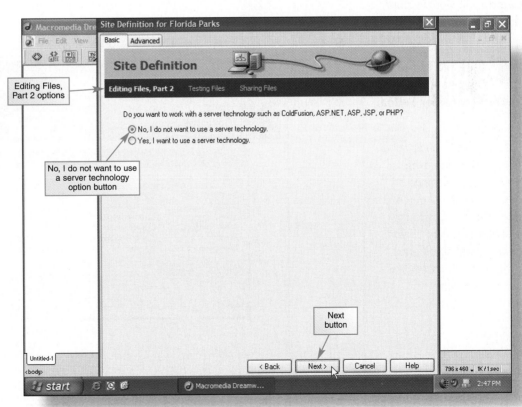

FIGURE 1-12

5 **Click the Next button. If necessary, click Edit local copies on my machine, then upload to server when ready (recommended). If necessary, change the Where on your computer do you want to store your files? path to C:\ or the location designated by your instructor. Point to the Folder icon to the right of the Where on your computer do you want to store your files? text box.**

The Site Definition dialog box displays the Editing Files, Part 3 options (Figure 1-13). The path in the Where on your computer do you want to store your files? text box is C:\.

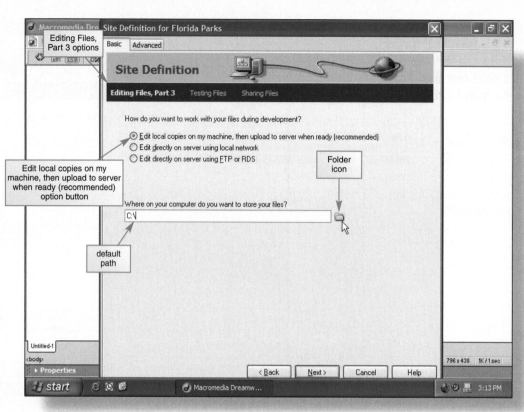

FIGURE 1-13

6 **Click the folder icon. Point to the Create New Folder button.**

The Choose Local Root Folder for Site Florida Parks dialog box is displayed (Figure 1-14). Settings on your computer will determine what displays in the Select box. Folders on your computer will be different. In Figure 1-14, Local Disk (C:) is the default.

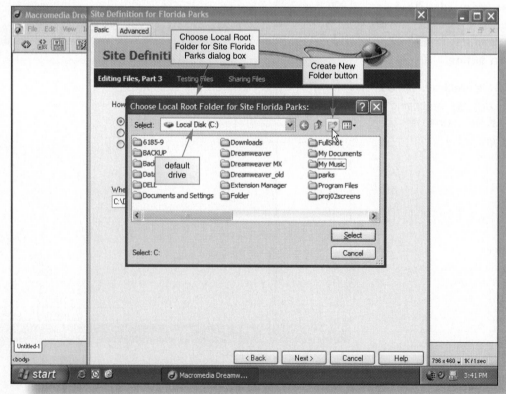

FIGURE 1-14

7 **Click the Create New Folder button.**

The New Folder text box is displayed (Figure 1-15). New Folder is highlighted.

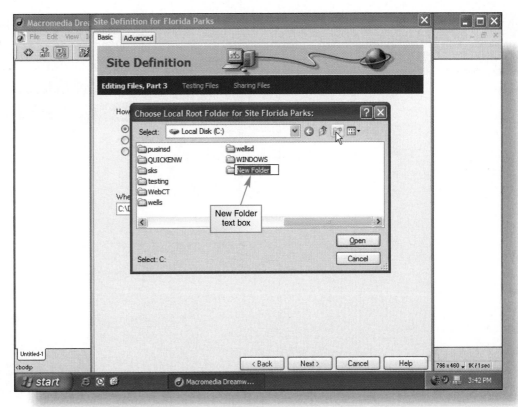

FIGURE 1-15

8 **Type your last name and first initial as the folder name and then press the ENTER key to select the folder. Point to the Open button.**

The last name and first initial of the Web page author are displayed (Figure 1-16). As shown in Figure 1-16, jonesw is the author in this project. Within the your name folder, you create a subfolder for each Web site you define. All of your projects, including end-of-project exercises, will be saved in subfolders under the your name folder.

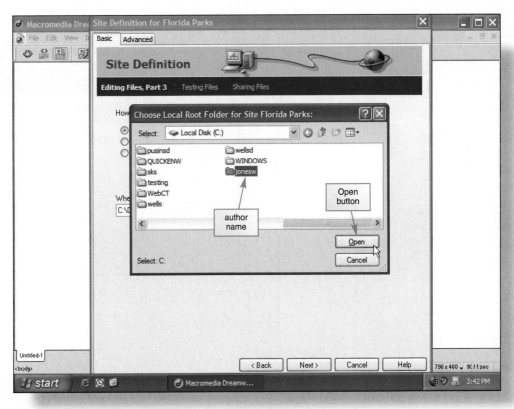

FIGURE 1-16

9 **Click the Open button and then point to the Create New Folder button (Figure 1-17).**

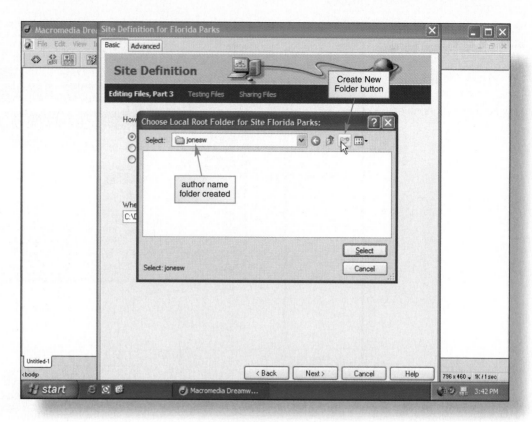

FIGURE 1-17

10 **Click the Create New Folder button.**

The New Folder text box is displayed (Figure 1-18).

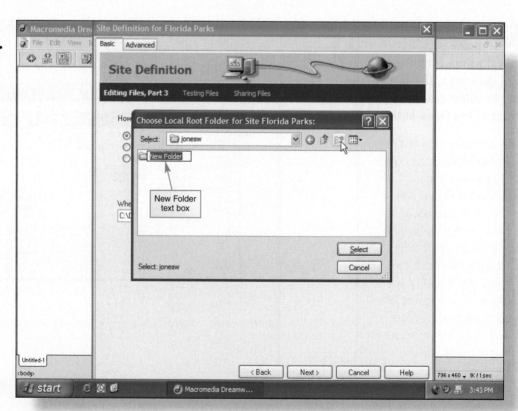

FIGURE 1-18

11 **Type** parks **in the New Folder text box and then press the ENTER key to select the folder. Point to the Open button.**

The parks subfolder is created (Figure 1-19).

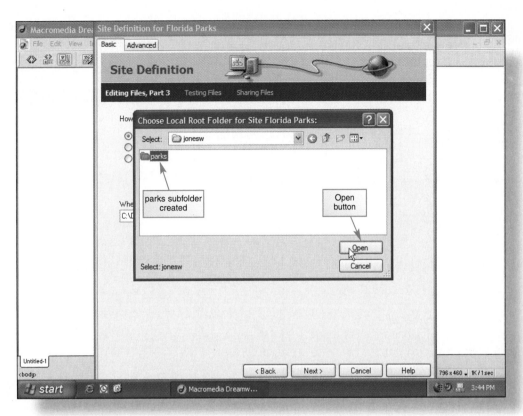

FIGURE 1-19

12 **Click the Open button and then point to the Select button.**

The parks subfolder name displays in the Select box (Figure 1-20). You have created a local root folder for the Florida Parks Web site. All subfolders and files pertaining to the parks site will be saved in this local root folder.

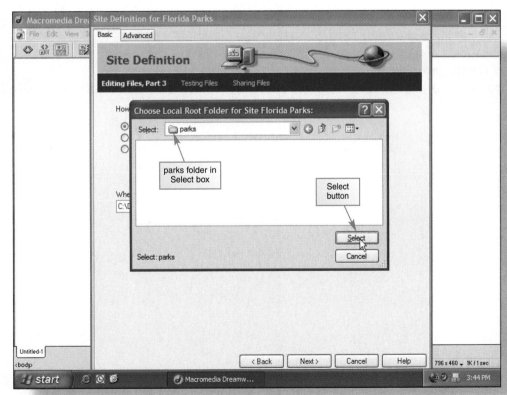

FIGURE 1-20

13 **Click the Select button and then point to the Next button.**

The Site Definition dialog box displays the Editing Files, Part 3 options with C:\jonesw\parks\ displayed in the Where on your computer do you want to store your files? text box (Figure 1-21). Your name and initial will display instead of jonesw. The path C:\jonesw\parks is the name of the local root folder. The folder jonesw is an organizational folder for this Web site and any additional Web sites you create.

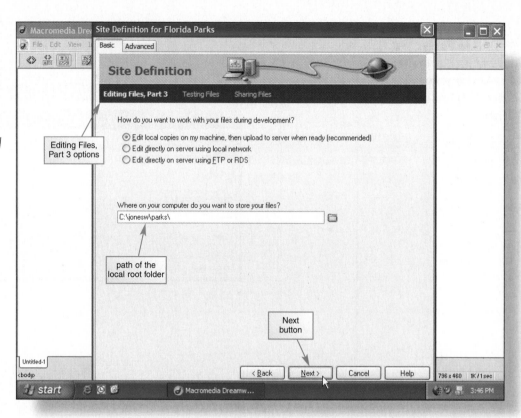

FIGURE 1-21

14 **Click the Next button. Point to the How do you connect to your remote server? box arrow.**

The Site Definition dialog box displays the Sharing Files options (Figure 1-22).

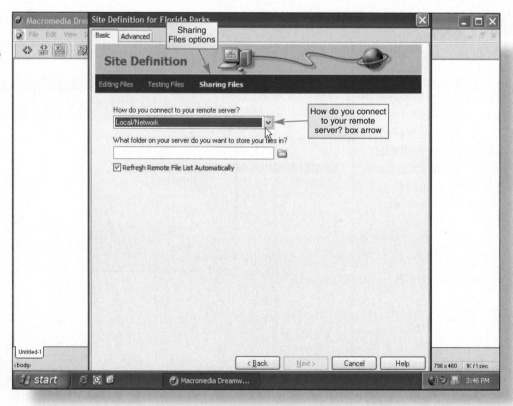

FIGURE 1-22

15 **Click the How do you connect to your remote server? box arrow and then point to None in the list.**

None is highlighted in the list (Figure 1-23).

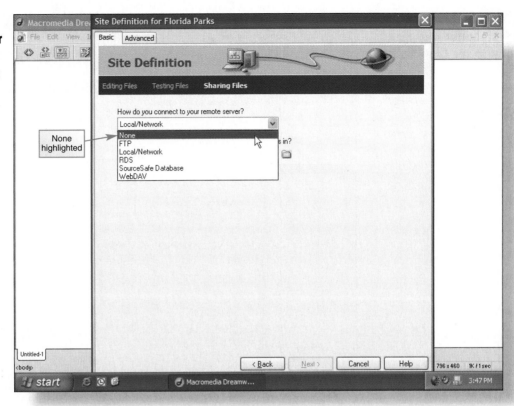

FIGURE 1-23

16 **Click None and then point to the Next button.**

Selecting None means that you are not connecting to a server at this time (Figure 1-24).

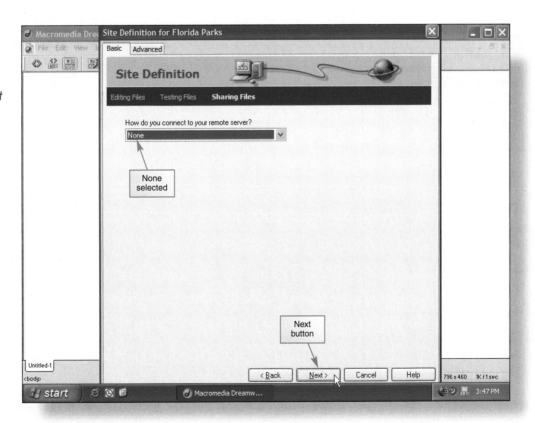

FIGURE 1-24

17 Click the Next button and then point to the Done button.

The Site Definition dialog box displays the Summary options (Figure 1-25). A summary of your selected settings is shown.

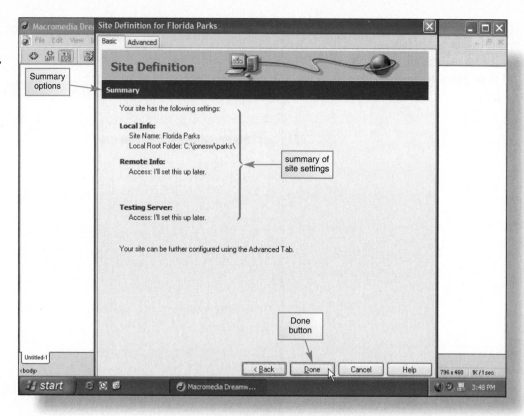

FIGURE 1-25

18 Click the Done button.

Dreamweaver displays the Document window and the Site panel in the Files panel group (Figure 1-26). The path to the Florida Parks site is displayed in the Site panel.

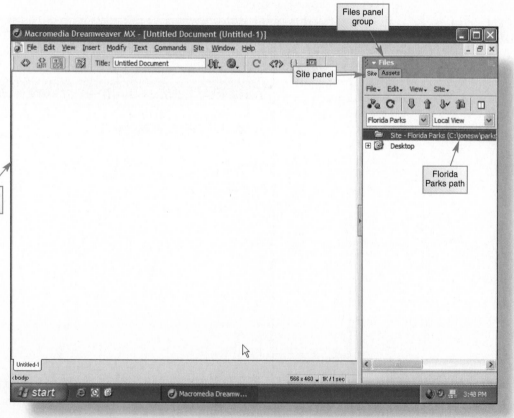

FIGURE 1-26

Other Ways

1. On Site menu click New Site, click Advanced tab

Deleting or Editing a Web Site

For various reasons, such as simply starting over, you may need to delete or edit a Web site. To delete or edit a Web site, click Site on the menu bar and then click Edit Sites. Invoking the **Edit Sites command** displays the Edit Sites dialog box (Figure 1-27). Select the site name and then click the Remove button to delete the site. Dreamweaver displays a Macromedia Dreamweaver MX caution dialog box providing you with an opportunity to cancel. Click the No button to cancel. Otherwise, click the Yes button and Dreamweaver deletes the site. To edit a site, click the site name and then click the Edit button. Dreamweaver displays the Site Definition dialog box, and from there, you can change any of the options you selected when you first created the site (Figure 1-27). Deleting a site in Dreamweaver removes the settings for the site. The files and folders remain and must be deleted separately.

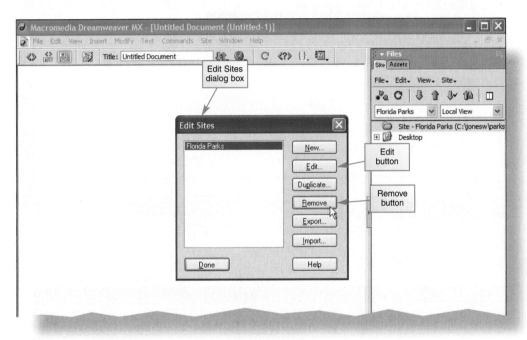

FIGURE 1-27

Color Schemes

Most Web pages display with a default white or gray background. Generally, the browser used to display the Web page determines the default background. You can enhance your Web page by adding a background image and/or background color. You add a background color by applying a color scheme in this project and add a background image in Project 2.

When you use a background color, you want to use Web-safe colors. **Web-safe colors** are colors that will display correctly on the computer screen when someone is viewing your Web page in a browser.

Adding a Color Scheme

Dreamweaver provides a series of Web-safe preset color schemes. Each scheme includes a background, text, active links, and visited links colors. Complete the steps on the next two pages to add a color scheme to the Florida Parks Web page.

Steps To Add a Color Scheme

1 **Click Commands on the menu bar and then point to Set Color Scheme.**

The Commands menu is displayed (Figure 1-28).

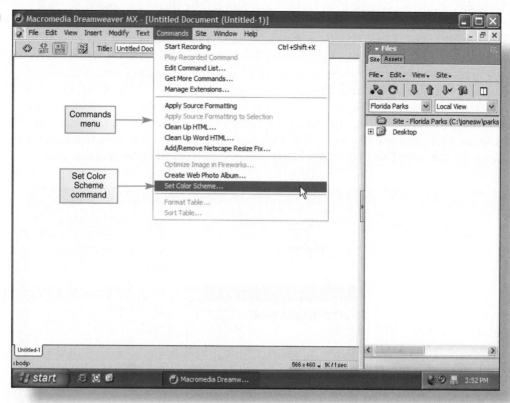

FIGURE 1-28

2 **Click Set Color Scheme and then point to Green in the Background list.**

The Set Color Scheme Command dialog box is displayed (Figure 1-29).

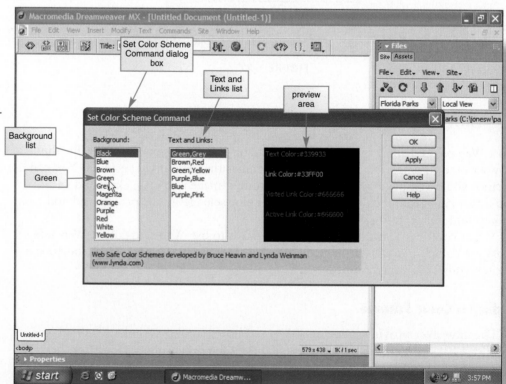

FIGURE 1-29

3 Click Green in the Background list and then click Blue, Brown,Green in the Text and Links list. Point to the OK button.

The Green background and the Blue,Brown,Green Text and Links are selected (Figure 1-30).

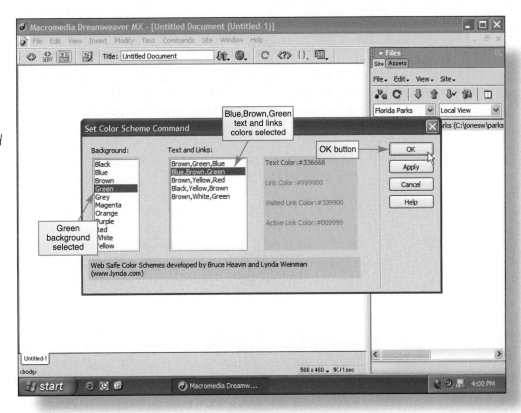

FIGURE 1-30

4 Click the OK button.

The background color is applied to the Document window (Figure 1-31). As you type text and insert links, the selected colors will be applied.

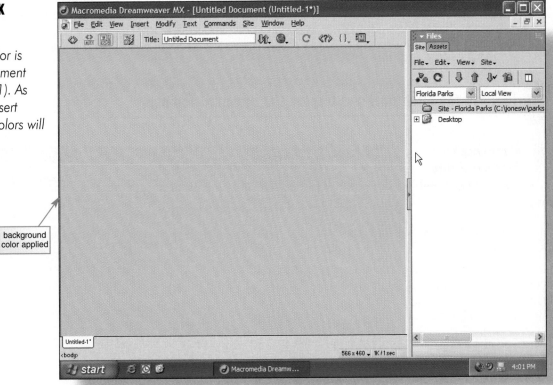

FIGURE 1-31

Web Page Creation

In Dreamweaver, you can create a Web page in several ways: (1) you can type a new document; (2) you can open an existing HTML document, even if it was not created in Dreamweaver; (3) you can copy and paste text; and (4) you can import a Word document.

In this project, you create the index page for Florida Parks Web page by typing the text in the Document window. Entering text into a Dreamweaver document is similar to typing text in a word processing document. You can position the insertion point at the top left of the Document window or within another element containing text, such as a table cell. Pressing the ENTER key creates a new paragraph and inserts a blank line. Web browsers automatically insert a blank line of space between paragraphs. To start a new single line without a blank line between lines of text requires a **line break**. You can insert a line break by holding down the SHIFT key and then pressing the ENTER key or by clicking the Line Break button on the Insert bar.

If you type a wrong letter and notice the error before pressing the ENTER key, press the BACKSPACE key to erase all the characters back to and including the one that is incorrect. If you mistakenly press the ENTER key and then discover the error, simply press the BACKSPACE key to return the insertion point to the previous line. Clicking the **Undo** button on the Standard toolbar reverses the most recent steps. The **Redo** button reverses the last undo action. The Undo and Redo commands also are accessible through the Edit menu.

Organizing Your Workspace

To organize your workspace, you close the Site panel and display the Standard toolbar. This gives you the maximum window space in the Dreamweaver Document window and gives you access to Standard toolbar buttons.

Complete the following steps to organize your workspace.

 To Close the Site Panel and Display the Standard Toolbar

1 **Right-click the Files panel title bar. Point to Close Panel Group.**

Dreamweaver displays the Files panel context menu. The Close Panel Groups command is highlighted (Figure 1-32).

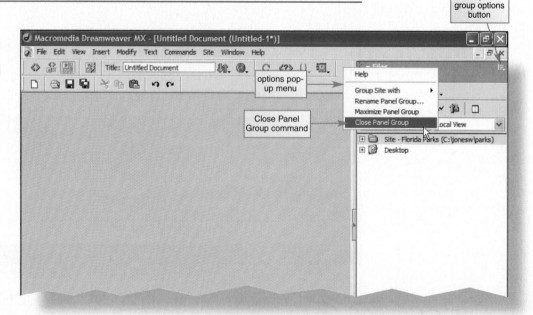

FIGURE 1-32

2 **Click Close Panel Group.**

The Files panel closes (Figure 1-33).

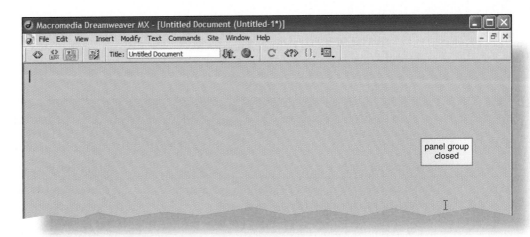

FIGURE 1-33

3 **Click View on the menu bar, point to Toolbars, and then point to Standard on the Toolbars submenu.**

Dreamweaver displays the View menu and the Toolbars submenu (Figure 1-34).

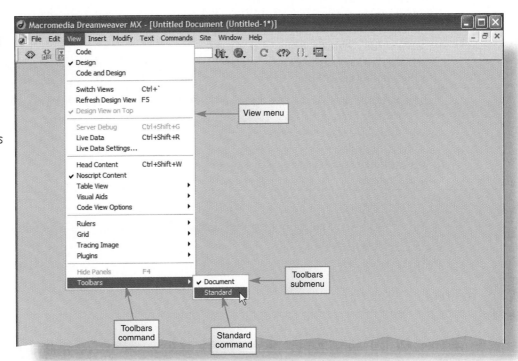

FIGURE 1-34

4 **Click Standard.**

The Standard toolbar is displayed in the Document window (Figure 1-35).

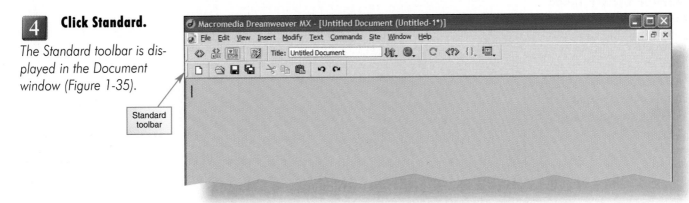

FIGURE 1-35

Adding Text

Table 1-1 includes the text for the Florida Parks Web page. After typing the sections of the document, you will press the ENTER key to insert a blank line.

Table 1-1 Discovering Scenic Florida Web Page Text

SECTION	HEADING, PART 1 AND PART 2	SECTION	PART 3, ITEMS FOR BULLETED LIST, AND CLOSING
Heading	Discovering Scenic Florida	Part 3	When planning your trip, consider the following:
Part 1	Florida is one of the nation's renowned vacationlands. Tourism is Florida's number one industry. Visitors flock to Walt Disney World, Epcot, Universal Studios, and other recreational attractions. Many vacationers, however, do not realize the diversity of Florida. In addition to the theme parks, Florida's appeal extends from the vast expanse of the Everglades in the south to notable cities such as Saint Augustine and Pensacola in the north. Florida's historic and natural sites offer travelers an opportunity to view a totally different side of Florida.	Items list	Biscayne, Everglades, and Dry Tortugas National Parks are located in southern Florida. Six of the top 20 beaches in America are located in Florida state parks. The state park system includes state preserves, state parks, state archeological sites, state museums, and others. Florida has 6 national wildlife refuges and 3 national forests in which many national wilderness areas are located.
Part 2	Florida has approximately 150 state parks and 3 national parks. Visitors to these parks can enjoy such activities as swimming, camping, hiking, fishing, boating, scuba diving, or simply reflecting on Florida's natural and cultural resources.	Closing	Park entrance fees vary throughout the state and are subject to change.

The following steps create the Web page and insert blank lines between sections of text.

Steps To Create a Web Page

1 Type the heading Discovering Scenic Florida **as shown in Table 1-1, and then press the ENTER key.**

The heading is entered in the Document window (Figure 1-36). The text color is blue. Pressing the ENTER key creates a new paragraph.

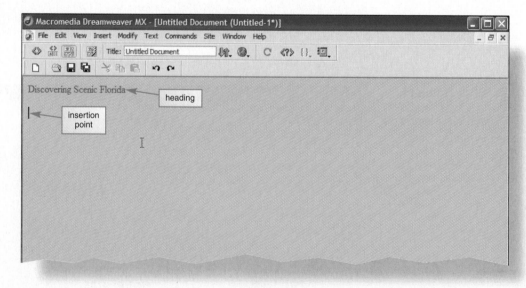

FIGURE 1-36

2 **Type the text of Part 1 shown in Table 1-1 and then press the ENTER key.**

The introductory paragraph is entered (Figure 1-37). Pressing the ENTER key creates a new paragraph.

Part 1

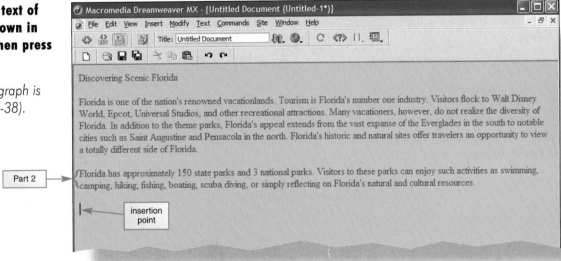

FIGURE 1-37

3 **Type the text of Part 2 shown in Table 1-1 and then press the ENTER key.**

The second paragraph is entered (Figure 1-38).

Part 2

FIGURE 1-38

4 **Type the text of Part 3 shown in Table 1-1 and then press the ENTER key.**

The third paragraph is entered (Figure 1-39).

Part 3

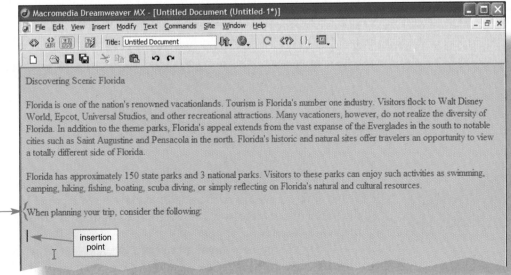

FIGURE 1-39

5 Type the four items for the bulleted list shown in Table 1-1. Press the ENTER key after each entry.

The items for the bulleted list are entered (Figure 1-40). Later in this project, you will format the list so that it becomes a bulleted list.

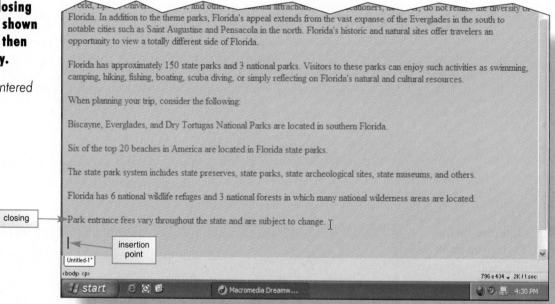

FIGURE 1-40

6 Type the closing paragraph shown in Table 1-1, and then press the ENTER key.

The paragraph is entered (Figure 1-41).

FIGURE 1-41

If you feel you need to start over for any reason, Dreamweaver makes it easy to delete a Web page. Save the page, display the Site panel by pressing the F8 key, click the name of the page you want to delete, right-click to display the context menu, and then click Delete.

The next step is to format the text. Dreamweaver provides two options for formatting text: the Text menu and the Property inspector. To format the Discovering Scenic Florida Web page, you will use the Property inspector.

The Property Inspector

The Property inspector is one of the panels you will use most often when creating Web pages. The **Property inspector** initially displays the more commonly used attributes, or properties, of the selected object. The object can be text, graphics, layers, frames, or hotspots. A **layer** is a container you create on your Web page to hold text, images, or other content. Dreamweaver enables you to stack layers on top of other layers. A **hotspot** is a clickable area on an image map. Options within the Property inspector change relative to the selected object. Perform the following steps to open the Property inspector.

More About

The Property Inspector

The Property inspector initially displays the most commonly used properties of the selected object. Click the expander arrow in the lower-right corner of the Property inspector to see more of the element's properties.

Steps **To Open the Property Inspector**

1 **Click Window on the menu bar and then point to Properties.**

The Window menu is displayed (Figure 1-42).

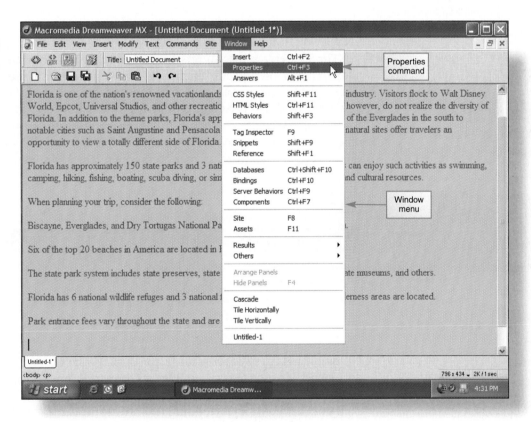

FIGURE 1-42

<table>
<tr>
<td>

2 **Click Properties. If necessary, click the expander arrow to collapse the Property inspector.**

Dreamweaver opens the Property inspector below the Document window (Figure 1-43).

</td>
</tr>
</table>

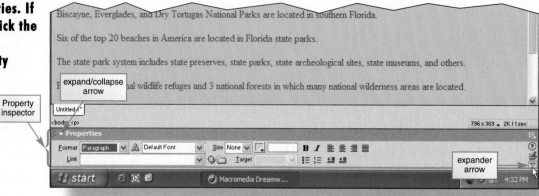

FIGURE 1-43

Other **Ways**

1. Press CTRL+F3

Property Inspector Features

The Property inspector lets you see the current properties of an element and allows you to alter or edit them. The Property inspector is divided into two sections. Clicking the expander arrow in the lower-right corner of the Property inspector collapses the Property inspector to show only the more commonly used properties for the selected element or expands the Property inspector to show more options. Some objects, such as text, do not contain additional properties within the expanded panel (Figure 1-44). The question mark icon opens the Help window.

FIGURE 1-44

By default, the Property inspector displays the properties for text on a blank document. Most changes you make to properties are applied immediately in the Document window. For some properties, however, changes are not applied until you click outside the property-editing text fields, press the ENTER key, or press the TAB key to switch to another property. The following section describes the text-related features of the Property inspector (Figure 1-45).

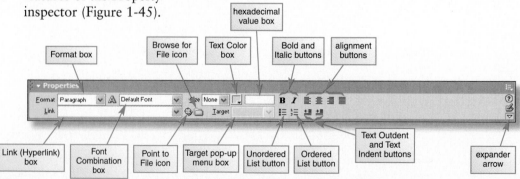

FIGURE 1-45

FORMAT   The **Format box** allows you to apply a Paragraph, Heading, or Preformatted style to the text. Clicking the Format box displays a pop-up menu from which you can select a style.

The **Paragraph style** is the normal default style for text on a Web page. **Paragraph formatting** is the process of changing the appearance of a paragraph. **Heading styles** are used to create divisions and separate one segment of text from another. The Heading numbers range from 1 through 6 and correspond to the HTML elements H1, H2, and so on. The smaller the number of the heading, the bigger the text displayed when viewed in a Web browser. These formats are displayed based on how different browsers interpret the tags, offering little consistency and control over layout and appearance. When you apply a heading tag to a paragraph, Dreamweaver automatically adds the next line of text as a standard paragraph. Use the **Preformatted style** when you do not want a Web browser to change the line of text in any way.

Font combination applies the selected font combination to the text and determines how a browser displays text on your Web page. The browser uses the first font in the combination that is installed on the user's system. If none of the fonts in the combination are installed, the browser displays the text as specified by the user's browser preferences. Most font faces in common usage on the Web are serif, sans-serif, or monospace fonts. The default font used on most Web pages is Times (also called Times New Roman or New Times), which is a serif font. The most commonly used sans-serif fonts are Arial, Helvetica, Geneva, and Verdana, while the most commonly used monospace font is Courier (also called Courier New). Use the Font Combination pop-up menu to apply a font combination.

SIZE   The **Text Size box** provides options that allow you to apply a font size to a single character or to an entire page of text. Font sizes in HTML range from 1 through 7, with size 7 being the largest. The default HTML font size, or **BASEFONT**, is 3, which equates to 12 points in a word processing document. A way to specify a particular point size for fonts in an HTML tag is not available. One method, however, that you can use is to set approximate sizes. Using the **relative size method**, the FONT tag can be used with the SIZE attribute to define text sizes in terms relative to the base font. Relative sizes can range from +1 through +7 or from -1 through -7. For example, the tag <FONT SIZE=+3> tells the browser to use a font size that is three times higher than the base font. The tag <FONT SIZE = -1> tells the browser to use a font size that is one time less than the base font.

TEXT COLOR   When you create a new document in Dreamweaver, the default text color is black. The **Text Color** box contains palettes of colors you can apply to emphasize, differentiate, and highlight topics. To display the text in a selected Web-safe color, click the Text Color box to access the different methods of selecting preset colors or creating custom ones. Colors also are represented by a hexadecimal value (for example, #FF0000) in the adjacent text field.

BOLD AND ITALIC   The **Bold button** and the **Italic button** allow you to format text using these two font styles in the Property inspector. These are the two more commonly used styles. Dreamweaver also supports a variety of other font styles available through the Text menu. To view these other styles, click Text on the menu bar and then point to Style.

LEFT, CENTER, RIGHT ALIGN, AND JUSTIFY   In Dreamweaver, the default alignment for text is left alignment. To change the default alignment, select the text you want to align or simply position the mouse pointer at the beginning of the text. Click an alignment button: Align Center, Align Right, or Justify. You can align and center complete blocks of text, but you cannot align or center part of a heading or part of a paragraph.

LINK   The **Link (Hyperlink) box** allows you to make selected text or other objects a hyperlink to a specified URL or Web page. To select the URL or Web page, you can click the Point to File or Browse for File icon to the right of the Link box to browse to a page in your Web site and then type the URL, or drag a file from the site window into the Link box. Links are covered in detail in Project 2.

TARGET   In the **Target pop-up menu box,** you specify the frame or window in which the linked page should load. If you are using frames, the names of all of the frames in the current document are displayed in the list. If the specified frame does not exist when the current document is opened in a browser, the linked page loads in a new window with the name you specified. Once this window exists, other files can be targeted to it.

UNORDERED LIST   Web developers often use a list to structure a page. An unordered list turns the selected paragraph or heading into an item in a bulleted list. If no text is selected before clicking the **Unordered List button**, a new bulleted list is started.

ORDERED LIST   An ordered list is similar to an unordered list. This type of list, however, turns the selected paragraph or heading into an item in a numbered list. If no text is selected before clicking the **Ordered List button**, a new numbered list is started.

INDENT AND OUTDENT   To set off a block quote, you can use the Indent feature. The **Text Indent button** will indent a line or a paragraph from both margins. In HTML, this is the BLOCKQUOTE tag. The **Text Outdent button** removes the indentation from the selected text by removing the BLOCKQUOTE tag. In a list, indenting creates a nested list and removing the indentation unnests the list. A **nested list** is one list inside another list.

Formatting Text

The text for your Web page is displayed in the Document window. The next step in creating your Web page is to format this text. **Formatting** means to apply different fonts, change heading styles, insert special characters, and insert other such elements that enhance the appearance of the Web page. You use commands from the Property inspector to format the text.

Within Dreamweaver, you can format text before you type, or you can apply new formats after you type. If you have used word processing software, you will find many of the Dreamweaver formatting commands similar to the commands within a word processing program. Your Web page contains only text, so the Property inspector displays attributes related to text.

To set block formatting, such as formatting a heading or an unordered list, position the insertion point in the line or paragraph and then format the text. To set character formatting, such as choosing a font or font size, however, you first must select the character, word, or words.

Web Page Design

Web pages reach a global audience. Therefore, to limit access to certain kinds of information, avoid including any confidential data. In particular, do not include your home address, telephone number, or other personal information.

Formatting Text Headings

Just as in a word processing document, the heading structure in a Web page is used to set apart document or section titles. The six levels of headings in this structure are Heading 1 through Heading 6. **Heading 1** (**H1**) produces the largest text and **Heading 6** (**H6**) the smallest. By default, browsers will display the six heading levels in the same font, with the point size decreasing as the importance of the heading decreases. Complete the following steps to format the heading.

> **More About**
>
> **Text Size**
>
> You can set the size of the text in your Web page, but viewers of your Web page also can change the size through their browser. When creating a page, use the font size that looks right for the page you are creating.

 To Format Text with Heading 1

1 If necessary, scroll up and then position the insertion point anywhere in the heading text, Discovering Scenic Florida (Figure 1-46). Point to the Format box arrow in the Property inspector.

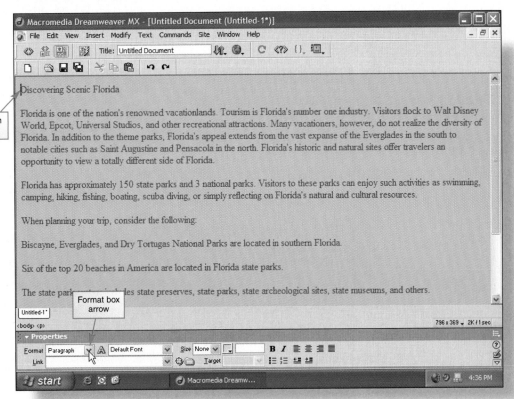

FIGURE 1-46

2   **Click the Format box arrow in the Property inspector and then point to Heading 1.**

The Format pop-up menu displays a list of formatting styles. Heading 1 is highlighted in the list (Figure 1-47).

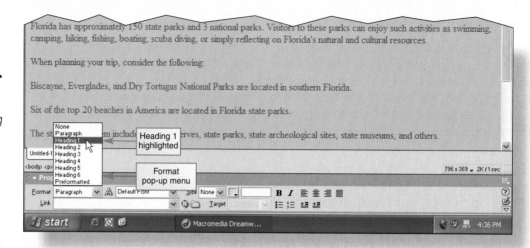

FIGURE 1-47

3   **Click Heading 1.**

The Heading 1 style is applied to the Discovering Scenic Florida heading (Figure 1-48).

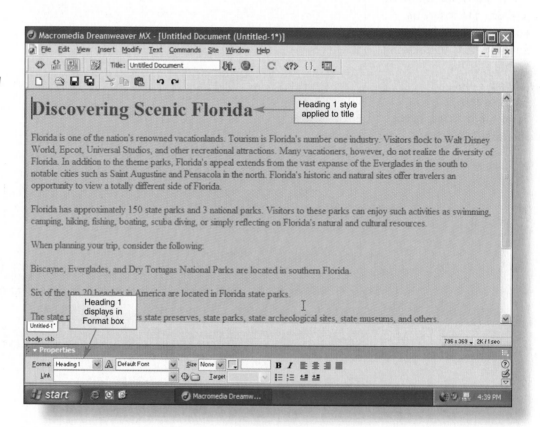

FIGURE 1-48

Centering Text

Using the **Align Center button** in the Property inspector allows you to center text. This button is very similar to the Center button in a word processing program. To center a single line or a paragraph, position the mouse pointer in the line or paragraph, and then click the button to center the text. You do not need to select a single line or single paragraph to center it. To center more than one paragraph at a time, however, you must select all paragraphs. The following step illustrates centering the heading.

Steps To Center the Web Page Heading

1 If necessary, click somewhere in the heading, Discovering Scenic Florida. Click the **Align Center button in the Property inspector.**

The heading, Discovering Scenic Florida, is centered (Figure 1-49).

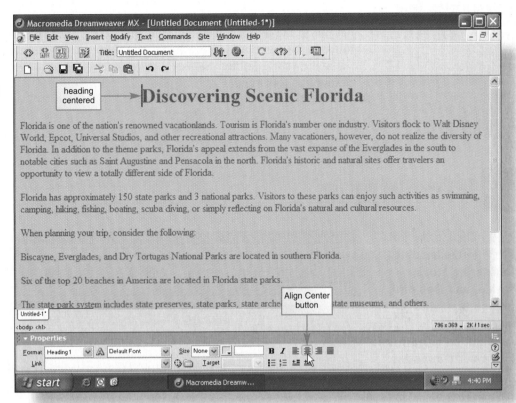

FIGURE 1-49

Other Ways

1. On Text menu click Align, click Center on Align submenu
2. Right-click selected text, point to Align on context menu, click Center on Align submenu
3. Press CTRL+ALT+SHIFT+C

Text is one of the more important elements of most any Web page. How the text displays on a Web page can attract or detract from the overall appearance. Using the appropriate font type can enhance and entice viewers to browse your Web site.

Specifying the Font Type

Type is important because it attracts attention, sets the style and tone of a Web page, influences how readers interpret the words, and defines the feeling of the page. The **font type** refers to the basic design of the lettering. Several methods are used to classify fonts. The most common way is to place them in different families based on shared characteristics. The five basic font type families are:

1. Serif, such as Times or Times New Roman
2. Sans-serif, such as Helvetica and Arial
3. Monospace, such as Courier
4. Cursive, such as Brush Script
5. Decorative and fantasy

Two general categories of typefaces are serif and sans-serif. **Sans-serif** typefaces are composed of simple lines, whereas **serif** typefaces use small decorative marks to embellish characters and make them easier to read. Helvetica and Arial are sans-serif types and Times New Roman is a serif type. A **monospace** font, such as Courier, is one in which every character takes up the same amount of horizontal space. **Cursive** font styles emulate handwritten letterforms. **Decorative and fantasy** is a family for fonts that do not fit any of the other families.

More About

Formatting Text

Research shows that people read text on-screen differently than they read the printed word. They are more apt to scan and look for the important concepts. Many changes in formatting could make the site confusing.

Most Web pages use only the first three families. Dreamweaver provides a font combination feature available in the Property inspector. **Font combinations** determine how a browser displays your Web page's text. In the Property inspector, you can select one of six font combinations. A browser looks for the first font in the combination on the user's computer, then the second, and then the third. If none of the fonts in the combination are installed on the user's computer, the browser displays the text as specified by the user's browser preferences. Perform the following steps to change the font type.

 To Change the Font Type

1 Click to the left of the heading, **Discovering Scenic Florida**, and then drag through the entire heading. Point to the Font Combination box arrow in the Property inspector.

The heading is selected (Figure 1-50).

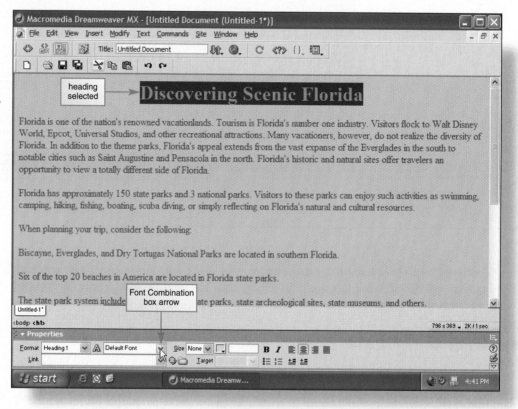

FIGURE 1-50

2 **Click the font combination box arrow and then point to Verdana, Arial, Helvetica.**

The Font Combination pop-up menu is displayed and the Verdana, Arial, Helvetica combination is highlighted (Figure 1-51). The menu includes six different font combinations and the default font.

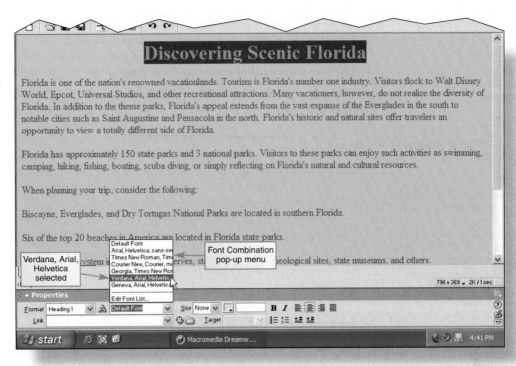

FIGURE 1-51

3 **Click Verdana, Arial, Helvetica.**

The new font type is applied to the selected heading (Figure 1-52).

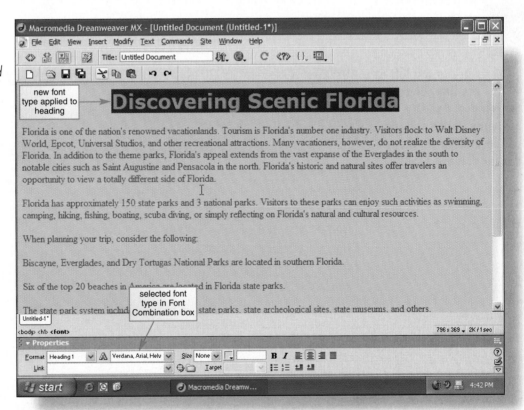

FIGURE 1-52

In addition to headings and font type attributes, other text design options are available. Presenting information in small chunks, such as bulleted or numbered lists, is a design element used by many Web page authors. Dreamweaver makes it easy to add lists such as these to your Web page.

Types of Lists

More About

Lists

You can remove the bullets or numbers from a formatted list just as easily as you added them. Select the formatted list. Click the button in the Properties inspector that you used originally to apply the formatting.

One way to group and organize information is by using lists. Web pages can have three types of lists: ordered or numbered, unordered or bulleted, and definition. **Ordered lists** contain text preceded by numbered steps. **Unordered lists** contain text preceded by bullets (dots or other symbols) or image bullets. You use an unordered list if the list items need not be listed in any particular order.

Definition lists do not use leading characters such as bullet points or numbers. Glossaries and descriptions often use this type of list. The Unordered List and Ordered List buttons are available in the Property inspector. The Definition List is not available in the Property inspector. You access this type of list command through the Text menu.

Creating an Unordered List

You can create a new list or you can create a list using existing text. Perform the following steps to create an unordered list using existing text.

Steps **To Create an Unordered List**

1 **Click to the left of the line, Biscayne, Everglades, and Dry Tortugas National Parks are located in southern Florida (Figure 1-53).**

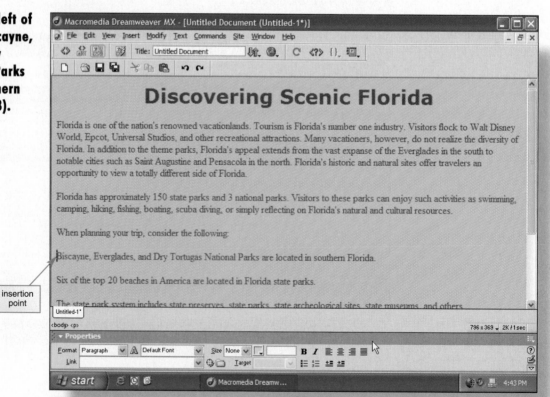

FIGURE 1-53

2 **Drag to select the text, Biscayne, Everglades, and Dry Tortugas National Parks are located in southern Florida, and the next three lines. Point to the Unordered List button in the Property inspector.**

The text is selected (Figure 1-54).

list items selected

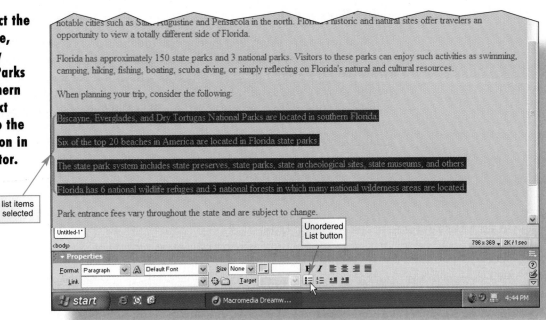

FIGURE 1-54

3 **Click the Unordered List button.**

A bullet is added to each line, the four lines are indented, and the space between each item is deleted (Figure 1-55). Later in this project, you will insert a blank line between each of the bulleted items.

bullets applied to list items

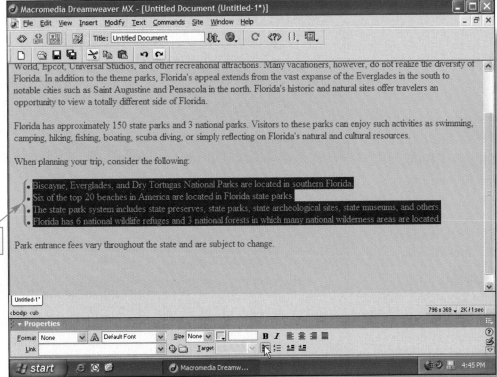

FIGURE 1-55

To emphasize the bulleted items further, you can use Text Indent. Text Indent will indent a line or a paragraph from both margins.

Other **Ways**

1. On Text menu point to List, click Unordered List on List submenu

Using Text Indent

When you are using **Text Indent**, the indentation takes place from both the left and right margins. Each side of the paragraph will move in by the same amount — two spaces for each indention. The text within the paragraph will rewrap to account for the shorter line length. In HTML, this is the BLOCKQUOTE tag. Text Outdent is the opposite of Text Indent. Clicking **Text Outdent** moves the paragraph back two spaces toward the margin for each indention. When you use Text Indent with a bulleted list, the shape of the bullet changes. Clicking the Text Indent button within a bulleted list, however, does not create a BLOCKQUOTE tag. Instead, a nested list is created. A **nested list** is one list inside of another.

 To Use Text Indent to Indent a Bulleted List

1 If necessary, select the bulleted list. Point to the Text Indent button in the Property inspector (Figure 1-56).

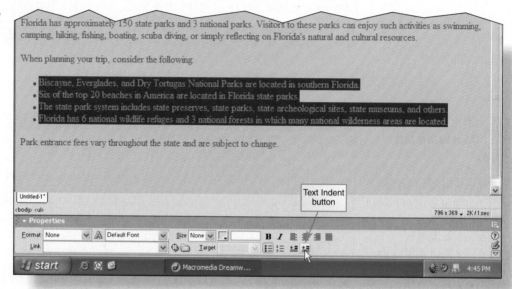

FIGURE 1-56

2 Click the Text Indent button.

The bulleted list indents and the shape of the bullet changes from a filled circle to a hollow circle (Figure 1-57).

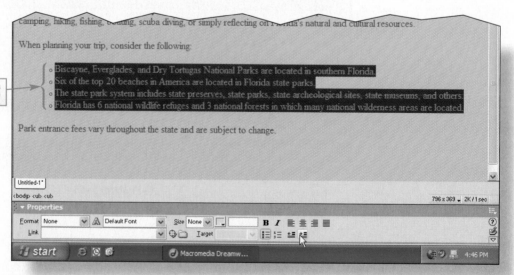

FIGURE 1-57

Other text formatting options are applying bold or italic styles to text. **Bold** characters display somewhat thicker and darker than those that are not bold. **Italic** characters slant to the right. The Property inspector contains buttons for both bold and italic font styles.

Applying Bold Formatting

To bold text within Dreamweaver is a simple procedure. If you have used word processing software, you are familiar with this process. The next step is to emphasize a sentence by applying bold formatting.

 To Bold Text

1 **If necessary, scroll down to display the closing paragraph. Drag through the text to select the entire paragraph (Figure 1-58). Point to the Bold button in the Property inspector.**

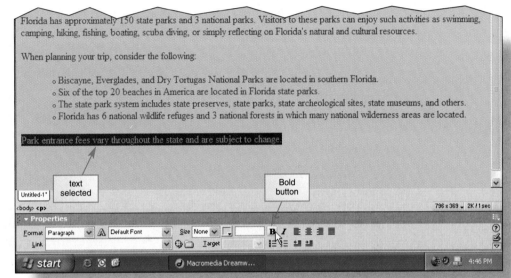

FIGURE 1-58

2 **Click the Bold button and then click anywhere in the Document window to deselect the text.**

Bold formatting is applied to the paragraph (Figure 1-59).

FIGURE 1-59

You also can use color for emphasis. Adding color to text can attract attention to important information.

Web-Safe Colors

It is easy to change the color of an individual character, a word, a line, a paragraph, or the text of an entire document. In HTML, colors are expressed either as hexadecimal values (for example, #FF0000) or as color names (red).

Use the **color picker** to select the colors for your page or text. Through the Property inspector, Dreamweaver provides access to five different color palettes: Color Cubes, Continuous Tone, Windows OS, Mac OS, and Grayscale. Color Cubes is the default color palette. Figure 1-60 shows the Color Cubes color palette available on the color palette pop-up menu.

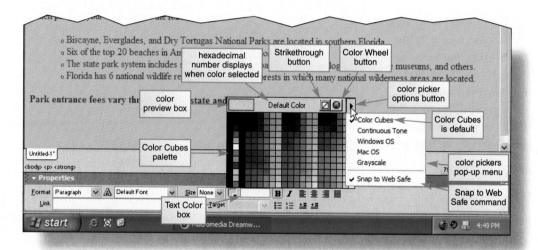

FIGURE 1-60

Two of the color palettes, Color Cubes and Continuous Tone, display Web-safe colors. Recall that Web-safe colors are colors that display correctly on the screen when someone is viewing your Web page through a browser. A Web-safe color is one that appears the same in Netscape Navigator and Microsoft Internet Explorer on both Windows and Macintosh systems. Most experts agree that approximately 212 to 216 Web-safe colors exist. Testing by experts, however, suggests that Internet Explorer renders only 212 Web-safe colors. Table 1-2 contains a list of the color picker options.

Table 1-2 Color Picker Options	
OPTION	FUNCTION
Color preview box	Provides a preview of the currently selected color or the color picked up by the eyedropper
Hex value area	Displays the hexadecimal value of the current color or the color picked up by the eyedropper
Strikethrough button	Clears current color and retains default color
Color Wheel button	Opens the system color pickers via the operating system Color dialog box
Option button	Displays a pop-up menu from which you can select five color pickers and Snap to Web Safe command
Snap to Web Safe command	Automatically changes non-Web-safe colors to the nearest Web-safe values

Dreamweaver has an **eyedropper** feature that lets you select colors and make perfect color matches. When you are working with color palettes, you can use the eyedropper to choose a color from anywhere on the screen, including outside of Dreamweaver, and apply the color to a selected object in the Document window. You place the eyedropper over the color you want to select and then click the mouse button. As soon as you click the mouse button, the color automatically is applied to the selected object. If you move the eyedropper to an object outside of Dreamweaver, the eyedropper changes to the block arrow mouse pointer shape until you move it back into the Dreamweaver window. Clicking the color picker options button and then selecting the Snap to Web Safe command will ensure the selected color is a Web-safe color.

Changing Text Color

The default color for Dreamweaver text is black. Adding a color scheme, however, changed the default text color to the color specified in the color scheme. The color scheme applied to the Web page changed the text color to a shade of blue. The colors for the supplied color schemes come from the Continuous Tone color picker. Perform the following steps to change the text color of the last sentence to dark blue. This color is a darker shade of the current text color.

 To Change the Text Color

1 **Select the closing paragraph and then click the Text Color box in the Property inspector.**

The Continuous Tone color palette is displayed (Figure 1-61). The color palette includes Web-safe colors, the color preview box, and the six-digit hexadecimal number that represents the selected color. In Figure 1-61, the hexadecimal number is #336666. This is the color of the text within this selected color scheme.

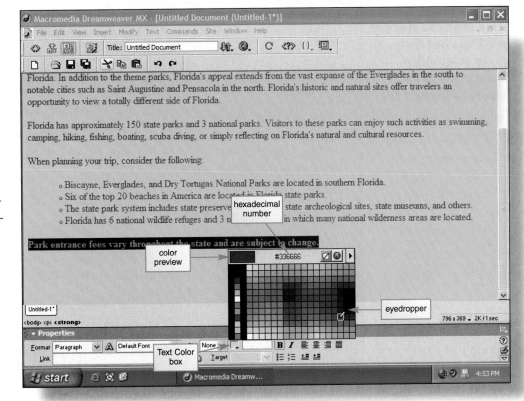

FIGURE 1-61

2 **Position the eyedropper on the shade of blue represented by hexadecimal number #333366 (row 5 from the bottom and column 3 from the right).**

The selected color appears in the color preview box, and the hexadecimal value area displays the number for the color (Figure 1-62).

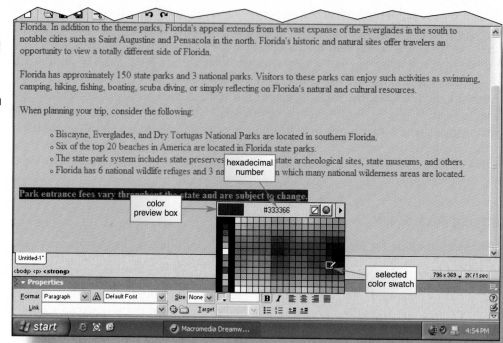

FIGURE 1-62

3 **Click the eyedropper to apply the color to the selected text and then close the color picker. Click anywhere in the document to deselect the text.**

The color is applied to the text. The paragraph is displayed in the dark blue color (Figure 1-63). Occasionally you may have to press the ESC key to close the picker.

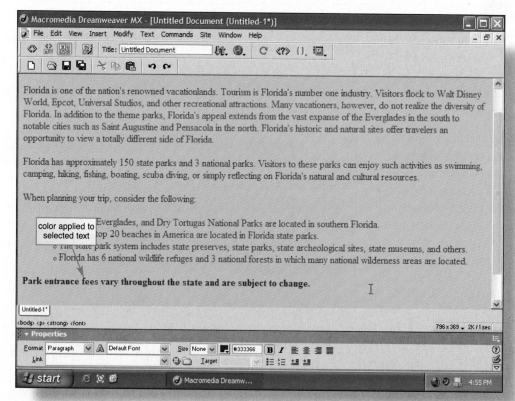

FIGURE 1-63

To add additional details to the Florida Parks Web page, a horizontal rule is inserted. Many Web designers use a horizontal rule to divide a Web page into sections and as a style element.

Horizontal Rules

A **horizontal rule** (or line) is useful for organizing information and visually separating text and objects. You can specify the width and height of the rule in pixels or as a percentage of the page size. The rule can be aligned to the left, center, or right, and you can add shading or draw the line in a solid color. These attributes are available in the Property inspector. The HTML tag for a horizontal rule is <HR>.

Inserting a Horizontal Rule

On the Discovering Scenic Florida Web page, you will insert a horizontal rule between the document heading and text. You will use the default shaded line, but change the width and the height of the rule and then center the rule.

 Steps **To Insert a Horizontal Rule**

1 **If necessary, scroll to the top of the page. Click to the right of the heading, Discovering Scenic Florida, and then press the END key.**

Pressing the END key moves the insertion point outside the HTML tags surrounding the heading (Figure 1-64).

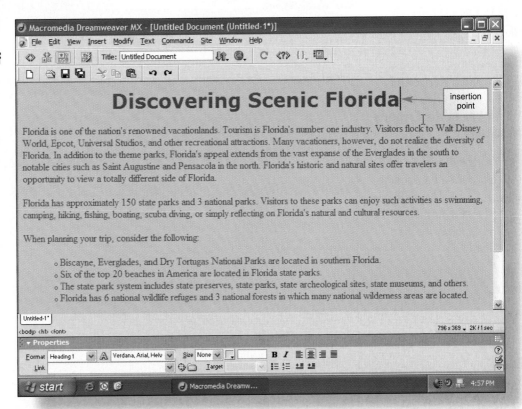

FIGURE 1-64

Dreamweaver MX

2 **Click Insert on the menu bar and point to Horizontal Rule (Figure 1-65).**

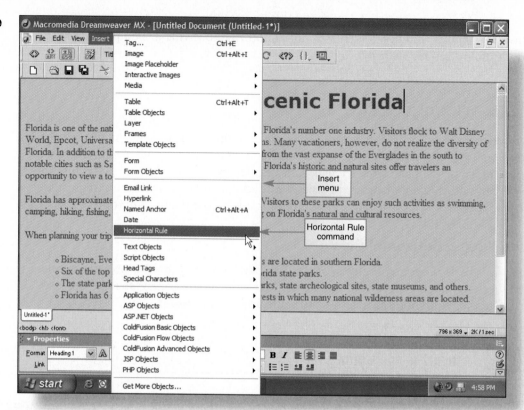

FIGURE 1-65

3 **Click Horizontal Rule. Click the Width box in the Property inspector.**

The horizontal rule is inserted below the heading (Figure 1-66). The attributes in the Property inspector change to those for the horizontal rule.

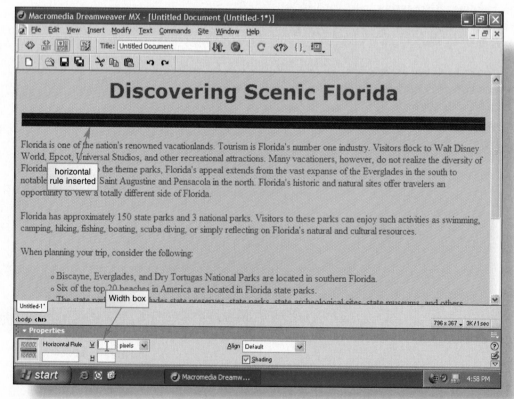

FIGURE 1-66

4 **Type** 500 **and then press the ENTER key. Click the Height box.**

The width of the line decreases (Figure 1-67).

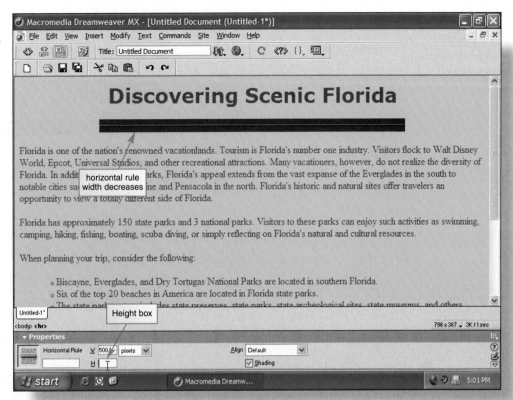

FIGURE 1-67

5 **Type** 6 **and then press the ENTER key. Point to the Align box arrow.**

The height of the line increases (Figure 1-68).

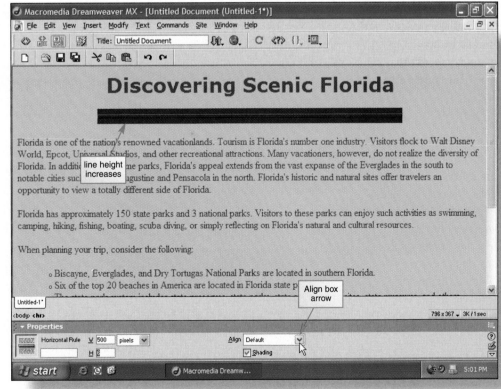

FIGURE 1-68

6 **Click the Align box arrow and then point to Center (Figure 1-69).**

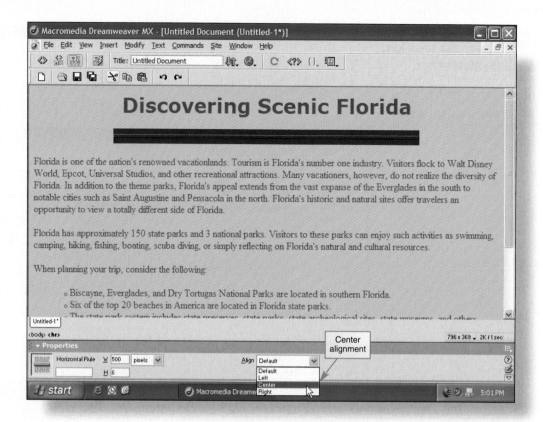

FIGURE 1-69

7 **Click Center and then click anywhere in the Document window to deselect the horizontal rule.**

The rule is centered (Figure 1-70). Even though the rule appeared centered before applying the Center attribute, it would not necessarily appear centered when viewed in all browsers. Adding the Center attribute assures that it always will be centered below the heading.

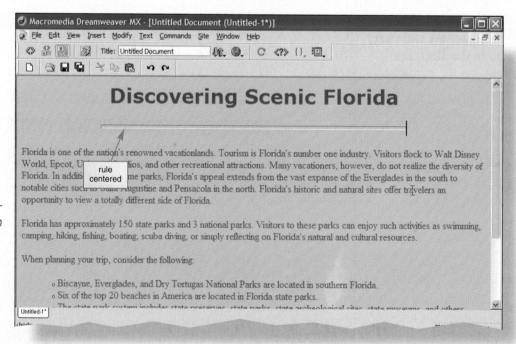

FIGURE 1-70

The next step illustrates using the Insert bar to insert a line break between the bulleted items.

he Insert Bar

The **Insert bar** is a panel consisting of 12 categories organized into tabs. Within each category are buttons for inserting common page elements. Clicking a tab accesses the buttons for that category. The **Characters category** includes the Line Break button and other buttons that allow you to insert a variety of symbols into your Web pages. A **line break** starts a new line of text at the exact point at which the LINE BREAK tag is encountered. The HTML tag for a line break is <BR>.

Perform the following steps to display the Insert bar.

Steps To Display the Insert Bar

1 **Click Window on the menu bar and then point to Insert.**

The Window menu is displayed and the Insert command is highlighted (Figure 1-71).

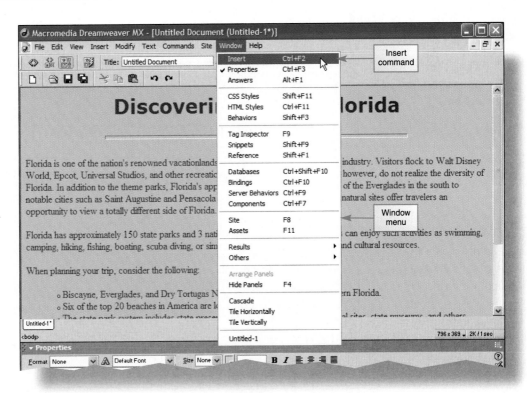

FIGURE 1-71

2 **Click Insert.**

Dreamweaver displays the Insert bar in the Document window (Figure 1-72). The Insert bar can display to the right of the Standard toolbar or above or below the Standard toolbar. Monitor resolution and the settings within the Dreamweaver window determine where the Insert bar is displayed.

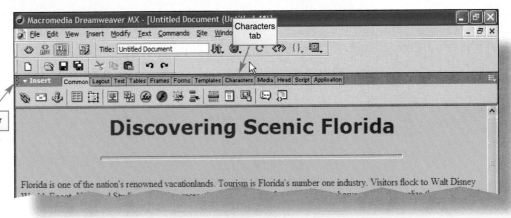

FIGURE 1-72

HTML

For more information about HTML, visit the Dreamweaver MX More About Web page (scsite.com/ dreamweavermx/ more.htm) and then click HTML.

Inserting a Line Break

When you added bullets to the items list earlier in this project, the blank line between each item was removed. Removing the blank line between items is a result of how Dreamweaver interprets the HTML code. A blank line between the bulleted items, however, will provide better spacing and readability when the Web page is viewed through a browser. You can add blank lines in several ways. You might assume that pressing the ENTER key at the end of each line would be the quickest way to accomplish this. Pressing the ENTER key, however, adds another bullet. The easiest way to accomplish the task of adding blank lines is to insert line breaks. Recall that the line break starts a new single line without inserting a blank line between lines of text. Inserting two line breaks, however, adds a single blank line. Perform the following steps to add a blank line between each of the bulleted items.

 To Add a Line Break

1 **Click the Characters tab in the Insert bar.**

The Characters tab displays buttons with special characters (Figure 1-73). The Line Break button inserts a line break rather than a blank line. As soon as the browser encounters a <BR> tag, it starts a new line with the text that follows the tag. Adding two consecutive <BR> tags will create a blank line.

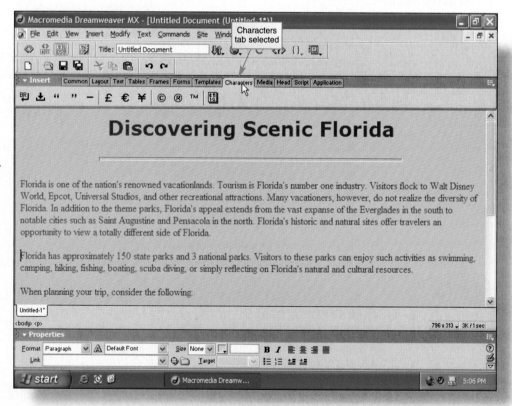

FIGURE 1-73

2 If necessary, scroll down and then click at the end of the first bulleted item. Point to the Line Break button on the Characters tab in the Insert bar (Figure 1-74).

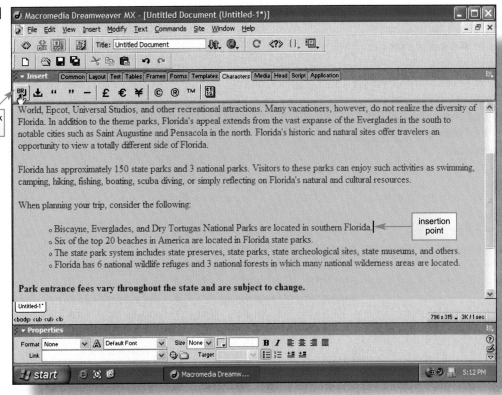

FIGURE 1-74

3 Click the Line Break button two times.

Two line breaks are inserted (Figure 1-75). When the Web page is viewed in Dreamweaver, it appears that two blank lines are inserted. When viewed in a browser, however, only one blank line will be displayed between each item. You will view your Web page in a browser later in this project.

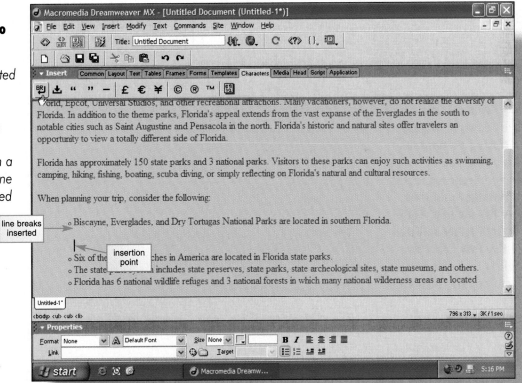

FIGURE 1-75

4 **Click the Line Break button two times at the end of the second and third bulleted items to insert blank lines between the second and third and the third and fourth bulleted list items.**

The bulleted items display with two blank lines between them in the Document window (Figure 1-76).

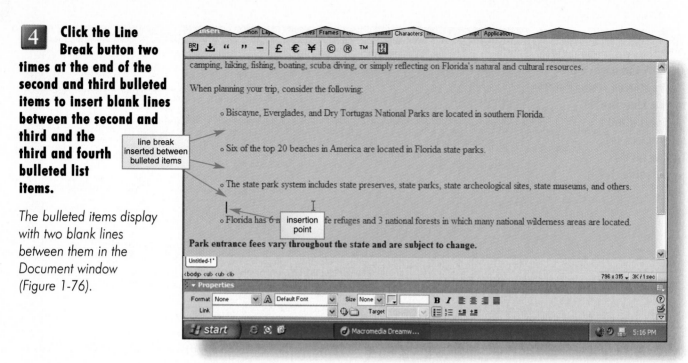

line break inserted between bulleted items

insertion point

FIGURE 1-76

When creating a Web document, it is a good idea to add your name and current date to the document. Insert a single line break between your name and the date. Complete the following steps to add this information.

 To Add Your Name and Current Date

1 **If necessary, scroll down to display the closing paragraph. Click at the end of the closing paragraph. Press the ENTER key and then press the END key. Verify that Bold is not selected and the Text Color box displays the correct color in the Property inspector.**

The insertion point moves to the next paragraph (Figure 1-77). Pressing the END key insures that you are not within the HTML code used to bold and add color to the closing line.

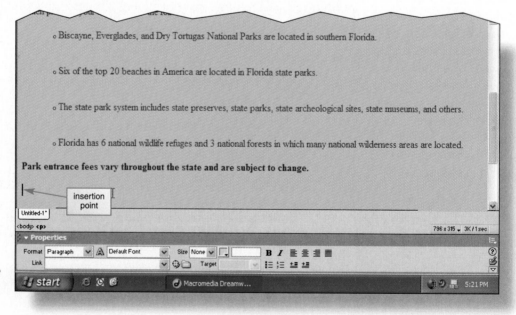

insertion point

FIGURE 1-77

2 Type your name. Do not press the ENTER key. Point to the Line Break button (Figure 1-78).

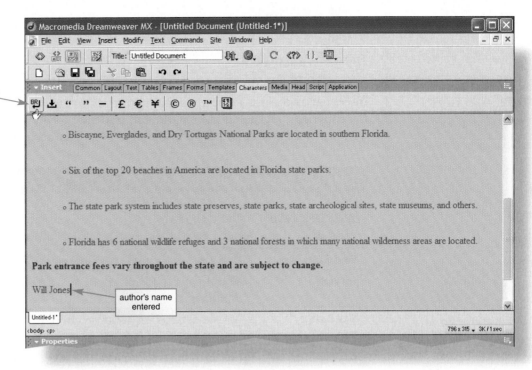

FIGURE 1-78

3 Click the Line Break button. Type the current date and then press the ENTER key.

The insertion point moves to the next line (Figure 1-79). No line space displays between the name and the date.

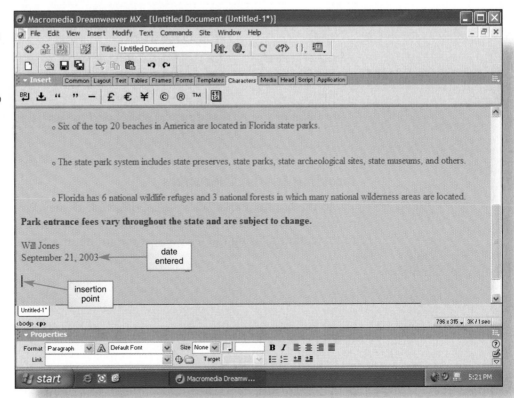

FIGURE 1-79

Other Ways

1. Press CTRL+ENTER

You now will use the Insert bar to add special characters to your Web page.

Special Characters

In addition to the line break character you used earlier, the Characters tab in the Insert bar also contains buttons that allow you to enter special characters, including the copyright, registered trademark, and trademark symbols. Table 1-3 lists all the button names and descriptions available on the Characters tab.

Table 1-3 Buttons on the Characters Tab		
BUTTON NAME	*DESCRIPTION*	*HTML TAGS AND CHARACTER ENTITIES*
Line Break	Places a line break at the insertion point	
Non-Breaking Space	Places a non-breaking space at the insertion point	
Left Quote	Places opening, curved double quotation marks at the insertion point	&#147;
Right Quote	Places closing, curved double quotation marks at the insertion point	&#148;
Em Dash	Places an em dash at the insertion point	&#151;
Pound	Places a pound (currency) symbol at the insertion point	&pound;
Euro	Places a euro (currency) symbol at the insertion point	&euro;
Yen	Places a yen (currency) symbol at the insertion point	&yen;
Copyright	Places a copyright symbol at the insertion point	&copy;
Registered Trademark	Places a registered trademark symbol at the insertion point	&reg;
Trademark	Places a trademark symbol at the insertion point	&#153;
Other Characters	Provides a set of special characters from which to select	Other ASCII characters

Inserting Special Characters

In the Florida Parks Web page, both Walt Disney World® and Epcot® are registered names. The following steps insert the registered trademark symbol next to these names, using the Characters tab in the Insert bar.

To Insert a Registered Trademark Character

1 Scroll up to display the first paragraph in the Web page. Click to the right of World (in Walt Disney World) and before the comma and then point to the Registered Trademark button on the Characters tab (Figure 1-80).

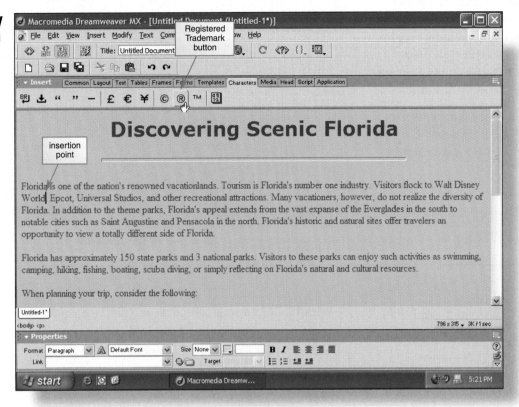

FIGURE 1-80

2 Click the Registered Trademark button.

The registered trademark symbol is inserted into the document (Figure 1-81).

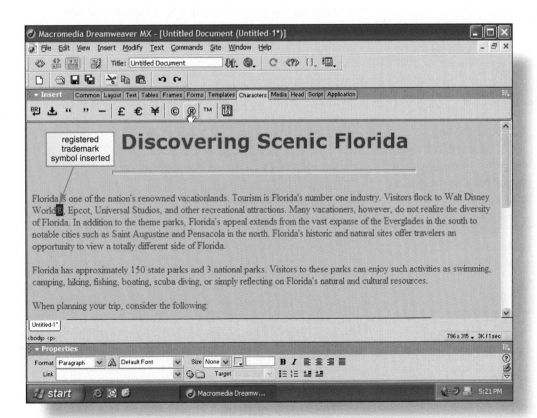

FIGURE 1-81

3 Click to the right of Epcot and before the comma and then click the Registered Trademark button on the Characters tab. Click anywhere in the document to deselect the symbol.

The registered trademark symbol is inserted into the document (Figure 1-82).

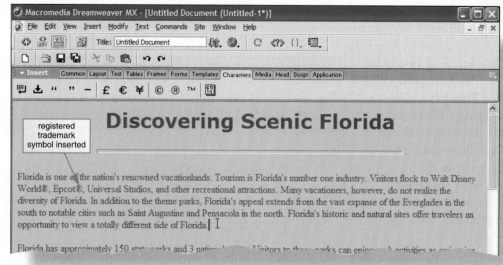

FIGURE 1-82

With the formatting complete, the next step is to collapse the Property inspector.

Collapsing the Property Inspector

Panels such as the Property inspector displaying in the Dreamweaver window require considerable space. If you are finished working with a panel, generally it is better to collapse or close it. **Collapsing** it leaves the title bar in the window, which allows you to expand it easily by clicking the expand/collapse arrow instead of using the Properties command on the Window menu. **Closing** it removes it completely from the Document window. The following step collapses the Property inspector.

 To Collapse the Property Inspector

1 Click the expand/collapse arrow on the left corner of the Property inspector title bar.

The Property inspector collapses (minimizes) (Figure 1-83).

FIGURE 1-83

One of the more important elements of your Web page is the title. An appropriate and meaningful title adds value to a Web page.

Web Page Titles

A **Web page title** helps Web site visitors keep track of what they are viewing as they browse. It is important to give your Web page an appropriate title. When visitors to your Web page create bookmarks or add the Web page to their Favorites lists, the title is used for the reference. If you do not title a page, the page will appear in the browser window, Favorites lists, and history lists as Untitled Document. Because many search engines use the Web page title, it is important to use a creative and meaningful name. (Giving the document a file name by saving it is not the same as giving the page a title.)

Changing a Web Page Title

The current title of your Web page is Untitled Document. Unless you change the title of the Web page, this name will be displayed on the browser title bar when the page is opened in a browser window. Perform the following steps to change the name of the Web page to Florida Parks.

 Steps To Change the Web Page Title

1 **Drag through the text, Untitled Document, in the Title text box on the Document toolbar.**

The text is highlighted to indicate that it is selected (Figure 1-84).

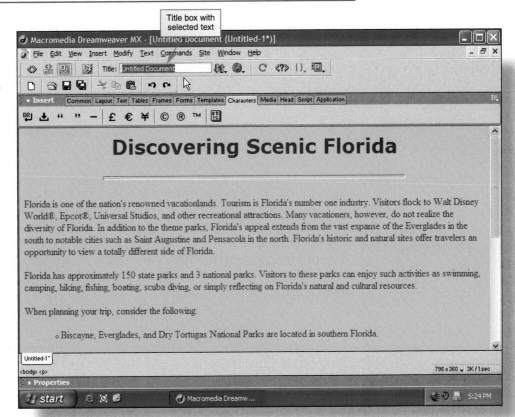

FIGURE 1-84

2 **Type** Florida Parks **in the Title text box and then press the ENTER key.**

The new name, Florida Parks, is displayed in the Title text box and on the Dreamweaver title bar (Figure 1-85).

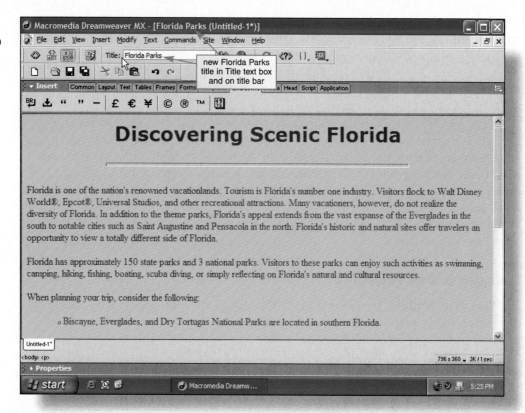

FIGURE 1-85

With all the text of the document entered, you can check the spelling of the document.

Checking Spelling

After you create a Web page, you should check it visually for spelling errors. In addition, you can use Dreamweaver's Check Spelling command to identify possible misspellings. The Check Spelling command ignores HTML tags and attributes. Recall from the Introduction that attributes are additional information contained within an HTML tag.

Perform the following steps to start the Check Spelling command and check your entire document. Your Web page may contain different misspelled words depending on the accuracy of your typing.

 **To Check Spelling**

1 **Click Text on the menu bar and then point to Check Spelling.**

Dreamweaver displays the Text menu (Figure 1-86).

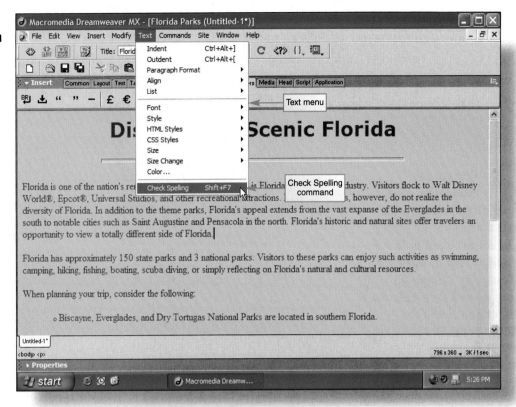

FIGURE 1-86

2 **Click Check Spelling. Point to the Ignore button.**

The Check Spelling dialog box is displayed (Figure 1-87). The Dreamweaver spelling checker displays the word, Epcot, in the Word not found in dictionary box. Suggestions for the correct spelling are displayed in the Suggestions list.

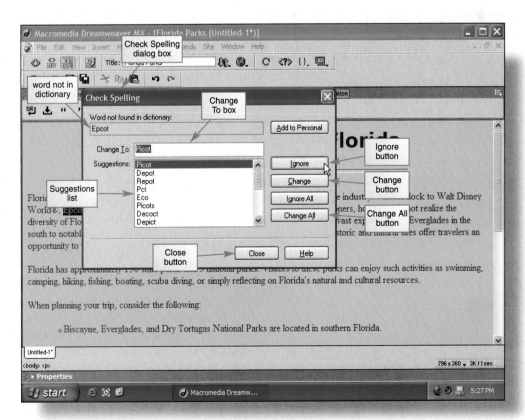

FIGURE 1-87

3 **Click the Ignore button.**

The spelling checker ignores the word, Epcot, and continues searching for additional misspelled words. If the spelling checker identifies a word that is spelled correctly, clicking the Ignore button skips the word.

4 **Correct any misspelled word by accepting the suggested replacement or by typing the correct word in the Change To box. Click the Change or Change All button, and then point to the OK button in the Macromedia Dreamweaver MX dialog box.**

When Dreamweaver has checked all text for misspellings, it displays the Macromedia Dreamweaver MX dialog box informing you that the spelling check is complete (Figure 1-88).

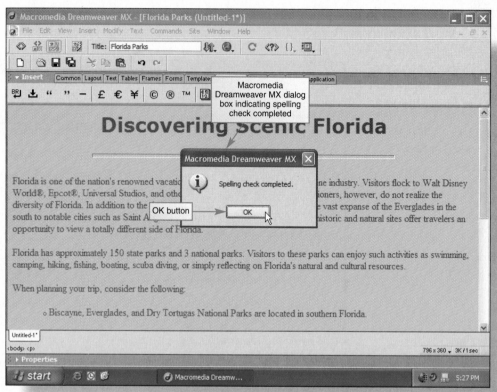

FIGURE 1-88

5 **Click the OK button.**

Dreamweaver closes the Check Spelling dialog box and displays the Document window.

Other Ways

1. Press SHIFT+F7

Types of Links

Links are a distinguishing feature of the World Wide Web. A **link**, also referred to as a **hyperlink**, is the path to another document, to another part of the same document, or to other media such as an image or a movie. Most links are displayed as colored and/or underlined text, although you also can link from an image or other object. Clicking a link accesses the corresponding document, other media, or another place within the same document. If you place the mouse pointer over the link, the link address or path usually appears at the bottom of the window on the status bar.

Three types of link paths are available: absolute, relative, and root-relative. An **absolute link** provides the complete URL of the document. This type of link also is referred to as an **external link**. Absolute links contain the protocol (such as http://) and primarily are used to link to documents on other servers. Project 2 contains detailed information on the other types of links. In the following steps, you enter text and create an absolute link to a Florida environmental Web site. The link will be between the closing paragraph and your name. You will create the link using the Property inspector Link box.

 **To Create an Absolute Link**

1 **Click the expand/collapse arrow in the Property inspector. Position the insertion point at the end of the closing paragraph, press the ENTER key, and then press the END key.**

The Property inspector is displayed and the insertion point is between the closing line and your name (Figure 1-89).

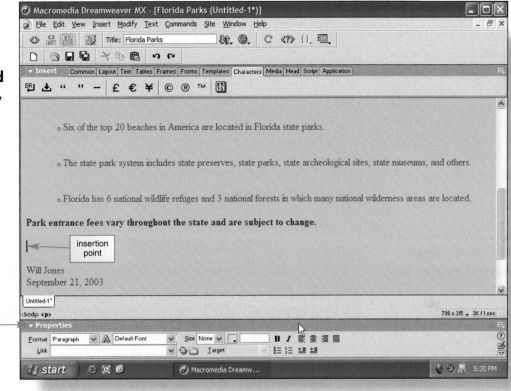

FIGURE 1-89

2 **Type** Florida Environmental Information **and then drag to select the text you typed. Click the Link box in the Property inspector.**

The text for the link is selected (Figure 1-90).

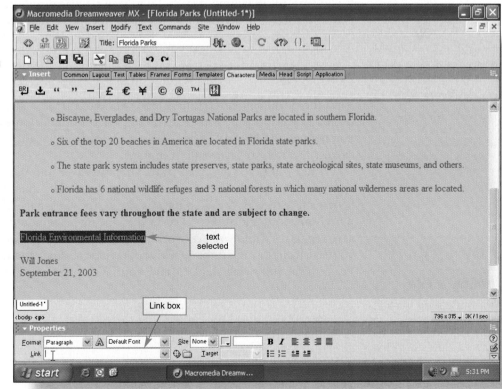

FIGURE 1-90

3 **Type**
http://www.dep
.state.fl.us **and then
press the ENTER key.**

*The link text is highlighted
and underlined in the
Document window. The link
is displayed in the Link box
(Figure 1-91). The link color
is part of the color scheme.
Later in this project, you will
test the link when you preview the Web page in a
browser.*

4 **Click anywhere in
the Document**
**window to deselect the
link.**

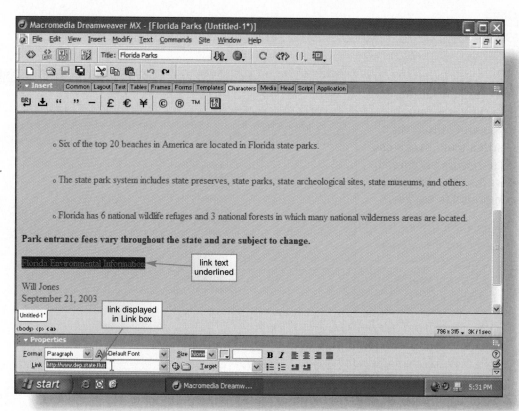

FIGURE 1-91

As you create a Web page in Dreamweaver, the computer stores it in memory.
If you turn off the computer or if you lose electrical power, the document in memory
is lost. Hence, it is necessary to save any document that you will use later.

More About

Saving Your File

It is a good idea to save
your file as soon as you
have created it. Continue
to save the file as you add
more content.

More About

Naming a File

When saving a file, use a
meaningful file name. Do
not put spaces in the file
name. To prevent problems
with any server, use no
more than eight lowercase
letters in the file name.

Saving the Web Page

With the document entered and spell checked, the next step is to save the Web page.
Earlier in this project, you created the parks subfolder on the Local Disk (C:) when
you defined the Florida Parks Web site. Verify with your instructor that this is the
correct location to save your Web page.

When you save your Web page, Dreamweaver automatically appends the
extension .htm to the file name. Documents with the **.htm** extension display in Web
browsers. Although the Web page is saved, the Web page also remains in your computer's memory and is displayed in the Document window. It is a good practice to
save regularly while you are working in Dreamweaver. By doing so, you protect
yourself from losing all the work you have done since the last time you saved.
Perform the following steps to save your Web page within the parks subfolder.

To Save a Web Page

1 Click the Save button on the Standard toolbar (Figure 1-92).

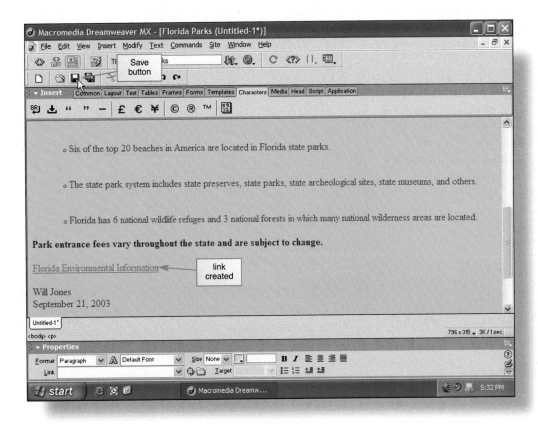

FIGURE 1-92

2 Type index **in the File name text box and then point to the Save button in the Save As dialog box.**

The Save As dialog is displayed (Figure 1-93). The parks folder name is displayed in the Save in box. The index file name is displayed in the File name box.

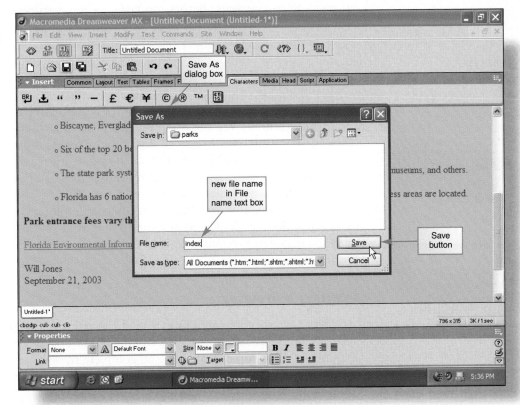

FIGURE 1-93

3 **Click the Save button and then press the F8 key to display the Site panel.**

Dreamweaver displays the Document window and the Site panel (Figure 1-94). The Florida Parks index.htm page is saved in the parks local folder. The path to the index file is C:\jonesw\ parks\index.htm.

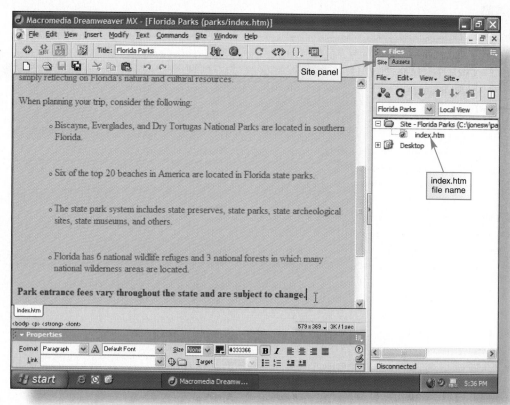

FIGURE 1-94

Other Ways

1. Press CTRL+S

With your Web page ready to share with the world, you next must select browsers to ensure your visitors can view the page properly. The two more popular browsers are Internet Explorer and Netscape.

Selecting Primary and Secondary Target Browsers

After you have created a Web page, it is a good practice to test your Web pages by previewing them in Web browsers to ensure they display correctly. Using this strategy helps you catch errors so you will not copy or repeat them.

As you create your Web page, you should be aware of the variety of available Web browsers. More than 24 different Web browsers are in use, most of which have been released in more than one version. Most Web developers target recent versions of Netscape Navigator and Microsoft Internet Explorer, which are used by the majority of Web users. You also should know that visitors viewing your Web page might have earlier versions of these browsers. You can define up to 20 browsers for previewing.

Selecting a Browser

The browser preferences are selected through the Preferences dialog box. Perform the following steps to select your target browsers: Microsoft Internet Explorer and Netscape Navigator. To complete these steps requires that you have both Internet Explorer and Netscape installed on your computer.

More About

Browsers

Just as you determined a primary and secondary browser, you also can remove a browser from your list. Click Edit on the menu bar and then click Preferences. Select the name of the browser you want to remove and then click the minus (–) button.

To Select Primary and Secondary Target Browsers

1 **Right-click the Files panel menu bar and close the panel group. Click File on the menu bar, point to Preview in Browser, and then point to Edit Browser List on the Preview in Browser submenu.**

Dreamweaver displays the File menu and Preview in Browser submenu (Figure 1-95).

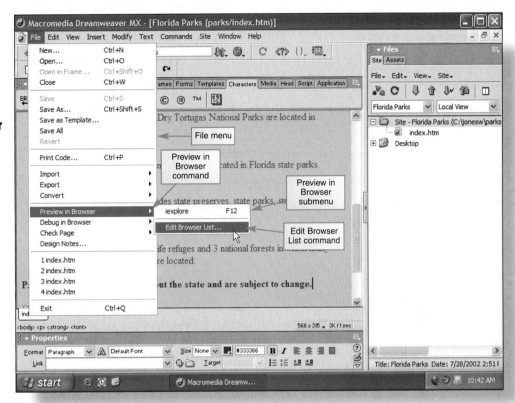

FIGURE 1-95

2 **Click Edit Browser List and point to the plus (+) button.**

The Preferences dialog box is displayed and the Preview in Browser category is selected (Figure 1-96). The primary browser was selected when Dreamweaver was installed on your computer. In this book, the primary browser is Internet Explorer. The browser name, iexplore, was selected automatically during the Dreamweaver installation.

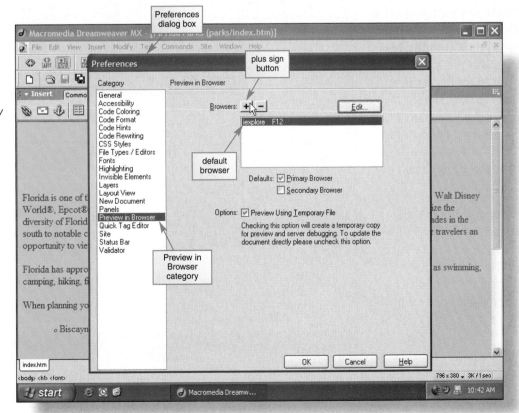

FIGURE 1-96

3 Click the plus (+) button in the Preview in Browser area. Point to the Browse button.

Dreamweaver displays the Add Browser dialog box (Figure 1-97).

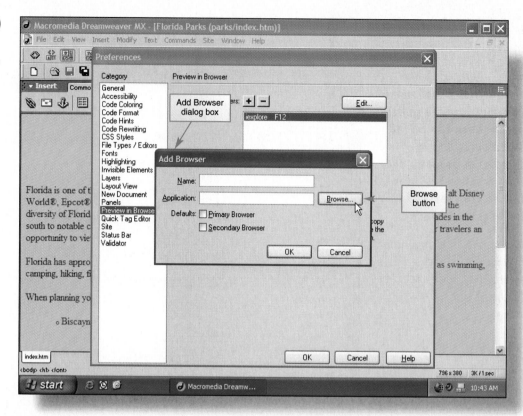

FIGURE 1-97

4 Click the Browse button and then locate the Netscp.exe file. Most likely this file is located on Local Drive (C:). Use the following path to locate the file: C:\Program Files\ Netscape\Netscape\ Netscp.exe. Point to the Open button in the Select Browser dialog box.

The Select Browser dialog box is displayed (Figure 1-98). The Netscp.exe file is selected. Different versions of Netscape may display a different file name or a different path.

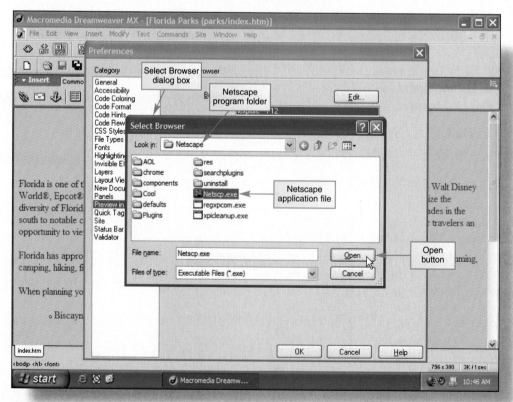

FIGURE 1-98

5 Click the Open button. Click Secondary Browser and then point to the OK button in the Add Browser dialog box.

The Name box displays Netscp.exe. The Application box displays the path and file name (Figure 1-99). The path and spelling of Netscape on your computer may be different from those shown.

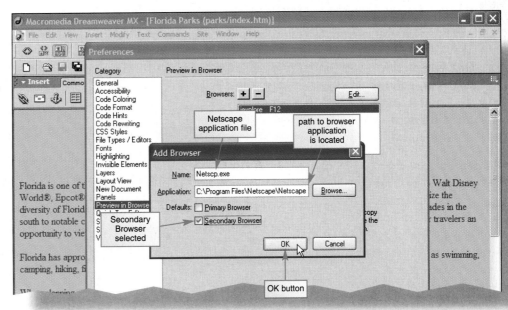

FIGURE 1-99

6 Click the OK button. If necessary, click Preview Using Temporary File to select it. Point to the OK button in the Preferences dialog box.

Netscape is added as the secondary browser (Figure 1-100).

7 Click the OK button.

The target browsers are selected, and Dreamweaver displays the Document window.

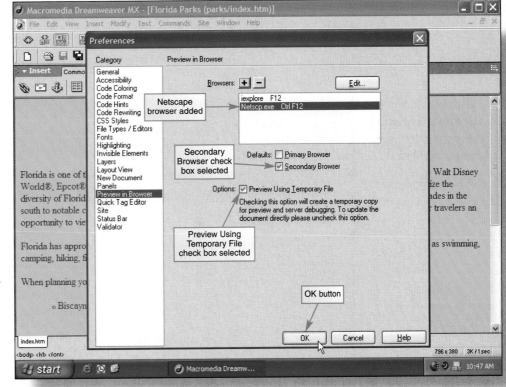

FIGURE 1-100

Previewing a Web Page in a Browser

With the target browsers set up, you can preview your Web pages in the browsers at any time. You do not have to save the document first. The steps on the next two pages illustrate how to preview a Web page.

To Preview the Web Page

1 **Click File on the menu bar, point to Preview in Browser, and then point to iexplore.**

The File menu and Preview in Browser submenu are displayed (Figure 1-101). The Preview in Browser submenu includes the names of both your primary and secondary browsers and the Edit Browser List command. Clicking the Edit Browser List command displays the Preferences dialog box.

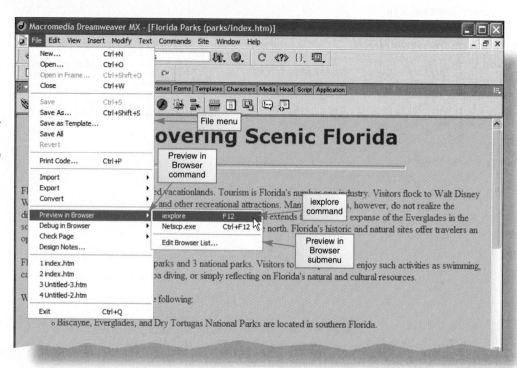

FIGURE 1-101

2 **Click iexplore (Internet Explorer). If necessary, maximize your browser window.**

Internet Explorer starts and displays the Web page in a browser window (Figure 1-102). Your browser name may be different. The file name displayed in the Address bar is a temporary name.

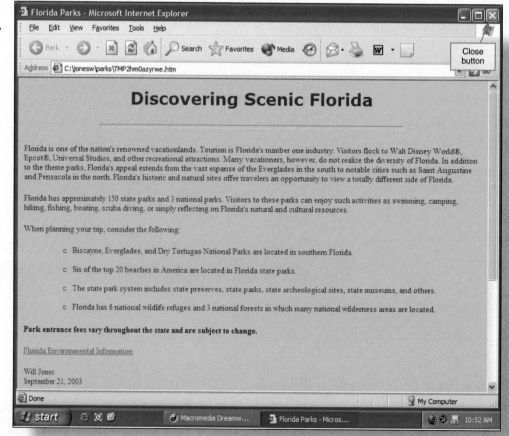

FIGURE 1-102

3 **Click Internet Explorer's Close button. Click File on the menu bar, point to Preview in Browser, and then click Netscp.exe on the Preview in Browser submenu.**

Netscape opens and displays the Web page in a browser window (Figure 1-103). Your browser name may be different. Compare how the files display in the two browsers.

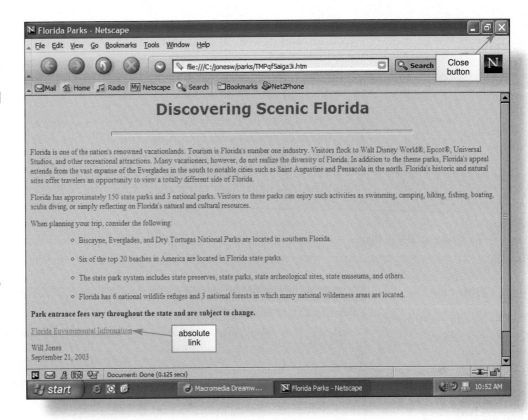

FIGURE 1-103

4 **If necessary, scroll down the page and click the absolute link to the Florida Environmental Information Web site.**

The Florida Department of Environmental Protection Web site is displayed (Figure 1-104). You must be online to complete this step.

5 **Click Netscape's Close button. If necessary, click the Dreamweaver button on the taskbar.**

The Dreamweaver Document window is displayed.

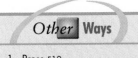

1. Press F12
2. Press CTRL+F12

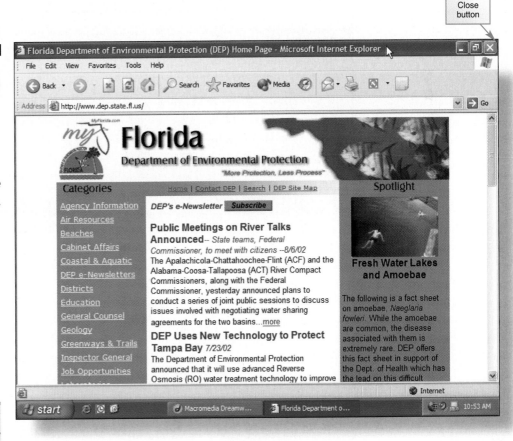

FIGURE 1-104

Your instructor may require that you print a copy of your Web page. The next step illustrates how to print a page.

Printing a Web Page

A variety of reasons exists why you may want to print a Web page. Interestingly, Dreamweaver provides an option to print code, but does not provide a print option to print the Design view. To print a Web page, first you must preview it in a browser. Printing a page from your browser is similar to printing a word processing document. The following steps illustrate printing the Web page in the browser.

Steps To Print a Web Page

1 **Press F12.**

The Web page is displayed in Internet Explorer.

2 **Click File on the menu bar and then point to Print (Figure 1-105).**

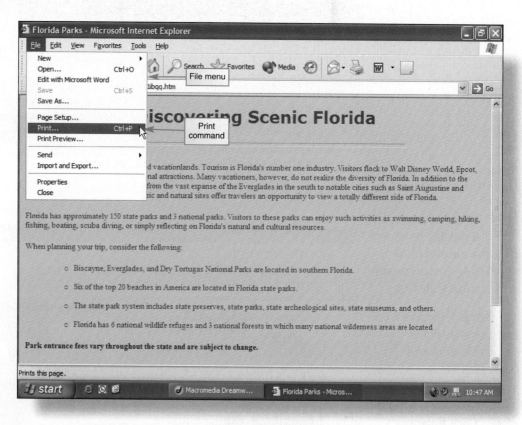

FIGURE 1-105

3   **Click Print. If necessary, select an appropriate printer. Point to the Print button.**

Internet Explorer displays the Print dialog box (Figure 1-106). Your selected printer is likely to be different from the one shown in Figure 1-106.

4   **Click the Print button.**

The Print dialog box closes and your Web page is sent to the printer.

5   **Retrieve the printout and then click Internet Explorer's Close button.**

The browser closes and Dreamweaver displays the Document window.

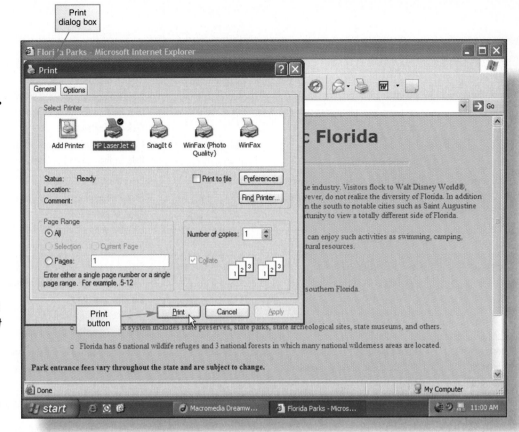

FIGURE 1-106

Dreamweaver Help System

Reference materials and other forms of assistance are available using the Dreamweaver Help system. You can display these materials, print them, or copy them to a word processing document. Table 1-4 on the next page summarizes the categories of online Help available. Several methods are available to activate the first four types listed in the table. Appendix A provides detailed instructions on using Dreamweaver Help.

Table 1-4 Dreamweaver Help System

TYPE	DESCRIPTION	HOW TO ACTIVATE
Contents sheet	Use the Contents sheet to view information organized by topic and then by subtopic, as you would in the table of contents of a book.	• Press the F1 key. Click the Contents tab. • Click Help on the menu bar and then click Using Dreamweaver. Click the Contents tab. • Click the options button on the title bar of a panel group and then click Help on the options pop-up menu. Click the Contents tab.
Index sheet	Use the Index sheet to look up specific terms or concepts, as you would in the index of a book.	• Press the F1 key. Click the Index tab. • Click Help on the menu bar and then click Using Dreamweaver. Click the Index tab. • Click the options button on the title bar of a panel group and then click Help on the options pop-up menu. Click the Index tab.
Search sheet	Use the Search sheet to find any character string, anywhere in the text of the Help system.	• Press the F1 key. Click the Search tab. • Click Help on the menu bar and then click Using Dreamweaver. Click the Search tab. • Click the options button on the title bar of a panel group and then click Help on the options pop-up menu. Click the Search tab.
Question Mark button or Help icon	Clicking the Question Mark button provides context-sensitive help in dialog boxes and inspectors.	• Click a Help button or Question Mark button in a dialog box. • Click the Help icon in an inspector or other kind of window.
Tutorials	Step-by-step lessons that focus on a specific Web design feature or topic.	• Click Help on the menu bar and then click Tutorials.
Dreamweaver online tutorials	Step-by-step online tutorials	• Access the Dreamweaver tutorial Web site at macromedia.com/desdev/mx/dreamweaver/index.html

Quitting Dreamweaver

After you create, save, preview, and print the Florida Parks Web page and review how to use Help, Project 1 is complete. To close the Web page, quit Dreamweaver MX, and return control to Windows, perform the following step.

Other Ways

1. On File menu click Exit
2. Press CTRL+W

TO CLOSE THE WEB SITE AND QUIT DREAMWEAVER

1 Click the Close button on the right corner of the Dreamweaver title bar.

The Dreamweaver window, the Document window, and Florida Parks Web site all close. If you have unsaved changes, Dreamweaver will prompt you to save the changes. Clicking the Yes button in the Dreamweaver MX dialog box saves the changes.

CASE PERSPECTIVE SUMMARY

The local Web site and Web page are complete. Will is pleased that he now can share his affection for Florida's Parks with others on the Internet. During the process, Will learned a lot about using Dreamweaver to define a Web site and to create simple, yet informative Web pages. He was amazed at how easy it was to add a color scheme, format and add color to text, create a bulleted list, and insert a rule to add variety to the elements of the page. He was happy to learn about absolute links and that visitors using virtually any Web browser would be able to view his Web page once it was uploaded to a server. He is looking forward to doing more with this Web site using these and other Dreamweaver tools.

Opening a Web Page

Opening a Web page in Dreamweaver is much the same as opening an existing document in most other software applications: that is, you use the File menu and Open command. If, however, the page is part of a Dreamweaver Web site, you also can open the file from the Site panel.

To open a Web page from the Site panel, you must select the appropriate Web site. The site pop-up menu in the Site panel lists sites you have defined. When you open the site, a list of pages and subfolders within the site displays. To open the page, double-click the file name. After opening the page, you can modify text, images, tables, and any other elements.

Project Summary

Project 1 introduced you to starting Dreamweaver, defining a Web site, and creating a Web page. You added a color scheme and used Dreamweaver's Property inspector to format text, change font color, and center text. You also learned how to apply color to text, add a horizontal rule, and use an unordered list to organize information. You used the Insert bar to add line breaks and special characters. Using the Property inspector, you added an absolute link. Once your Web page was completed, you learned to save the Web page, preview it in a browser, and test your absolute link. You learned how to print using the browser. To enhance your knowledge of Dreamweaver further, you learned basics about the Dreamweaver Help system.

What You Should Know

Having completed this project, you now should be able to perform the tasks shown in Table 1-5.

Table 1-5   Project 1 What You Should Know

TASK NUMBER	TASK	PAGE NUMBER	TASK NUMBER	TASK	PAGE NUMBER
1	Start Dreamweaver	DW 1.04	15	Insert a Horizontal Rule	DW 1.45
2	Close All Open Panels	DW 1.10	16	Display the Insert Bar	DW 1.49
3	Use the Site Definition Wizard to Create a Local Web Site	DW 1.12	17	Add a Line Break	DW 1.50
			18	Add Your Name and Current Date	DW 1.52
4	Add a Color Scheme	DW 1.22	19	Insert a Registered Trademark Character	DW 1.55
5	Close the Site Panel and Display the Standard Toolbar	DW 1.24			
6	Create a Web Page	DW 1.26	20	Collapse the Property Inspector	DW 1.56
7	Open the Property Inspector	DW 1.29	21	Change the Web Page Title	DW 1.57
8	Format Text with Heading 1	DW 1.33	22	Check Spelling	DW 1.59
9	Center the Web Page Heading	DW 1.35	23	Create an Absolute Link	DW 1.61
10	Change the Font Type	DW 1.36	24	Save a Web Page	DW 1.63
11	Create an Unordered List	DW 1.38	25	Select Primary and Secondary Target Browsers	DW 1.65
12	Use Text Indent to Indent a Bulleted List	DW 1.40	26	Preview the Web Page	DW 1.68
			27	Print a Web Page	DW 1.70
13	Bold Text	DW 1.41	28	Close the Web Site and Quit Dreamweaver	DW 1.72
14	Change the Text Color	DW 1.43			

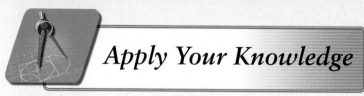

Apply Your Knowledge

1 Defining a Web Site and Creating a Web Page

Instructions: Start Dreamweaver. Perform the following tasks to define a Web site and create and format a Web page for B & B Lawn Service. The Web page as it displays in a browser is shown in Figure 1-107. The text for the Web site is shown in Table 1-6.

Software and hardware settings determine how a Web page is displayed in the browser. Your Web pages may display differently in your browser than those in the figures. For an updated list of links, visit the Dreamweaver MX Links Web page (scsite.com/dreamweavermx/links) and then click Project 1 Links.

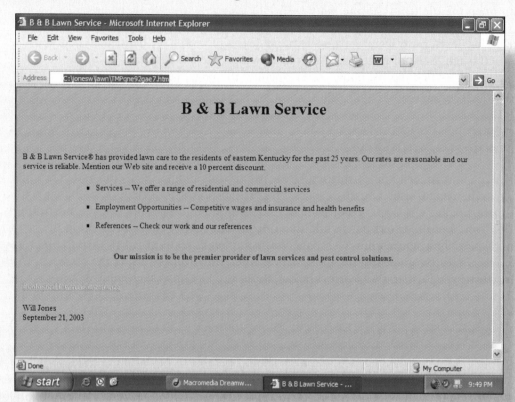

FIGURE 1-107

Table 1-6	B & B Lawn Service Web Page
SECTION	**WEB PAGE TEXT**
Heading	B & B Lawn Service
Introductory Paragraph	B & B Lawn Service has provided lawn care to the residents of eastern Kentucky for the past 25 years. Our rates are reasonable and our service is reliable. Mention our Web site and receive a 10 percent discount.
List Item 1	Services -- We offer a range of residential and commercial services
List Item 2	Employment Opportunities -- Competitive wages and insurance and health benefits
List Item 3	References -- Check our work and our references
Closing	Our mission is to be the premier provider of lawn services and pest control solutions.
Link Text	Ecological Lawn Maintenance

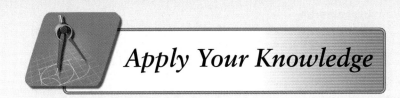

Apply Your Knowledge

1. Press F4 to close all open panels. Click Site on the menu bar and then click New Site. Use the Site Definition Wizard to create a local Web site under the your name folder. In Site Definition Editing Files options, name the site Lawn Service. Click the Next button. In the Site Definition Editing Files, Part 2 options, click No, I do not want to use a server technology. Click the Next button. In the Site Definition Editing Files, Part 3 options, create a new subfolder under jonesw (your name), and name the new subfolder lawn. The path will be C:\jonesw\lawn. Click the Next button. In the Site Definition Sharing options, select None in the How do you connect to your remote server? list. Click the Next button. In the Site Definition Summary options, click the Done button.

2. Click Commands on the menu bar and then click Set Color Scheme. Select the Green background and Brown, Yellow, Red for text and links.

3. Click in the Document window. Type the Web page text in Table 1-6. Press the ENTER key after typing the text in each section and after each one of the list items in the table.

4. Click Window on the menu bar and then click Properties to display the Property inspector. Select the heading text and then apply Heading 1. Click the Align Center button in the Property inspector to center the heading.

5. Select the three list items. Click the Unordered List button in the Property inspector to create a bulleted list with these three items. Click the Text Indent button in the Property inspector two times.

6. Select the closing paragraph. Click the Align Center button and then click the Bold button in the Property inspector. Do not deselect the sentence.

7. Click the Text Color box and select hexadecimal color #993333. This color swatch is located in the 5th column from the right and 5th row from the bottom.

8. Click at the end of the heading and then press the END key. Click Insert on the menu bar and then click Horizontal Rule. Specify a width of 450 pixels, a height of 4, center alignment, and no shading.

9. Click Window on the menu bar and then click Insert to display the Insert bar. Click the Characters tab. Click to the right of B & B Lawn Service in the first paragraph. Insert a registered trademark symbol.

10. Click at the end of the first bulleted item. Insert two line breaks between the first and second bulleted items and then insert two line breaks between the second and third bulleted items.

11. Title the Web page, B & B Lawn Service, using the Title text box on the Document toolbar.

12. Select the link text. Create an absolute link. Type http://www.eap.mcgill.ca/Publications/EAP68.htm in the Link box.

13. Click to the right of the inserted link, press the END key, and then press the ENTER key to insert a blank line after the linked text.

14. Type your name. Insert a line break and then type the current date.

15. Click Text on the menu bar and then click Check Spelling. Spell check your document and correct any errors.

16. Click File on the menu bar and then click Save to save the Web page in the C:\jonesw\lawn folder (use the your name folder). Type index in the File name text box and then click the Save button in the Save As dialog box.

17. Click Site on the menu bar and then click Site Files to verify that you saved the file correctly.

18. Press the F12 key to view the Web page in the browser. Test the link. Print a copy if required and hand it in to your instructor. Click the browser's Close button.

19. Click the Dreamweaver Close button to quit Dreamweaver.

In the Lab

1 Creating a Business Web Site

Problem: A friend of yours, Mary Stewart, is starting her own business selling candles. She has asked you to assist her in preparing a Web page to help her advertise her candles (Figure 1-108).

Software and hardware settings determine how a Web page is displayed in the browser. Your Web pages may display differently in your browser than those in the figures. For an updated list of links, visit the Dreamweaver MX Links Web page (scsite.com/ dreamweavermx/ links) and then click Project 1 Links.

Instructions: Start Dreamweaver. Perform the following tasks to define a Web site and

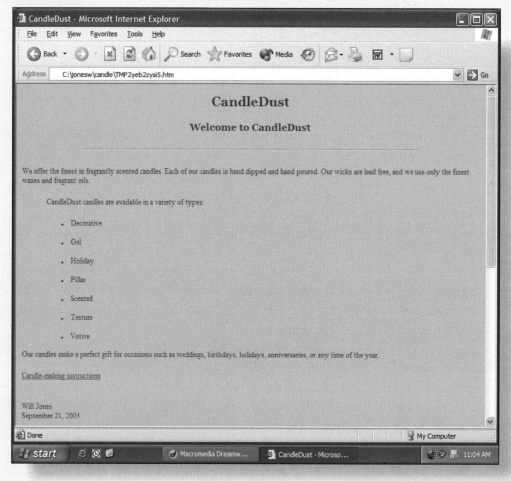

FIGURE 1-108

create and format a Web page for CandleDust. The text for the Web page is shown in Table 1-7.

1. Press F4 to close all open panels. Click Site on the menu bar and then click New Site. Use the Site Definition Wizard to create a local Web site under the your name folder. In Site Definition Wizard Editing Files options, name the site CandleDust. In the Editing Files, Part 3 options, create a new subfolder under the your name folder and name the new subfolder candle. All other selections in the Site Definition Wizard are the same as those for the parks Web site.

2. Set the Color Scheme to a Purple background and Blue,Purple,Green for text and links.

3. Click in the Document window and then type the Web page text in Table 1-7. Press the ENTER key after typing each section and after each list item in the table.

In the Lab

Table 1-7   CandleDust Web Page

SECTION	WEB PAGE TEXT
Heading	CandleDust
Subheading	Welcome to CandleDust
Introductory Paragraph	We offer the finest in fragrantly scented candles. Each of our candles is hand dipped and hand poured. Our wicks are lead free, and we use only the finest waxes and fragrant oils.
Second Paragraph	CandleDust candles are available in a variety of types:
List Item 1	Decorative
List Item 2	Gel
List Item 3	Holiday
List Item 4	Pillar
List Item 5	Scented
List Item 6	Texture
List Item 7	Votive
Closing	Our candles make a perfect gift for occasions such as weddings, birthdays, holidays, anniversaries, or any time of the year.

4. Display the Property inspector. Select the heading text and apply Heading 1. Select the subheading text and apply Heading 2. Select both headings and then click the Align Center button in the Property inspector to center the titles. Change the font type to Georgia, Times New Roman.

5. Select the introductory paragraph text. Click the Text Indent button in the Property inspector to indent the paragraph. Select the list items. Click the Unordered List button in the Property inspector and then click the Text Indent button in the Property inspector two times.

6. Click at the end of CandleDust and then press the END key. Click Insert on the menu bar and then click Horizontal Rule. Change the width to 550 pixels, and align center.

7. Click Window on the menu bar and then click Insert to display the Insert bar. Click the Characters tab. Click at the end of the first bulleted item. Click the Line Break button on the Characters tab two times to insert two line breaks between the first and second bulleted list items. Insert two line breaks between the other bulleted list items.

8. Select the text in the Title text box on the Document toolbar. Type CandleDust as the title.

9. Click at the end of the closing paragraph and then press the ENTER key. Type Candle-making instructions as the link text.

10. Select the link text and create an absolute link using the Link box in the Property inspector. Type http://candleandsoap.about.com/cs/candlemaking1/ for the URL.

11. Click to the right of the link, press the END key, and then press the ENTER key to insert a blank line after the last line.

12. Type your name. Insert a line break and then type the current date.

13. Spell check your document and correct any errors.

(continued)

In the Lab

Creating a Business Web Site *(continued)*

14. Click File on the menu bar and then click Save to save the Web page in the C:\jonesw\candle folder (use the your name folder). Type index in the File name text box and then click the Save button in the Save As dialog box.
15. Click Site on the menu bar and then click Site Files to verify that you saved the file correctly.
16. View the Web page in the browser. Test the link. Print a copy if required and hand it in to your instructor. Close the browser.
17. Quit Dreamweaver.

2 Credit Protection Web Page

Problem: Marcy Cantu is an intern in a small law practice. She recently lost her wallet, which contained all of her credit cards. She called the credit card companies and canceled her credit cards. One of the attorneys suggested she also call the three credit bureaus to make them aware of this problem. Because searching for the names, telephone numbers, and addresses of the three credit bureaus was quite time consuming, Marcy decided she wants to have this information readily available in the event she needs it again and for others who might find themselves in a similar situation. She has asked you to prepare the Web page shown in Figure 1-109.

Software and hardware settings determine how a Web page is displayed in the browser. Your Web pages may display differently in your browser than those in the figures. For an updated list of links, visit the Dreamweaver MX Links Web page (scsite.com/dreamweavermx/links) and then click Project 1 Links.

Instructions: Start Dreamweaver. Perform the following tasks to define a Web site and create and format an informational Web page on credit protection. The text for the Web page is shown in Table 1-8.

Table 1-8	Credit Protection Web Page
SECTION	**WEB PAGE TEXT**
Heading	Credit Protection
Introductory Paragraph	A credit card can be a great financial tool, but it also is a big responsibility. Applying for and receiving a credit card generally is an easy procedure. Offers from credit card companies arrive frequently in the regular mail.
Second Paragraph	Many people, particularly first-time users, do not fully understand the implications of a credit card. They may charge more than they can repay. This can damage a credit rating and create credit problems that can be difficult to fix.
Third Paragraph	Before you submit a credit application, obtain a copy of your credit report from one of the three major credit reporting agencies to make sure it is accurate.
List Item 1	Equifax Information Services, LLC P.O. Box 740241 Atlanta, GA 30374
List Item 2	Experian Consumer Opt-Out 701 Experian Parkway Allen, TX 75013
List Item 3	TransUnion LLC's Name Removal Option P.O. Box 97328 Jackson, MS 39288-7328

In the Lab

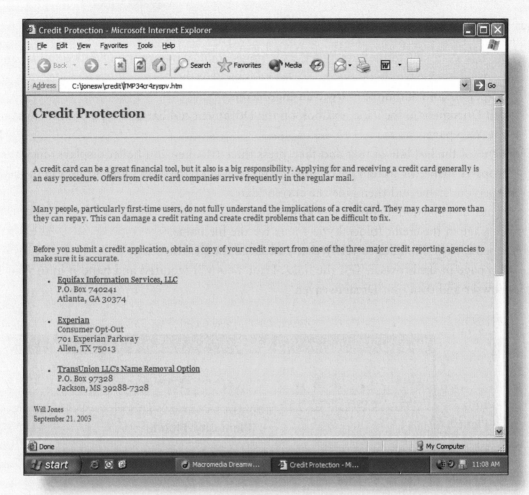

FIGURE 1-109

1. Close all open panels. Use the Site Definition Wizard to create a local Web site under the your name folder. Name the site Credit Protection. Create a new subfolder under your name and name the new subfolder credit. All other selections in the Site Definition Wizard are the same as those for the parks Web site.

2. Set the Color Scheme to a Yellow background and Green,Blue,Purple for text and links.

3. Type the heading and first three paragraphs of the Web page text in Table 1-8. Press the ENTER key after typing each section of the text in the table.

4. Type list item 1. Insert a line break after the company name and after the address. Press the ENTER key after the city and state. Type list items 2 and 3. Insert a line break after the company name and address and press the ENTER key after the city and state.

5. Display the Property inspector. Select the heading text and apply Heading 1. Align to the left (to ensure the heading is displayed properly in the browser). Insert a horizontal rule following the heading.

6. Click Edit on the menu bar and then click Select All. Change the font type to Georgia, Times New Roman for all the text on the Web page.

7. Select the three list items (companies and addresses) and create an unordered (bulleted) list. If necessary, use the Line Break button to add a blank line between the bulleted items.

(continued)

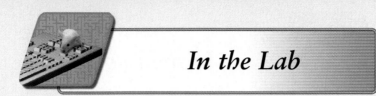

In the Lab

Credit Protection Web Page *(continued)*

8. Select the name of company in the first bulleted list item (Equifax Information Services, LLC) and create an absolute link using http://www.equifax.com. Create a link from the other two company names, using http://www.experian.com and http://www.transunion.com.

9. Select Untitled Document in the Title text box on the Document toolbar and type Credit Protection as the title of the Web page.

10. Click at the end of the last line of text and then press the ENTER key. If a bullet displays, click the Bullet button in the Property inspector to remove the bullet and then click the Text Outdent button in the Property inspector. Type your name and then type the current date.

11. Spell check your document and correct any errors.

12. Save the Web page in the credit folder. Type index for the file name.

13. On the Site menu, click Site Files to verify that you saved the file correctly.

14. View the Web page in the browser. Test the links. Print a copy if required and hand it in to your instructor. Close the browser and then quit Dreamweaver.

3 Plant City Web Page

Problem: Juan Benito recently moved to Plant City, Florida. He has discovered that Plant City has a colorful history and that many consider the city to be the Strawberry Capital of the United States. He has asked you to help prepare a Web page (Figure 1-110) so he can share information with friends, relatives, and visitors to Florida about the city's historical facts.

Software and hardware settings determine how a Web page is displayed in the browser. Your Web pages may display differently in your browser than those in the figures. For an updated list of links, visit the Dreamweaver MX Links Web page (scsite.com/dreamweavermx/links) and then click Project 1 Links.

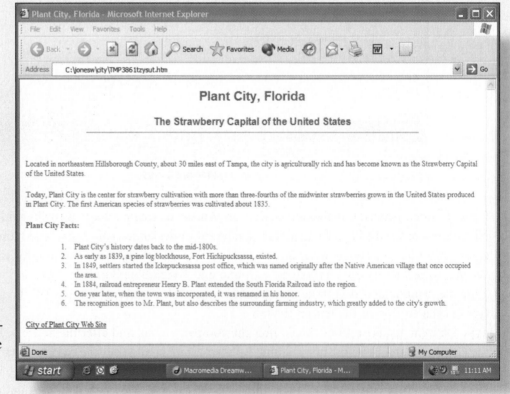

FIGURE 1-110

In the Lab

Instructions: Start Dreamweaver. Perform the following tasks to define a Web site and create and format an informational Web page on Plant City, Florida. The text of the Web page is shown in Table 1-9.

Table 1-9	Plant City, Florida Web Site
SECTION	**WEB PAGE TEXT**
Heading	Plant City, Florida
Subheading	The Strawberry Capital of the United States
Introductory Paragraph	Located in northeastern Hillsborough County, about 30 miles east of Tampa, the city is agriculturally rich and has become known as the Strawberry Capital of the United States.
Second Paragraph	Today, Plant City is the center for strawberry cultivation with more than three-fourths of the midwinter strawberries grown in the United States produced in Plant City. The first American species of strawberries was cultivated about 1835.
Third Paragraph	Plant City Facts:
List Item 1	Plant City's history dates back to the mid-1800s.
List Item 2	As early as 1839, a pine log blockhouse, Fort Hichipucksassa, existed.
List Item 3	In 1849, settlers started the Ickepuckesassa post office, which was named originally after the Native American village that once occupied the area.
List Item 4	In 1884, railroad entrepreneur Henry B. Plant extended the South Florida Railroad into the region.
List Item 5	One year later, when the town was incorporated, it was renamed in his honor.
List Item 6	The recognition goes to Mr. Plant, but also describes the surrounding farming industry, which greatly added to the city's growth.
Link Text	City of Plant City Web Site

1. Close all open panels. Use the Site Definition Wizard to create a local Web site under the your name folder. Name the site Plant City. Create a subfolder and name it city. All other selections in the Site Definition Wizard are the same as those for the parks Web site.

2. Set the Color Scheme to a White background and Brown,Red,Orange for text and links.

3. Click in the Document window and then type the Web page text in Table 1-9. Press the ENTER key after typing the text in each section in the table.

4. Display the Property inspector. Select the heading text and apply Heading 1. Select the subheading text and apply Heading 2. Center both headings. Change the heading font type to Arial, Helvetica, sans-serif.

5. Insert a centered horizontal line, 550 pixels in width, below the subtitle.

6. Select the third paragraph, Plant City Facts, and then apply bold formatting to the text.

7. Select the list items 1 through 6 and apply an ordered list. Text Indent one time.

8. Change the Web page title to Plant City, Florida.

9. Select the link text and then create an absolute link using http://www.ci.plant-city.fl.us/ as the URL.

10. Insert your name and the current date on the Web page.

11. Spell check your document and correct any errors. Save the Web page in the C:\jonesw\city folder. Type index for the file name.

12. Check the Site Files to verify that you saved the file correctly.

13. View the Web page in the browser. Test the link. Print a copy if required and hand it in to your instructor. Close the browser. Quit Dreamweaver.

Cases and Places

The difficulty of these case studies varies:
▶ are the least difficult; ▶▶ are more difficult; and ▶▶▶ are the most difficult.

1 ▶ Define a Web site named Favorite Sports with a subfolder named sports. Prepare a Web page listing your favorite sports and favorite teams. Include a title for your Web page. Bold and center the title, and then apply the Heading 1 style. Include a sentence or two explaining why you like the sport and why you like the teams. Bold and italicize the names of the teams and the sports. Give the Web page a meaningful title. Apply a color scheme to your Web page. Spell check the document. Use the concepts and techniques presented in the project to format the text. Save the file in the sports folder.

2 ▶ Your instructor has asked you to create a Web page about one of your hobbies. Define the Web site using Hobbies for the site name and hobby for the subfolder name. Italicize and center the title, and then apply the Heading 2 style. Type a paragraph of three or four sentences explaining why you selected the subject. Select and center the paragraph. Add a list of three items and create an ordered list from the three items. Include line breaks between each numbered item. Title the Web page the name of the hobby you selected. Spell check your document. Use the concepts and techniques presented in the project to format the text.

3 ▶▶ Define a Web site and create a Web page that gives a description and information about your favorite type of music. Name the Web site Favorite Music and the subfolder music. Apply a color scheme to the Web page. Include a left-aligned heading formatted with the Heading 1 style. Include a subheading formatted with Heading 2. Insert a horizontal rule following the subheading. List four facts about why you selected this type of music. Include the names of three of your favorite songs and the names of the artists. Bold and italicize the name of the songs and artists and apply a font color of your choice. Create an ordered list from the four facts. Text Indent your list. Title the Web page `Favorite Music`. Save the file as `index` in the music folder. Use the concepts and techniques presented in the project to format the text.

4 ▶▶ Assume you are running for office in your city's local government. Define a Web site using the name of the city in which you live and a subfolder named office. Include the following information in your Web page: Your name, centered, with Heading 1 and a font color of your choice; the name of the office for which you are running, bold and italicized; and a paragraph about the duties of the office in Courier font. Create a bulleted list within your Web page. Change the title of the Web page from Untitled Document to your name. Locate a related site online and create an absolute link to the site. Use the concepts and techniques presented in the project to format the text.

5 ▶▶ Your school has a budget for student trips. Your assignment is to put together a Web site and Web page, listing locations and trips from which the student body can select. Apply a color scheme. Include a title, formatted with Heading 1, and a subtitle, formatted with Heading 2. Insert a shaded horizontal line following the subtitle. List three locations. Bold and apply a font color to each location name and use Text Indent on the three items. Add a bullet to each location name. Include information about each location. Title the page `Student Government`. Add an absolute link to a related Web site. Use the concepts and techniques presented in the project to format the text.

Macromedia Dreamweaver MX

Adding Web Pages, Links, and Images

You will have mastered the material in this project when you can:

O B J E C T I V E S

- Copy files and folders using the integrated file browser
- Set a home page
- Add pages to a Web site
- Describe image file formats
- Add a background image to a Web page
- Insert, resize, and align images within a Web page
- Describe the different types of links
- Create a relative, absolute, and e-mail link
- Change the color of links
- Edit and delete links
- Describe and display the Site Map
- Use the Link Checker
- Describe Code View and Design View
- Use Code View to modify HTML code

Macromedia Dreamweaver MX

Adding Web Pages, Links, and Images

PROJECT

2

C A S E   P E R S P E C T I V E

A coworker at the state environmental agency, Joan Komisky, who also is interested in Florida's parks, viewed the Web page that you and Will created. She has offered some suggestions and asked to help with the design. Both you and Will agreed, and the three of you have become a team.

Joan suggests adding images to the home page. Will proposes that the Web site should include a page for Florida's three national parks and another page with information about his three favorite state parks located in northwest Florida. You explain to Will and Joan that the addition of each new page will require hyperlinks from the home page and links from each page back to the home page. You assure them that Dreamweaver includes all the tools they need to add many types of links to other related Web sites as well as e-mail links. You create a navigation map to illustrate how the links will work among the three pages. All team members agree that these two new pages should be added and will include images and links. With the addition of these two pages, the Web page will become a Web site.

Introduction

Project 2 introduces the addition of Web pages to the local site created in Project 1 and the integration of links and graphics into the Web pages that make up the site. Recall from Project 1 that a site or a Web site is a set of linked documents with shared attributes, such as related topics, a similar design, or a shared purpose.

The site structure feature provides a way to maintain and organize your files. A Web page essentially is a text document and a collection of HTML code. The HTML (HyperText Markup Language) defines the structure and layout of a Web document and is generated automatically by Dreamweaver. Images and other media content are separate files. For example, a page that displays text and three images consists of four separate files — one for the text document and one for each of the three images.

Most Web site builders include images on their Web pages. It is important that you take the time to learn about images, image properties, and the types of images best suited for a particular situation. Image properties, such as alternative text for accessibility issues, alignment, and changing the size, help you to understand the effects of using images on Web pages.

When a file or image is referenced within the HTML document, a link (or hyperlink) exists within the HTML code to the external file or image. Recall from Project 1 that a link (hyperlink) is a Web page element that, when clicked, accesses another Web page, or a different place within the existing Web page. A Web page can contain different types of links: internal or relative, absolute (the type you created in Project 1), e-mail, and links to a specific place within a document. This project discusses how to create these links.

Project Two — Adding Links and Images to the Florida Parks Web Site

In this project, you continue with the creation of the Florida Parks Web site. You add two additional Web pages and add an image background, page images, and links to the index page (Figure 2-1a) and the two new pages (Figure 2-1b on the next page) and (Figure 2-1c on the next page).

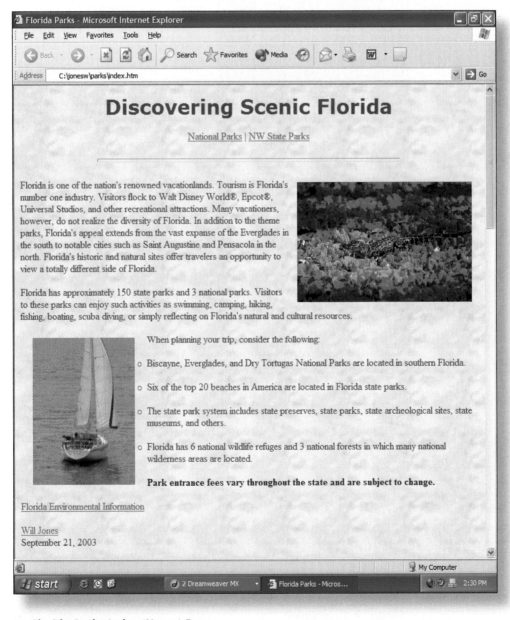

(a) Florida Parks Index (Home) Page

FIGURE 2-1

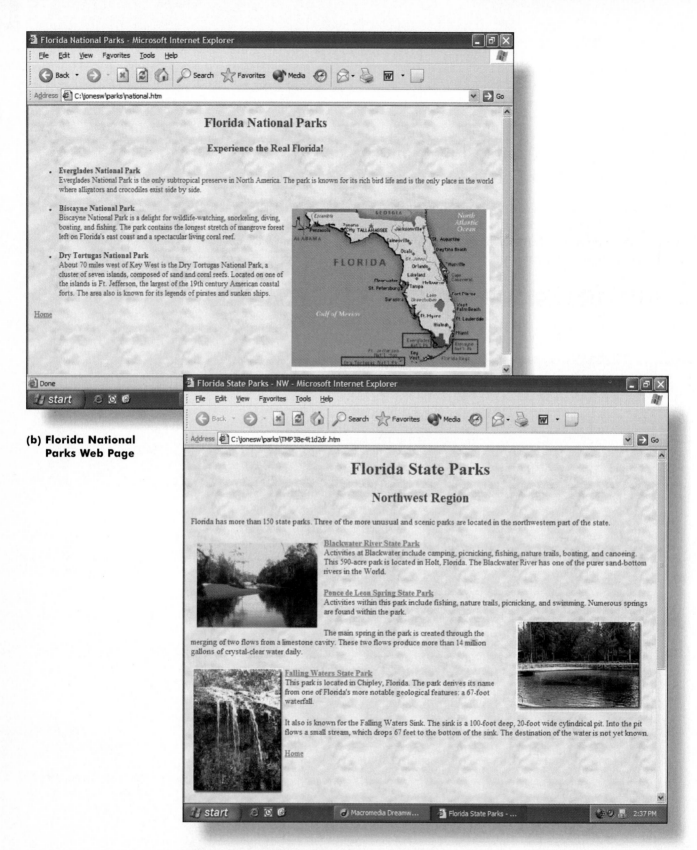

(b) Florida National Parks Web Page

(c) Florida State Parks Web Page

FIGURE 2-1 (continued)

In the Introduction (page I-13), four types of Web structures were illustrated: linear, hierarchical, web or random, and grid. This project uses a hierarchical structure (Figure 2-2). The index page is the home page, or entrance to the Web site. From this page, the visitor to this site can link to a page about Florida national parks or to a page about state parks in northwest Florida.

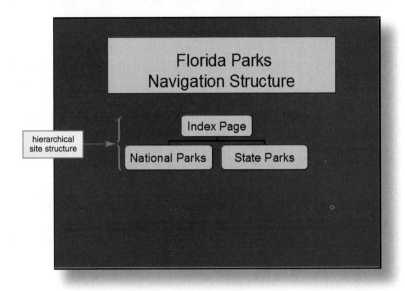

FIGURE 2-2

Managing a Web Site

Organization is a key element of Web design. Dreamweaver works best with entire sites rather than individual Web pages and has many built-in tools to make site creation easy, such as checking links and organizing files. You defined the parks Web site in Project 1 and created the index page. You can add pages to your site by creating a new page and saving it as part of the site or by opening an existing page from another source and saving it as part of the site. In this project, you will create two new pages.

Almost all Web sites have a home page. Compare the home page to your front door. Generally, the front door is the first thing guests see when they visit you. The same applies to a Web site's home page. When someone visits a Web site, he or she usually enters through the home page.

The home page is named **index.htm** or **index.html**. This file name has special significance. Most Web servers recognize index.htm (or index.html) as the default home page and automatically display this page without requiring that the user type the full Uniform Resource Locator (URL), or Web address. For example, if you type http://www.scseries.com into a Web browser address box and access the Web site, what you see is http://www.scseries.com/index.htm, even though you did not type it as such.

Organizing and using Dreamweaver's site management features can assure you that the media within your Web page will display correctly. Bringing all of these elements together will start you on your way to becoming a successful Web site developer.

Starting Dreamweaver and Closing Open Panels

When you start Dreamweaver, generally most or all of the panels are displayed by default. Closing unused panels provides uncluttered workspace in the Document window. To organize your workspace, you close or collapse the open panels. This gives you the maximum window space in the Dreamweaver Document window.

TO START DREAMWEAVER AND CLOSE OPEN PANELS

1. Click the Start button on the Windows taskbar. Point to All Programs on the Start menu, point to Macromedia on the All Programs submenu, and then click Macromedia Dreamweaver MX on the Macromedia submenu.

2. If necessary, maximize the Document window and then press the F4 key.

Dreamweaver displays the maximized Document window and closes all the open panels (Figure 2-3).

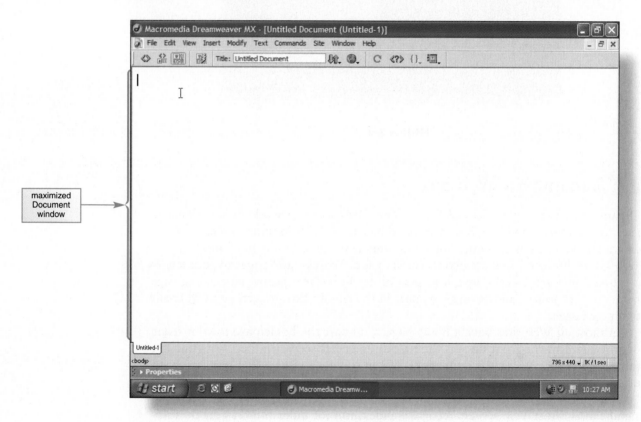

FIGURE 2-3

Accessing a Web Site and Opening a Web Page

Once you have created and saved a Web page or copied a Web page to a Web site, you often will have reason to retrieve it from disk. Opening an existing Web page in Dreamweaver is much the same as opening an existing document in most other software applications; that is, you use the File menu and Open command. If, however, the page is part of a Dreamweaver Web site, you also can open the file from the Site panel.

To open a Web page from the Site panel, you must switch to the appropriate Web site. The **site pop-up menu** in the Site panel lists sites you have defined. When you open the site, a list of pages and subfolders within the site displays. After opening the page, you can modify text, images, tables, and any other elements.

The following steps illustrate how to access a Web site and open a Web page from a local site in the Site panel.

 Steps To Access a Web Site and Open a Web Page from a Local Web Site

1 Press the F8 key to display the Site panel. If necessary, click the Site box arrow and then point to Florida Parks on the site pop-up menu (Figure 2-4).

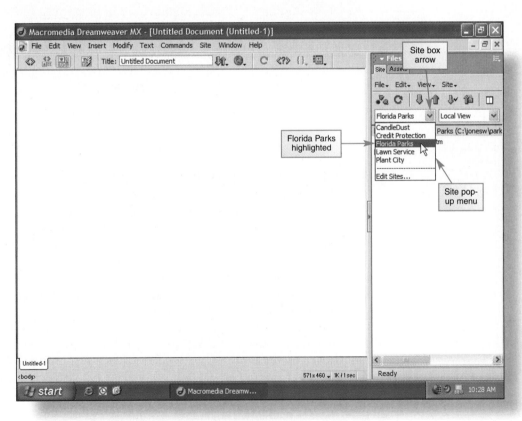

FIGURE 2-4

2 **Click Florida Parks. Double-click index.htm in the Site panel.**

The Florida Parks index page is displayed in the Document window and the name of the page is displayed on the tab at the bottom of the window (Figure 2-5). The tab for the initial Document window, (Untitled-1), displays to the left of the index.htm tab.

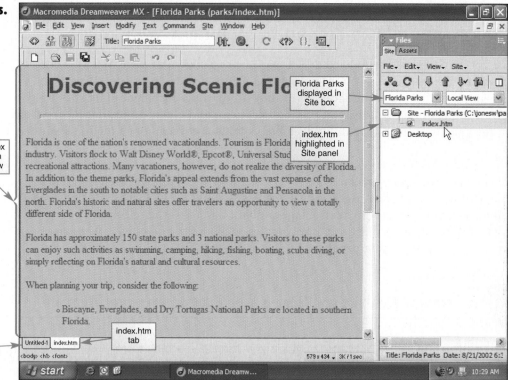

FIGURE 2-5

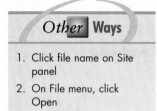

1. Click file name on Site panel
2. On File menu, click Open

The Integrated File Browser

Organization is one of the keys to a successful Web site. Creating documents without considering where in the folder hierarchy they should go generally creates a difficult-to-manage Web site. The Dreamweaver integrated file browser provides a view of the devices and folders on your computer and shows how these devices and folders are organized. You can create new folders and files for your site through the integrated file browser, which is similar to the Windows XP file organization. You also can use the **integrated file browser** to drag or copy and paste files to your Web site.

The main directory of a disk is called the **root directory** or the **top-level directory**. A small device icon or folder icon is displayed next to each object in the list. The **device icon** represents a device such as the Desktop or a disk drive, and the **folder icon** represents a folder. Many of these icons have a plus or minus sign next to them, which indicates whether the device or folder contains additional folders. Windows XP arranges all of these objects — root directory, folders, subfolders, and files — in a hierarchy. The plus and minus signs are controls that you can click to expand or collapse the view of the file hierarchy. In the integrated file browser, Dreamweaver uses the same hierarchy arrangement, but site folders appear in a different color than non-site folders so that you easily can distinguish between the two.

Copying Data Files to the Local Web Site

Your Data Disk contains images for Project 2. These images are in an Images folder. You use the integrated file browser to copy the Project 2 Images folder to your parks local root folder. The Images folder will become a subfolder within the parks Web site. See the inside back cover for instructions for downloading the Data Disk or see your instructor for information about accessing the files required for this book.

The Data Files folder for this project is stored at Local Disk (C:). The location on your computer may be different. If necessary, verify with your instructor the location of the Data Files folder. Complete the following steps to copy the files to the parks local root folder.

More About

Refreshing the Site Panel

To refresh the Site panel, click the Refresh button on the Site panel toolbar, click View on the menu bar and then click the Refresh command, or press the F5 key.

 To Copy Data Files to the Parks Web Site

1 Point to the plus sign (+) located to the left of the Desktop icon in the Site panel (Figure 2-6).

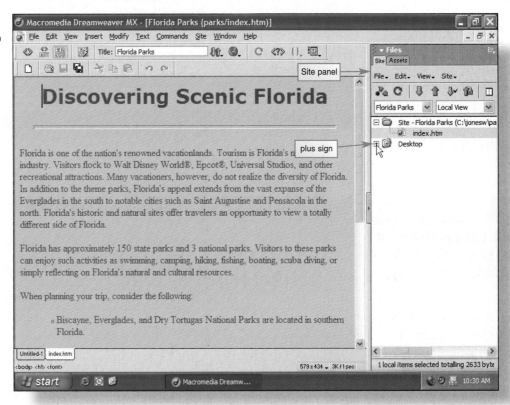

FIGURE 2-6

2 **Click the plus sign (+) to the left of the Desktop icon in the Site panel. Click the plus sign to the left of the My Computer icon and then point to the plus sign to the left of Local Disk (C:).**

A list of devices on your computer is displayed (Figure 2-7). The list on your computer will be different.

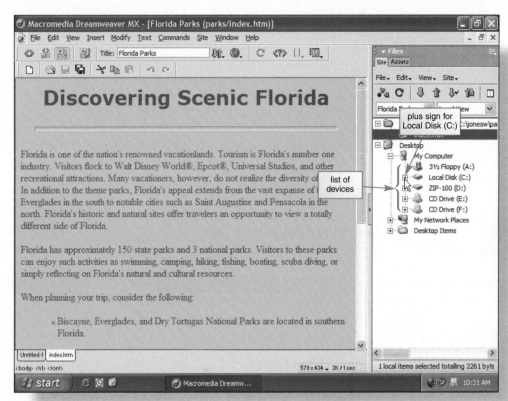

FIGURE 2-7

3 **Click the plus sign to the left of Local Disk (C:) and then point to the plus sign to the left of Data Files.**

The view of the file hierarchy is expanded and the list of folders is displayed (Figure 2-8). The list on your computer will be different.

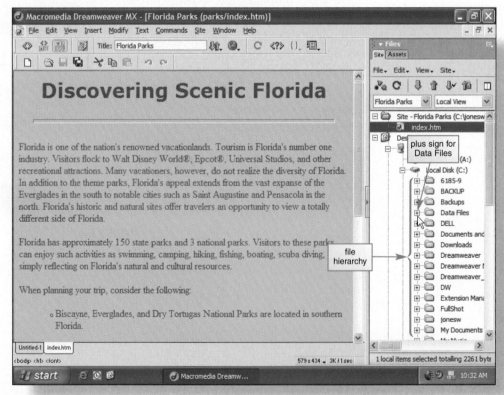

FIGURE 2-8

4 **Click the plus sign to the left of the Data Files folder. Point to the plus sign to the left of the Proj02 folder.**

The file hierarchy expands to display two subfolders: Proj02, and Proj03 (Figure 2-9).

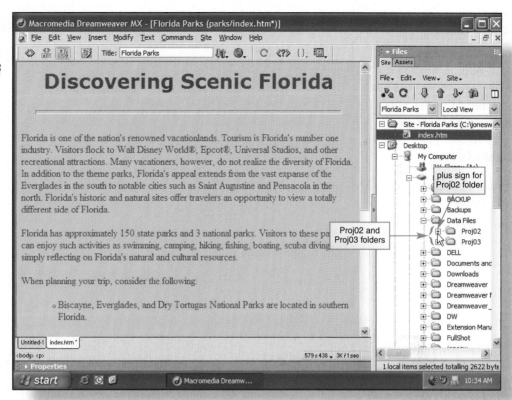

FIGURE 2-9

5 **Click the Proj02 plus sign.**

The Proj02 folder is expanded and contains the Images folders for the parks Web site and the four end-of-project exercises (Figure 2-10).

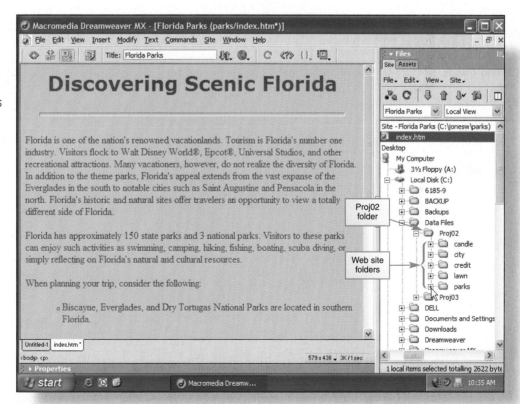

FIGURE 2-10

6 If necessary, use the Site panel horizontal and vertical scroll bars to display the folder list, so you can see it better. Click the plus sign to the left of the parks folder. Point to the Images folder.

The file hierarchy of the parks folder expands to display the Images folder (Figure 2-11).

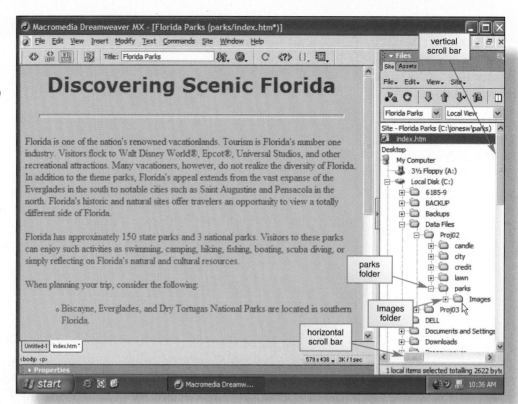

FIGURE 2-11

7 Right-click the Images folder and then point to Copy on the context menu.

The context menu is displayed (Figure 2-12). The files in the Images folder will be copied to the Florida Parks Web site.

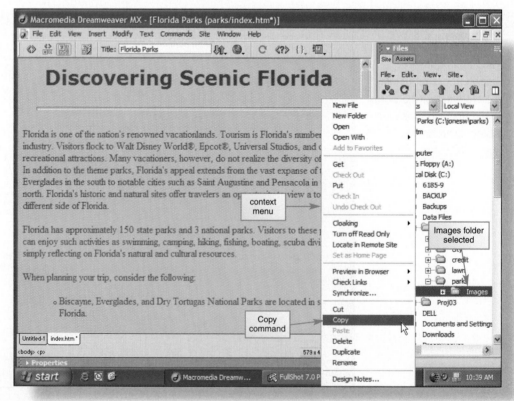

FIGURE 2-12

8 **Click Copy. If necessary, scroll to the top of the Site panel. Right-click Site - Florida Parks and then use the scroll bars to display the parks Web site hierarchy. Point to Paste on the context menu.**

The context menu is displayed (Figure 2-13).

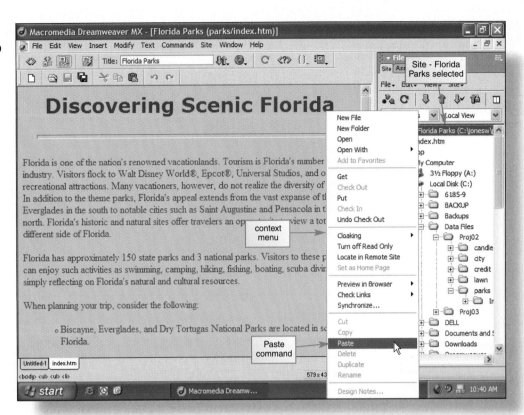

FIGURE 2-13

9 **Click Paste. Point to the minus sign to the left of the Desktop icon.**

The Images folder is copied to the Florida Parks site (Figure 2-14) and becomes a subfolder within the site.

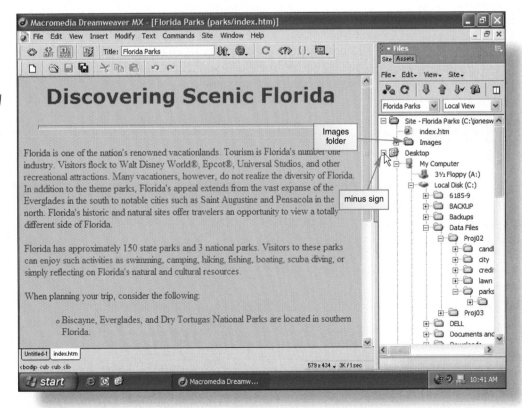

FIGURE 2-14

10 Click the minus sign to collapse the file list.

The list of files displaying below Desktop is closed (Figure 2-15).

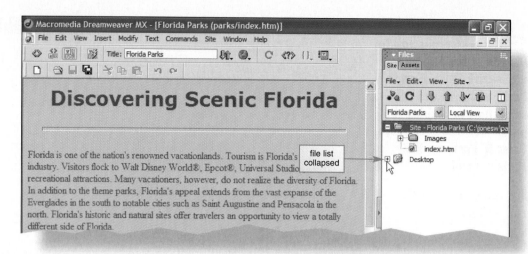

FIGURE 2-15

1 Select folder, on Site panel Edit menu click Copy, select folder to copy to, on Site panel Edit menu click Paste

Most Web sites have a starting point, called a home page. In a personal home page within a Web site, for example, you would probably list your name, your e-mail address, some personal information, and links to other information on your Web site. The index page you created in Project 1 is the home page for the parks Web site. The next section sets the home page.

Setting a Home Page

Each Web site you create within Dreamweaver should have a home page. A **home page** is similar to a table of contents or an index in a book. The home page generally contains links to all pages within the Web site. Most home pages are named index.htm or index.html. Complete the following steps to define the home page through the Site panel.

Steps **To Set a Home Page**

1 Click the index.htm file name in the Site panel. Point to Site on the Site panel menu bar.

The index.htm file name is highlighted (Figure 2-16).

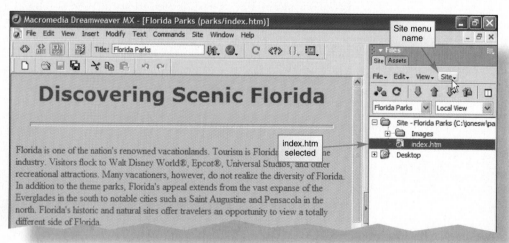

FIGURE 2-16

2 Click Site on the Site panel menu bar and then point to Set as Home Page.

The Site menu is displayed (Figure 2-17).

3 Click Set as Home Page.

The index.htm file is set as the home page for the parks Web site. In the files list, however, no changes are evident.

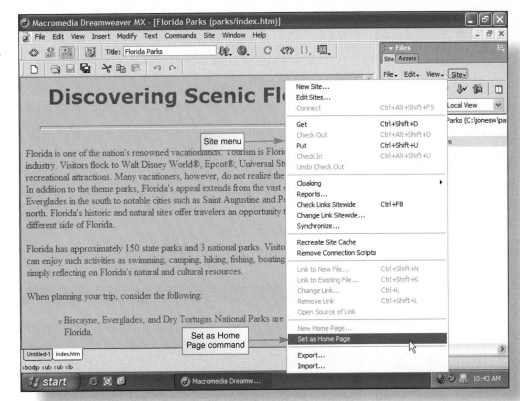

FIGURE 2-17

Although you cannot tell which page in a Web site is the home page by viewing the site files, Dreamweaver provides a graphical option to view the home page — the Site Map. You access the Site Map through the Site panel. You will use the Site Map to view the Web site later in this project.

Dreamweaver can have any number of open Document windows. When you started Dreamweaver, a blank untitled Document window opened. You will use this Document window to create a new Web page.

Adding Pages to a Web Site

You copied the images necessary to begin creating your Web site to the parks local root folder in the Site panel. It is time to start building and enhancing your site. You will add two additional pages to the Web site: Florida National Parks and Florida State Parks. You will add links, a background image, and page images to the index page and to the two new pages.

Dreamweaver offers many tools, such as the Standard toolbar, Property inspector, and Insert bar, to help you create a Web page. The tools you display in one Document window display in all other open Document windows. Complete the steps on the next page to prepare the workspace and to select the Untitled-1 Document window.

More *About*

Site Organization

Critical to Web development is the hierarchy of folders and files in a Web site. Even for the very simplest of sites, you should create a separate folder for the images. The folder name can be any name you choose, but it is best to use a descriptive, meaningful name.

TO PREPARE THE WORKSPACE

1 If necessary, click View on the menu bar, point to Toolbars, and then click Standard on the View submenu to display the Standard toolbar.

2 Click Window on the menu bar and then click Properties.

3 Click Window on the menu bar and then click Insert to display the Insert bar.

4 Right-click the Files title bar and then click the Close Panel Group command.

5 Click the Untitled-1 tab.

The Untitled-1 Document window, toolbar, and panels are displayed and the Files Panel group is closed (Figure 2-18).

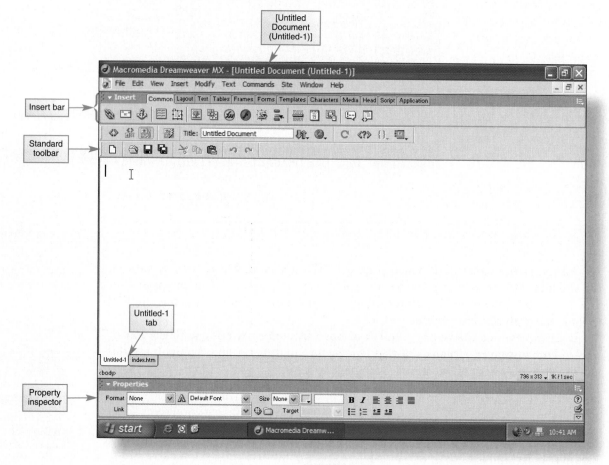

FIGURE 2-18

With the workspace prepared and the Document window displayed, you can begin creating the Web page for Florida National Parks.

Creating the National Parks Web Page

To create the page for Florida National Parks, you type the text in the untitled Document window. Table 2-1 includes the text for the Florida National Parks Web page. Press the ENTER key or insert a line break <BR> as indicated in the instructions in Table 2-1.

Table 2-1	Florida National Parks Web Page Text
SECTION	**WEB PAGE TEXT**
Heading	Florida National Parks <ENTER>
Subheading	Experience the Real Florida! <ENTER>
Part 1	Everglades National Park Everglades National Park is the only subtropical preserve in North America. The park is known for its rich bird life and is the only place in the world where alligators and crocodiles exist side by side. <ENTER>
Part 2	Biscayne National Park Biscayne National Park is a delight for wildlife-watching, snorkeling, diving, boating, and fishing. The park contains the longest stretch of mangrove forest left on Florida's east coast and a spectacular living coral reef. <ENTER>
Part 3	Dry Tortugas National Park About 70 miles west of Key West is the Dry Tortugas National Park, a cluster of seven islands, composed of sand and coral reefs. Located on one of the islands is Ft. Jefferson, the largest of the 19th century American coastal forts. The area also is known for its legends of pirates and sunken ships. <ENTER>
Closing	Home <ENTER>

More About

Using the Keyboard Shortcut Editor

For more information about using the Keyboard Shortcut Editor to create your own shortcut keys, edit existing shortcuts, or use a predetermined set of shortcuts, visit the Dreamweaver MX More About Web page (scsite.com/dreamweavermx/more) and then click Dreamweaver MX Shortcut Editor.

The following steps create the Web page and insert blank lines and line breaks between sections of text.

Steps **To Create the National Parks Web Page**

1 **Type the heading** Florida National Parks **as shown in Table 2-1. Press the ENTER key.**

The heading is entered in the Document window (Figure 2-19). Pressing the ENTER key creates a new paragraph.

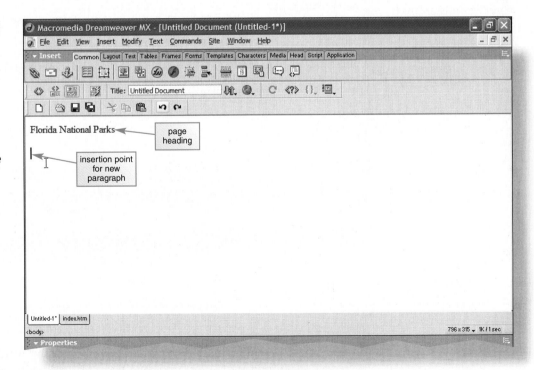

FIGURE 2-19

2 **Type the subheading**
Experience the Real Florida! **as shown in Table 2-1, and then press the ENTER key.**

The subheading is entered in the Document window (Figure 2-20).

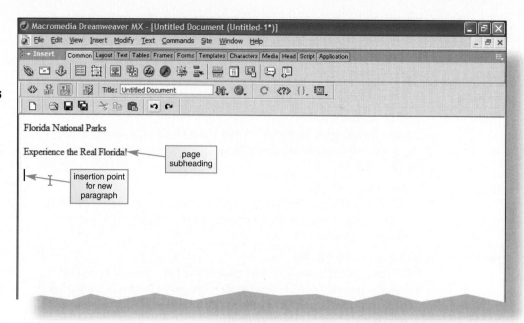

FIGURE 2-20

3 **Type the rest of the text in Table 2-1. Press the ENTER key or insert a line break as indicated in the instructions.**

The text for the Florida National Parks is entered (Figure 2-21).

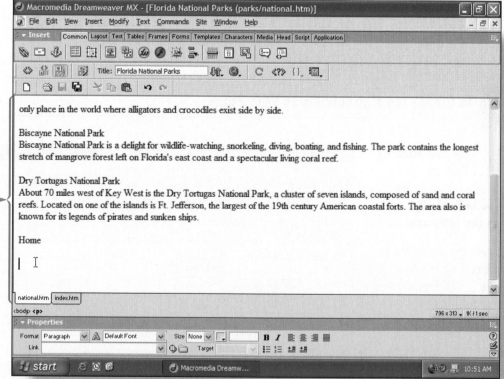

FIGURE 2-21

In Project 1, you formatted the index page by adding headings and bullets, centering, using text indent, and bolding text. The following steps apply similar formatting to the national parks page.

TO FORMAT THE FLORIDA NATIONAL PARKS PAGE

1 If necessary, scroll up to the top of the Web page and then apply Heading 1 to the heading text.

2 Apply Heading 2 to the subheading text.

3 Center the heading and subheading.

4 Add bullets to the following three lines: Everglades National Park, Biscayne National Park, and Dry Tortugas National Park.

5 Bold each of these three lines: Everglades National Park, Biscayne National Park, and Dry Tortugas National Park.

6 Add two line breaks after the text describing the Everglades National Park and the Biscayne National Park.

7 Type Florida National Parks for the title.

8 Press F12 to view the page in the browser and to verify the line spacing is correct as shown in Figure 2-22. Close the browser.

9 Save the Web page as national in the parks folder.

The Florida National Parks Web page text is entered, formatted, and saved.

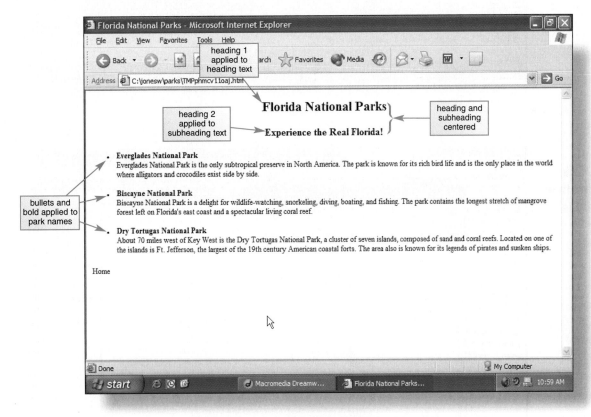

FIGURE 2-22

When you created the Florida National Parks Web page, you used the Untitled-1 page that displayed when you opened Dreamweaver. For the Florida States Park Web page, you need to open a new Document window. Complete the steps on the next two pages to open a new blank Document window.

Dreamweaver MX

 Steps **To Open a New Document Window**

1 **Click File on the menu bar and then point to New.**

The File menu is displayed (Figure 2-23).

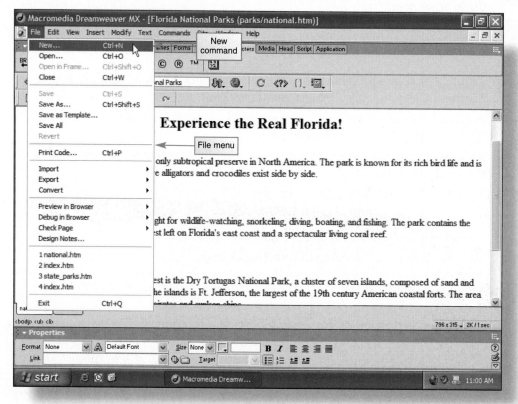

FIGURE 2-23

2 **Click New. If necessary, click the General tab and then click Basic Page in the Category list. Point to the Create button.**

The New Document dialog box is displayed (Figure 2-24). Basic Page is highlighted in the Category list. HTML is the default in the Basic Page list.

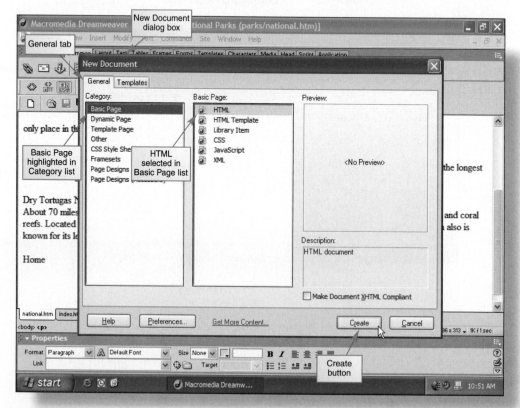

FIGURE 2-24

3 **Click the Create button.**

A new Untitled-2 Document window displays (Figure 2-25).

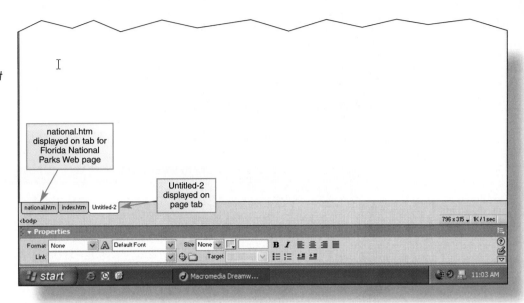

national.htm displayed on tab for Florida National Parks Web page

Untitled-2 displayed on page tab

national.htm index.htm Untitled-2

<body>

796 x 315 ▾ 1K / 1 sec

FIGURE 2-25

Creating the State Parks Web Page

You created the page for Florida National Parks by typing the text in the untitled Document window that displayed when you started Dreamweaver. You will enter the text for the Florida State Page the same way you entered text for the Florida National Parks page. Table 2-2 includes all the text for the Florida State Web page.

Table 2-2 Florida State Parks Web Page Text	
SECTION	*WEB PAGE TEXT*
Heading	Florida State Parks <ENTER>
Subheading	Northwest Region <ENTER>
Part 1	Florida has more than 150 state parks. Three of the more unusual and scenic parks are located in the northwestern part of the state. <ENTER>
Part 2	Blackwater River State Park Activities at Blackwater include camping, picnicking, fishing, nature trails, boating, and canoeing. This 590-acre park is located in Holt, Florida. The Blackwater River has one of the purer sand-bottom rivers in the world. <ENTER>
Part 3	Ponce de Leon Spring State Park Activities within this park include fishing, nature trails, picnicking, and swimming. Numerous springs are found within the park.<ENTER> The main spring in the park is created through the merging of two flows from a limestone cavity. These two flows produce more than 14 million gallons of crystal-clear water daily. <ENTER>
Part 4	Falling Waters State Park This park is located in Chipley, Florida. The park derives its name from one of Florida's more notable geological features: a 67-foot waterfall. <ENTER> It also is known for the Falling Waters Sink. The sink is a 100-foot deep, 20-foot wide cylindrical pit. Into the pit flows a small stream, which drops 67 feet to the bottom of the sink. The destination of the water is not yet known. <ENTER>
Closing	Home <ENTER>

More *About*

Accessibility Issues

For more information about authoring for accessibility, visit the Dreamweaver MX More About Web page (scsite.com/ dreamweavermx/more) and then click Dreamweaver MX Accessibility Issues.

Type the text for the State Parks Web page using Table 2-2 and the following step. Press the ENTER key or insert a line break <BR> as indicated in the table.

TO CREATE THE STATE PARKS WEB PAGE

1 Type the text of the Web page shown in Table 2-2.

The text for Florida State Parks is entered (Figure 2-26).

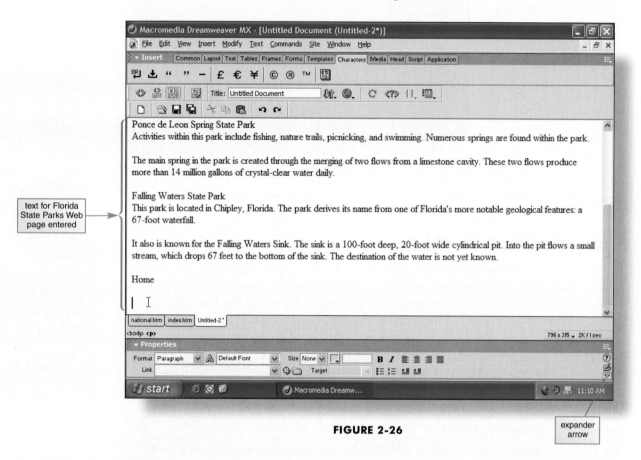

text for Florida State Parks Web page entered

FIGURE 2-26

expander arrow

TO FORMAT THE FLORIDA STATE PARKS PAGE

1 If necessary, scroll to the top of the Web page and then apply Heading 1 to the heading.

2 Apply Heading 2 to the subheading.

3 Center the heading and subheading.

4 Bold the names of each of the three parks where they are used as subtitles.

5 Type Florida State Parks - NW for the title.

6 Press F12 to view the page in the browser and to verify the line spacing is correct as shown in Figure 2-27. Close the browser.

7 Save the Web page as state_parks in the parks folder.

The text for the Florida State Parks page is entered, formatted, and saved.

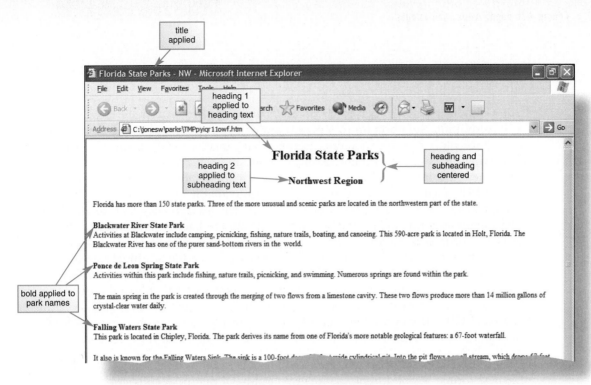

FIGURE 2-27

You have completed entering and formatting the text for the two new pages and copied the images to the parks local root folder in the Site panel. It is time to start enhancing your site. You will add a background image, page images, and links to the Web pages. You begin by adding images.

Images

If used correctly and with an understanding of the Web site audience, images add excitement and interest to a Web page. When selecting images for a Web site, it is important to understand that the size and type of image or images used within a Web page affect how fast the Web page downloads and displays in the viewer's Web browser. A Web page that downloads too slowly will turn away visitors.

Image File Formats

Graphical images used on the Web are in one of two broad categories: vector and bitmap. **Vector** images are composed of key points and paths, which define shapes and coloring instructions, such as line and fill colors. The vector file contains a description of the image expressed mathematically. The file describes the image to the computer and the computer draws it. This type of image generally is associated with Macromedia's Flash or Adobe's LiveMotion animation programs. One of the benefits of vector images is file size, particularly relative to the file size of bitmap images. Dreamweaver contains a feature that allows the user to modify the properties and content of Flash objects.

Bitmap images are the more common type of image file. Bitmap files map out or plot the image on a pixel-by-pixel basis. A **pixel**, or **picture element**, is the smallest point in a graphical image. Graphic monitors display images by dividing the display screen into thousands (or millions) of pixels, arranged in a **grid** of rows and columns. The pixels appear connected because they are so close together. This grid of pixels is a **bitmap**. The **bit-resolution** of an image is described by the number of bits used to represent each pixel. An 8-bit image supports up to 256 colors, and a 24- or 32-bit image supports up to 16.7 million colors.

Web browsers currently support three bitmap image file types: GIF, JPEG, and PNG.

GIF GIF (.gif) is an acronym for **Graphics Interchange Format**. The GIF format uses 8-bit resolution, supports up to a maximum of 256 colors, and uses combinations of these 256 colors to simulate colors beyond that range. The GIF format is best for displaying images such as logos, icons, buttons and other images with even colors and tones. GIF images come in two different versions: GIF87 and GIF89a format. The GIF89a format contains three features not available in the GIF87 or JPEG formats: transparency, interlacing, and animation. The **transparency** feature allows the user to specify a transparency color, which allows the background color or image to display. The **interlacing** feature lets the browser begin to build a low-resolution version of the full-sized GIF picture on the screen while the file is still downloading. Using an animated GIF editor, GIF89a images can be **animated**. Animated GIF images are simply a number of GIF images saved into a single file and looped, or repeated over and over. A number of shareware GIF editors are available to create animated GIFs. If you do not want to create your own animations, you can find thousands of free animated GIFs on the Internet available for downloading.

JPEG JPEG (.jpg) is an acronym for **Joint Photographic Experts Group**. JPEG files are the best format for photographic images because JPEG files can contain up to 16.7 million colors. **Progressive JPEG** is a new variation of the JPEG image format. This image format supports a gradually built display such as the interlaced GIFs. Older browsers do not support progressive JPEG files.

PNG PNG stands for **Portable Network Graphics**. PNG is the native file format of Macromedia Fireworks. PNG files retain all the original layer, vector, color, and effect information (such as a drop shadow), and all elements are fully editable at all times. This format is not supported by many browsers without a special plug-in. Generally, it is better to use GIF or JPEG images in your Web pages.

When developing a Web site that consists of many pages, you should maintain a consistent, professional layout and design throughout all of the pages. The pages in a site, for example, should use similar features such as background colors or images, margins, and headings.

Adding a Background Color and Background Image

Background Images

If you add a background image to your Web page, select an image that does not clash with the text and other content. The background image should not overwhelm the Web page.

Most Web pages display with a default white or gray background. Generally, the browser used to display the Web page determines the default background. You can enhance your Web page by adding a background image and/or background color. In Project 1, you added a color scheme and part of the scheme included the background color.

You can add a background color, however, without applying a color scheme. If you use a background color, the same cautions apply to background color as they do to text color. You want to use Web-safe colors, such as those in the Dreamweaver color schemes. This means the colors will display correctly on the computer screen when someone is viewing your Web page. To define an image or color for the page background, you use the Page Properties dialog box. When you display the Page Properties dialog box, you will see the color scheme selections you made in Project 1.

Background images are used to add texture and interesting color to a Web page. If you use both a background image and a background color, the color appears while the image downloads, and then the image covers up the color. Use background images cautiously. Web page images displayed on top of a busy background image may not mix well, and text may be difficult to read. Complete the following steps to add a background image to the index page. You will begin by closing the Insert bar and collapsing the Property inspector to provide additional workspace.

To Add a Background Image to the Index Page

1 **Click Window on the menu bar, click insert, and then click the Property inspector expander arrow.**

Dreamweaver closes the Insert bar and collapses the Property inspector.

2 **Click the index.htm tab to select the home page in the Document window. Click Modify on the menu bar and then point to Page Properties.**

Dreamweaver displays the index.htm page and the Modify menu (Figure 2-28).

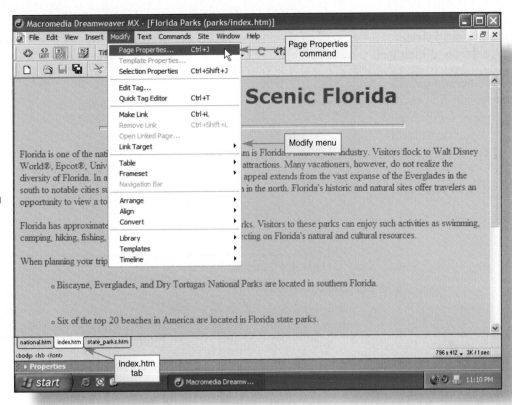

FIGURE 2-28

3 **Click Page Properties. Point to the Browse button in the Page Properties dialog box.**

The Page Properties dialog box displays (Figure 2-29). The colors and hexadecimal numbers are displayed for the Background, Text, Links, Visited Links, and Active Links. This is the result of the color scheme applied in Project 1.

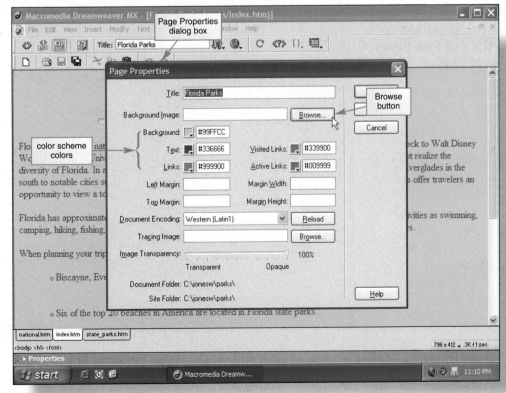

FIGURE 2-29

4 **Click the Browse button and then click the Images folder name. Point to the OK button in the Select Image Source dialog box.**

Dreamweaver displays the Select Image Source dialog box (Figure 2-30). The parks folder name is displayed in the Look in box and the Images folder is highlighted.

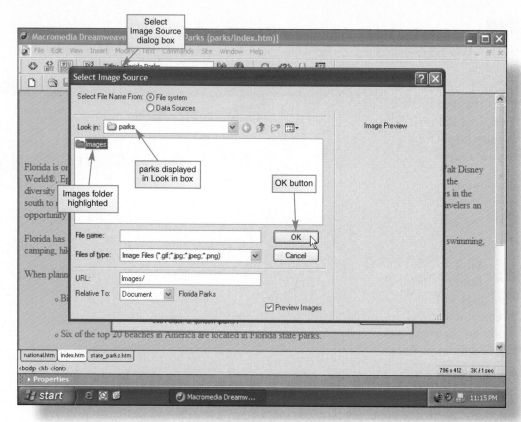

FIGURE 2-30

5 **Click the OK button. Click background.jpg. If necessary, click the Preview Images box to select it and then point to the OK button.**

The Images folder is opened and a list of file images is displayed (Figure 2-31). The file name, background.jpg, is displayed in the File name text box. A preview of the image is displayed in the Image Preview area. The dimensions of the image, type of image, file size, and download time are listed below the image.

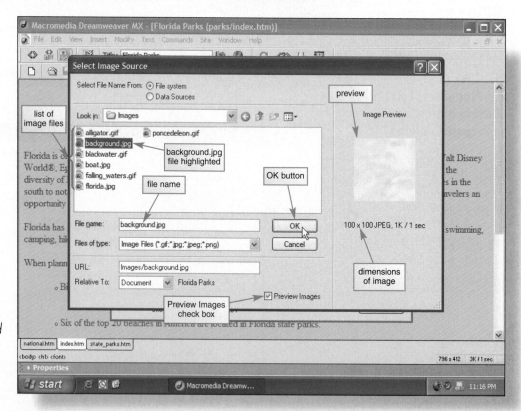

FIGURE 2-31

6 Click the OK button in the Select Image Source dialog box and then point to the OK button in the Page Properties dialog box.

The Page Properties dialog box displays the folder and file name in the Background Image box (Figure 2-32).

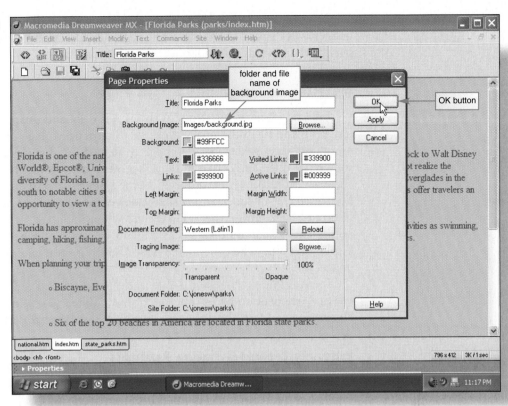

FIGURE 2-32

7 Click the OK button.

The background image is applied to the Florida Parks index page (Figure 2-33). The background color displays only during the downloading process when viewed through a browser.

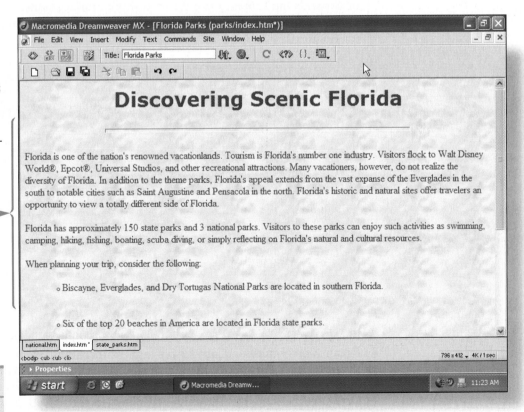

FIGURE 2-33

To enhance your index Web page further, you will add two images. One of the images will display at the top right of the document and the second image will display at the bottom to the left of the bulleted list.

Inserting an Image into a Web Page

Inserting images into your Web page is easy and quick with Dreamweaver — just drag and drop the image from the Site panel. Image placement, however, can be more complex. When the Web page is viewed in a browser, the image may display somewhat differently than in the Document window. If the images do not display correctly, you can select and modify the images directly in the Document window. Dreamweaver includes an **invisible element marker** that shows the location of the inserted image within the HTML code when the image is moved from the insertion point. This visual aid displays as a small yellow icon when the image is selected and displays as blue when the image is not selected. You can drag the icon to move the image.

In addition to the visual aid feature, you use the Property inspector to help with image placement and add other attributes. When you select an image within the Document window, the Property inspector displays properties specific to the image.

Property Inspector Image Features

The Property inspector lets you see the current properties of the selected element. The Property inspector is divided into two sections. Clicking the expand/collapse arrow in the lower-right corner of the Property inspector collapses the Property inspector to show only the most commonly used properties for the selected element or expands the Property inspector to show more options.

The following section describes the image-related features of the Property inspector (Figure 2-34).

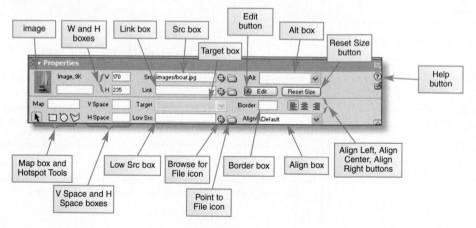

FIGURE 2-34

W AND H The **W** and **H** boxes indicate the width and height of the image, in pixels. Dreamweaver automatically displays the dimensions when a image is inserted into the page. You can specify the image size in the following units: pc (picas), pt (points), in (inches), mm (millimeters), cm (centimeters), and combinations, such as 2in+5mm. Dreamweaver converts the values to pixels in the HTML source code.

LINK   The **Link** box allows you to make a selected image a hyperlink to a specified URL or Web page. To create a link, you can click the Point to File or Browse for File icon to the right of the Link box to browse to a page in your Web site, or drag a file from the site window into the Link box. For an external link, you can type the URL directly into the Link box or use copy and paste.

ALIGN   **Align** sets the alignment of an image in relation to other elements in the same paragraph, table, or line. Align is discussed in more detail later in this project.

ALT   **Alt** specifies alternative text that appears in place of the image for text-only browsers or for browsers that have been set to download images manually. For visually impaired users who use speech synthesizers with text-only browsers, the text is spoken out loud. In some browsers, this text also appears when the pointer is over the image.

MAP NAME AND HOTSPOT TOOLS   Use **Map Name** and the **Hotspot tools** to label and create a client-side image map.

V SPACE AND H SPACE   V Space and H Space add space, in pixels, along the sides of the image. **V Space** adds space along the top and bottom of an image. **H Space** adds space along the left and right of an image.

TARGET   **Target** specifies the frame or window in which the linked page should load. This option is not available when the image is linked to another file.

LOW SRC   **Low Src** specifies the image that should load before the main image. Many designers use a small black and white version of the main image because it loads quickly and gives visitors an idea of what they will see.

BORDER   **Border** is the width, in pixels, of the image's border. The default is no border.

EDIT   **Edit** launches an external image editor, such as Macromedia Fireworks.

RESET SIZE   If an image size is changed, **Reset Size** resets the W and H values to the original size of the image.

LEFT, CENTER, AND RIGHT ALIGN   In Dreamweaver, the default alignment for an image is left alignment. To change the default alignment, select the image you want to align. Click an alignment button: Align Center, Align Right, or Justify.

SRC   **Src** specifies the source file for the image.

   To insert images in the home page, complete the steps on the next two pages.

To Insert an Image into the Index Page

1 **Click the expander arrow in the Properties inspector.**

The Property inspector expands and displays a lower panel (Figure 2-35). The Document window contains text only; therefore, no additional attributes display in the expanded Property inspector at this time.

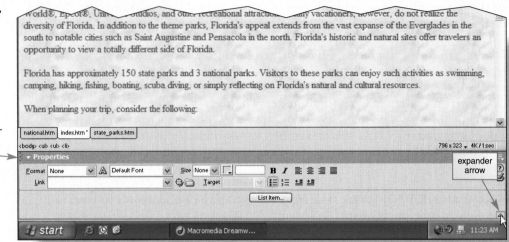

FIGURE 2-35

2 **Press F8. Point to the plus (+) sign to the left of the Images folder in the Site panel.**

The Site panel is displayed (Figure 2-36).

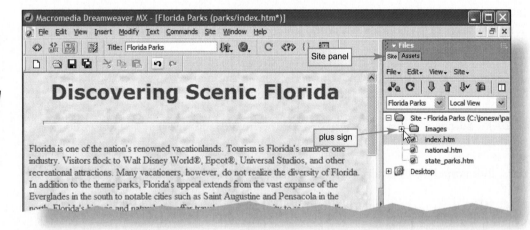

FIGURE 2-36

3 **Click the plus (+) sign to open the Images folder.**

The Images folder is opened and displays a list of seven images (Figure 2-37). Some of the images are gif files and others are jpg files. One of the files is the background image. All other images will be inserted into the three Web site pages.

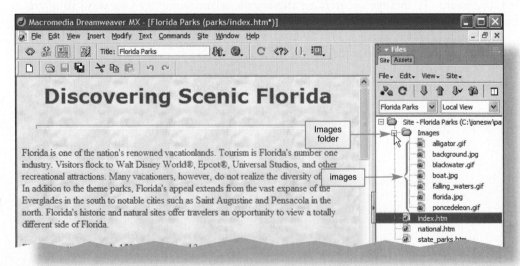

FIGURE 2-37

4   **If necessary, scroll to the top of the page in the Document window and position the insertion point so that it is to the left of the first line of the first paragraph (Figure 2-38). Drag alligator.gif from the Site panel file list to the insertion point. Do not release the mouse button.**

When you start to drag, a page icon displays next to the mouse pointer (Figure 2-38), indicating the image is being dragged.

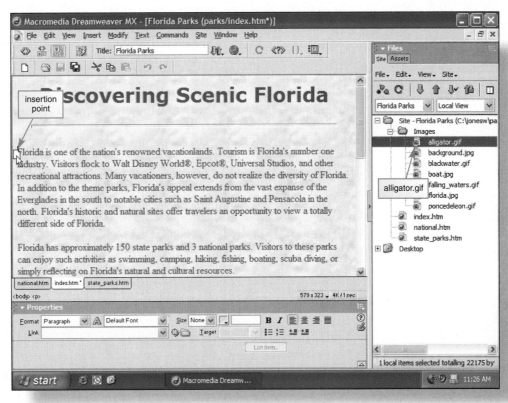

FIGURE 2-38

5   **Release the mouse button and then click the alligator image to select it.**

The border and handles around the image indicate it is selected. The attributes change in the Property inspector to reflect the selected object (Figure 2-39).

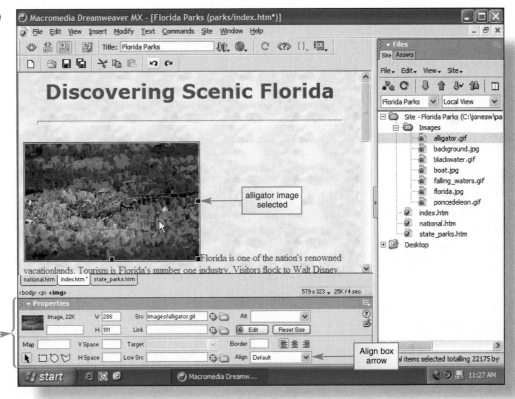

FIGURE 2-39

Aligning an Image

When you insert an image into a Web page, by default, the text around the image aligns to the bottom of the image. The image alignment options on the Align pop-up menu in the Property inspector let you set the alignment for the image in relation to other page content. Dreamweaver provides ten alignment options for images. Table 2-3 describes these image alignment options.

Table 2-3 Image Alignment Options	
ALIGNMENT OPTION	DESCRIPTION
Default	Aligns the image with the baseline of the text in most browser default settings
Baseline	Aligns the image with the baseline of the text regardless of the browser setting
Top	Aligns the image with the top of the item; item can be text or another object
Middle	Aligns the image with the baseline of the text or object at the vertical middle of the image
Bottom	Aligns the image with the baseline of the text or the bottom of another image regardless of the browser setting
Text Top	Aligns the image with the top of the tallest character in a line of text
Absolute Middle	Aligns the image with the middle of the current line of text
Absolute Bottom	Aligns the image with the bottom of the current line of text or another object
Left	Aligns the image at the left margin
Right	Aligns the image at the right margin

As indicated in Table 2-3, the Align pop-up menu contains ten alignment options. The more widely used options are left, right, and center. Complete the following steps to align the alligator image to the right and create text wrapping to the left of the image.

1 **If necessary, click the alligator image to select it and then click the Align box arrow in the Property inspector. Point to Right on the pop-up menu.**

The Align pop-up menu is displayed and Right is highlighted (Figure 2-40).

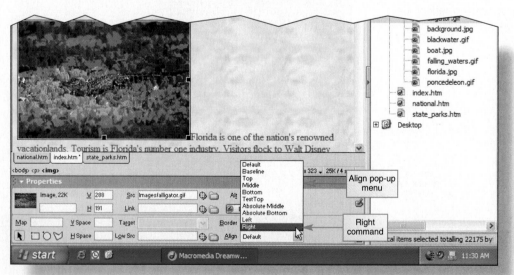

FIGURE 2-40

2 Click Right.

The image moves to the right side of the window (Figure 2-41). A visual aid displays to indicate the location of the insertion point.

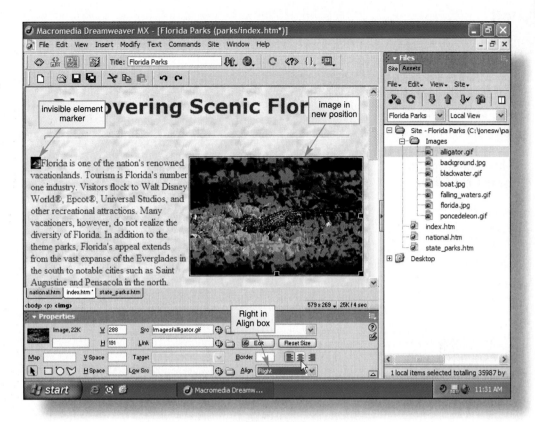

FIGURE 2-41

The spacing between the text and the image is very small. You can add vertical and horizontal spacing between the image and text, however, to display the Web page proportionally. In the next steps, you adjust the horizontal and vertical spacing around the image.

Adjusting Space Around Images

When aligning an image, by default, only about three pixels of space are inserted between the image and adjacent text. You can adjust the amount of vertical and horizontal space between the image and text through the V Space and H Space settings. The V Space setting controls the vertical space above or below an image. The H Space setting controls horizontal space to the left or right side of the image. You add vertical and horizontal spacing in the step on the next page.

Steps ## To Adjust the Horizontal and Vertical Space

1 **Click the V Space text box and then type** 6 **as the vertical space. Click the H Space box and then type** 12 **as the horizontal space. Press the ENTER key.**

Dreamweaver adds additional horizontal and vertical space between the image and the text (Figure 2-42).

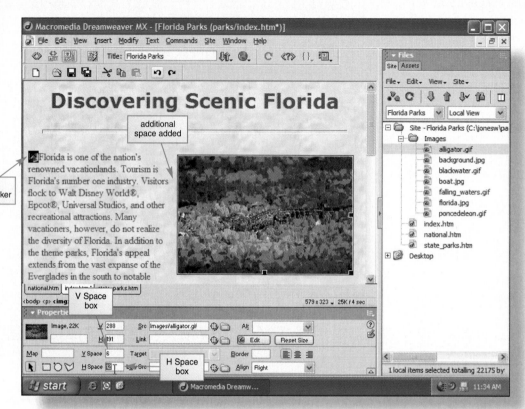

FIGURE 2-42

Another feature within the Property inspector is Alt text. For individuals who are visually impaired, the Alt text can be interpreted by their screen readers. Dreamweaver supports two screen readers — JAWS and Window-Eyes.

Specifying the Alt Text

The **Alt** text is short for **Alternative Text** and provides an alterative source of information about the image. The text typed in the Alt box displays as the image is downloading. This text also appears as a ScreenTip as the mouse pointer is moved over the image when it is displayed in some browsers. Complete the following step to add Alt text to the alligator image.

To Add Alt Text

1 **If necessary, click the alligator image to select it. Click the Alt box and then type** Florida alligator **as the alternate text. Press the ENTER key.**

The Alt text is entered in the Alt text box (Figure 2-43).

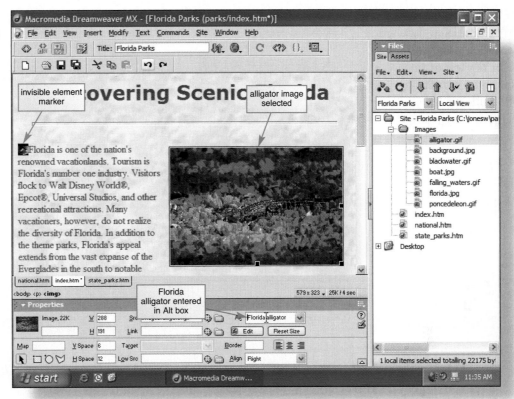

FIGURE 2-43

To enhance your Web page further, you will add a second image of a sailboat. This image is displayed on the left side of the page, to the left of the bulleted items. Perform the steps on the next four pages to insert an image of a sailboat in the Web page.

To Insert a Second Image

1 Scroll down and position the insertion point so that it is to the left of the sentence introducing the bulleted list (Figure 2-44).

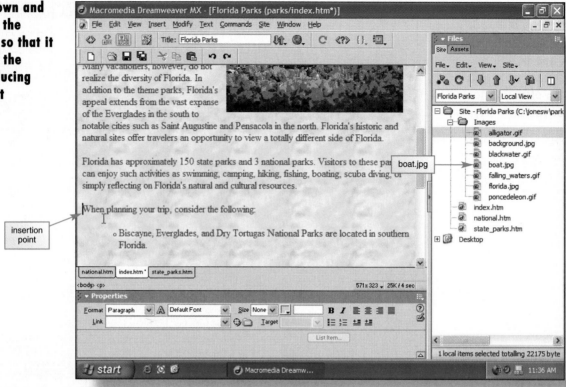

FIGURE 2-44

2 Drag the boat.jpg image from the Site panel to the insertion point and then click the image to select it. Point to the Align box arrow in the Property inspector.

The image is displayed (Figure 2-45). The border and handles around the image indicate it is selected.

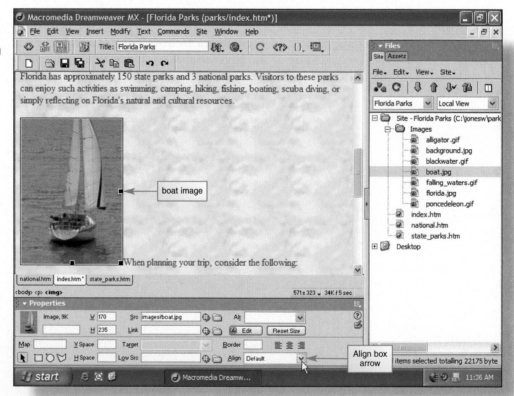

FIGURE 2-45

3 Click the Align box arrow and then click Left in the Align pop-up menu.

The image moves to the left side of the window and the text adjusts to the right side (Figure 2-46). The bullets do not display and some of the text is hidden by the image. Adjusting the spacing will display the bullets and text.

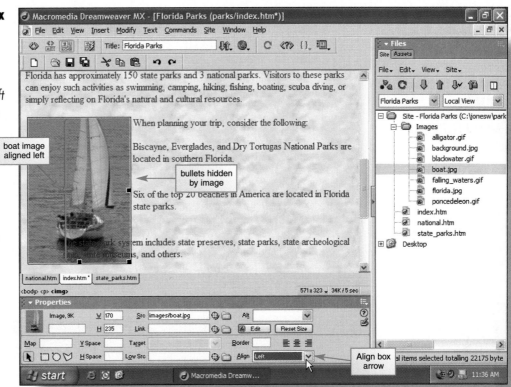

FIGURE 2-46

4 Click the V Space box and then type 6 as the vertical space. Click the H Space box and then type 20 as the horizontal space. Press the ENTER key. Click anywhere in the Document window.

Additional horizontal and vertical space is added between the image and the text, and the bullets are displayed (Figure 2-47).

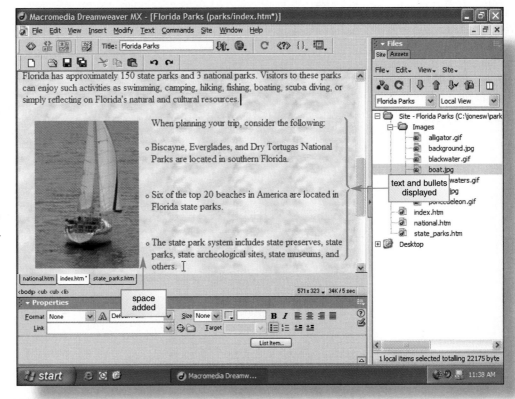

FIGURE 2-47

5 Click the image to select it. Click the Alt box and then type Sailboat as the alternate text. Press the ENTER key.

The Alt text is applied (Figure 2-48).

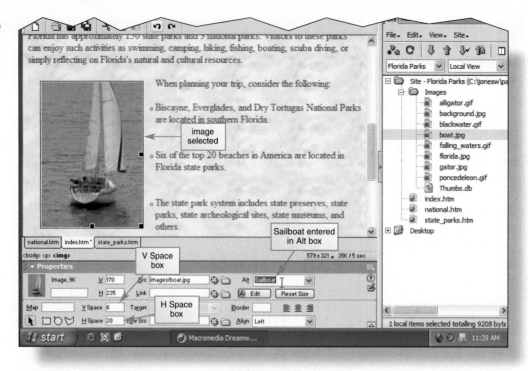

FIGURE 2-48

6 Press the F12 key.

The index page displays in your browser (Figure 2-49). Web pages may display differently in your browser. The browser and selected text size affect how a Web page displays.

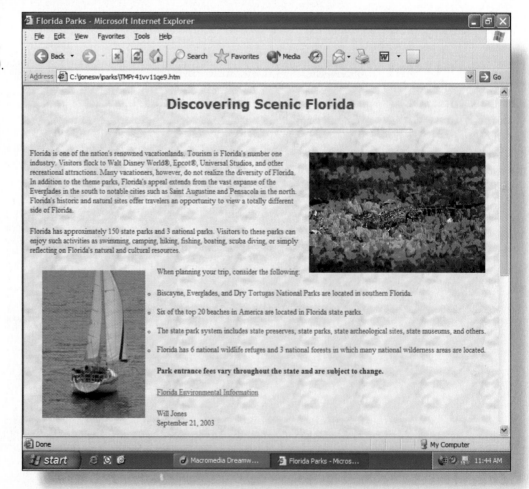

FIGURE 2-49

7 **Close the browser to return to Dreamweaver. Click the Save button on the Standard toolbar.**

All changes to the index page are saved (Figure 2-50). The asterisk no longer displays to the right of the file name in the index.htm tab or on the title bar.

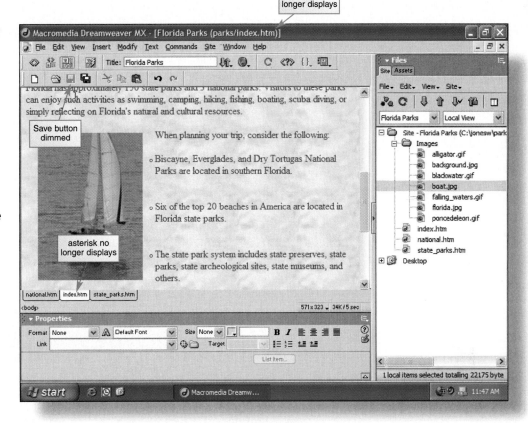

FIGURE 2-50

Consistency in Web pages ties the Web site together. Using the same color scheme and background image on all pages within the site is one way to achieve consistency. Next, you will add the same color scheme and background images to the national parks Web page that you applied to the index page. Complete the following steps to add the color scheme and background image to the Web page.

TO ADD A COLOR SCHEME AND BACKGROUND IMAGE TO THE NATIONAL PARKS WEB PAGE

1 Click the national.htm tab. Click Commands on the menu bar and then click Set Color Scheme.

2 Select Green in the Background list and Blue,Brown,Green in the Text and Links list. Click the OK button.

3 Click Modify on the menu bar and then click Page Properties. Click the Browse button to the right of the Background Image box.

4 Click background.jpg and then click the OK button in the Select Image Source dialog box.

5 Click the OK button in the Page Properties dialog box.

The background image and color scheme are applied to the National Parks page (Figure 2-51 on the next page).

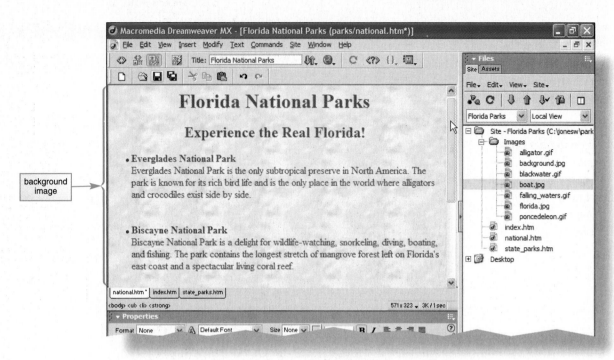

FIGURE 2-51

To develop the national parks page further and add information showing the location of the three Florida national parks, you will add a Florida map. References to each park are contained on the map. Complete the following steps to add the Florida map image to the national parks Web page.

To Insert an Image in the National Parks Web Page

1 If necessary, scroll to the top of the page. Position the insertion point between the bullet and the text heading of the second bulleted item (Biscayne National Park).

The insertion point is positioned to the left of Biscayne National Park and to the right of the bullet (Figure 2-52).

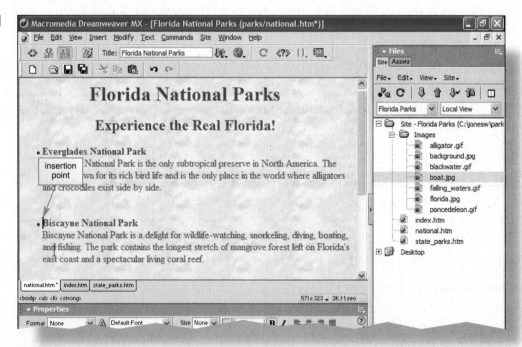

FIGURE 2-52

2 Drag the florida.jpg file from the Site panel to the insertion point and then click the image to select it. Point to the Align box arrow in the Property inspector.

The border and handles around the image indicate it is selected (Figure 2-53). The attributes change in the Property inspector to reflect the selected object.

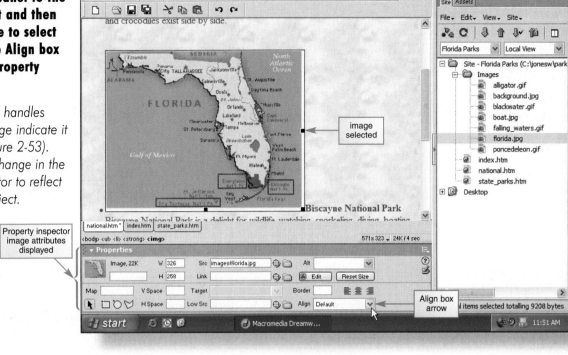

FIGURE 2-53

3 Click the Align box arrow and then click Right.

The image is aligned to the right in the Document window (Figure 2-54).

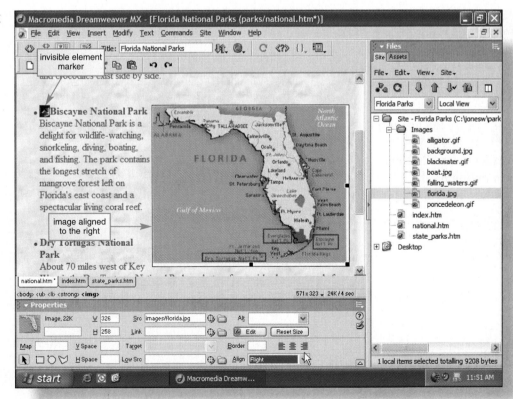

FIGURE 2-54

4 Click the Alt box and then type Florida Map as the alternate text. Click the V Space box and then type 8 as the vertical space. Click the H Space box and then type 10 as the horizontal space. Press the ENTER key (Figure 2-55).

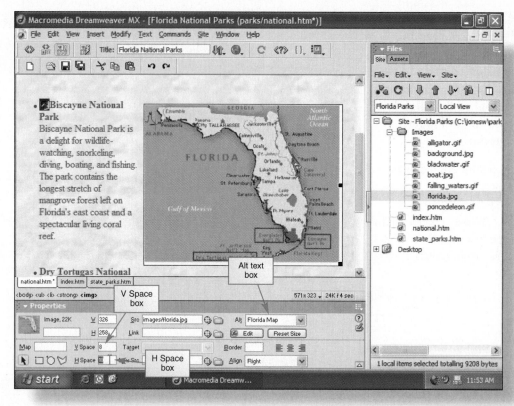

FIGURE 2-55

5 Press the F12 key.

The Florida National Parks Web page is displayed in the browser (Figure 2-56).

6 Close the browser to return to Dreamweaver. Click the Save button on the Standard toolbar.

The Florida National Parks Web page is saved.

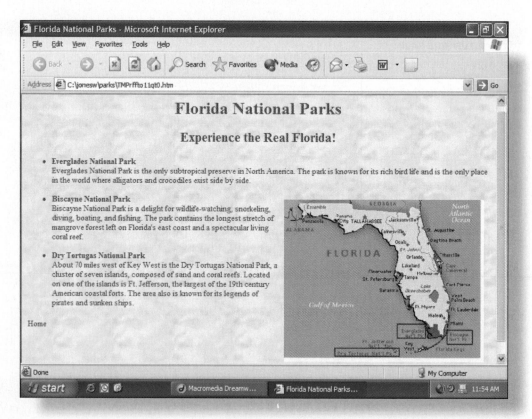

FIGURE 2-56

The third page in your Web site is northwest Florida state parks. Again, you need to add the color scheme and background image to this page. To add interest to the page, you will add three images. You will align two of the images to the left and one to the right. Complete the following steps to add the color scheme and background image to the northwest state parks Web page.

TO ADD A COLOR SCHEME AND BACKGROUND IMAGE TO THE STATE PARKS WEB PAGE

1 Click the state_parks.htm tab. Click Commands on the menu bar and then click Set Color Scheme.

2 Select Green in the Background list and Blue,Brown,Green in the Text and Links list. Click the OK button.

3 Click Modify on the menu bar and then click Page Properties. Click the Browse button to the right of the Background Image box.

4 Click background.jpg and then click the OK button in the Select Image Source dialog box.

5 Click the OK button in the Page Properties dialog box.

The color scheme and background image are applied to the northwest state parks page (Figure 2-57).

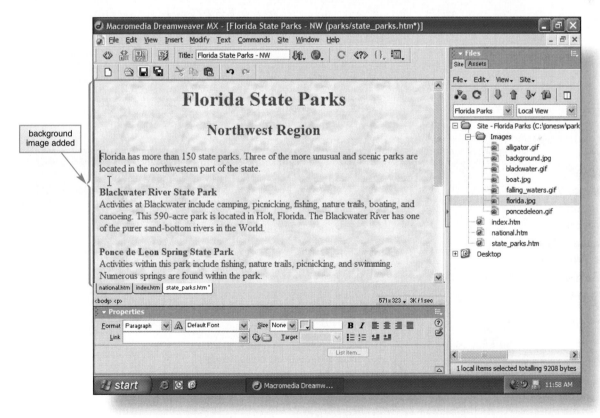

FIGURE 2-57

Next, you will add the three images to the state parks page. Complete the steps on the next five pages to insert and align the images.

Steps | **To Insert and Align Images in the State Parks Web Page**

1 If necessary, scroll to the top of the document. Position the insertion point to the left of Blackwater River State Park (Figure 2-58).

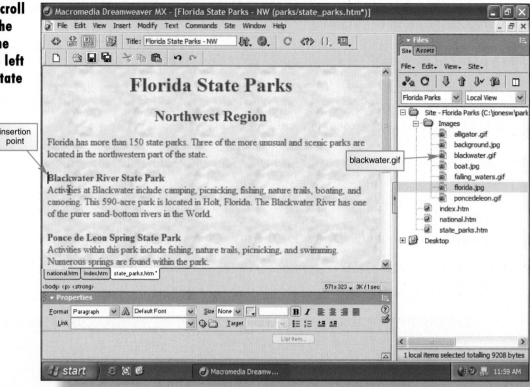

FIGURE 2-58

2 Drag the blackwater.gif file from the Site panel to the insertion point. Click the image to select it and then click the Align box arrow in the Property inspector. Click Left on the Align pop-up menu.

The image aligns to the left (Figure 2-59).

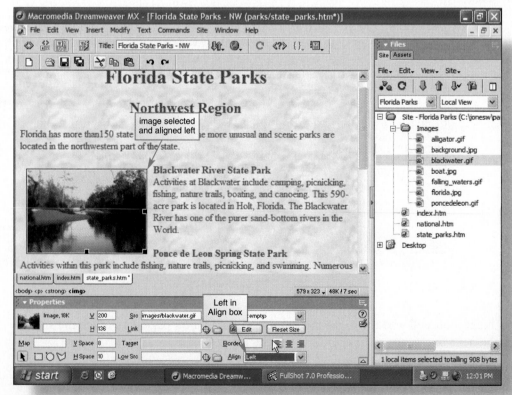

FIGURE 2-59

3 Click the V Space box and then type 8 as the vertical space. Click the H Space box and then type 10 as the horizontal space. Press the ENTER key. Click the Alt box, type Blackwater River State Park as the alternate text, and then press the ENTER key.

The image is selected. The Alt text, V Space, and H Space attributes are added to the state parks Web page (Figure 2-60).

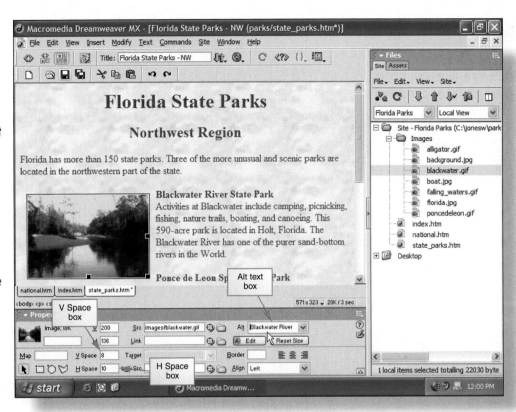

FIGURE 2-60

4 If necessary, scroll down and then position the insertion point to the right of the word, park, in the last line in the Ponce de Leon Spring State Park paragraph.

The insertion point is to the right of the last sentence in the third paragraph (Figure 2-61).

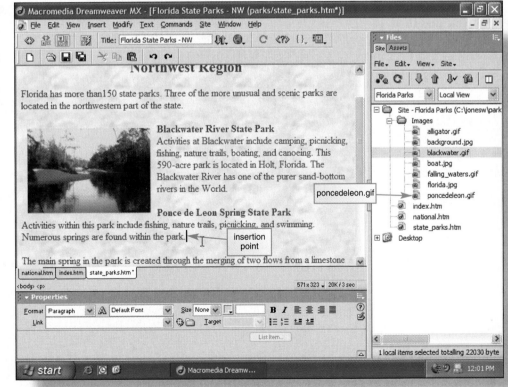

FIGURE 2-61

5 **Drag the poncedeleon.gif image to the insertion point and then select the image. Point to the Align box arrow.**

The image is selected (Figure 2-62).

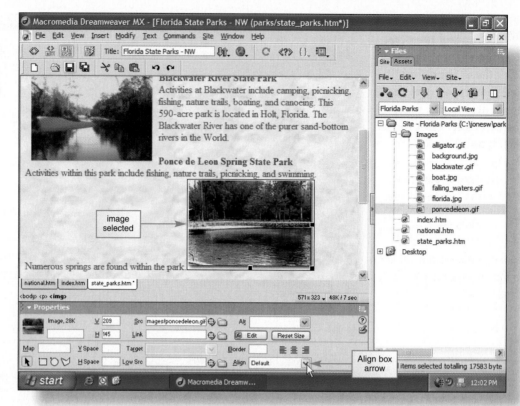

FIGURE 2-62

6 **Click the Align box arrow and then click Right on the Align pop-up menu.**

The poncedeleon.gif image moves to the right side of the window (Figure 2-63). The visual aid displays because the image is aligned to the right.

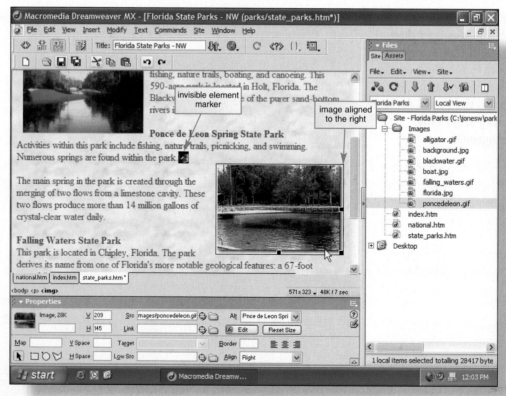

FIGURE 2-63

7 Click the **V Space box** and then type **6** as the vertical space. Click the **H Space box** and then type **12** as the horizontal space. Click the **Alt box**, type Ponce de Leon Spring State Park as the alternate text, and then press the ENTER key. Position the insertion point to the left of Falling Waters State Park.

The image is positioned on the page (Figure 2-64).

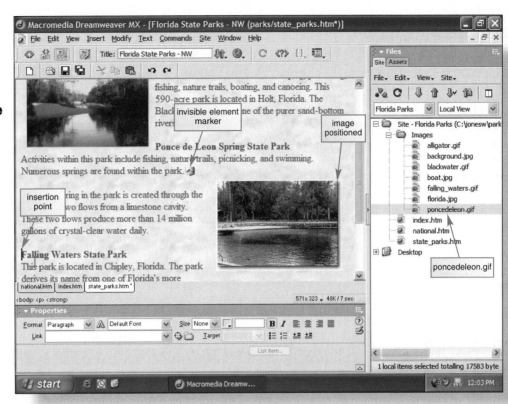

FIGURE 2-64

8 Drag the **falling_waters.gif** from the Site panel to the insertion point and then select the image. Click the **Align box arrow** and then click **Left** on the Align pop-up menu.

The Falling Waters image is aligned to the left (Figure 2-65).

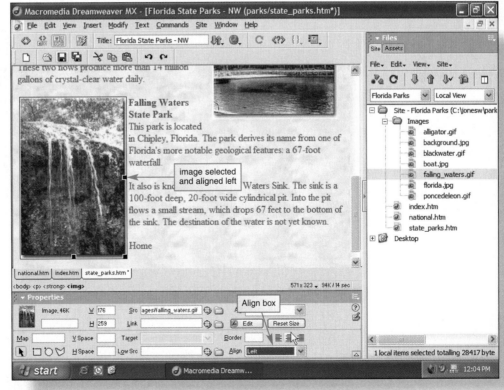

FIGURE 2-65

9 Click the V Space box and then type 8 as the vertical space. Click the H Space box and then type 12 as the horizontal space. Click the Alt box, type Falling Waters State Park as the alternate text, and then press the ENTER key.

The image is positioned on the page (Figure 2-66).

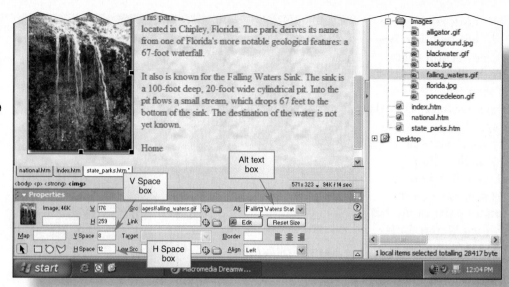

FIGURE 2-66

10 Press the F12 key.

The state parks page is displayed in the browser (Figure 2-67).

11 Close the browser.

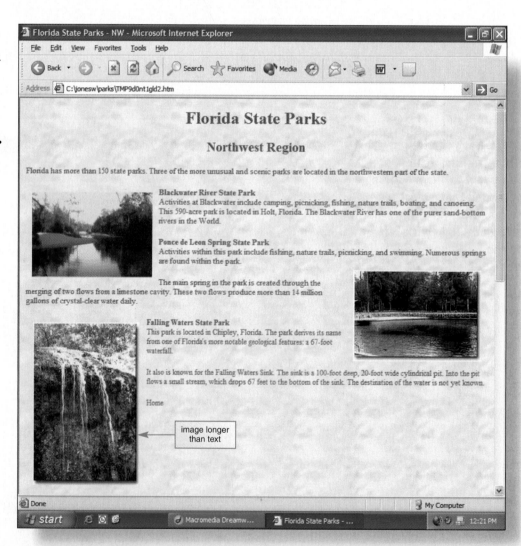

FIGURE 2-67

In Figure 2-67, the height of the Falling Waters image makes the Web page appear out of balance. The image needs to be resized. Resizing images, in this case, the Falling Waters image, will balance the image and the text so they are displayed attractively spaced in the browser.

Resizing Images

Dreamweaver provides two methods to resize an image: visual and numeric. When a file is resized, the image displays at a different size, but the size of the image does not change. If you have several images to resize, it is best to do this in a graphics and photo editor program such as Macromedia Fireworks, Adobe® Photoshop®, or Jasc® PaintShop Pro®.

When an image is selected, resize handles appear at the bottom and right sides of the image and in the bottom-right corner. To resize the image visually, do one of the following:

▶ To adjust the width of the image, drag the selection handle on the right side.
▶ To adjust the height of the image, drag the bottom selection handle.
▶ To adjust the width and the height of the image at the same time, drag the corner selection handle.
▶ To preserve the image's proportions (its width-to-height ratio) as you adjust its dimensions, hold down the SHIFT key and drag the corner selection handle.

To resize an image numerically, change the W and H fields in the Property inspector. To return an image to its original size, click the Property inspector Reset Size button.

After you insert the image into the Web page and then select it, the Property inspector displays features specific to images. As discussed earlier, alignment is one of these features. **Alignment** determines where on the page the image displays and if and how text wraps around the image. The following steps resize an image.

More About

Editing Images

To edit an image from within Dreamweaver, simply click the image name in the Site panel, and an external editing program will open. Fireworks is the default program within Dreamweaver, but you can change this to an image editing program of your choice by selecting Edit on the menu bar, choosing the Preferences command, and then selecting File Types / Editors in the Category list in the Preferences dialog box.

Steps To Resize an Image

1 If necessary, select the Falling Waters image. Double-click the W box and then type 150 as the new value. Double-click the H box and then type 200 as the new value. Press the ENTER key.

The image size is reduced on the screen (Figure 2-68). The values in the W box and H box are displayed bold to indicate that the image size was changed.

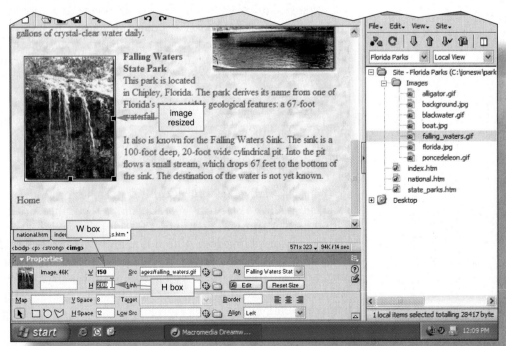

FIGURE 2-68

2 Press the F12 key to view the resized image (Figure 2-69).

3 Close the browser to return to the Dreamweaver window. Click the Save button on the Standard toolbar.

The state parks page is saved.

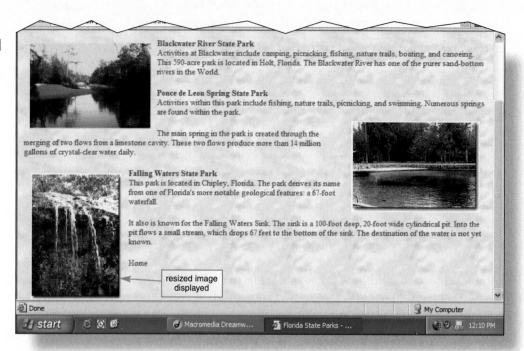

FIGURE 2-69

To connect the pages within the Web site and to display the navigation structure of the pages in the Site Map, they must be linked. In the next section, the different types of links are discussed.

Understanding Different Types of Links

Links are the distinguishing feature of the World Wide Web. A link, also referred to as a hyperlink, is the path to another document, to another part of the same document, or to other media such as an image or a movie. Most links display as colored and/or underlined text, although you also can link from an image or other object. Clicking a link accesses the corresponding document, other media, or another place within the same document. If you place the mouse pointer over the link, the Web address of the link, or path, usually appears at the bottom of the window on the status bar.

Three types of link paths are available: absolute, relative, and root-relative. An **absolute link** (created in Project 1) provides the complete URL of the document. This type of link also is referred to as an **external link**. Absolute links generally contain the protocol (such as http://) and primarily are used to link to documents on other servers.

You use **relative links** for local links. This type of link also is referred to as a **document-relative link** or an **internal link**. If the linked documents are in the same folder, such as those in your parks folder, this is the best type of link to use. You also can use a relative link to link to a document in another folder, such as the images folder. All the files you see in the Site panel Local View are internal files and are referenced as relative links. You accomplish this by specifying the path through the folder hierarchy from the current document to the linked document. Consider the following examples.

- To link to another file in the same folder, specify the file name. Example: everglades.htm
- To link to a file in a subfolder of the current Web site folder (such as the Images folder), the link path would consist of the name of the subfolder, a forward slash (/), and then the file name. Example: Images/gator.jpg.

You use the **root-relative link** primarily when working with a large Web site that requires several servers. Web developers generally use this type of link when they must move HTML files from one folder or server to another folder or server. Root-relative links are beyond the scope of this book.

Two other types of links are named anchor and e-mail. A **named anchor** lets the user link to a specific location within a document. An **e-mail link** creates a blank e-mail message containing the recipient's address. A third type of link is a **null**, or **script, link**. This type of link provides for attaching behaviors to an object or executes JavaScript code.

Relative Links

Another Dreamweaver feature is the variety of ways in which to create a relative link. Two of the more commonly used methods are drag-and-drop and browse for file. The **drag-and-drop method** requires that the Property inspector be open and that the site files display in the Site panel. The **browse for file method** is accomplished through a dialog box. The next step is to add the text to create the relative links between the home page and the national and state park pages. You will then use drag and drop to create a relative link from the text to a specific Web page.

Adding Text for the Relative Links

To create relative links from the index page, you add text to the index page and use the text to create the links to the other two Web pages in your Web site. You will center the text directly below the Discovering Scenic Florida heading. You add the text for the links in the following steps.

Steps **To Add Text for Relative Links**

1 **Click the index.htm tab. If necessary, scroll to the top of the page and then position the insertion point at the end of the title, Discovering Scenic Florida. Press the ENTER key and then press the END key.**

The insertion point is centered below the title (Figure 2-70). Pressing the END key positions the insertion point outside of the heading </H1> tag.

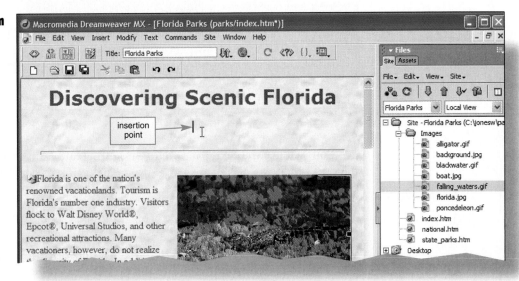

FIGURE 2-70

2 **Type** National
Parks **and then
press the SPACEBAR.**

*The text for the first link,
National Parks, is displayed
in the Document window
(Figure 2-71).*

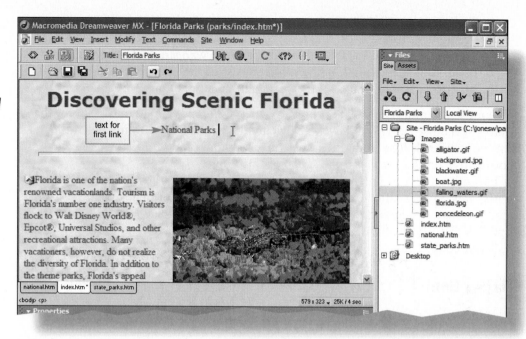

FIGURE 2-71

3 **Hold down the
SHIFT key and then
press the VERTICAL LINE KEY
(|). Press the SPACEBAR and
then type** NW State
Parks **for the second
link.**

*Text for both links is dis-
played in the Document
window (Figure 2-72).*

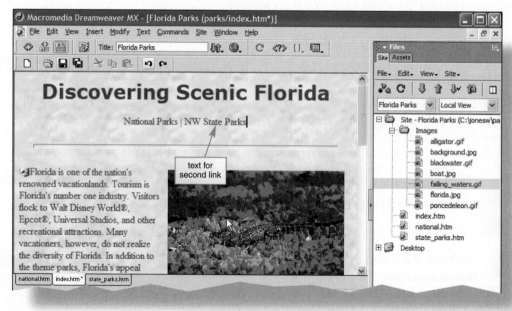

FIGURE 2-72

You will use the text, National Parks, to create a link to the national parks Web
page and the text, NW State Parks, to create a link to the northwest state parks
page.

Creating a Relative Link Using Drag and Drop

A relative link is used to create links between local files or files within one Web
site. The drag-and-drop method requires that the Property inspector be displayed.
Complete the following steps to use the drag-and-drop method to create a relative
link from the Florida Parks home page to the national parks Web page.

To Create a Relative Link Using Drag and Drop

1 **Click the expander arrow in the lower-left corner of the Property inspector to collapse it. Drag to select the text National Parks.**

The National Parks text is highlighted (Figure 2-73).

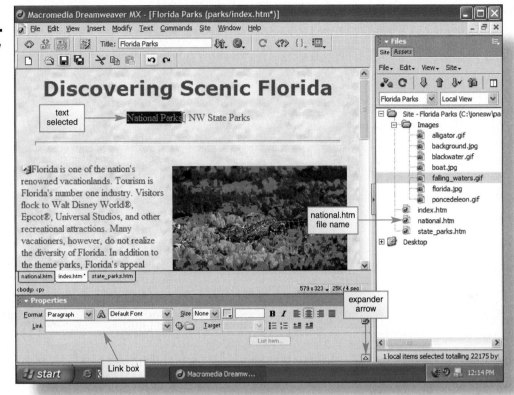

FIGURE 2-73

2 **Drag the national.htm file to the Link box in the Property inspector.**

When you start to drag, a page icon displays next to the mouse pointer, indicating the link is being copied. When the mouse pointer is over the Link box, it changes to a circle with a centered line (Figure 2-74). This circle indicates the link is established.

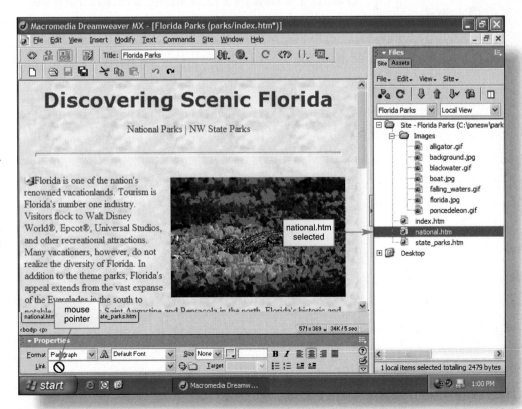

FIGURE 2-74

3 **Release the mouse button. Click National Parks to display the linked text.**

The linked text displays underlined and in a different color in the Document window, and the link text displays in the Link box (Figure 2-75). If you click anywhere else in the document, the linked document name does not display in the Link box.

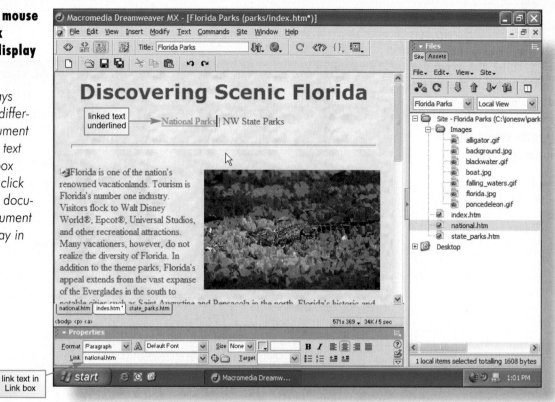

FIGURE 2-75

More About

Images as Links

It is easy to create a link from an image. Just select the image and then type or drag the file name into the Property inspector Link box.

Creating a Relative Link Using Browse for File

The **Browse for File method** is a second way to create a link. Using this method, you select the file name from the Select File dialog box. In the following steps, you use the Browse for File method to create a link to the state parks page.

Steps **To Create a Relative Link Using Browse for File**

1 **Drag to select NW State Parks and then point to the Browse for File icon in the Property inspector.**

The text NW State Parks is highlighted (Figure 2-76).

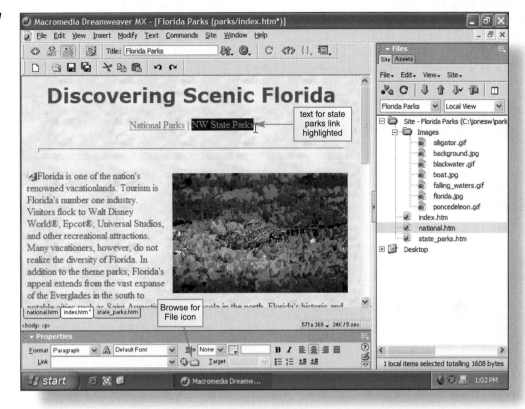

FIGURE 2-76

2 **Click the Browse for File icon and then click state_parks.htm. Point to the OK button.**

The Select File dialog box is displayed (Figure 2-77).

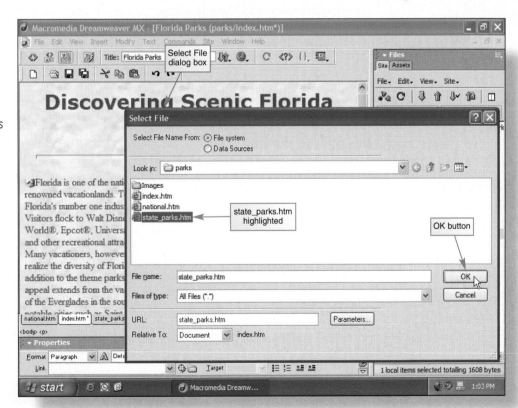

FIGURE 2-77

3 Click the OK button and then click the selected text, NW State Parks, to display the link.

The linked text displays underlined and in a different color in the Document window and the link text displays in the Link box (Figure 2-78). If you click anywhere else in the document, the linked document name does not display in the Link box.

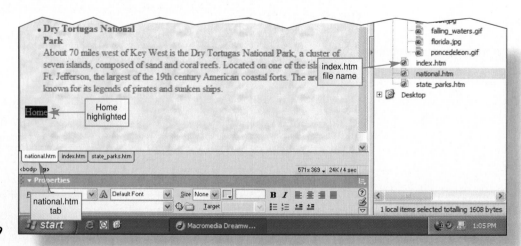

FIGURE 2-78

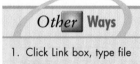

1. Click Link box, type file name
2. Click Point to File icon in Property inspector, drag to file name

Creating Relative Links to the Home Page and the Three National Parks Pages

You created a relative link from the home page to each of the other two pages within the Web site. Visitors can enter a Web site at any point, however, so it is important always to include a link from each page within the site back to the home page. Complete the following steps to create a link from the national parks page and a link from the state parks page to the home page.

Then, on the national parks page, create links from the three park names to the respective park pages. These links will be activated in Project 3 when you create the three pages for the three national parks.

Steps **To Create a Relative Link to the Home Page**

1 Click the national.htm tab and then scroll to the bottom of the page. Drag to select Home.

The text, Home, is highlighted (Figure 2-79). This text will become a link.

• **Dry Tortugas National Park**
About 70 miles west of Key West is the Dry Tortugas National Park, a cluster of seven islands, composed of sand and coral reefs. Located on one of the islands, Ft. Jefferson, the largest of the 19th century American coastal forts. The area is known for its legends of pirates and sunken ships.

FIGURE 2-79

2 Drag the index.htm file name from the Site panel to the Link box. Click the text, Home, to display the link. Click the Save button on the Standard toolbar. Point to the state_parks.htm tab.

The link is created and index.htm displays in the Link box (Figure 2-80). The national parks page is saved and the asterisk no longer displays on the tab or title bar.

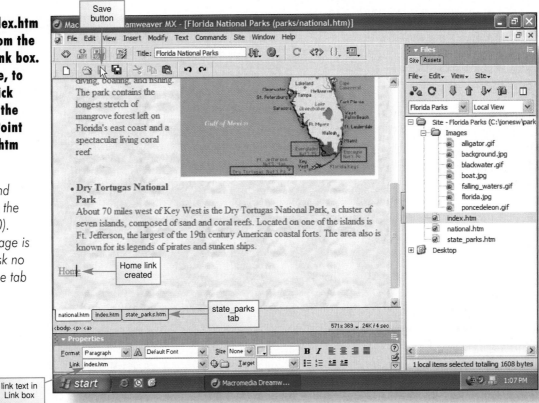

FIGURE 2-80

3 Click the state_parks.htm tab. If necessary, scroll to the end of the document and then drag to select the text, Home (Figure 2-81).

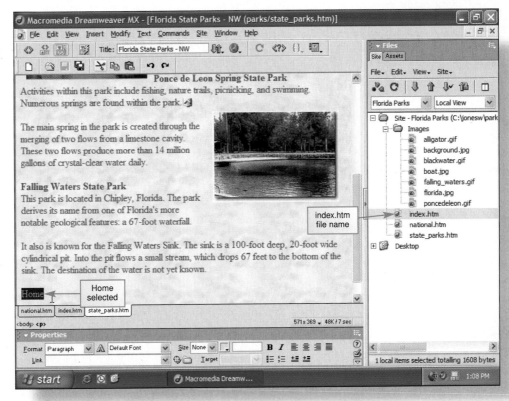

FIGURE 2-81

4 Drag the index.htm file name from the Site panel to the Link box. Click the Save button on the Standard toolbar.

The link is created and index.htm displays in the Link box (Figure 2-82). The state parks page is saved.

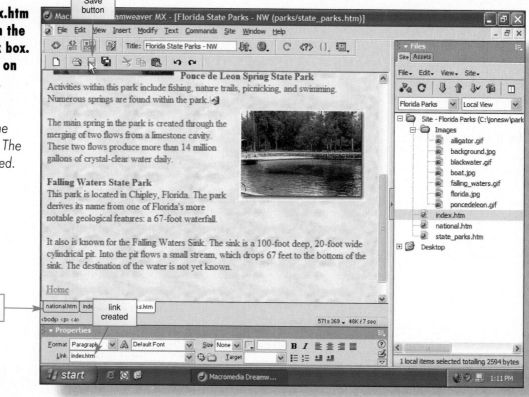

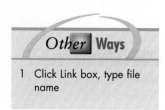

FIGURE 2-82

Other **Ways**

1 Click Link box, type file name

The following steps create relative links to the national parks pages.

TO CREATE RELATIVE LINKS TO THE THREE NATIONAL PARKS PAGES

1 Click the national.htm tab.

2 Drag to select the bulleted text, Everglades National Park.

3 Click the Link box and then type `everglades.htm` for the link text.

4 Drag to select the bulleted text, Biscayne National Park.

5 Click the Link box and then type `biscayne.htm` for the link text.

6 If necessary, scroll down. Drag to select the bulleted text, Dry Tortugas National Park.

7 Click the Link box and then type `dry_tortugas.htm` for the link text.

8 Click the Save button on the Standard toolbar.

The three relative links are added to the Florida National Parks page and the Web page is saved. You create the pages for these links in Project 3.

Absolute Links

In Project 1, you created an absolute link from the index page to the Florida Environmental Department. To create an absolute link, you must know the URL or the path of the external site to which you want to link. You can type the link in the Link box or copy and paste the link.

Creating an Absolute Link

You now will create three absolute (external) links in the NW State Parks page. These links are from the name of each of the three parks to a Web page about the selected park. Perform the following steps to create the three absolute links.

TO CREATE AN ABSOLUTE LINK

1 If necessary, scroll to the top of the page. Drag to select the text, Blackwater River State Park.

2 Click the Link box and then type `http://www.dep.state.fl.us/parks/district1/blackwater/index.asp`.

3 Drag to select the text, Ponce de Leon Spring State Park. Click the Link box and then type `http://www.dep.state.fl.us/parks/district1/poncedeleon/index.asp`.

4 If necessary, scroll down and then drag to select the text, Falling Waters State park. Click the Link box and then type `http://www.dep.state.fl.us/parks/district1/fallingwaters/index.asp`.

5 Click the Save button on the Standard toolbar.

The three absolute links are added to the respective state parks page (Figure 2-83) and the Web page is saved.

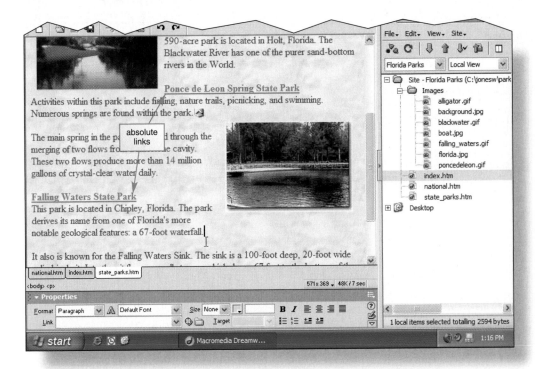

FIGURE 2-83

More About

Absolute Links

When you add an absolute link to a Web page, generally you have no control over the Web pages to which you have linked. If the name of the linked page is changed or removed, your visitors will receive an error message when they click the link. Maintain your site by testing your links periodically.

Other Ways

1 Start browser, open Web page, select URL, copy URL, close browser, paste in Link box

E-mail Links

An **e-mail link** is one of the foundation elements of any successful Web site. It is important for visitors to be able to contact you for additional information or to comment on the Web page or Web site. When visitors click an e-mail link, their default e-mail program opens to a new e-mail message. The e-mail address you specify is inserted automatically in the To box.

Creating an E-mail Link

The next steps create an e-mail link for your home page using your name as the linked text. You do this through the Insert menu.

 To Add an E-mail Link

1 **Click the index.htm tab, scroll down, and then drag to select your name. Click Insert on the menu bar and then point to Email Link.**

Your name is highlighted and the Insert menu is displayed (Figure 2-84).

FIGURE 2-84

2 **Click Email Link.**

The Email link dialog box is displayed. Will Jones is highlighted in the Text text box (Figure 2-85). On your computer, your name is displayed in the Text box.

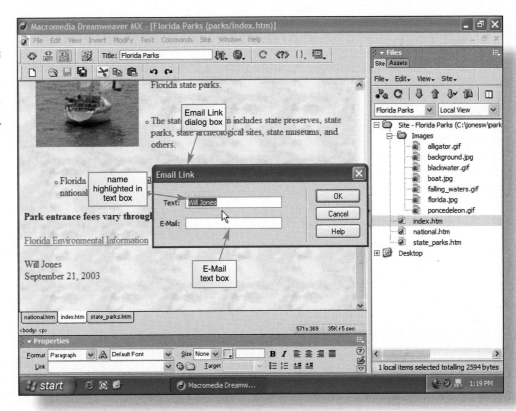

FIGURE 2-85

3 **Click the E-Mail text box and then type your e-mail address. Point to the OK button.**

The e-mail address for Will Jones is displayed in the E-Mail text box. On your computer, Dreamweaver displays your e-mail address (Figure 2-86).

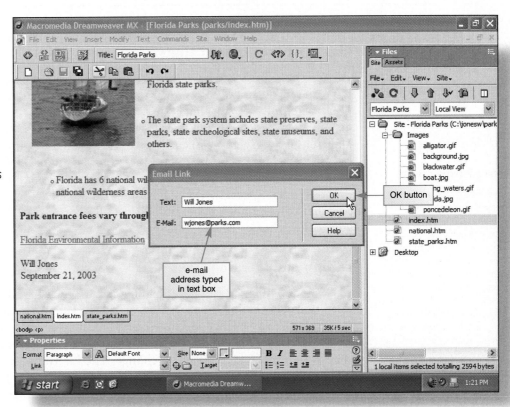

FIGURE 2-86

4 **Click the OK button. Click the Save button on the Standard toolbar and then click the highlighted text (your name).**

The selected text for the e-mail link, Will Jones, is displayed as linked text. The Link box displays the e-mail address (Figure 2-87). On your computer, Dreamweaver displays your name as the linked text.

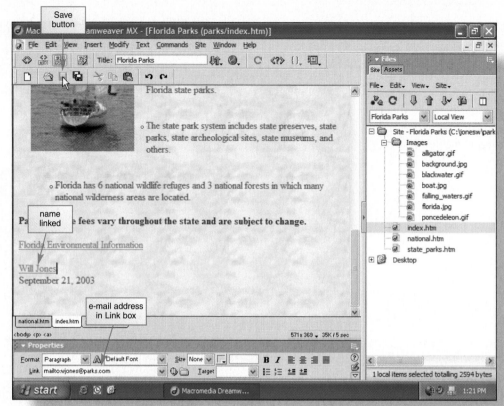

FIGURE 2-87

Changing the Color of Links

Web page links can have three colors: Link (the link has not been clicked), Active Link (the link changes color when the user clicks it), and Visited Link (the link has been visited). By default, linked text follows the color scheme established in your default Web browser. In Internet Explorer, linked text is blue and visited links are dark red. It is easy to make changes to these default settings and select colors that complement the background and other colors you are using on your Web pages. This is accomplished through the Page Properties dialog box. You display the Page Properties dialog box by clicking Modify on the menu bar. You then can click the box that corresponds to one of the three types of links and select a color to match your color scheme.

Editing and Deleting Links

Web development is a never-ending process. At some point, it will be necessary to edit or delete a link. For instance, an e-mail address may change, a URL to an external link may change, or an existing link may contain an error.

Dreamweaver makes it easy to edit or delete a link. First, select the link or click within the link you want to change. The linked document name displays in the Link box in the Property inspector. To delete the link without deleting the text, delete the text from the Link box. To edit the link, make the change in the Link box.

A second method to edit or delete a link is to use the context menu. Right-click within the link you want to change and then click Remove Link on the context menu to eliminate the link; click Change Link on the context menu to edit the link.

Targeting Links

By default, when you click a link, the Web page will open in the current browser window. You can specify, however, to open a linked Web page in a new browser window. First, select the item and create the link. Then, in the expanded Property inspector, click the Target box arrow and click _blank on the Target pop-up menu. When you view the page in a browser and click the link, it will display in a new window.

The Site Map

Dreamweaver provides a visual site map for viewing the relationships among files. The **site map** is a graphical representation of the structure of a Web site. You visually can design and modify the Web site structure through the site map. The home page displays at the top level of the map, and linked pages display at the lower levels. The site map view allows you to create, change, display, save, and print a Web site's structure and navigation. As previously discussed, a Web site structure is the relationships among the pages in a Web site.

Viewing the Site Map

The home page now contains links to other pages in the site and each page in the site contains links back to the home page. The state parks page contains a link to three external Web sites outside of the local site and located on a different server. The index page also contains a link to an external Web site.

You created links from the home page to the two other pages in the Web site (national parks and state parks) and links from these two pages back to the home page. You can use the site map to view a graphical image of these links. In addition to viewing the site map, Dreamweaver also has an option that lets you view your file list and site map simultaneously.

Displaying the Site Map and Local Files

The site map shows the pages as icons and displays links in the order in which they are encountered in the HTML source code. Starting from the home page, the site map default displays the site structure two levels deep. The relative links have a plus sign to their left. If you click the plus (+) sign, pages below the second level display. Some pages have a minus sign to their left. If you click the minus (−) sign, pages linked below the second level are hidden. Text displayed in blue and marked with a globe icon indicates a file on another site or a special link such as an e-mail link. Text displayed in red indicates a broken link. You access the site map through the Site panel. Complete the following steps to display the newly created links among the pages in the Florida Parks Web site.

 To Display the Site Map and Local Files List

1 Click the View box arrow and then point to Map View in the View pop-up menu (Figure 2-88).

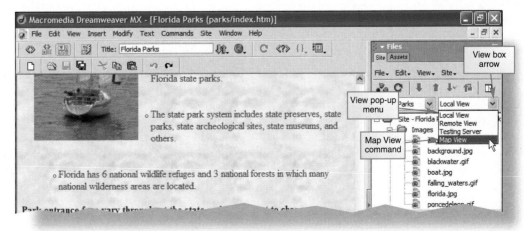

FIGURE 2-88

2 **Click Map View and then point to the Expand/Collapse button on the Site panel toolbar.**

Dreamweaver displays a graphical view of the Web site in the Site panel (Figure 2-89).

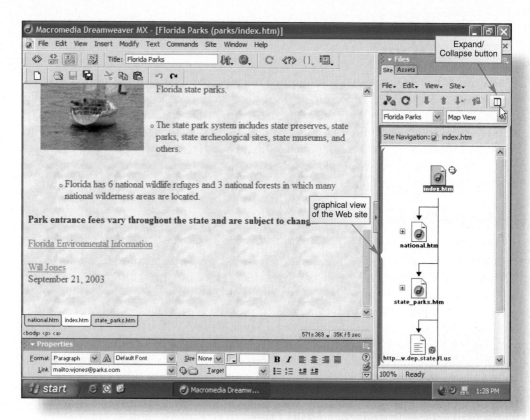

FIGURE 2-89

3 **Click the Expand/ Collapse button. Point to the plus sign to the left of the national.htm icon.**

The site map expands and displays a graphical structure of the links between the index page and the other two pages and external links (Figure 2-90). The plus signs to the left of the national.htm and state_parks.htm pages indicate that additional files or links are below those pages. The files list is displayed on the right in the Local Files panel.

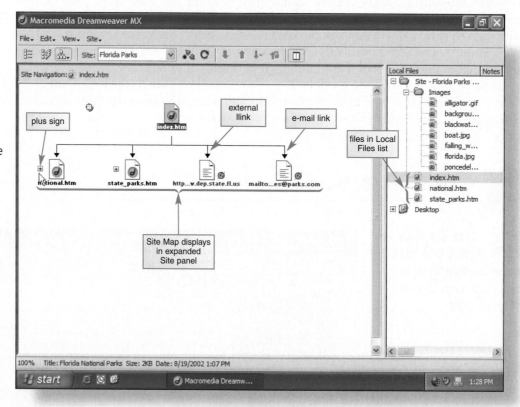

FIGURE 2-90

4 Click the plus sign to the left of the national.htm icon and then point to the plus sign to the left of the state_parks.htm icon.

The structure further expands and displays the relative link to the index page from the national.htm page (Figure 2-91).

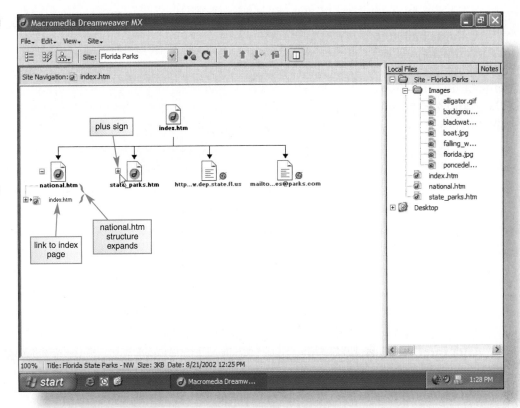

FIGURE 2-91

5 Click the plus sign to the left of the state_parks.htm icon and then point to the Expand/Collapse button on the expanded Site map toolbar.

The structure further expands and displays the relative link to the index page from the state parks page and the external links (Figure 2-92).

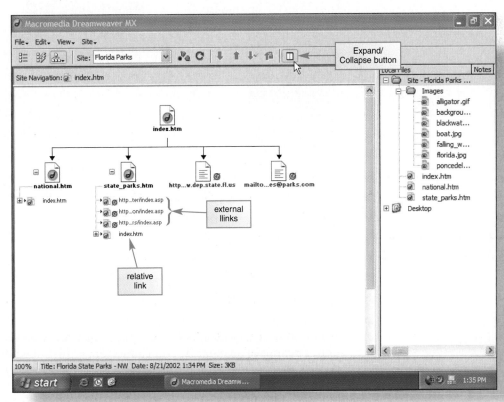

FIGURE 2-92

6 **Click the Expand/ Collapse button to close the site map. Click the View box arrow and then point to Local View in the View pop-up menu (Figure 2-93).**

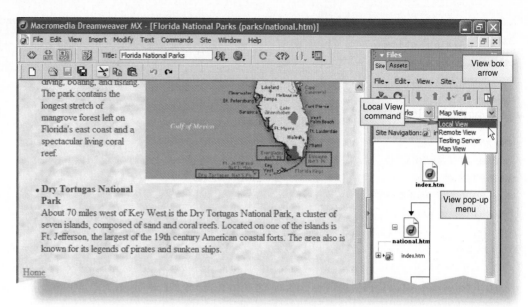

FIGURE 2-93

7 **Click Local View.**

The Site - Florida Parks file hierarchy displays (Figure 2-94).

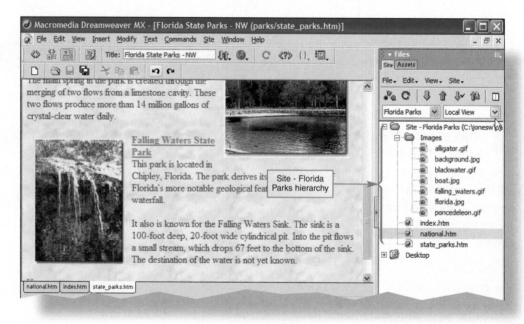

FIGURE 2-94

Verifying Links

It is important that you check and verify that your links work. Links are not active within Dreamweaver; that is, you cannot open the linked document by clicking the link in the Document window. You can check any type of link by displaying the page in a browser. Using a browser is the only available option for absolute or external and e-mail links. For relative or internal links, Dreamweaver provides the Link Checker feature. Use the Link Checker to check internal links in a document, folder, or entire site.

Using the Link Checker

A large Web site can contain hundreds of links that can change over time. Dreamweaver's **Link Checker** searches for broken links and unreferenced files in a portion of a local site or throughout an entire local site. This feature is limited, however, because it verifies internal links only. A list of external links is compiled, but not verified. External links are checked through a browser.

The Link Checker does have advantages, however. When you use this feature, the Link Checker displays a statistical report that includes broken links, orphaned files, and external links. An **orphaned file** is a file that is not connected to any page within the Web site. The orphaned file option is for informational purposes only. The orphaned file report, however, is particularly valuable for a large site since it displays a list of all files not part of the Web site. Deleting unused files from a Web site increases disk space and streamlines your site. You can use the Link Checker to check links throughout your entire site from any Web page within your site. The following steps verify internal links using the Link Checker.

 To Verify Internal Links with the Link Checker

1 **Click the Site menu in the Site panel and then point to Check Links Sitewide (Figure 2-95).**

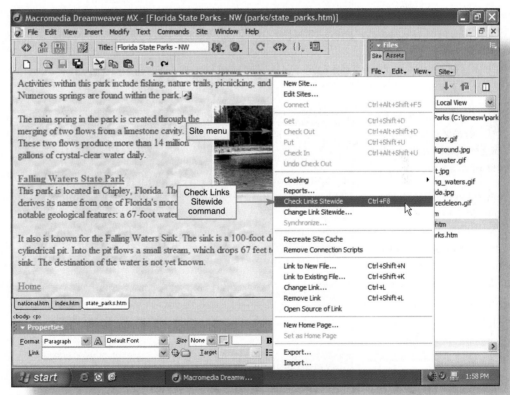

FIGURE 2-95

2 **Click Check Links Sitewide.**

The Results panel is displayed. The report shows a total of 10 files within the site, including 10 Total, 3 HTML, 8 Orphaned, 15 All Links, 0 Broken, and 5 External links (Figure 2-96). External links are not verified. Your report may include different results.

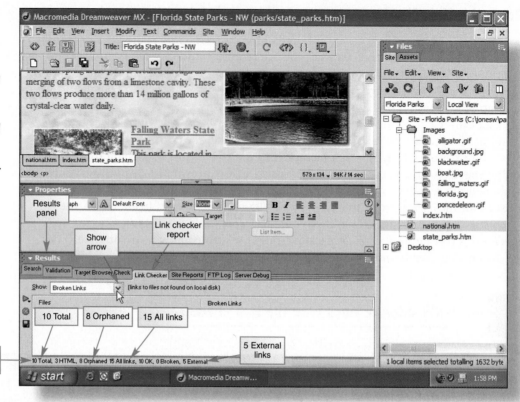

FIGURE 2-96

3 **Click the Show box arrow and then click External Links in the Show pop-up menu.**

The five external links are displayed (Figure 2-97). These are links to absolute Web site and e-mail links. External links are not verified through the Link Checker.

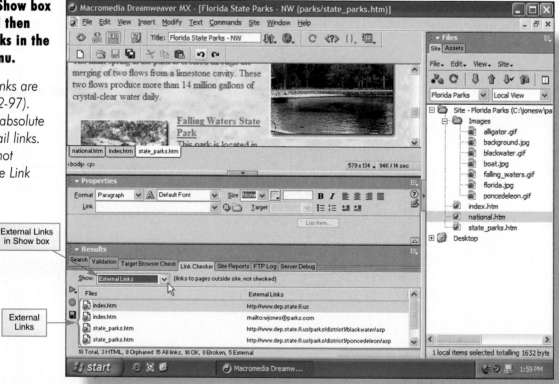

FIGURE 2-97

4 Click the Show down arrow and then point to and click Orphaned Files. Point to the Options button on the Results panel.

The list of orphaned files is displayed (Figure 2-98). Orphaned files are files that are not linked to any file in the site or links to external sites.

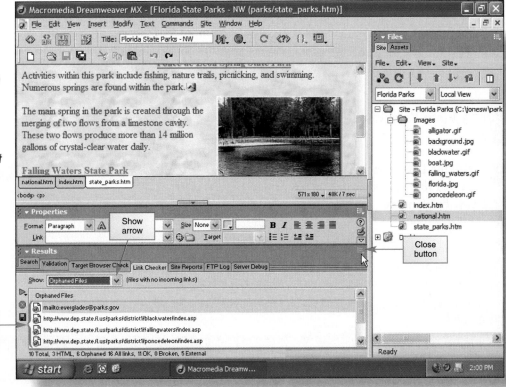

FIGURE 2-98

5 Click the Options button and then click the Close Panel Group to close the Results window (Figure 2-99).

The Results panel closes.

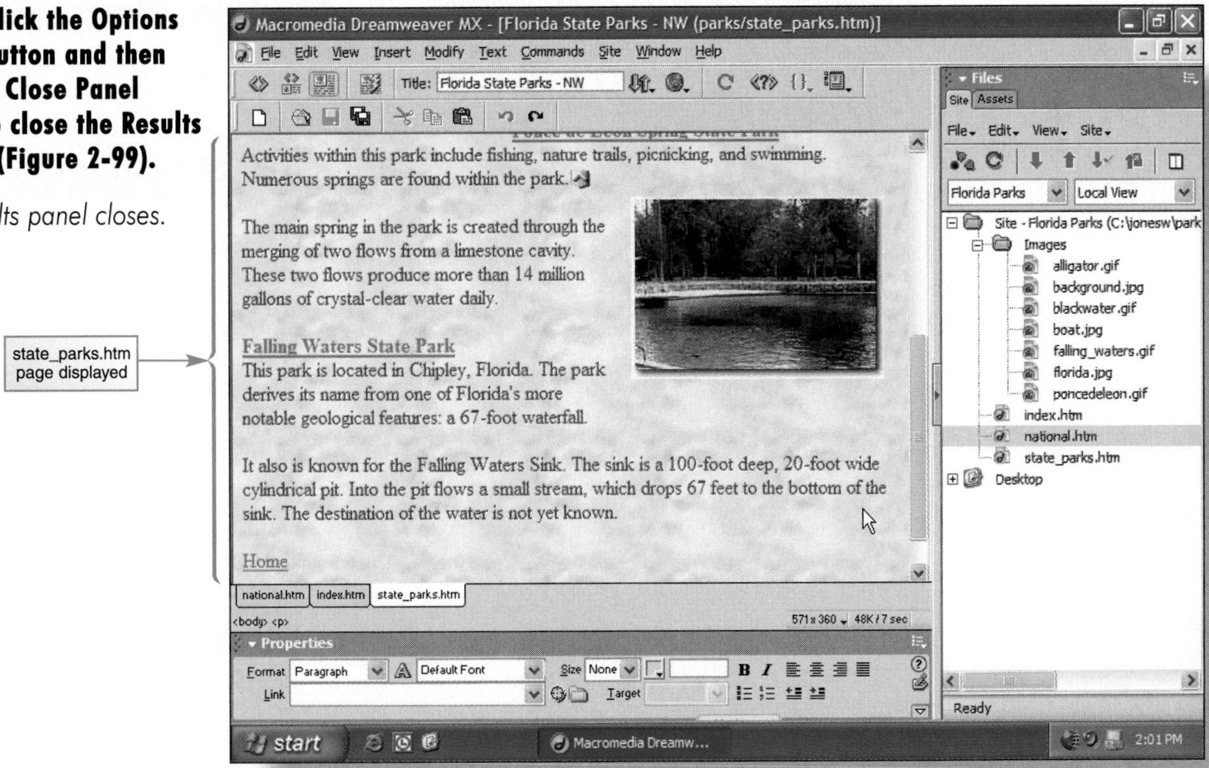

FIGURE 2-99

Viewing Your Site in a Browser

Now that you have completed adding images and verifying links in your Web pages, you will view them through a browser. Complete the following steps to view your Web pages and test your external links.

Steps **To View Your Web Site in a Browser**

1 **Click the index.htm tab and then press the F12 key. Point to the National Parks link.**

The browser displays your index page (Figure 2-100). When you point to a link, the mouse changes to a pointing hand.

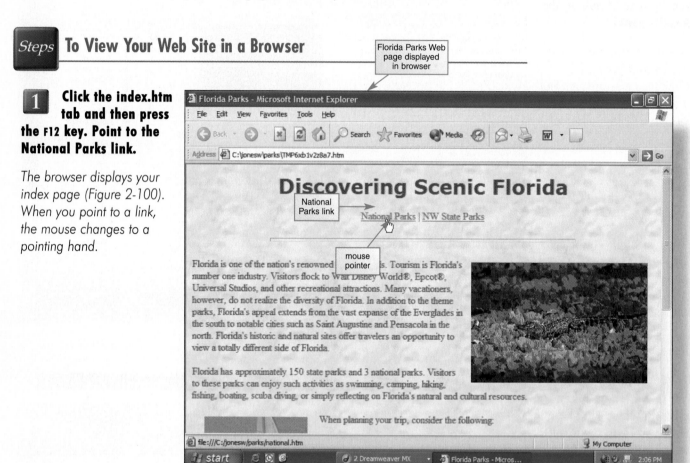

FIGURE 2-100

2 Click the National Parks link.

The Florida National Parks page is displayed in the browser (Figure 2-101).

Florida National Parks Web page displayed in browser

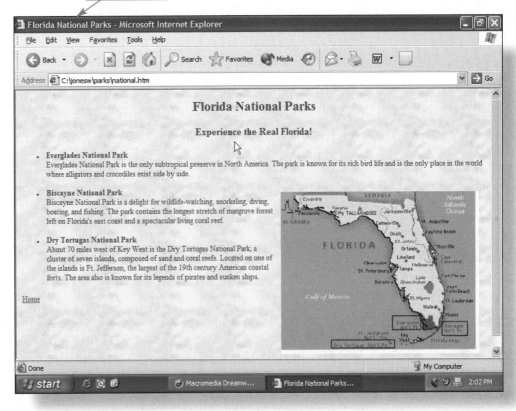

FIGURE 2-101

3 Scroll down and click the Home link to return to the index page. Click the NW State Parks link.

The state parks Web page displays (Figure 2-102).

4 Click each of the three absolute (external) links to view the state park Web sites. Click the browser Back button after you view each page.

5 Click Home to return to the index page. Click the browser Close button to close the browser.

Florida State Parks Web page displayed in browser

Close button

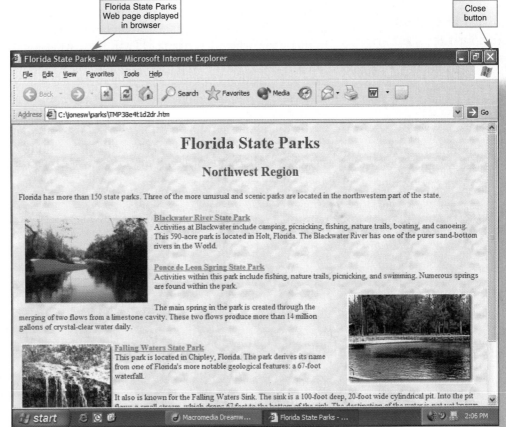

FIGURE 2-102

HTML Code View

Dreamweaver provides two views, or *ways*, to look at a document: **Design view** and **Code view**. Thus far, you have been working in Design view. As you create and work with documents, Dreamweaver automatically generates the underlying HTML code. Recall that the HTML code defines the structure and layout of a Web document by using a variety of tags and attributes. Even though Dreamweaver generates the code, occasions occur that necessitate the tweaking or modifying of code.

Dreamweaver provides several options for viewing and working with HTML code. You can split the Document window so that it displays both the Code view and the Design view. You can display only the Code view in the Document window, or you can open the Code inspector. The **Code inspector** opens in a separate window, so you can keep the whole Document window reserved for Design view.

Using Code View and Design View

In Code view and Design view, you work in a split-screen environment. You can see the design and the code at the same time. Splitting the Document window to view the code makes it easier to view the visual design while you make changes in the HTML code. When you make a change in Design view, the HTML code also is changed. Viewing the code at this early stage may not seem important, but the more code you learn, the more productive you will become.

Within the HTML code, tags can be entered in uppercase, lowercase, or a combination of upper- and lowercase. The letter combination has no effect on how the browser displays the output. When you view the code in Code view in Dreamweaver, some HTML tags display in lowercase letters and some attributes in uppercase letters. This is the Dreamweaver default.

In this book when describing HTML tags, we use uppercase letters for tags and attributes to make it easier to differentiate from the other text. Entering tags as uppercase also is the standard used by many Web page authors who write their own HTML code. Within the steps, however, we use lowercase letters to match the displayed code.

In the following steps, you use the Code View and Design View option to look at the code for the
 (line break) and <P> (paragraph) tags. The paragraph tag has an opening tag <P> and a closing tag </P>. The
 (line break) tag does not have a closing tag.

Using the Quick Tag Editor

For more information about using the Quick Tag Editor to review and edit HTML tags, visit the Dreamweaver MX More About Web page (scsite.com/dreamweavermx/more) and then click Dreamweaver MX Quick Tag Editor.

Steps **To View Design View and Code View Simultaneously**

1 **Collapse the Property inspector and close the Site panel. Position the insertion point to the left of the heading, Florida State Parks. Point to the Show Code and Design Views button on the Document toolbar (Figure 2-103).**

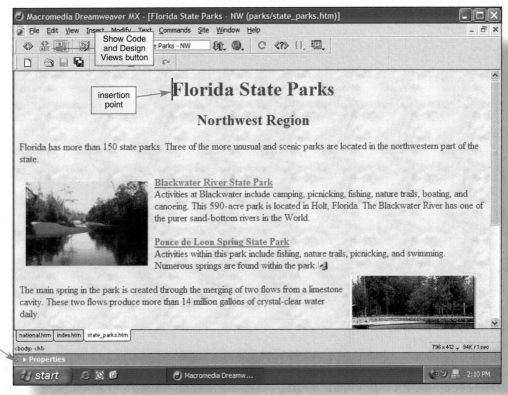

FIGURE 2-103

2 **Click the Show Code and Design Views button. If necessary, click the View menu, point to Code View Options, and then click Line Numbers.**

The window splits. The upper window displays Code view and the lower window displays Design view (Figure 2-104). The insertion point is displayed in Code view in the same location as in Design view (to the left of the heading). The lines are numbered in Code view. The HTML code is displayed in color and in lowercase surrounded by < (less than) and > (greater than) symbols. Your window may display Design view in the upper window and Code view in the lower window.

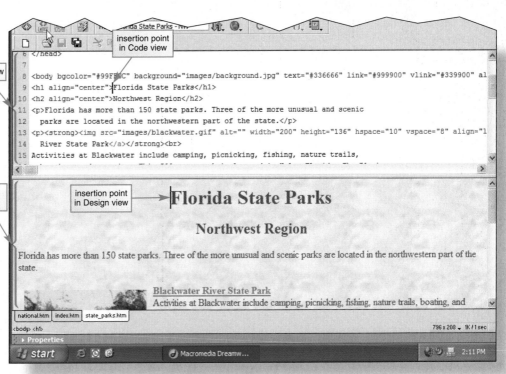

FIGURE 2-104

Modifying HTML Code

One of the more common problems within Dreamweaver and the HTML code is related to line breaks and paragraphs. Occasionally, you inadvertently press the ENTER key or insert a line break and need to remove the tag. Or, you may copy and paste or open a text file that contains unneeded paragraphs or line breaks.

Pressing the BACKSPACE key or DELETE key may return you to the previous line, but does not always delete the line break or paragraph tag within the HTML code. The deletion of these tags is determined by the position of the insertion point when you press the BACKSPACE or DELETE keys. If the insertion point is still inside the HTML code, pressing the BACKSPACE key will not delete these tags and your page will not display correctly.

In the following steps, you practice deleting a line break and a paragraph tag. Then you use Undo to restore them to their original position.

 To Delete and Restore the Line Break Tag and the Paragraph Tag

---

1 **In Code view, position the insertion point to the right of the <br> tag in line 14 as shown in Figure 2-105.**

The insertion point is to the right of the <br> tag in Code view in Line 14 (Figure 2-105). This is the line break tag between the paragraph heading, Blackwater River State Park, and the paragraph describing the park. The line number may be different on your screen.

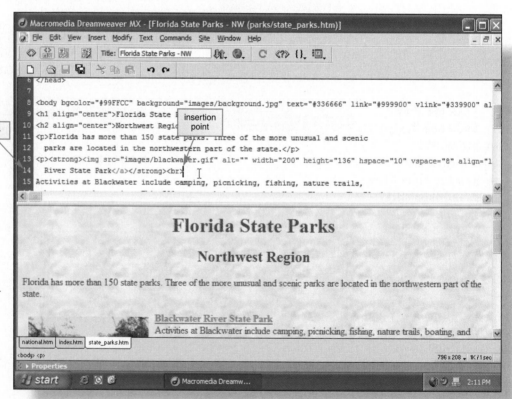

FIGURE 2-105

2 Press the BACKSPACE key four times or the number of times necessary to delete the <br> tag.

The <br> tag is deleted and the insertion point is to the left of the </strong> tag (Figure 2-106). Dreamweaver uses the <strong> tag to indicate bold.

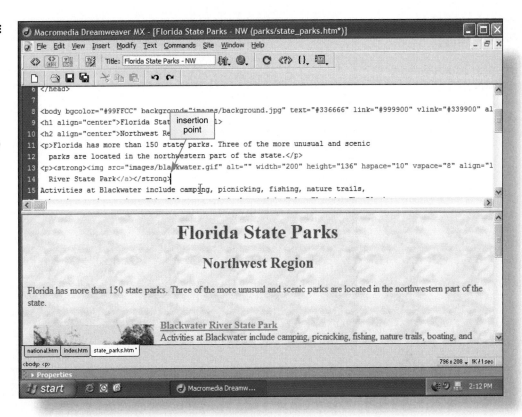

FIGURE 2-106

3 Click anywhere in Design view. Point to the Undo button on the Standard toolbar.

The line break between the paragraph heading and the paragraph is deleted and the paragraph heading is displayed on the same line with the paragraph. The insertion point displays at the same location in both Design view and Code view (Figure 2-107).

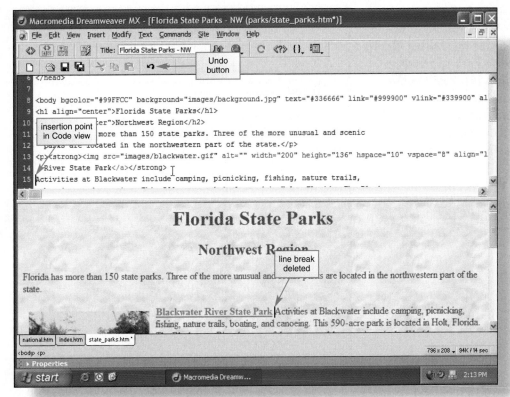

FIGURE 2-107

4 Click the Undo
button.

*The Web page returns to
its original format
(Figure 2-108).*

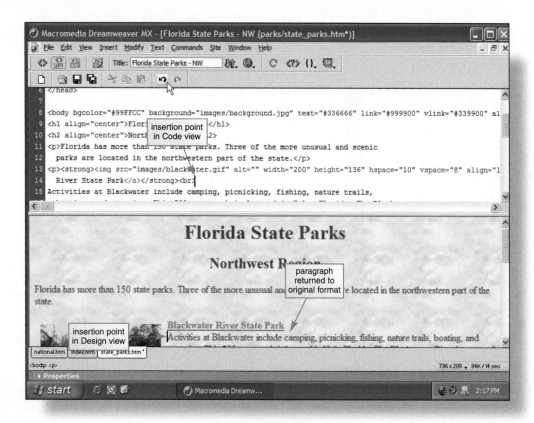

FIGURE 2-108

5 In Code view,
scroll down to
display the Falling Waters
State Park information
(line 29). Position the
insertion point to
the right of the
<p> tag as shown
in Figure 2-109.

*The insertion point is
positioned to the right of
the<p> tag (Figure 2-109).*

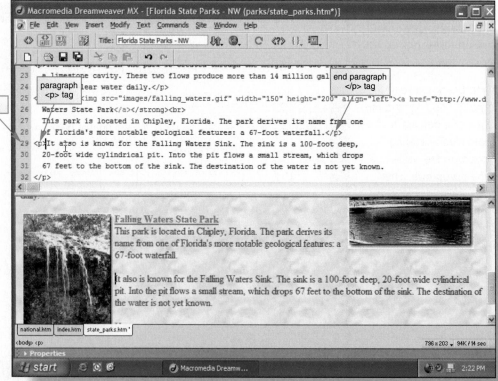

FIGURE 2-109

6 Press the BACKSPACE key until you have deleted both the **<p>** and **</p>** tags. Click anywhere in Design view. Point to the Undo button on the Standard toolbar.

The line between the two paragraphs is deleted (Figure 2-110).

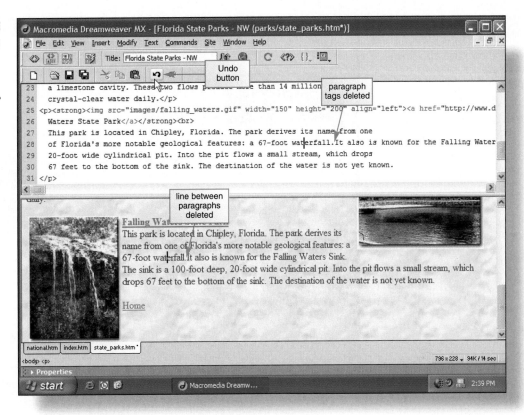

FIGURE 2-110

7 Click the Undo button and then click anywhere in Design view. Point to the Show Design View button on the Document toolbar.

The page is restored to its original format (Figure 2-111).

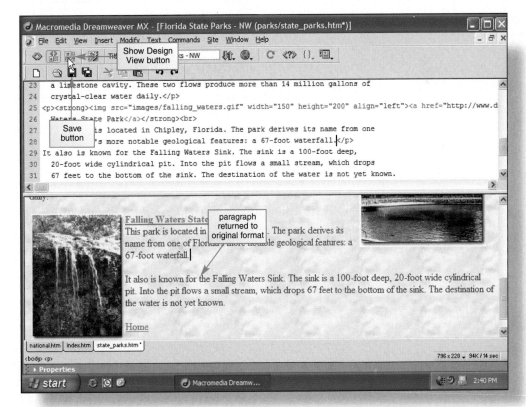

FIGURE 2-111

8 **Click the Show Design View button and then click the Save button.**

The split window is removed and the page is displayed in Design view (Figure 2-112). The Web page is saved.

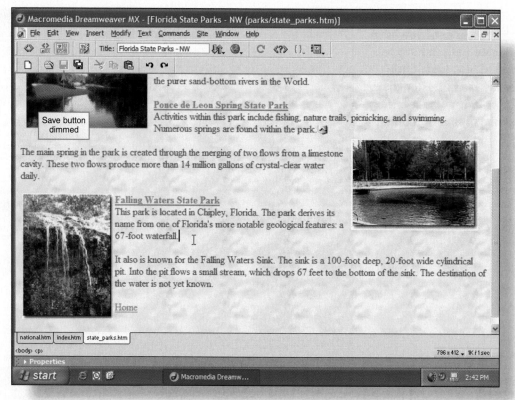

FIGURE 2-112

Quitting Dreamweaver

After you add pages to your Web site, including images and links, and then verify links using the site map and Link Checker, Project 2 is complete. To close the Web site, quit Dreamweaver MX, and return control to Windows, perform the following step.

TO CLOSE THE WEB SITE AND QUIT DREAMWEAVER

1 Click the Close button on the right corner of the Dreamweaver title bar.

The Dreamweaver window, the Document window, and the Florida Parks Web site all close. If you have unsaved changes, Dreamweaver will prompt you to save the changes. Clicking the Yes button in the Dreamweaver MX dialog box saves the changes.

CASE PERSPECTIVE SUMMARY

Will and Joan work well together and are a good team. They are pleased with the new pages on Florida's national and state parks. Both expressed great enthusiasm about learning how to add images and links to a Web page. Joan was particularly impressed with the site map and Link Checker features. Will was surprised at how easy it was to modify the HTML code and is looking forward to learning more about other HTML code revision. Will and Joan are anxious to get started on the next project.

Project Summary

Project 2 introduced you to images, links, the site map, and how to view and modify HTML code. You began the project by using Dreamweaver's integrated file browser to copy data files to the local site. You added two new pages — one for Florida national parks and one for Florida state parks — to the Web site you created in Project 1. Next, you added a background image and page images to the index page. Following that, you applied a color scheme, a background image, and page images to the national and state parks pages. Then, you added relative links to all three pages. You added an e-mail link to the home page and three absolute links to the state parks page. You learned to use the site map and the Link Checker. Finally, you learned how to view and modify HTML code.

What You Should Know

Having completed this project, you now should be able to perform the tasks shown in Table 2-4.

Table 2-4   Project 2 What You Should Know

TASK NUMBER	TASK	PAGE NUMBER	TASK NUMBER	TASK	PAGE NUMBER
1	Start Dreamweaver and Close Open Panels	DW 2.06	19	Add a Color Scheme and Background Image to the State Parks Web Page	DW 2.43
2	Access a Web Site and Open a Web Site from a Local Web Site	DW 2.07	20	Insert and Align Images in the State Parks Web Page	DW 2.44
3	Copy Data Files to the Parks Web Site	DW 2.09	21	Resize an Image	DW 2.49
4	Set a Home Page	DW 2.14	22	Add Text for Relative Links	DW 2.51
5	Prepare the Workspace	DW 2.16	23	Create a Relative Link Using Drag and Drop	DW 2.53
6	Create the National Parks Web Page	DW 2.17	24	Create a Relative Link Using Browse for File	DW 2.55
7	Format the Florida National Parks Page	DW 2.19	25	Create a Relative Link to the Home Page	DW 2.57
8	Open a New Document Window	DW 2.20	26	Create an Absolute Link	DW 2.59
9	Create the State Parks Web Page	DW 2.22	27	Add an E-mail Link	DW 2.60
10	Format the Florida State Parks Page	DW 2.22	28	Display the Site Map and Local Files List	DW 2.63
11	Add a Background Image to the Index Page	DW 2.25	29	Verify Internal Links with the Link Checker	DW 2.67
12	Insert an Image into the Index Page	DW 2.30	30	View Your Web Site in a Browser	DW 2.70
13	Align an Image	DW 2.32	31	View Design View and Code View Simultaneously	DW 2.73
14	Adjust the Horizontal and Vertical Space	DW 2.34	32	Delete and Restore the Line Break Tag and the Paragraph Tag	DW 2.74
15	Add Alt Text	DW 2.35	33	Close the Web Site and Quit Dreamweaver	DW 2.78
16	Insert a Second Image	DW 2.36			
17	Add a Color Scheme and Background Image to the National Parks Web Page	DW 2.39			
18	Insert an Image in the National Parks Web Page	DW 2.40			

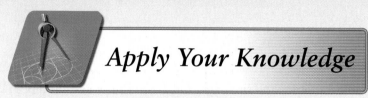

Apply Your Knowledge

1 Modifying the B & B Lawn Service Web Site

Instructions: Start Dreamweaver. If the panels display, press the F4 key to close all panels. Data and image files for the B & B Lawn Service Web site are included on the Data Disk. See the inside back cover of this book for instructions for downloading the Data Disk or see your instructor for information on accessing the files in this book.

You add three new pages to the B & B Lawn Service Web site: a services page, an employment page, and a references page. In this exercise, you add relative and absolute links to each page. You apply a color scheme to each new page and then add a background image to all pages. Next, you insert images on all pages and use the settings in Table 2-5 to align the images and enter the Alt text. You then add an e-mail link to the home page and relative links from the three new pages to the home page. The pages for the Web site are shown in Figures 2-113a through 2-113d.

Software and hardware settings determine how a Web page is displayed in the browser. Your Web pages may display differently in your browser than those in the figures. For an updated list of links, visit the Dreamweaver MX Links Web page (scsite.com/dreamweavermx/links) and then click Project 2 Links.

Table 2-5	Image Property Settings for the B & B Lawn Service Web Site					
IMAGE NAME	W	H	PROPERTY/ALT TEXT V SPACE	H SPACE	ALIGN	ALT
trimming2.gif	174	193	6	6	Right	Tree trimming
shovel.gif	124	166	6	8	Left	Shovel
mowing.gif	120	135	None	20	Left	Grass mowing
shakehands.gif	200	170	None	150	Right	Shaking hands
planting.gif	186	165	6	None	Right	Tree planting
planting2.gif	122	125	8	8	Left	Tree planting

Perform the following tasks:
1. Display the Site panel. Select Lawn Service on the Site pop-up menu in the Site panel. Double-click the index.htm file in the Site panel. Display the Property inspector. Click the expander arrow to expand the Property inspector. If necessary, display the Standard toolbar.
2. Use Dreamweaver's integrated file browser to copy the Images folder and data files to your Proj02 lawn folder. Click the plus sign to the left of the Desktop icon and then navigate through the file hierarchy to the Data Files folder as you did for Florida Parks. Click the Images folder. Hold down the SHIFT key and then click services.htm. Copy the Images folder and the three htm files to the jonesw/lawn folder using Copy and Paste on the context menu.
3. Click Modify on the menu bar and then click Page Properties. Click the Links box arrow and change the color to hexadecimal #CC3333 (row 5 from the bottom, column 11 from the left). Click the Browse button in the Page Properties dialog box, double-click the Images folder, and then select the background.gif image. Click the OK button in the Select Image Source dialog box and in the Page Properties dialog box. Click index.htm in the Site panel to select it. Use the Site panel Site menu to set the index.htm page as the home page.

Apply Your Knowledge

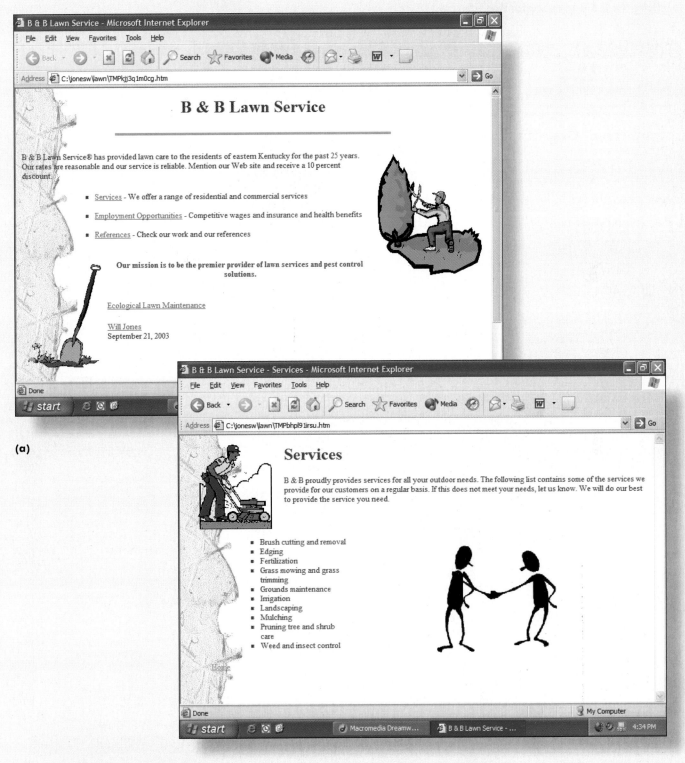

(a)

(b)

FIGURE 2-113

(continued)

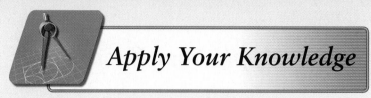

Apply Your Knowledge

Modifying the B & B Lawn Service Web Site *(continued)*

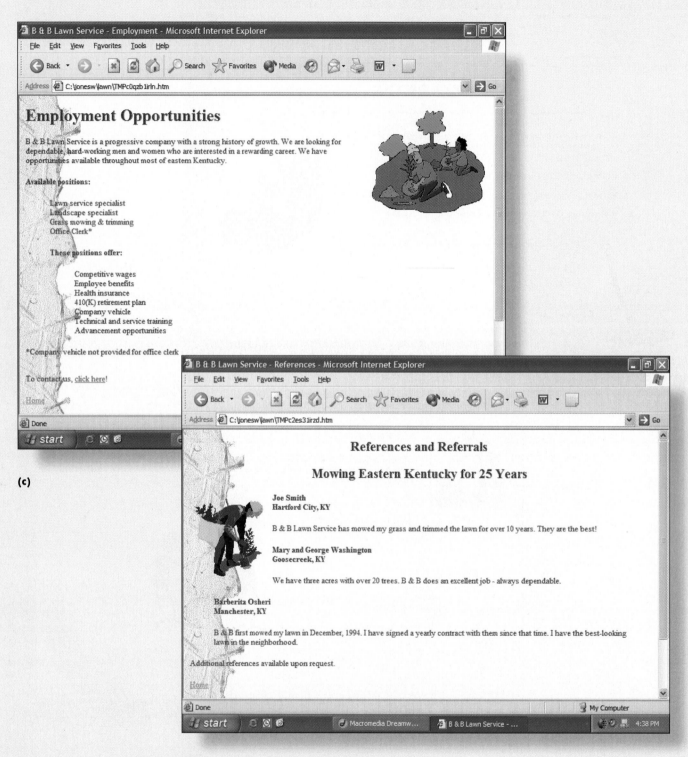

(c)

(d)

FIGURE 2-113 *(continued)*

Apply Your Knowledge

4. Position the insertion point to the left of the first line of the first paragraph. Drag the trimming2.gif image to the insertion point and then select the image. Apply the settings in Table 2-5 on page DW 2.80 to align the image and enter the Alt text. If necessary, scroll down. Position the insertion point to the left of the last sentence on the Web page. Drag the shovel.gif image to the insertion point and then select the image. Apply the settings in Table 2-5.

5. If necessary, scroll up. Select Services (the first bulleted item heading). Use either the drag-and-drop or Browse for File method to create a link to the services page. Repeat this process to add links from Employment Opportunities and References (the second and third bulleted item headings) to the respective Web pages. Select your name. Use the Insert menu to create an e-mail link using your name. Save the index page (Figure 2-113a).

6. Open services.htm. Use the Commands menu to apply the color scheme (Green background and Brown, Yellow, Red text and links) you added in Project 1 to the index page. Display the Page Properties dialog box. Change the Links color to hexadecimal #CC3333 and add the background image to the services.htm page as you did in step 3 to the index.htm page.

7. Position the insertion point to the left of the page heading, drag the mowing.gif image to the insertion point, and then select the image. Apply the settings in Table 2-5. Position the insertion point to the right of the first bulleted item and then drag the shakehands.gif to the insertion point. Select the image. Apply the settings in Table 2-5.

8. If necessary, scroll down. Select Home and then create a relative link to the index page. Title the page B & B Lawn Service - Services. Save the services page (Figure 2-113b).

9. Open employment.htm. Apply the same color scheme you applied to services.htm in step 6. Change the links color and add the background image to the employment page as you did in step 3 to the index.htm page.

10. Position the insertion point to the left of the heading and then drag the planting.gif image to the insertion point. Select the image. Apply the settings in Table 2-5.

11. Scroll to the bottom of the page. Select the words, click here, in the last sentence on the page, To contact us, click here! Use the Insert menu to create an e-mail link using your e-mail address. Select Home at the bottom of the page and then drag index.htm to the Link box in the Property inspector to create a relative link to the index.htm file. Title the page B & B Lawn Service - Employment. Save the employment page (Figure 2-113c).

12. Open references.htm. Apply the same color scheme and background image you applied to the other pages in this Web site. Change the links color as you did in step 3 to the index.htm page.

13. Create a link from Home to the index page.

14. Position the insertion point to the left of the text, Joe Smith. Drag the planting2.gif image to the insertion point. Select the image. Apply the settings in Table 2-5. Title the page B & B Lawn Service - References. Save the references page (Figure 2-113d).

15. View the Web site in your browser. Check each link to verify that it works. Print a copy of each page if required and hand the copies in to your instructor. Close the browser. Quit Dreamweaver.

In the Lab

1 Modifying the CandleDust Web Site

Problem: Mary Stewart, for whom you created the CandleDust Web site and Web page, is very pleased with the response she has received. She has asked you to create a second page with links and images added to the index page. Mary wants the new page to include information about her company's history. The revised Web site is shown in Figures 2-114a and 2-114b. Table 2-6 includes the settings and Alt text for the images. Software and hardware settings determine how a Web page displays in the browser. Your Web pages may display differently in your browser than those in the figures. For an updated list of links, visit the Dreamweaver MX Links Web page (scsite.com/dreamweavermx/links) and then click Project 2 Links.

Table 2-6	Image Property Settings for the CandleDust Web Site						
IMAGE NAME	**W**	**H**	**PROPERTY/ALT TEXT**				
			V SPACE	**H SPACE**	**ALIGN**	**ALT**	
candle1.gif	126	192	6	15	Left	Logo	
candle2.gif	192	178	None	75	Right	Candles	
candle_dip.gif	164	191	10	50	Left	Candle dipping	

Instructions: Perform the following tasks:

1. Start Dreamweaver. Display the Site panel. Select CandleDust on the Site pop-up menu in the Site panel. Double-click the index.htm file in the Site panel. Display the Property inspector. Click the expander arrow to expand the Property inspector. If necessary, display the Standard toolbar.

2. Use Dreamweaver's integrated file browser to copy the Images folder and data file to your candle folder. Click the plus sign to the left of the Desktop icon and then navigate through the file hierarchy to the candle folder in Proj02. Click the plus sign to the left of candle and then select and copy the Images folder and data file to the jonesw/candle folder using Copy and Paste on the context menu.

3. Click Modify on the menu bar and then click Page Properties. Click the Browse button in the Page Properties dialog box, click the Images folder, and then select the background.gif image. Click the OK button in the Select Image Source dialog box and in the Page Properties dialog box. Click index.htm in the Site panel to select it. Click Site on the Site panel menu bar and then set the index.htm page as the home page.

4. Position the insertion point to the left of the heading and then drag the candle1.gif to the insertion point. Select the image. Apply the settings in Table 2-6 to align the image and enter the Alt text.

5. Position the insertion point to the right of CandleDust candles are available in a variety of types: and then drag the candle2.gif to the insertion point. Select the image and then apply the settings in Table 2-6.

6. Scroll to the bottom of the page and then drag through the text, company history. Use the drag-and-drop method to create a link to the history.htm page. Use the Insert menu to create an e-mail link using your e-mail address. Save the index page (Figure 2-114a).

7. Open history.htm. Use the Command menu to apply the color scheme, Purple background and Blue,Purple,Green for text and links (the same color scheme you applied to the index page in Project 1). Apply the background image to the history page as you did in step 3 to the index page.

In the Lab

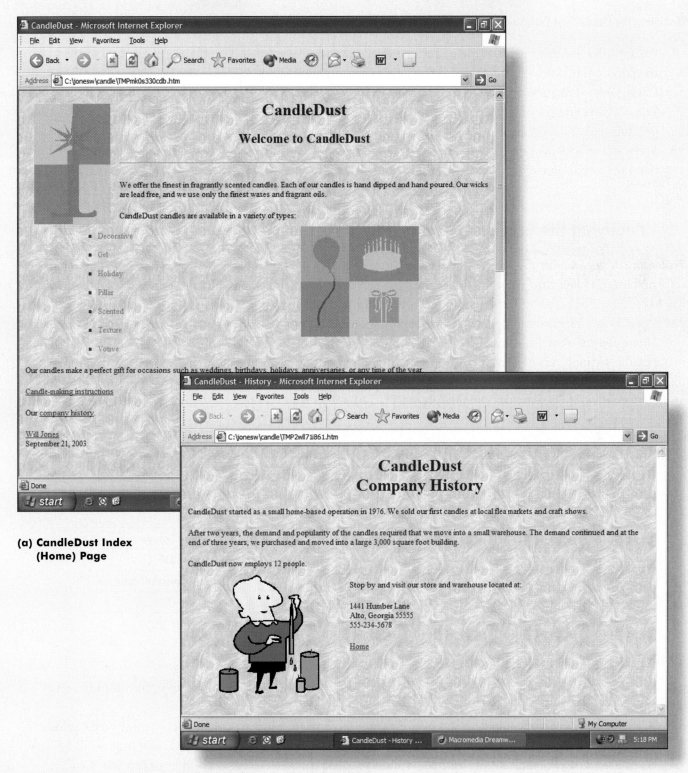

(a) CandleDust Index (Home) Page

(b) CandleDust - History Web Page

FIGURE 2-114

(continued)

In the Lab

Modifying the CandleDust Web Site (continued)

8. Position the insertion point at the end of the third paragraph and then drag the candle_dip.gif to the insertion point. Select the image and then apply the settings in Table 2-6 on page DW 2.84. Title the page CandleDust - History.

9. Select Home and then create a relative link to the index page. Save the history page (Figure 2-114b on the previous page).

10. View your pages in your browser and verify that your links work. Print a copy of each page if required and hand the copies in to your instructor. Close your browser. Quit Dreamweaver.

2 Modifying the Credit Protection Web Site

Problem: Marcy Cantu has received favorable comments about the Web page and site you created about credit information. Her law firm wants to utilize the Web site to provide additional information to its clients. Marcy has asked you if you would be willing to work with her and another intern at the firm to create two more Web pages in the site. They want one of the pages to discuss credit protection and the other page to contain information about identity theft. The revised Web site is shown in Figures 2-115a, 2-115b, and 2-115c. Table 2-7 includes the settings and Alt text for the images. Software and hardware settings determine how a Web page displays in the browser. Your Web pages may display differently in your browser than those in the figures. For an updated list of links, visit the Dreamweaver MX Links Web page (scsite.com/dreamweavermx/links) and then click Project 2 Links.

Table 2-7	Image Property Settings for the Credit Protection Web Site					
IMAGE NAME	W	H	PROPERTY/ALT TEXT V SPACE	H SPACE	ALIGN	ALT
money1.gif	174	110	None	20	Absolute Middle	Money
answer.gif	202	176	None	200	Right	Reporting options
protection.gif	240	170	14	20	Left	Identity theft
theft.gif	172	169	20	75	Right	Protect personal information
question.gif	148	366	None	15	Right	Questions?

Instructions: Perform the following tasks:

1. Start Dreamweaver. Display the Site panel. Select Credit Protection on the Site pop-up menu in the Site panel. Open index.htm.

2. Use Dreamweaver's integrated file browser to copy the Images folder and data files to your credit folder. The data files consist of the Images folder and two data files — questions.htm and theft.htm.

3. If necessary, display the Property inspector and the Standard toolbar. Expand the Property inspector.

4. Click the index.htm file and set the page as the home page. Apply the background.jpg image (located in the Images folder) to the index page.

In the Lab

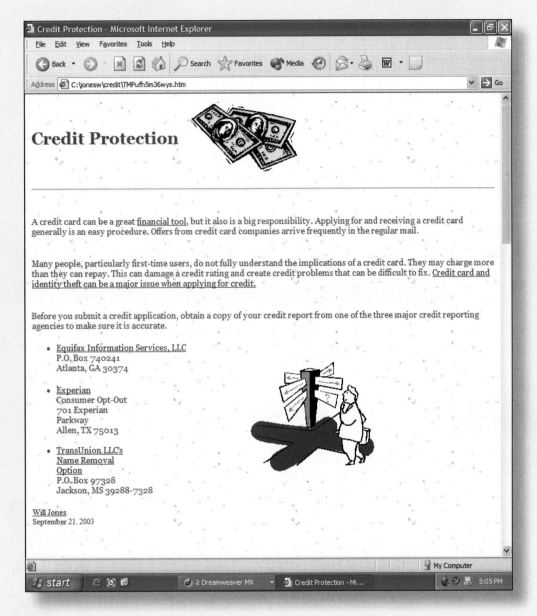

(a) Credit Protection Index (Home) Page

FIGURE 2-115

5. Position the insertion point to the right of the heading and then drag the money1.gif image to the insertion point. Select the image and then apply the settings in Table 2-7. Position the insertion point to the right of the text, Equifax Information Services, LLC. Drag the answer.gif image to the insertion point and then select the image. Apply the settings in Table 2-7.

6. Select the text, financial tool, located in the first sentence of the first paragraph. Create a relative link from the selected text to questions.htm.

(continued)

In the Lab

Modifying the Credit Protection Web Site *(continued)*

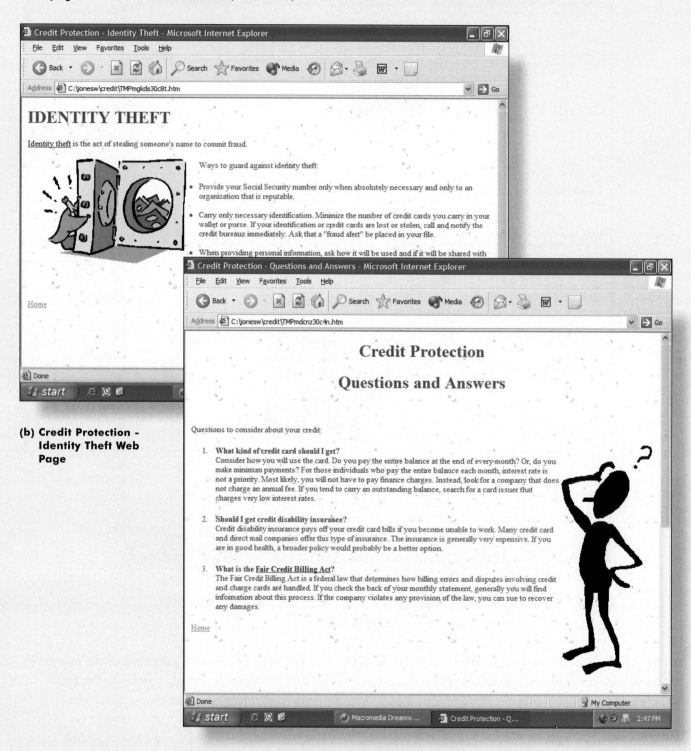

(b) Credit Protection – Identity Theft Web Page

(c) Credit Protection - Questions and Answers Web Page

FIGURE 2-115 *(continued)*

In the Lab

7. Position the insertion point at the end of the second paragraph. Press the SPACEBAR. Type Credit card and identity theft can be a major issue when applying for credit. Select the text you just typed and then create a relative link to the theft.htm file. Save the index page (Figure 2-115a on page DW 2.87).

8. Open theft.htm and then apply the same color scheme (Yellow background and Green,Blue,Purple for text and links) you applied to the index.htm page in Project 1. Apply the background image to the theft.htm page as you did in step 4 to the index.htm page.

9. Position the insertion point to the left of the second line and then drag the protection.gif to the insertion point. Select the image. Apply the settings in Table 2-7 on page DW 2.86. Position the insertion point to the right of the third bulleted item and then drag the theft.gif to the insertion point. Select the image. Apply the settings in Table 2-7.

10. Drag to select the text, Identity theft, at the beginning of the first sentence and then create an absolute link using http://www.consumer.gov/idtheft/ for the URL. Create an absolute link from the protection.gif image using the same URL. Select the image and then type the URL in the Link box. Select Home and then create a relative link to the index.htm page. Title the page Credit Protection - Identity Theft. Save the theft page (Figure 2-115b).

11. Open questions.htm. Apply the same color scheme and background image that you added to the theft.htm page in step 8.

12. Position the insertion point to the right of the first line of text and then drag the question.gif image to the insertion point. Select the image. Apply the settings in Table 2-7.

13. Create an absolute link from the Fair Credit Billing Act text in question 3. Use http://www.ftc.gov/bcp/conline/pubs/credit/fcb.htm for the URL. Select Home and then create a relative link to the index page. Title the page Credit Protection - Questions and Answers. Save the questions page (Figure 2-115c).

14. Click Site on the Site panel menu bar and then click Check Links Sitewide. Use the Link Checker in the Results panel to check the relative links in your Web site. View the site in the site map. Modify the URLs to correct any link problems.

15. View the Web site in your browser and verify that your external links work. Hint: Click the image on the theft.htm page. Print a copy of each page if required and hand the copies in to your instructor. Close your browser and quit Dreamweaver.

3 Modifying the Plant City Web Page

Problem: Juan Benito recently became a member of a marketing group promoting Plant City's strawberry history. He wants to expand the Web site you created for him by adding two new Web pages that will highlight other features of Plant City, Florida. Juan explains that some members of the committee are not fond of the text color within the original color scheme, so they want you to change it. You inform Juan that you can create the new pages and make the changes to the color scheme. The revised Web site is displayed in Figures 2-116a, 2-116b, and 2-116c (on pages DW 2.91 and DW 2.92). Table 2-8 on the next page includes the settings and Alt text for the images. Software and hardware settings determine how a Web page displays in the browser. Your Web pages may display differently in your browser than those in the figures. For an updated list of links, visit the Dreamweaver MX Links Web page (scsite.com/dreamweavermx/links) and then click Project 2 Links.

(continued)

In the Lab

Modifying the Plant City Web Page *(continued)*

IMAGE NAME	W	H	PROPERTY/ALT TEXT V SPACE	H SPACE	ALIGN	ALT
strawberry01.gif	77	75	None	80	Right	Strawberry
train.gif	225	140	6	8	Right	Train
strawberry02.gif	200	145	None	25	Right	Strawberry

Table 2-8 Image Property Settings for the Plant City Web Site

Instructions: Perform the following tasks:

1. Start Dreamweaver. Display the Site panel. Select Plant City on the Site pop-up menu.
2. Use Dreamweaver's integrated file browser to copy the data files to the city folder. The data files consist of an Images folder and two Web pages — facts.htm and recipes.htm.
3. Open index.htm. If necessary, display the Property inspector and the Standard toolbar. Expand the Property inspector.
4. Select the index.htm file and set the index.htm page as the home page. Open the Page Properties dialog box and then click the Text box arrow. Change the text color to black. Apply the border.gif image as the background image. Click Edit on menu bar and then click Select All. Click the Text Indent button in the Property inspector two times.
5. Position the insertion point after the last numbered item (6) on the page and then press the ENTER key. Click the Ordered List button to deselect the numbered list and then click the Text Outdent button two times. Type Facts | Recipes as the link text.
6. Create a relative link from Facts to the facts.htm page and then create a relative link from Recipes to the recipes.htm page.
7. Position the insertion point to the right of the first line of the first paragraph and then drag the strawberry01.gif image to the insertion point. Select the image. Apply the settings in Table 2-8.
8. Insert the train.gif image to the right of the first numbered item. Apply the settings in Table 2-8. Use the Border box to add a 3-pixel border to the image. Save the index page (Figure 2-116a).
9. Open facts.htm and then select all of the text except for the heading. Click the Text Indent button in the Property inspector two times. Apply the border.gif image to the background. Display the Page Properties dialog box and change the Links color to hexadecimal #FF0000 (row 7, column 2 from the left).
10. Position the insertion point to the left of the heading and then drag the strawberry02.gif image to the insertion point. Select the image. Apply the settings in Table 2-8.
11. Scroll to the bottom of the page and then select Home. Create a relative link to the index.htm page. Click to the right of Home. Press the ENTER key and then type Strawberry Varieties. Select the text and create an absolute link to http://www.extension.umn.edu/extensionnews/2002/New StrawberryVarieties.html. Title the page Plant City, Florida - Strawberry Facts. Save the facts page (Figure 2-116b).

In the Lab

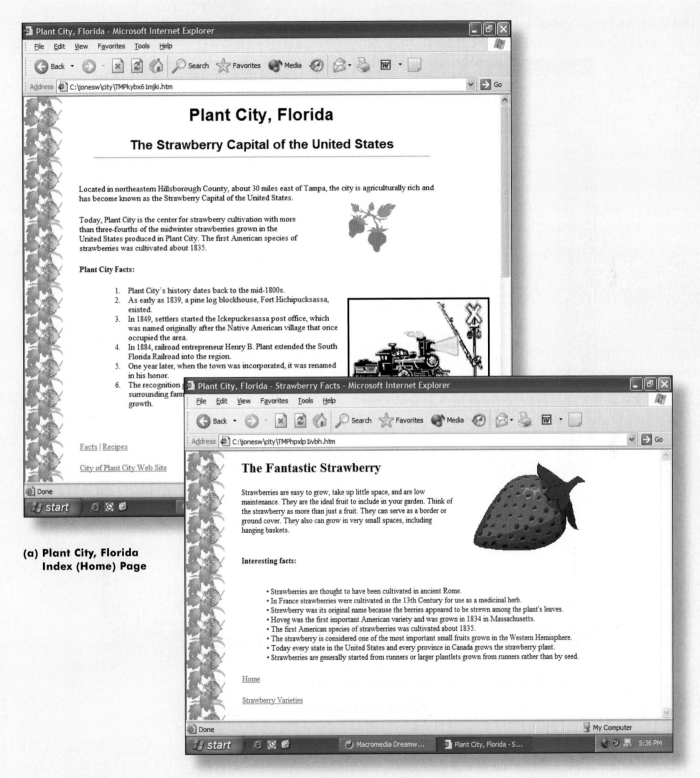

(a) Plant City, Florida Index (Home) Page

(b) Plant City, Florida - Strawberry Facts Web Page

FIGURE 2-116

(continued)

In the Lab

Modifying the Plant City Web Page *(continued)*

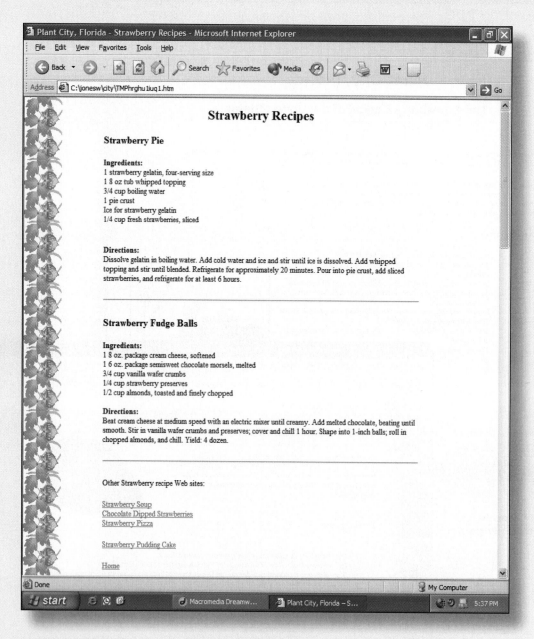

(c) Plant City, Florida - Strawberry Recipes Web Page

FIGURE 2-116 *(continued)*

In the Lab

12. Open recipes.htm. Select all the text except the heading and then click the Text Indent button in the Property inspector two times. Apply the border.gif image to the background. Display the Page Properties dialog box and change the Links color to hexadecimal #FF0000 (row 7, column 9 from the left).

13. Position the insertion point at the end of the second horizontal rule and then press the ENTER key. Type the following text. Press the ENTER key after typing each line of text:

    ```
    Strawberry Soup
    Chocolate Dipped Strawberries
    Strawberry Pizza
    ```

    Add absolute links to these three items as follows:

    For Strawberry Soup, type `http://www.sweettechnology.com/straw1.htm` as the URL; for Chocolate Dipped Strawberries, type `http://momo.essortment.com/recipestrawberr_pwh.htm` as the URL; and for Strawberry Pizza, type `http://www.pallensmith.com/features/recipes/strawpizza.htm` as the URL.

14. Use a search engine and find another Web site with strawberry recipes. Select a recipe you like and make a note of the URL. Position the insertion point at the end of the Web page. Type the name of the recipe you selected and then create an absolute link to the Web site.

15. Title the page Plant City, Florida - Strawberry Recipes. Save the recipes page (Figure 2-116c).

17. Use the Link Checker to verify the internal links. View the Web site in your browser and verify the external links. Close your browser and quit Dreamweaver.

Cases and Places

The difficulty of these case studies varies:
▶ are the least difficult; ▶▶ are more difficult; and ▶▶▶ are the most difficult.

1   ▶   In Project 1, you created a Web site and a Web page listing your favorite sport. Now, you want to add another page to the site. Create and format the page. The page should include general information about your selected sport. Create a relative link from the home page to the new page and from the new page to the home page. Add a background image to both pages and insert an image on one of the pages. Include an appropriate title for the page. Save the page in the sports subfolder. For a selection of images and backgrounds, visit the Dreamweaver MX Media Web page (scsite.com/dreamweavermx/media) and then click Media below Project 2.

Cases and Places

2 ▶ Several friends of yours were impressed with the Web page and Web site you created about your favorite hobby in Project 1. They have given you some topics they think you should include on the site. You decide to create an additional page that will consist of details about your hobby and the topics. Format the page. Add an absolute link to a related Web site and a relative link from the home page to the new page and from the new page to the home page. Add a background image to the index page and to the new page. Create an e-mail link on the index page. Title the page the name of the selected hobby. Save the page in the hobby subfolder. For a selection of images and backgrounds, visit the Dreamweaver MX Media Web page (scsite.com/dreamweavermx/media) and then click Media below Project 2.

3 ▶▶ Modify the favorite type of music Web site you created in Project 1 by creating a new page. Format the page. Discuss your favorite artist or band on the new page. Apply a color scheme to the new page and add an image to both pages. On the index page, align the image right, and on the new page, align the image left. Position each image appropriately on the page by adding H Space and V Space. Add appropriate Alt text for each image. Add an e-mail link on the index page and add text and a relative link from the new page to the index page. View your Web pages in your browser. Give the page a meaningful title and then save the page in your music subfolder. For a selection of images and backgrounds, visit the Dreamweaver MX Media Web page (scsite.com/dreamweavermx/media) and then click Media below Project 2.

4 ▶▶ In Project 1, you created a Web site and a Web page to publicize your running for office campaign. Develop two additional pages to add to the site. Apply a color scheme, and include a background image on all three pages. Apply appropriate formatting to the two new pages. Scan a picture of yourself or make a picture with a digital camera and include the picture on the index page. Add a second image illustrating one of your campaign promises. Include at least two images on one of the new pages and one image on the other new page. Add appropriate H Space and V Space to position the images and add Alt text for all images. Add a border to one of the images. Create e-mail links on all three pages, and create relative links from the home page to both pages and from each of the pages to the home page. Create an absolute link to a related site on one of the pages. Use the site map to verify your links. Give each page a meaningful title and then save the pages in the office subfolder. For a selection of images and backgrounds, visit the Dreamweaver MX Media Web page (scsite.com/dreamweavermx/media) and then click Media below Project 2.

5 ▶▶▶ The student trips Web site you created in Project 1 is a success. Students love it. The dean is so impressed that she asks if you will continue with the project. You create and format three additional Web pages — one for each of three possible locations for the trip. Add a background image to all pages. Add two images to each of the pages, including the index page. Resize one of the images. Add appropriate H Space and V Space to position each image and then add Alt text for each image. Create a link from the index page to each of the three new pages and a link from each page to the index page. Create an absolute link to a related informational Web site on each of the three new pages. Add an appropriate title to each page. Preview in a browser to verify the links. Save the pages in your trips subfolder. For a selection of images and backgrounds, visit the Dreamweaver MX Media Web page (scsite.com/dreamweavermx/media) and then click Media below Project 2.

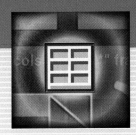

Macromedia Dreamweaver MX

Tables and
Page Layout

You will have mastered the material in this project when you can:

OBJECTIVES

- Understand and plan page layout
- Describe Standard view and Layout view
- Design a Web page using tables in Standard view
- Design a Web page using tables in Layout view
- Describe visual guides
- Modify a table structure
- Describe HTML table tags
- Add content to a table
- Format table content
- Format a table
- Create head content

Macromedia Dreamweaver MX

Tables and Page Layout

CASE PERSPECTIVE

The Florida Parks Web site has been very successful thus far. Will has received several e-mail messages asking for additional information about the three national parks. Joan suggests that a separate page on each park would be a good addition to the Web site. Both Will and you agree this is a good idea. The two of you volunteer to research various sources and to create the content for the three new pages.

Joan further suggests that, in addition to adding the same color scheme and background as the rest of the site, the three new pages also should have some consistency in the displayed information. The team decides that each page should include a header with the name of the park, that the information contained in the body content should describe the location and contain some interesting facts, and that each page should list the park's address, including an e-mail link. The footer will contain links to the home page and to the other two national parks pages. You all are eager to get started on this new addition to the Florida Parks Web site.

Introduction

Project 3 introduces the use of tables for page layout and the addition of head content elements. Page layout is an important part of Web design. Page layout refers to the way your page will display in the browser, which is one of the major challenges for any Web designer. Dreamweaver's table feature is a great tool for designing a Web page. The table feature is very similar to the table feature in word processing programs, such as Microsoft Word. A table allows you to add vertical and horizontal structure to a Web page. Using a table, you can put just about anything on your page and have it display in a specific location. You can lay out tabular data. You can create columns of text or navigation bars. You can delete, split, and merge rows and columns; modify table, row, or cell properties to add color and alignment; and copy and paste cells.

Dreamweaver provides two views, or ways, to use the table feature: Standard view and Layout view. Standard view uses the Insert Table dialog box, and Layout view is a free-form process in which you draw the table and the individual cells. This project discusses both views and the advantages and disadvantages of each. The second part of the project discusses the addition and value of head content.

When you create a Web page, the underlying HTML code is made up of two main sections: the head section and the body section. The body section contains the page content that displays in the browser. In Project 1 and Project 2, you created your Web pages in the body section. The head section contains a variety of information. With the exception of the page title, all head content is invisible when viewed in the Dreamweaver Document window or in a browser. Some head content is accessed by other programs, such as search engines, and some content is accessed by the browser. This project discusses the head content options and the importance of this content.

Project Three — Florida Parks Page Layout

In this project, you continue with the creation of the Florida Parks Web site. You use tables to create three new Web pages focusing on Florida's three national parks. You will add these new pages to the parks Web site and link to them from the national.htm Web page (Figure 3-1a, Figure 3-1b on the next page, and Figure 3-1c on page DW 3.05). When you complete your Web page additions, you will add keywords and a description as the head content.

(a) Everglades National Park Page

FIGURE 3-1

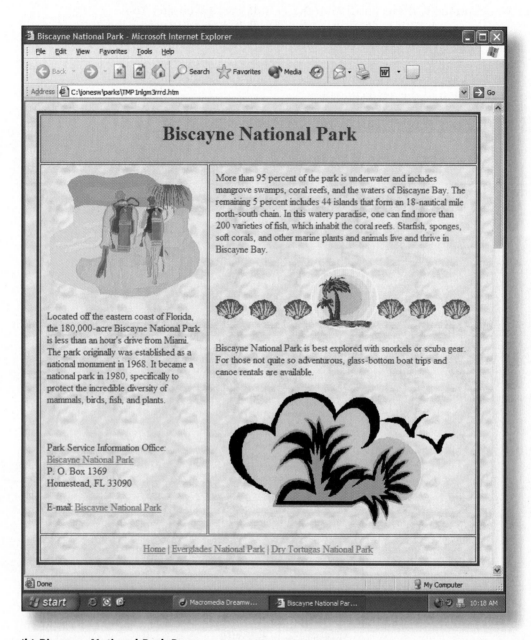

(b) Biscayne National Park Page

FIGURE 3-1 (continued)

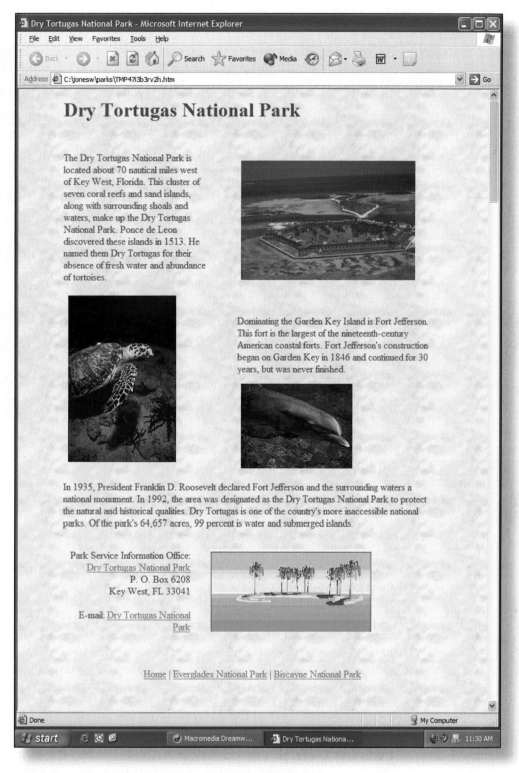

(c) Dry Tortugas National Park Page

FIGURE 3-1 (continued)

This project uses a hierarchical structure. The structure is now expanded to include the three new pages (Figure 3-2).

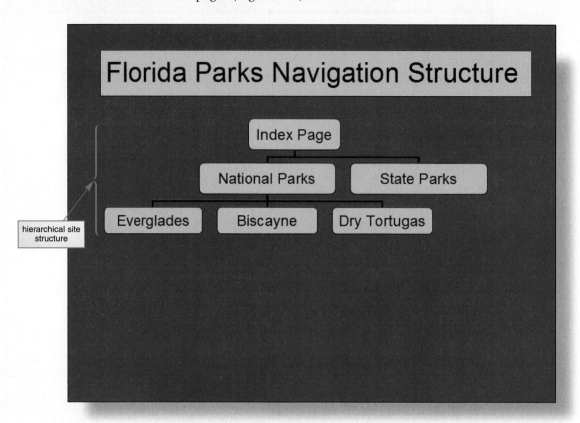

FIGURE 3-2

Understanding and Planning Page Layout

Page layout is the process of arranging the text, images, and other elements on the page. The basic rules of page layout are that your site should be easy to navigate, easy to read, and quick to download. Studies have indicated that visitors will lose interest quickly in your Web site if the majority of a page does not download within 15 seconds. One popular design element that downloads quickly is tables.

Tables download very fast because they are created with HTML code. They can be used anywhere — for the home page, menus, images, navigation bars, frames, and so on. Tables originally were intended for use in presenting data arranged by rows and columns, such as tabular data within a spreadsheet. Web designers, however, quickly seized upon the use of tables to produce specific layout effects. You can produce good designs by using tables creatively. Tables provide the ability to position elements on a Web page with much greater accuracy. Using tables for layout provides the Web page author with endless design possibilities.

A typical Web page is composed of three sections: the header, the body, and the footer (Figure 3-3). The **header**, generally located at the top of the page, can contain logos, images, or text that identifies the Web site. The header also may contain hyperlinks to other pages within the Web site.

The **body** of the Web page contains informational content about your site. This content may be in the form of text, graphics, animation, video, and audio.

The **footer** provides hyperlinks for contact information. Many Web designers also include navigational controls in the footer. This may be in addition to the navigation controls in the header. Other common items contained within a footer are the name and e-mail address of the author or of the webmaster. Sometimes, hyperlinks to other resources or to Help information are part of the footer. A typical Web page structure is displayed in Figure 3-3.

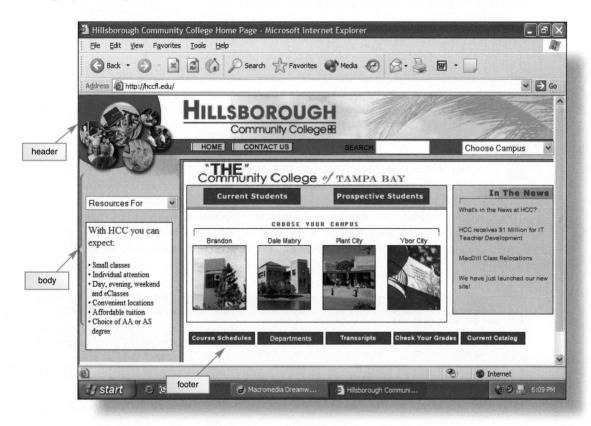

FIGURE 3-3

It is easy to create this header/body/footer structure with tables or to create any other layout structure applicable for your specific Web page needs. The entire structure can be contained within one table or a combination of multiple and nested tables. You will use a structure similar to Figure 3-3 to create the three new pages for the Florida Parks Web site.

Standard View and Layout View

Dreamweaver provides two options for creating tables: Standard view and Layout view. In **Standard view**, tables are presented as a grid of rows and columns. This view is similar to a Microsoft Excel spreadsheet or a table created in a word processing program such as Microsoft Word. In **Layout view**, you can draw, resize, and move boxes on the page while Dreamweaver still uses tables for the underlying structure. If you have used a desktop publishing program such as Microsoft Publisher or QuarkXPress, then you are familiar with the format in which layout tables are created. Using Layout view, you can place content at any location in the Document window.

Starting Dreamweaver and Closing Open Panels

When you start Dreamweaver, generally most of or all of the panels are displayed. Closing unused panels provides uncluttered workspace in the Document window. To organize your workspace, you close the open panels and then display the panels and toolbars you will use. This project includes using the Site panel, the Standard toolbar, the Insert bar, and the Property inspector.

TO START DREAMWEAVER AND CLOSE OPEN PANELS

1 Start Dreamweaver. If necessary, maximize the Document window. Press the F4 key to close all open panels.

2 Press the F8 key to display the Site panel. If necessary, select the Florida Parks site.

3 If necessary, use the View menu to display the Standard toolbar.

4 Use the Window menu to display the Property inspector, and then, if necessary, click the expander arrow to collapse the Property inspector.

Dreamweaver displays the maximized Document window, the Site panel, the Standard toolbar, and the Property inspector (Figure 3-4). Your toolbar may display above or below the Document toolbar or may be docked somewhere in another location.

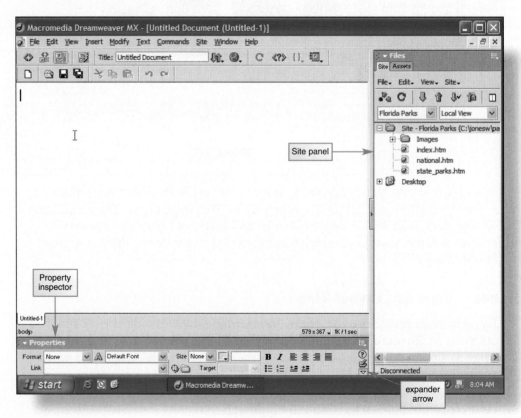

FIGURE 3-4

The Web pages you create in this project require additional images. These images need to be copied from the Data Files to the parks Web site.

Copying Data Files to the Local Web Site

Your Data Disk contains images for Project 3. These images are located in the Proj03 folder. You use Dreamweaver's integrated file browser to copy the Project 3 images to the parks Images folder you created in Project 2. The Images folder is a subfolder within the parks Web site.

The Data Files folder for this project is stored on Local Disk (C:). The location on your computer may be different. If necessary, verify with your instructor the location of the Data Files folder. Complete the following steps to copy the files to the parks local root folder.

TO COPY DATA FILES TO THE PARKS WEB SITE

1   Click the plus sign (+) to the left of the Desktop icon in the Site panel. Click the plus sign to the left of the My Computer icon and then navigate through the file hierarchy to the Data Files folder as you did in Project 2.

2   Click the plus sign to the left of the Proj03 folder and then click the plus sign to the left of the parks folder.

3   Click the plus sign to the left of the Images folder.

4   Click birds.gif. Hold down the SHIFT key and then click the turtle.jpg image.

5   Copy the ten images to the jonesw/parks/Images folder (your name folder) using Copy and Paste on the context menu (Figure 3-5).

6   Click the minus sign to the left of the Desktop icon to collapse the file list.

7   Click the minus sign to the left of the Images icon to collapse the Images folder.

The Project 3 images are pasted into the parks Images subfolder (Figure 3-5).

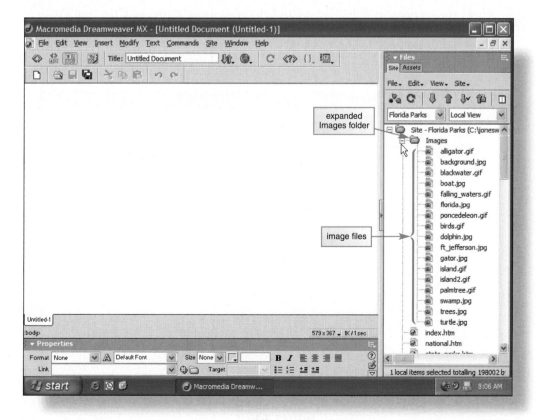

FIGURE 3-5

Adding Pages to a Web Site

You copied the images necessary to begin creating your new Web pages to the parks local root folder in the Site panel. You will add three additional pages to the Web site — Everglades, Biscayne, and Dry Tortugas national parks. You first create the Everglades National Park Web page. You will add a color scheme, the background image, and a heading to the new page. Then you will use Dreamweaver's Standard view to insert tables and add text, images, and links to the cells within the table. Table 3-1 lists the color scheme and image information to be used for all three Web pages.

Table 3-1	Color Scheme and Background Image for Florida Parks Web Pages
COLOR SCHEME	IMAGE
Commands menu, Set Color Scheme command	Modify menu, Page Properties command
Green background	Browse button/Images folder
Blue, Brown, Green text and links	background.jpg

Creating the Everglades National Park Web Page

You use the Untitled-1 default page that displayed when you started Dreamweaver to begin creating the Everglades page. You start by applying a color scheme and background image. This is the same color scheme and background image you used for the Florida Parks Web site pages in Projects 1 and 2.

TO ADD A COLOR SCHEME AND BACKGROUND IMAGE TO THE EVERGLADES NATIONAL PARK WEB PAGE

1. Apply the settings in Table 3-1 to add the color scheme and then click the OK button in the Set Color Scheme Command dialog box.

2. Apply the settings in Table 3-1 to add the background image. Click the OK button in the Page Properties dialog box.

The background image is applied to the Everglades National Park page (Figure 3-6).

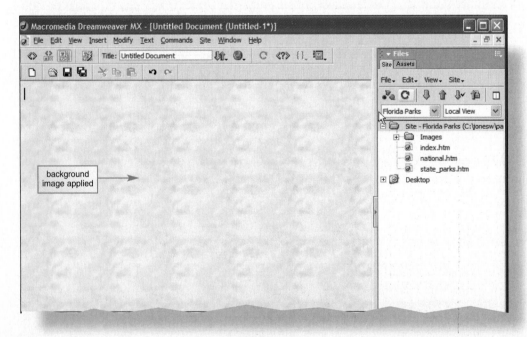

background image applied

FIGURE 3-6

Next, you will insert, center, and format a page heading. Then, you will add a page title and save the Web page. You close the Site panel to provide additional workspace and a better view of the Document window. Perform the following steps to insert and format the heading and close the Site panel.

TO INSERT AND FORMAT THE HEADING

1 Click the Document window. Type Everglades National Park.

2 Apply Heading 1, click the Align Center button in the Property inspector, and then press the ENTER key.

3 Click the Align Left button.

4 Title the page Everglades National Park.

5 Right-click the Files panel group title bar and then click Close Panel Group on the context menu.

6 Click the Save button on the Standard toolbar. Type everglades for the file name and then click the Save button in the Save As dialog box. The file is saved in the parks folder.

The heading is centered and formatted and the title is added (Figure 3-7). The Web page is saved in the parks folder.

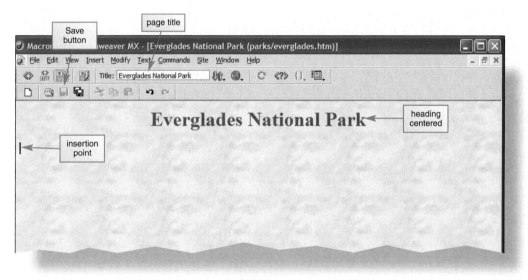

FIGURE 3-7

Understanding Tables

Tables have many uses in HTML design. The most obvious is a table of data, but tables also are used for page layout, such as placing text and graphics on a page at just the right location. Tables provide Web designers a method to add vertical and horizontal structure to a page. A **table** consists of three basic components: rows, columns, and cells. A **row** is a horizontal collection of cells, and a **column** is a vertical collection of cells. A **cell** is the container created when the row and column intersect. Each cell within the table can contain any standard element you use on a Web page. This includes text, images, and other objects.

Inserting a Table into the Everglades National Park Page

You will add two tables to the Everglades National Park page and then add text and images to the cells within the tables. The first table will consist of three rows and two columns with cell padding of 2 and cell spacing of 20. The border is set to 0. When the table displays in Dreamweaver, a border outline is displayed around the table. This outline, however, does not display when viewed in a browser when the border is set to 0.

The table width is 90 percent. When specifying the width, you can select percent or pixels. A table with width specified as a **percent** expands with the width of the window and monitor size in which it is being viewed. A table with width specified as **pixels** will remain the same size regardless of the window and monitor size. If you select percent and an image is larger than the selected percent, the cell and table will expand to accommodate the image. Likewise, if the **No Wrap** property is enabled and the text will not fit within the cell, the cell and table will expand to accommodate the text. It is not necessary to declare a table width. When no value is specified, the table is displayed as small as possible and then expands as content is added. If modifications are necessary to the original specified table values, these values can be changed in the Property inspector.

The second table is a one-cell table, consisting of one row and one column. This table will contain links to the Home page and to the other two national parks. You use the Insert bar with the Layout category and the Property inspector to control and format the tables. Complete the following step to display the Insert bar and select the Layout category.

TO DISPLAY THE INSERT BAR AND SELECT THE LAYOUT CATEGORY

1 Click Window on the menu bar and then click Insert. Click the Layout tab. The Insert bar may display in a different location on your screen.

The Insert bar is displayed. The Layout tab is selected (Figure 3-8).

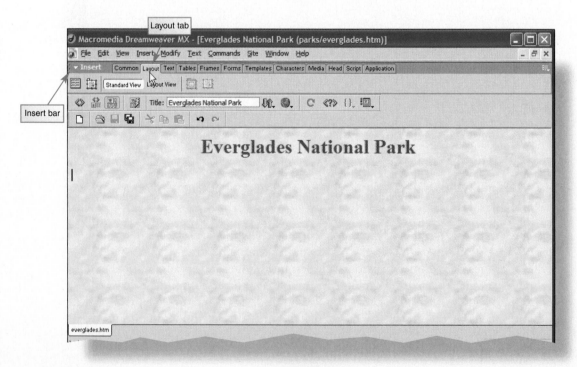

FIGURE 3-8

Table Views

The Layout category (Figure 3-9) enables you to work with tables and layers. Dreamweaver provides two ways to create tables — Standard view and Layout view. In Standard view, a table displays as a grid and expands as you add text and images. You define the structure of the table using the Insert Table dialog box. In Layout view, you create tables and cells by drawing them. You will work with Layout view later in this project. Table 3-2 lists the button names and descriptions available on the Layout tab.

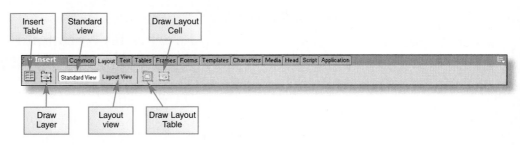

FIGURE 3-9

Table 3-2 Buttons on the Layout Tab	
BUTTON NAME	**DESCRIPTION**
Insert Table	Places a table at the insertion point
Draw Layer	Creates a layer
Standard View	Displays a table as a grid of lines
Layout View	Displays a table as boxes that can be drawn, dragged, and resized
Draw Layout Cell	Used to draw individual table cells in the Design view of the Document window
Draw Layout Table	Used to draw a table in the Design view of the Document window

More About

Dreamweaver Features

For more information about Dreamweaver MX table views, visit the Dreamweaver MX More About Web page (scsite.com/dreamweavermx/more.htm) and then click Dreamweaver MX Tables.

Perform the following steps to insert a table with 3 rows and 2 columns into the Everglades National Park Web page.

 To Insert a Table Using Standard View

1 Point to the Insert Table button on the Insert bar (Figure 3-10).

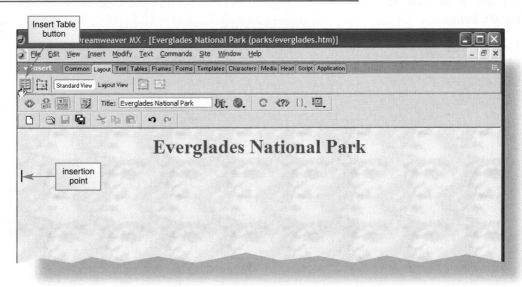

FIGURE 3-10

2 **Click the Insert Table button.**

The Insert Table dialog box is displayed (Figure 3-11). The settings displayed are the default settings from the last table created.

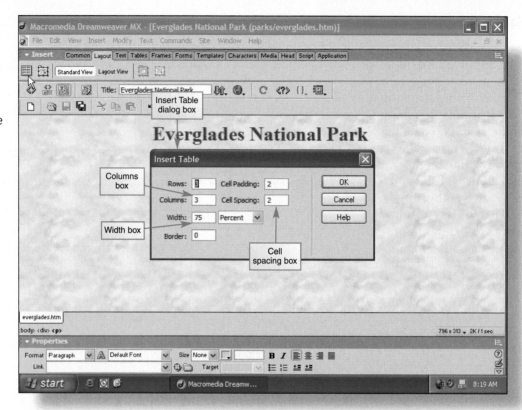

FIGURE 3-11

3 **Double-click the Columns box and then type 2 as the new value. Double-click the Cell Spacing box and then type 20 as the new value. Double-click the Width box and then type 90 as the new value. Point to the OK button.**

The Insert Table dialog box is displayed with the new settings as shown in Figure 3-12.

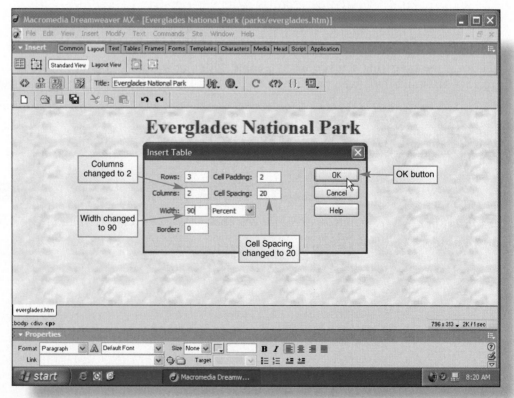

FIGURE 3-12

4 **Click the OK button. Point to the Property inspector expander arrow.**

The table is inserted into the Document window (Figure 3-13). The dark border around the table and the three handles on the lower and right borders indicate the table is selected. The <table> tag displays as bold in the tag selector, also indicating the table is selected. Cell spacing between each cell is 20 pixels. The default alignment for the table is left. The border is set to 0 and displays as an outline when viewed in Dreamweaver. When viewed in a browser, however, no border is displayed.

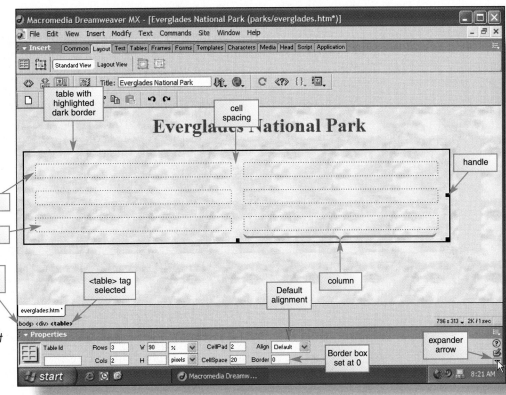

FIGURE 3-13

5 **Click the Property inspector expander arrow.**

The Property inspector expands to display additional table properties (Figure 3-14). The property settings you selected in the Insert Table dialog box display in the top half of the Property inspector.

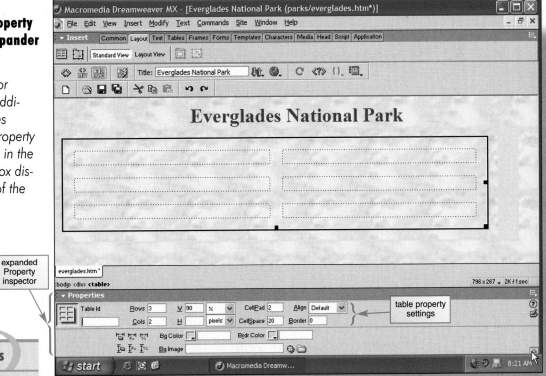

Other Ways

1. On Insert menu click Table, select table properties, click OK button

FIGURE 3-14

Property Inspector Table Features

As you have seen, the Property inspector options change depending on the selected object. You use the Property inspector to modify and add table attributes. When a table is selected, the Property inspector displays table properties. Properties are contained in both panels within the Property inspector when a table is selected. When another table element is selected — row, column, and cell — the displayed properties change and are determined by the selected element. The following section describes the table-related features of the Property inspector shown in Figure 3-15.

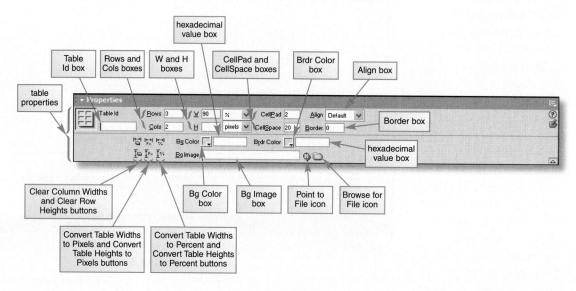

FIGURE 3-15

TABLE ID   An identifier used for cascading style sheets or for scripting; it is not required to assign a name.

ROWS AND COLS   The number of rows and columns in the table.

W   Used to specify the minimum width of the table in either pixels or percentage. If a size is not specified, the size can vary depending on the monitor and browser settings. A table width specified in pixels is displayed at the same size in all browsers. A table width specified in percentage is altered in appearance based on the user's monitor resolution and browser window size.

H   Used to specify the height of the table in either pixels or percentage. Generally, the height of a table consists of the height of the collective rows and is not specified.

CELLPAD   The number of pixels between the cell border and the cell content.

CELLSPACE   The number of pixels between adjacent table cells.

ALIGN   Determines where the table appears, relative to other elements in the same paragraph such as text or images. The default alignment is to the left.

BORDER   Specifies the border width in pixels.

CLEAR COLUMN WIDTHS AND CLEAR ROW HEIGHTS   Deletes all speacified row height or column width values from the table.

CONVERT TABLE WIDTHS TO PIXELS AND CONVERT TABLE HEIGHTS TO PIXELS Sets the width or height of each column in the table to its current width in pixels and also sets the width of the whole table to its current width in pixels.

CONVERT TABLE WIDTHS TO PERCENT AND CONVERT TABLE HEIGHTS TO PERCENT Sets the width or height of each column in the table to its current width expressed as a percentage of the Document window's width and also sets the width of the whole table to its current width as a percentage of the Document window's width.

BG COLOR The table background color.

BRDR COLOR The table border color.

BG IMAGE The table background image.

Row, Column, and Cell Properties

When a row, column, or cell is selected, the properties in the upper pane of the Property inspector are the same as the standard ones for text. You can use these properties to incorporate standard HTML formatting tags within a cell, row, or column. The part of the table selected determines which properties display in the lower pane of the Property inspector. The properties for all three features (row, column, and cell) are the same, except for one element — the icon displayed in the lower-left pane of the Property inspector. The following section describes the row-related features (Figure 3-16), column-related features (Figure 3-17), and cell-related features (Figure 3-18 on the next page) of the Property inspector.

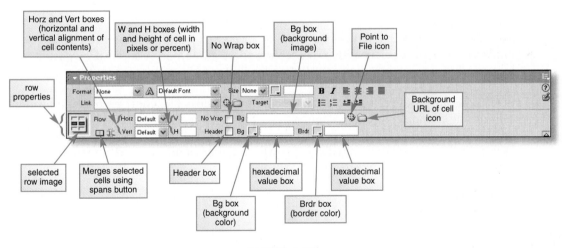

FIGURE 3-16

FIGURE 3-17

cell image

Splits cell into rows or columns button

FIGURE 3-18

HORZ Specifies the horizontal alignment of the contents of a cell, row, or column — contents can be aligned to the left, right, or center of the cells.

VERT Specifies the vertical alignment of the contents of a cell, row, or column — contents can be aligned to the top, middle, bottom, or baseline of the cells.

W AND H Specifies the width and height of selected cells in pixels or as a percentage of the entire table's width or height.

BG (UPPER TEXT FIELD) The file name of the background image for a cell, column, or row.

BG (LOWER COLOR BOX AND TEXT FIELD) The background color of a cell, column, or row, using the color picker.

BRDR The border color for the cells.

NO WRAP Prevents line wrapping, keeping all text in a given cell on a single line. If No Wrap is enabled, cells widen to accommodate all data as it is typed or pasted into a cell.

HEADER Formats the selected cells as table header cells. The contents of table header cells are bold and centered by default.

MERGE CELLS Combines selected cells, rows, or columns into one cell (available when rows or columns are selected).

SPLIT CELLS Divides a cell, creating two or more cells (available when a single cell is selected).

Table Formatting Conflicts

For more information about Dreamweaver MX table formatting conflicts, visit the Dreamweaver MX More About Web page (scsite.com/ dreamweavermx/ more.htm) and then click Dreamweaver MX Tables.

Table Formatting Conflicts

When formatting tables in Standard view, you can set properties for the entire table or for selected rows, columns, or cells in the table. When applying these properties, however, a potential for conflict exists. To resolve this potential conflict, HTML assigns levels of precedence. The order of precedence for table formatting is cells, rows, and table. When a property, such as background color or alignment, is set to one value for the whole table and another value for individual cells, cell formatting takes precedence over row formatting, which in turn takes precedence over table formatting.

If you set the background color for a single cell to green, and then set the background color of the entire table to red, for example, the green cell does not change to red, because cell formatting takes precedence over table formatting. Dreamweaver, however, does not always follow the precedence. The program will override the settings for a cell if you change the settings for the row that contains the cell. To eliminate this problem, you should change the cell settings last.

Understanding HTML Structure within a Table

As you work with and become more familiar with tables, it is helpful to have an understanding of the HTML structure within a table. Suppose, for example, you have a table with two rows and two columns, displaying a total of four cells, such as the following:

First cell	Second cell
Third cell	Fourth cell

The general syntax of the table is:

```
<TABLE>
<TR>
     <TD> First cell </TD>
     <TD> Second cell </TD>
</TR>
<TR>
     <TD> Third cell </TD>
     <TD> Fourth cell </TD>
</TR>
</TABLE>
```

When viewing your table in Dreamweaver, the tag selector displays the <table>, <td>, and <tr> tags. The <table> tag indicates the whole table. Clicking the <table> tag in the tag selector selects the whole table. The <td> indicates table data. Clicking the <td> tag in the tag selector selects the cell containing the insertion point. The <tr> tag indicates table row. Clicking the <tr> tag in the tag selector selects the row containing the insertion point.

Selecting the Table and Selecting Cells

The Property inspector displays table attributes only if the entire table is selected. You can select the table from within the Document window by clicking the upper-left corner of the table or by clicking anywhere on the right or lower edge. As discussed previously, another method for selecting a table is to click anywhere in the table and then click the <table> tag in the tag selector. When selected, the table will display with a dark border and selection handles on the table's lower and right edges (Figure 3-19 on the next page).

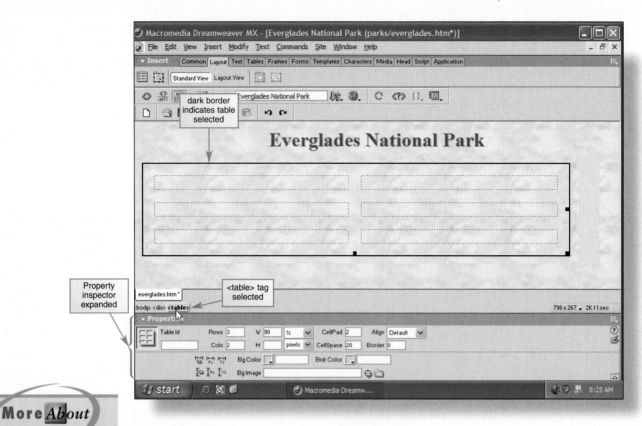

FIGURE 3-19

More *About*

Formatting a Table

Dreamweaver MX includes a number of preset table designs. To view these table designs, select the table, click Commands on the menu bar, and then click Format Table. Make your selections in the Format Table dialog box.

Selecting a row, column, or cell is easier than selecting the entire table. When a cell, row, or column is selected, the selected item has a dark border. To select a cell, click inside the cell. To select a row or column, click inside one of the cells in the row or column and drag to select the other cells. A second method for selecting a row or column is to point to the left edge of a row or the top edge of a column. When the pointer changes to a selection arrow, click to select the row or column. In Figure 3-20, the selection arrow is pointing to a row and the row is selected.

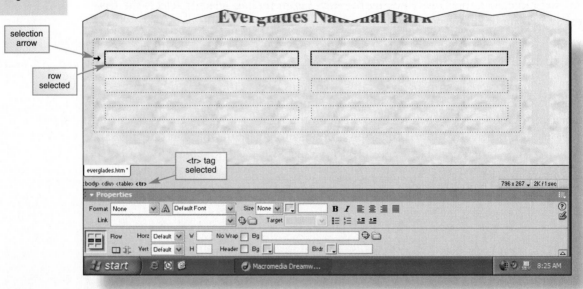

FIGURE 3-20

To select nonadjacent cells, click one cell, hold down the CTRL key and then click the other cells you want to select.

Centering a Table

When a table is inserted into the Document window with a specified width, it defaults to the left. Using the Property inspector, you can center the table by selecting it and then applying the Center command. Perform the following steps to select and center the table.

 To Select and Center a Table

1 Click row 1, column 1. Point to <table> in the tag selector.

The insertion point is in the first cell of the first row and the first column (Figure 3-21).

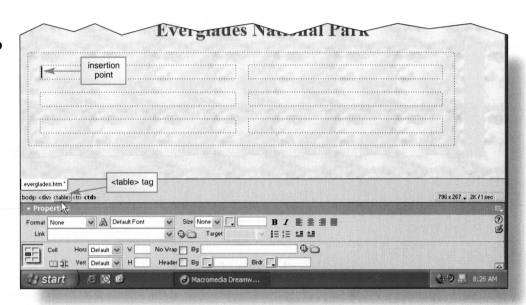

FIGURE 3-21

2 Click <table>. Click the Align box arrow in the Property inspector and then point to Center on the pop-up menu.

The table is selected and handles are displayed on the lower and right border of the table. The <table> tag is bold, indicating it is selected. Center is highlighted in the Align pop-up menu (Figure 3-22).

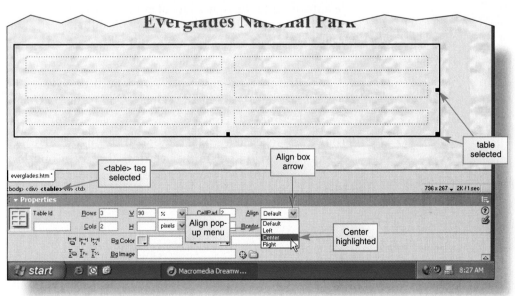

FIGURE 3-22

3 **Click Center.**

The table is centered in the Document window (Figure 3-23).

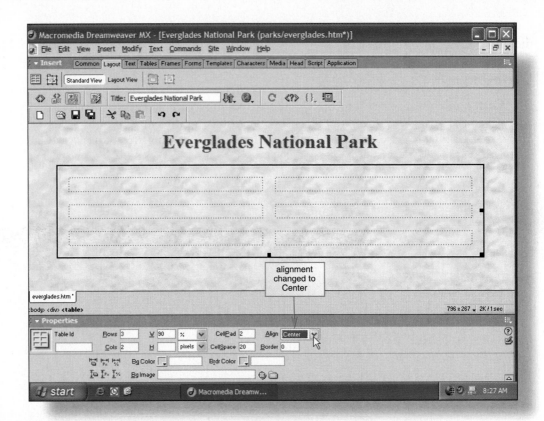

FIGURE 3-23

Changing the Default Cell Alignment

The default horizontal cell alignment is left. When you enter text or add an image to a cell, it defaults to the left margin of the cell. You can change the left alignment through the Property inspector by clicking the cell and then changing the default to center or right. The default vertical cell alignment is middle, which aligns the cell content in the middle of the cell. Other vertical alignment options include the following:

> Top — aligns the cell content at the top of the cell.
> Bottom — aligns the cell content at the bottom of the cell.
> Baseline — aligns the cell content at the bottom of the cell (same as Bottom).

You can change the vertical alignment through the Property inspector by clicking the cell and then selecting another vertical alignment option.

Complete the following steps to select the cells and change the default vertical alignment from middle to top.

To Change Vertical Alignment from Middle to Top

1 **Click row 1, column 1. Drag to select the three rows in the table. Click the Vert box arrow and then point to Top in the Vert pop-up menu.**

The three rows in the table are selected. The Property inspector changes to reflect the properties for a row. The Vert pop-up menu is displayed and Top is highlighted (Figure 3-24).

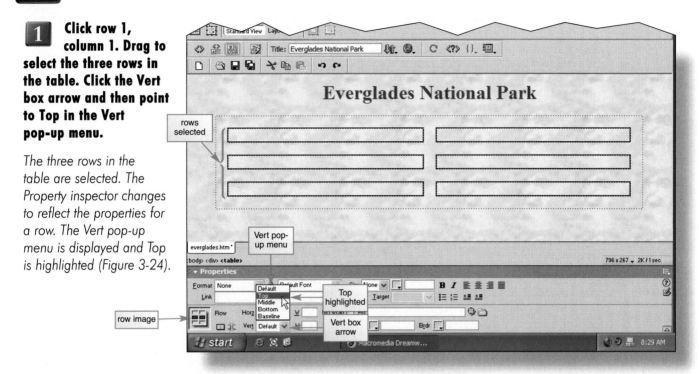

FIGURE 3-24

2 **Click Top.**

The vertical alignment is changed to Top (Figure 3-25). This change does not display in the Document window.

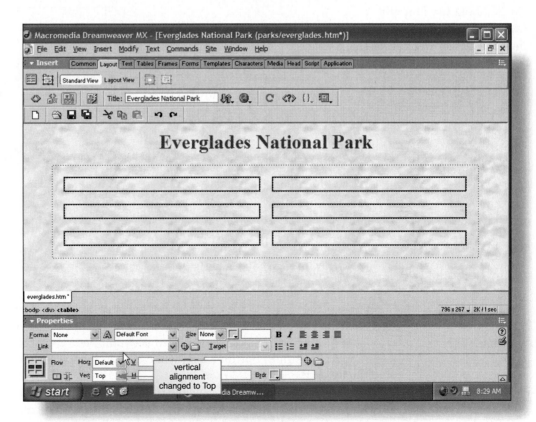

FIGURE 3-25

Specifying Column Width

When a table width is specified as a percentage, column width expands to accommodate the text or image. When adding content to the table, this expansion can distort the table appearance and make it difficult to visualize how the final page will display. You can control this expansion by setting the column width. The objective for the Everglades National Park page is to display the page in two columns of equal width or 50 percent.

Steps **To Specify Column Width**

1 **Click the cell in row 1, column 1 and then drag to select all cells in column 1. Click the W box in the Property inspector. Type 50% and then press the ENTER key.**

2 **Click the cell in row 1, column 2 and then drag to select all cells in column 2. Click the W box in the Property inspector. Type 50% and then press the ENTER key.**

The width for column 1 and column 2 is specified as 50% (Figure 3-26). This change does not display in the Document window.

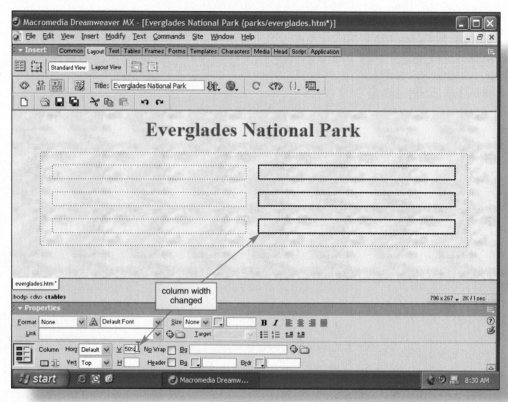

FIGURE 3-26

Adding Text to the Everglades National Park Web Page

Next, you will enter and format the text for the Everglades National Park Web page. Table 3-3 includes the text for the first table. The text is entered into the table cells. If you have not set the width and height of a cell, when you begin to enter text into a table cell, the cell expands to accommodate the text. The other cells may appear to shrink, but they also will expand when you type in the cells, or add an image to the cells.

Complete the following steps to add text to the Everglades National Park page. Press the ENTER key or insert a line break <BR> as indicated in the table. Press SHIFT+ENTER to insert a line break. Press the TAB key to move from cell to cell.

Table 3-3	Everglades National Park Web Page Text
SECTION	*TEXT FOR EVERGLADES NATIONAL PARK WEB PAGE*
Part 1	Everglades National Park, located at the southern tip of Florida, is the largest remaining subtropical wilderness in the United States. It is the only ecosystem of its kind on the planet and the only place in the world where alligators and crocodiles coexist.\<ENTER> A freshwater river, 50 miles wide and six-inches deep, flows from Lake Okeechobee through marshy grassland into Florida Bay. The Everglades National Park was created in 1947 by President Harry S. Truman to preserve the wetlands and this slow-moving "River of Grass." \<ENTER> The 1.5 million acres of Everglades National Park provide habitats for more than 1,600 varieties of plants and innumerable animals, including more than 350 species of tropical and temperate birds, 40 species of mammals, 50 species of reptiles, and 18 species of amphibians. The sea and wetland wilderness invites exploration by canoe or boat. Walking and tram tours are excellent ways to observe the extensive wildlife.
Part 2	The park is open year round. \<ENTER> Park Service Information Office \ Everglades National Park \ 40001 State Road 9336 \ Homestead, FL 33034 \<ENTER> E-mail: Everglades National Park \

Table Data

If you have a table that contains data that requires sorting, you can perform a simple table sort based on the contents of a single column, or you can perform a more complicated sort based on the contents of two columns. Click Commands on the menu bar and then click Sort Table.

Steps **To Add Everglades National Park Text**

1 Click the Insert bar expand/collapse arrow to collapse the Insert bar. Click the Property inspector expand/collapse arrow to collapse the Property inspector.

The Insert bar and Property inspector panels are collapsed (Figure 3-27). Additional workspace is provided in the Document window.

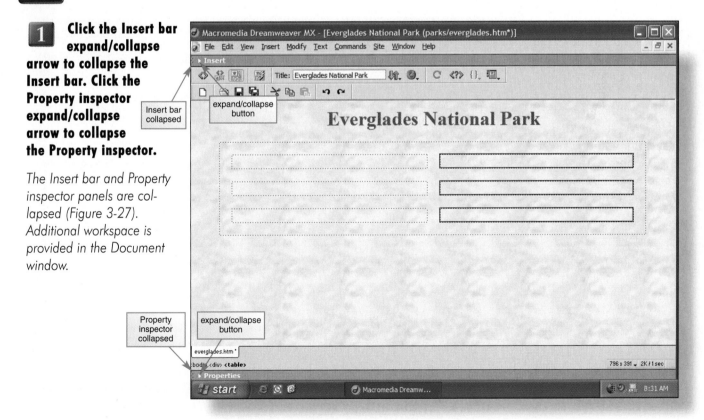

FIGURE 3-27

2 **Type the three paragraphs of Part 1 in Table 3-3 on the previous page in row 1, column 2 of the table in the Document window.**

The three paragraphs are entered into row 1, column 2 (Figure 3-28).

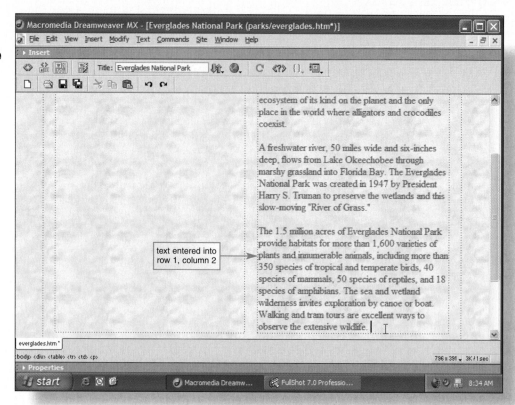

FIGURE 3-28

3 **If necessary, scroll down to display the rest of the table. Type the text of Part 2 in Table 3-3 in row 3, column 1 of the Document window. Use SHIFT+ENTER to insert the line breaks. Point to the Property inspector expand/collapse button.**

The text is entered (Figure 3-29). The insertion point is still within the cell and does not display because a line break was added. A line break moves the insertion point to the next line, but does not create a blank space such as when the ENTER key is pressed.

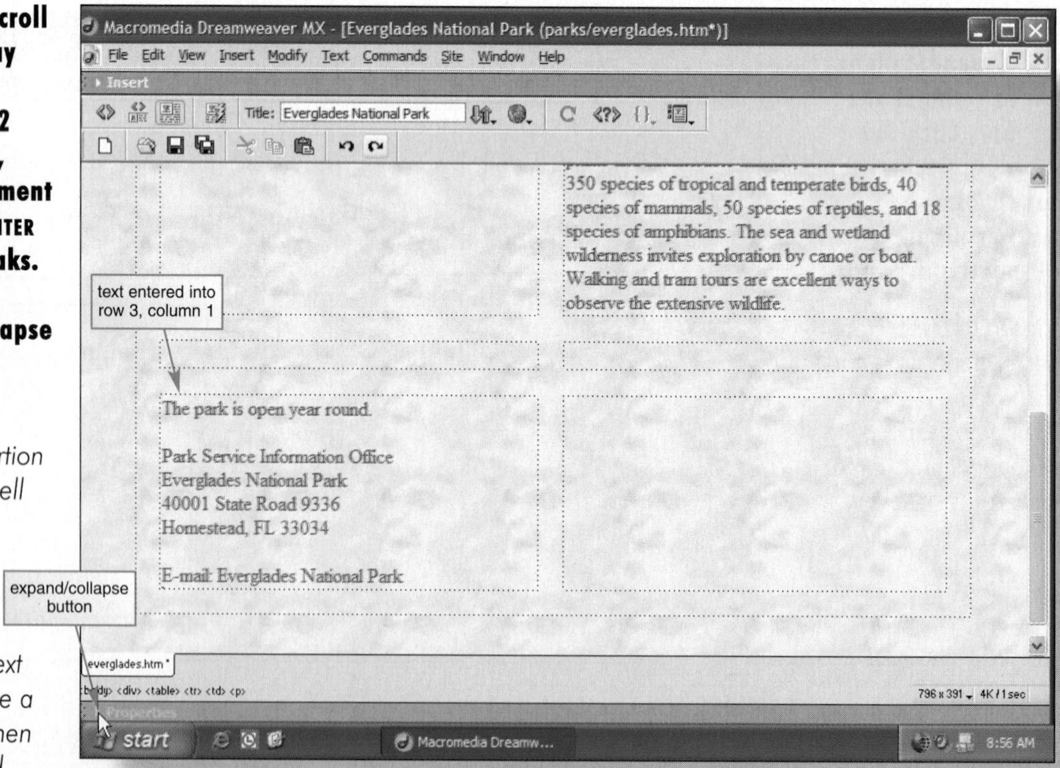

FIGURE 3-29

Click the expand/collapse button to display the Property inspector. Select the text in row 3, column 1. Click the Align Right button in the Property inspector.

The Property inspector is displayed and the text is aligned to the right in the cell (Figure 3-30).

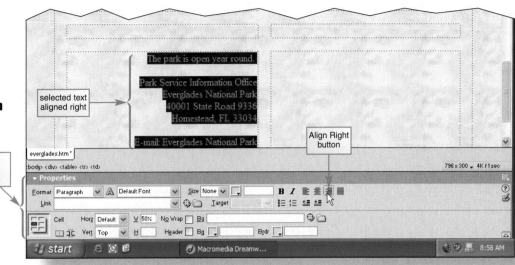

FIGURE 3-30

Other Ways

1. Right-click selected text, point to Align on context menu, click Right on Align submenu

Adding a Second Table to the Everglades National Park Web Page

Next, you will add a second table to the Everglades National Park Web page. This table will contain one row and one column and will serve as the footer for your Web page. The text is centered in the cell and will contain links to the home page and to the other two national parks Web pages. Complete the following steps to add the second table and text.

Steps | **To Add a Second Table to the Everglades National Park Web Page**

1 Click outside the right border of the existing table to position the insertion point outside the table.

The insertion point is located and blinking to the right of the table border (Figure 3-31).

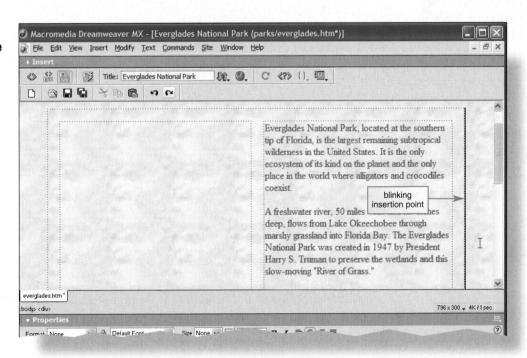

FIGURE 3-31

2 **Press the ENTER key. Point to the Insert bar expand/collapse arrow.**

The insertion point is centered below the first table (Figure 3-32). The insertion point is still within the centered HTML table tags. Otherwise, it would default to the left.

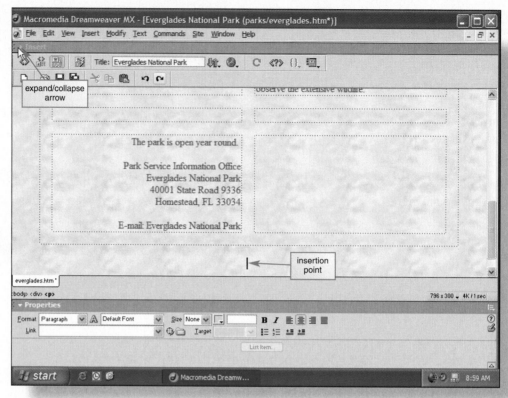

FIGURE 3-32

3 **Click the Insert bar expand/collapse button. If necessary, click the Layout tab and then click the Insert Table button.**

The Insert Table dialog box is displayed (Figure 3-33). The dialog box retains the settings from the first table. The dialog box on your computer may show different settings.

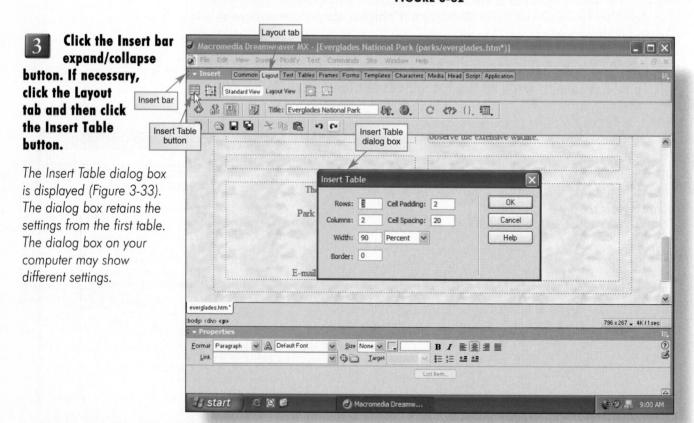

FIGURE 3-33

4 **Change the number of rows to 1, the number of columns to 1, cell spacing to 10, and width to 75. If necessary, change other settings to match the settings shown in Figure 3-34. Point to the OK button.**

The Insert Table dialog box displays the new table settings as shown in Figure 3-34.

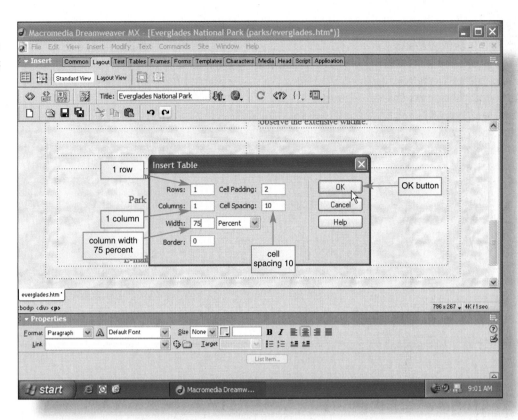

FIGURE 3-34

5 **Click the OK button.**

The table is inserted into the Document window (Figure 3-35). The dark border and handles indicate the table is selected.

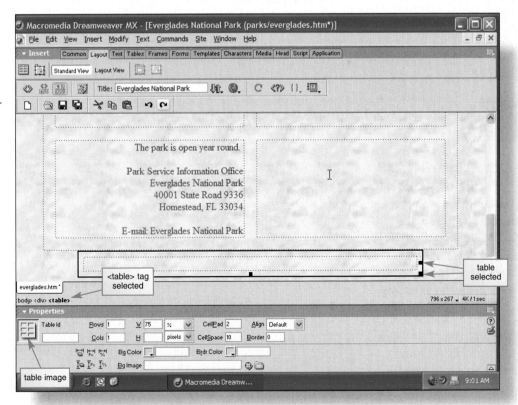

FIGURE 3-35

6 **Click the table. Type** Home **and then press the SPACEBAR. Press SHIFT + | (VERTICAL BAR) and then press the SPACEBAR. Type** Biscayne National Park **and then press the SPACEBAR. Press SHIFT + | and then press the SPACEBAR. Type** Dry Tortugas National Park **as the last link text.**

The text is entered into the table (Figure 3-36).

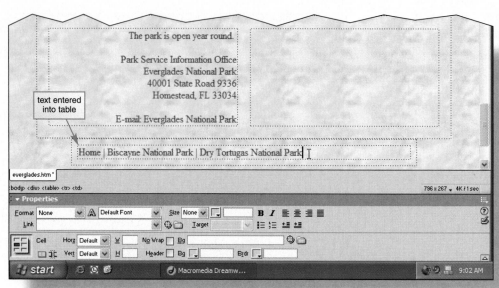

FIGURE 3-36

Adjusting the Table Width

Determining table width sometimes is a matter of judgment. You may overestimate or underestimate the table width when first inserting it into the Document window. When this happens, it is easy to make adjustments to the table width through the Property inspector. The table with the names that will contain links is too wide for the text it contains and needs to be adjusted. You adjust the table width by selecting the table and then changing the width in the Property inspector.

 To Adjust the Table Width

1 **If necessary, click the cell in table 2. Click <table> in the tag selector to select the table. Double-click the W box in the Property inspector. Type** 60 **and then press the ENTER key.**

The dark border around the table indicates the table is selected. The Property inspector displays table properties. The table width is decreased (Figure 3-37).

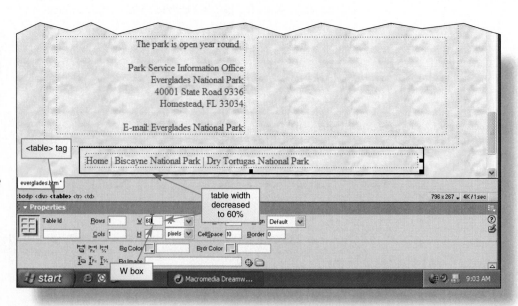

FIGURE 3-37

2 **Click the cell and then drag to select the text. Click the Align Center button in the Property inspector.**

The text is centered in the cell (Figure 3-38). This is a one-cell table, so the text also is centered in the table.

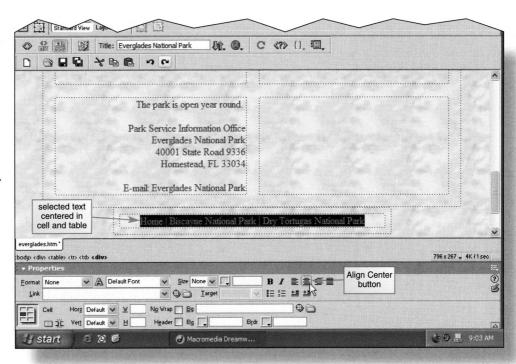

FIGURE 3-38

Next, you will add relative, absolute, and e-mail links to the Everglades National Park page. Perform the following steps to add the links.

TO ADD LINKS TO THE EVERGLADES NATIONAL PARK PAGE

1 Select the first instance of Everglades National Park located in the first table in row 3, column 1. Type `http://www.nps.gov/ever/` in the Link box to create an absolute link.

2 Select the second instance of Everglades National Park located in the first table, row 3, column 1. Click Insert on the menu bar and then click Email Link. When the Email Link dialog box is displayed, type `everglades@parks.gov` for the e-mail address. Click the OK button.

3 Select Home in the second table. Type `index.htm` in the Link box to create the relative link.

4 Select Biscayne National Park in the second table. Type `biscayne.htm` in the Link box to create the relative link.

5 Select Dry Tortugas National Park in the second table. Type `dry_tortugas.htm` in the Link box to create the relative link.

6 Click the Save button on the Standard toolbar.

7 Press the F12 key to view the Web page. Scroll down to view the links as shown in Figure 3-39 on the next page.

8 Close the browser and return to the Dreamweaver window.

The links are added to the Web page (Figure 3-39). The links for Biscayne National Park and Dry Tortugas National Park are not active at this point. You will add these two pages later in this project.

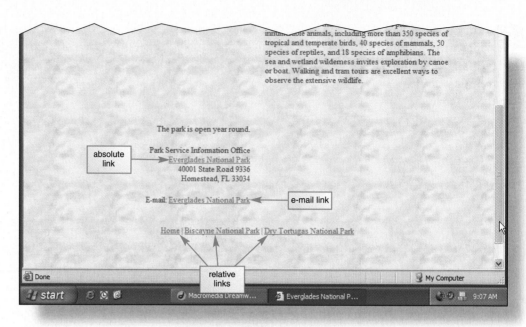

immumerable animals, including more than 350 species of tropical and temperate birds, 40 species of mammals, 50 species of reptiles, and 18 species of amphibians. The sea and wetland wilderness invites exploration by canoe or boat. Walking and tram tours are excellent ways to observe the extensive wildlife.

The park is open year round.

absolute link → Park Service Information Office
Everglades National Park
40001 State Road 9336
Homestead, FL 33034

E-mail: Everglades National Park ← e-mail link

Home | Biscayne National Park | Dry Tortugas National Park

relative links

FIGURE 3-39

Editing and Modifying Table Structure

Thus far, you have created two tables and made adjustments in Dreamweaver for the Everglades National Park Web page. For various reasons, as you create and develop Web sites, you will need to edit and modify a table, change the dimensions of a table, add rows and columns, or delete the table and start over. The following section describes how to accomplish editing, modifying, and deleting table elements within the structure.

DELETE A ROW OR COLUMN Select a row or column and then press the DELETE key. You also can delete a row or column by clicking a cell within the row or column, right-clicking to display the context menu, pointing to Table, and then clicking Delete Row or Delete Column on the Table submenu.

INSERT A ROW OR COLUMN To insert a row or column, click in a cell. Right-click to display the context menu, point to Table, and then click Insert Row or Insert Column on the Table submenu. To insert more than one row or column and to control the row or column insertion point, click in a cell, right-click to display the context menu, point to Table, and then click Insert Rows or Columns on the Table submenu to display the Insert Rows or Columns dialog box (Figure 3-40). Make your selections and then click the OK button. To add a row automatically, press the TAB key in the last cell of a table.

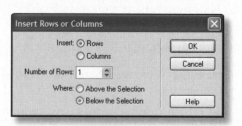

FIGURE 3-40

MERGE AND SPLIT CELLS By merging and splitting cells, you can set alignments more complex than straight rows and columns. To merge two or more cells, select the cells and then click Merge Cells in the Property inspector. The selected cells must be contiguous and in the shape of a rectangle. You can merge any number of adjacent cells as long as the entire selection is a line or a rectangle. To split a cell, click the cell and then click Split Cells in the Property inspector to display the Split Cell dialog box (Figure 3-41). In the Split Cell dialog box, specify how to split the cell and then click the OK button. You can split a cell into any number of rows or columns, regardless of whether it was previously merged. When you split a cell into two rows, the other cells in the same row as the split cell are not split. The same is true if a cell is split into two or more columns: the other cells in the same column are not split. To select a cell quickly, click the cell and then click the <td> tag on the tag selector.

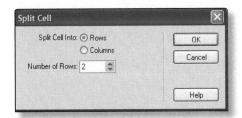

FIGURE 3-41

RESIZING A TABLE, COLUMNS, AND ROWS You can resize an entire table or resize individual rows and columns. To resize the table, select the table and change the W (width) in the Property inspector. A second method is to select the table and then drag one of the table selection handles. When you resize an entire table, all of the cells in the table change size proportionately. If you have assigned explicit widths or heights to a cell or cells within the table, resizing the table changes the visual size of the cells in the Document window but does not change the specified widths and heights of the cells. To resize a column or row, select the column or row and change the properties in the Property inspector. A second method to resize a column is to select the column and then drag the right border of the column. To resize a row, select the row and then drag the lower border of the row.

DELETE A TABLE You easily can delete a table. Select the table tag in the tag selector and then press the DELETE key. All table content is deleted along with the table.

Merging Cells and Adding Images

The concept of merging cells probably is familiar to you if you have worked with spreadsheets or word processing tables. In HTML, however, this is a complicated process. Dreamweaver makes this easy by hiding some complex HTML table restructuring code behind an easy-to-use interface in the Property inspector. Dreamweaver also makes it easy to add images to a table. When you add and then select an image in a table cell, the Property inspector displays the same properties as were displayed when you added and selected an image in the Document window in Project 2. When the image in the cell is not selected, the Property inspector displays the same properties as it does for any cell. These properties were described earlier in this project.

You will merge two cells (row 1, columns 1 and 2) and add three images to the Everglades National Park page. The first and second images go into the merged cells and the third image goes in row 3, column 2. Perform the steps on the next page to merge two cells.

More *About*

Splitting and Merging Cells

An alternative approach to merging and splitting cells is to increase or decrease the number of rows or columns spanned by a cell.

Steps **To Merge Two Cells**

1 **Click the expand/collapse arrow to collapse the Insert bar. Press F8 to display the Site panel. If necessary, scroll up and then click row 1, column 1. Drag to select the cells in rows 1 and 2 in column 1. Point to the Merge Cells button in the Property inspector.**

The two cells are selected (Figure 3-42). The Site panel is displayed.

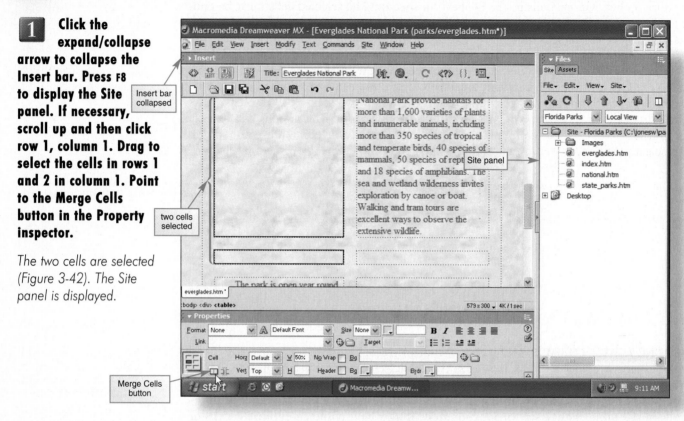

FIGURE 3-42

2 **Click the Merge Cells button.**

The two cells are merged (Figure 3-43).

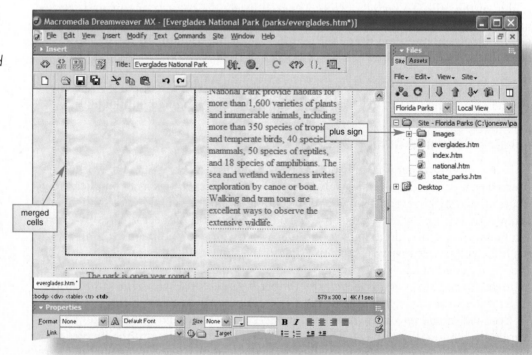

FIGURE 3-43

Next, you will add three images to the table. You align and modify the size of the images. Complete the following steps to display the image file names in the Site panel and then add, align, and modify images in a Standard view table.

Steps | To Add Images to a Standard View Table

1 **Click the plus sign (+) to the left of Images in the Site panel. Scroll to the top of the table and then click the cell in row 1, column 1.**

The Images folder is expanded and the insertion point is positioned in the merged cell (Figure 3-44). The gator.jpg image will be inserted at the location of the insertion point.

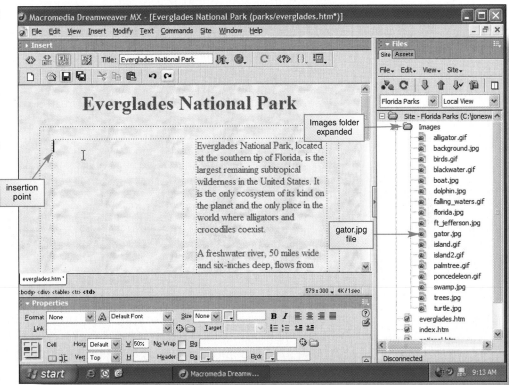

FIGURE 3-44

2 **Drag the gator.jpg image to the insertion point in the merged cell.**

The gator.jpg image is inserted in the cell (Figure 3-45). The insertion point is blinking to the right of the image.

FIGURE 3-45

3 **Press the ENTER key.**

The insertion point is displayed below the gator.jpg image (Figure 3-46). The swamp.jpg image will be inserted at the location of the insertion point.

FIGURE 3-46

4 **Drag the swamp.jpg image to the insertion point.**

The swamp.jpg image is displayed below the gator.jpg image and the insertion point is blinking to the right of the swamp.jpg image (Figure 3-47). The image is larger than the cell, and the cell expands to accommodate the image. The horizontal scroll bar may display because the full table width is no longer visible.

FIGURE 3-47

5 Click the gator.jpg image to select it.

The gator.jpg image is selected (Figure 3-48). The Property inspector displays image properties.

FIGURE 3-48

6 Double-click the W box in the Property inspector. Type 340 and then press the TAB key to move to the H box. Type 260 as the new value. Click the Alt box, type Florida alligator and then press the ENTER key.

The properties are applied to the gator.jpg image (Figure 3-49).

FIGURE 3-49

7 Scroll down and then click the swamp.jpg image to select it.

The swamp.jpg image is selected (Figure 3-50).

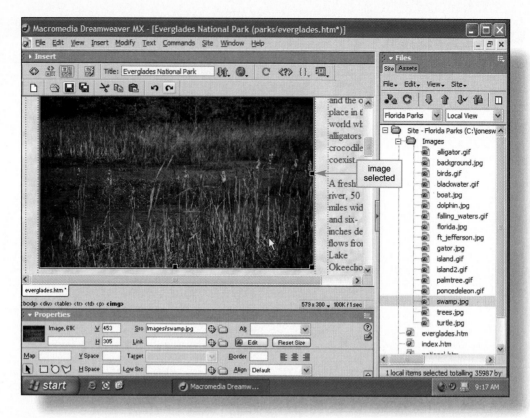

FIGURE 3-50

8 Double-click the W box in the Property inspector. Type 330 and then press the TAB key to move to the H box. Type 220 as the new value. Click the Alt box. Type Florida swamp and then press the ENTER key.

The properties are applied to the swamp.jpg image (Figure 3-51).

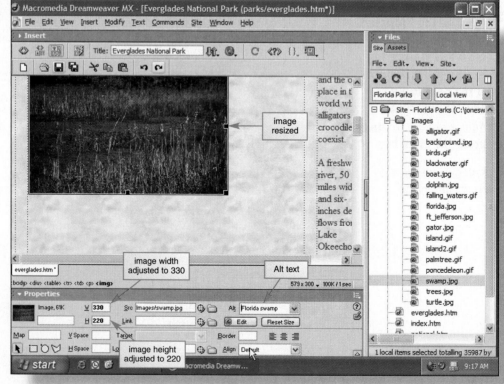

FIGURE 3-51

9 **Scroll down. Click row 3, column 2.**

The insertion point is displayed in the cell (Figure 3-52). The birds.gif image will be inserted at the location of the insertion point.

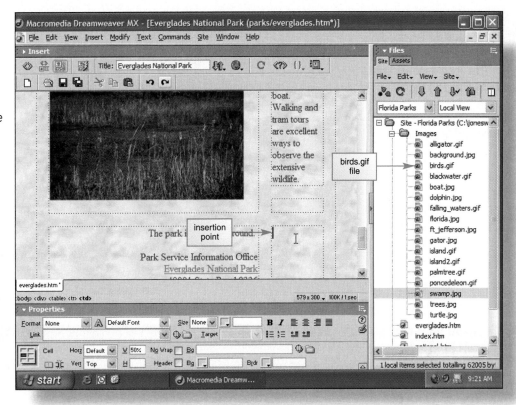

FIGURE 3-52

10 **Drag the birds.gif file to the insertion point in row 3, column 2.**

The birds.gif image is displayed in the cell (Figure 3-53). The cell expands to accommodate the image. The insertion point is blinking to the right of the image.

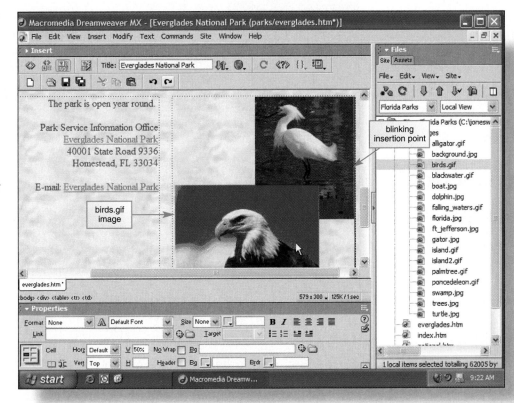

FIGURE 3-53

11 **Click the birds.gif image to select it. Click the Alt box. Type** Florida birds **and then press the ENTER key.**

The Alt text is entered (Figure 3-54).

FIGURE 3-54

12 **Scroll up. Click the cell in row 2, column 2 and then drag to select this cell and the cell in row 3, column 2.**

The two cells are selected (Figure 3-55).

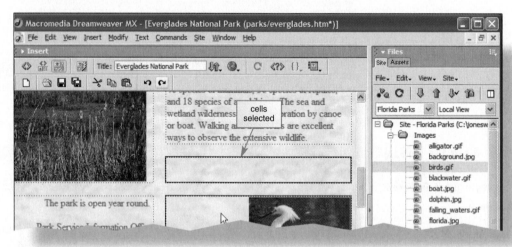

FIGURE 3-55

13 **Click the Merge Cells button.**

The two cells are merged and the top border of the newly merged cell moves up (Figure 3-56).

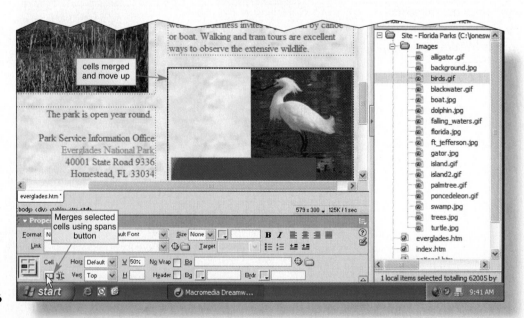

FIGURE 3-56

14 **Click the Save button on the Document toolbar and then press the F12 key to view the page in your browser.**

The Florida Everglades page displays in the browser (Figure 3-57).

15 **Close the browser window and then close the Site panel and the Everglades National Park Web page.**

FIGURE 3-57

Creating the Biscayne National Park Web Page

You used the Untitled-1 default page that displayed when you started Dreamweaver to begin creating the Everglades page. To create the Biscayne National Park Web page, you open a new Untitled Document window. You start by applying a color scheme and the background image. This is the same color scheme and background image you used for the Florida Parks Web site in Projects 1 and 2.

TO ADD A COLOR SCHEME AND BACKGROUND IMAGE TO THE BISCAYNE NATIONAL PARK WEB PAGE

1 Open a new Untitled window. Apply the settings in Table 3-1 on page DW 3.10 to add the color scheme and then click the OK button in the Set Color Scheme Command dialog box.

2 Apply the settings in Table 3-1 to add the background image. Click the OK button in the Page Properties dialog box.

3 Click the Save button on the Standard toolbar and save the Web page in the parks folder. Type biscayne for the file name.

The background image is applied to the Biscayne National Park page (Figure 3-58).

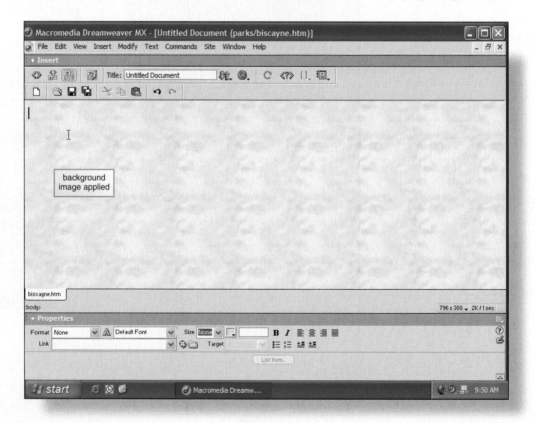

FIGURE 3-58

Next, you will insert and center a 3-row, 2-column table. Then you will add the page title — Biscayne National Park. Perform the following steps to insert and center the table and to add the title.

TO INSERT AND CENTER A TABLE

1 Click the Align Center button in the Property inspector.

2 If necessary, expand the Insert bar and then click the Layout tab. Click the Insert Table button.

3 In the Insert Table dialog box, change the following settings: Rows 3, Cell Padding 10, Columns 2, Cell Spacing 2, W 90 Percent, and Border 4. Press the OK button to insert the table.

4 Title the page Biscayne National Park.

5 Click the expand/collapse arrow to collapse the Insert bar.

6 Click the Save button on the Standard toolbar.

The centered table is added to the Web page (Figure 3-59). The Web page is saved in the parks folder.

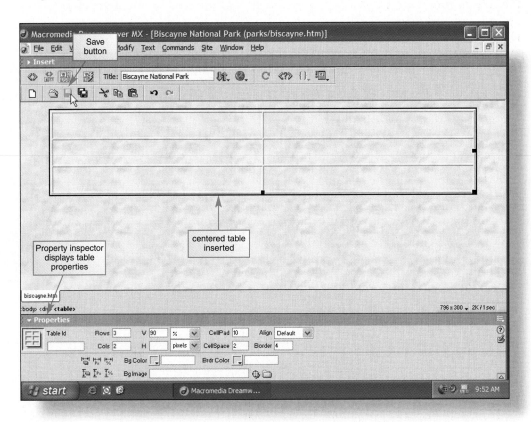

FIGURE 3-59

An understanding of HTML and how it relates to a table and to parts of a table provides you with the ability to select a table and table components and to modify a table through the code. Merging and varying the span of columns (as you did in the Everglades National Park page) and merging and varying the span of rows is helpful for grouping information, adding emphasis, or deleting empty cells. When you merge two cells in a row, you are spanning a column. Continuing with the <TABLE> example on page DW 3.19 and spanning the two cells in row 1, the HTML tags would be <TD COLSPAN="2">First cellSecond cell</TD>. When you merge two cells in a column, you are spanning a row. The attribute ROWSPAN would replace COLSPAN in the above example. Understanding COLSPAN and ROWSPAN will help you determine when and if two columns or two rows have been merged.

For the Everglades National Park page, you entered a heading outside the table and links to the other pages in a second table. For the Biscayne National Park page, you will merge the cells in row 1 and then merge the cells in row 3. You will enter a heading in row 1 and then enter text for the links to the home page and other national parks in row 3. Perform the following steps to merge the cells in row 1 and merge the cells in row 3.

TO MERGE CELLS IN ROWS 1 AND 3

1 Click row 1, column 1 and drag to select row 1.

2 Click the Merge Cells button in the Property inspector.

3 Click row 3, column 1 and drag to select row 3.

4 Click the Merge Cells button in the Property inspector.

The cells in row 1 are merged into one column and the cells in row 3 are merged into one column (Figure 3-60).

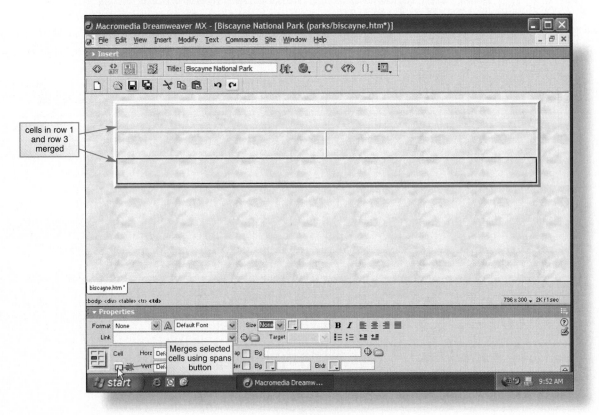

FIGURE 3-60

Next, you will add and center a heading. Complete the following steps to add and center the heading in row 1.

Steps **To Add a Heading to Row 1**

1 **Click row 1 and then click the Align Center button in the Property inspector.**

The insertion point is aligned in the middle of the row (Figure 3-61).

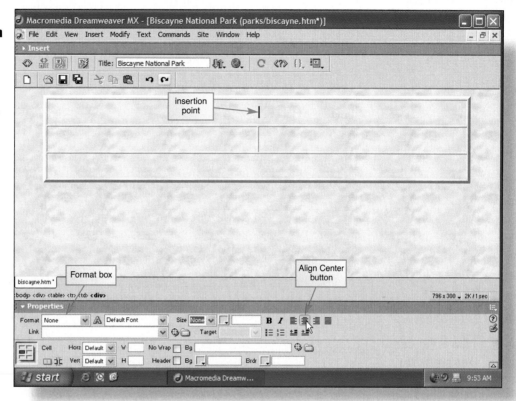

FIGURE 3-61

2 **Type** Biscayne National Park **and then use the Format pop-up menu to apply Heading 1.**

The heading is centered in row 1 and Heading 1 is applied to the text (Figure 3-62).

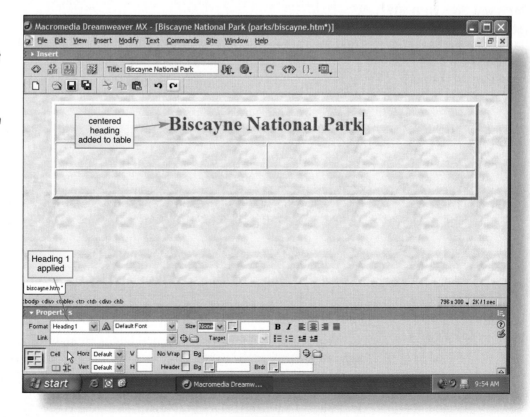

FIGURE 3-62

3 Click row 3 and then click the Align Center button in the Property inspector.

The insertion point is centered in row 3 (Figure 3-63).

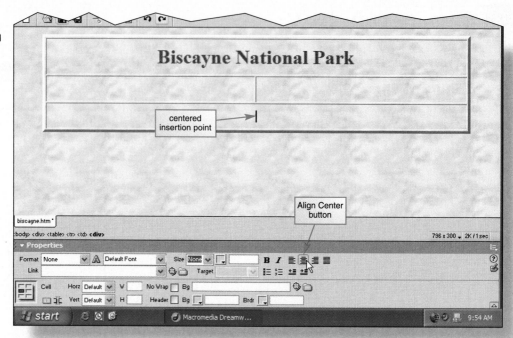

FIGURE 3-63

4 Type Home and then press the SPACEBAR. Press SHIFT+| (VERTICAL BAR) and then press the SPACEBAR. Type Everglades National Park and then press the SPACEBAR. Press SHIFT+| and then press the SPACEBAR. Type Dry Tortugas National Park as the last link text.

The text for the links is centered in the row (Figure 3-64).

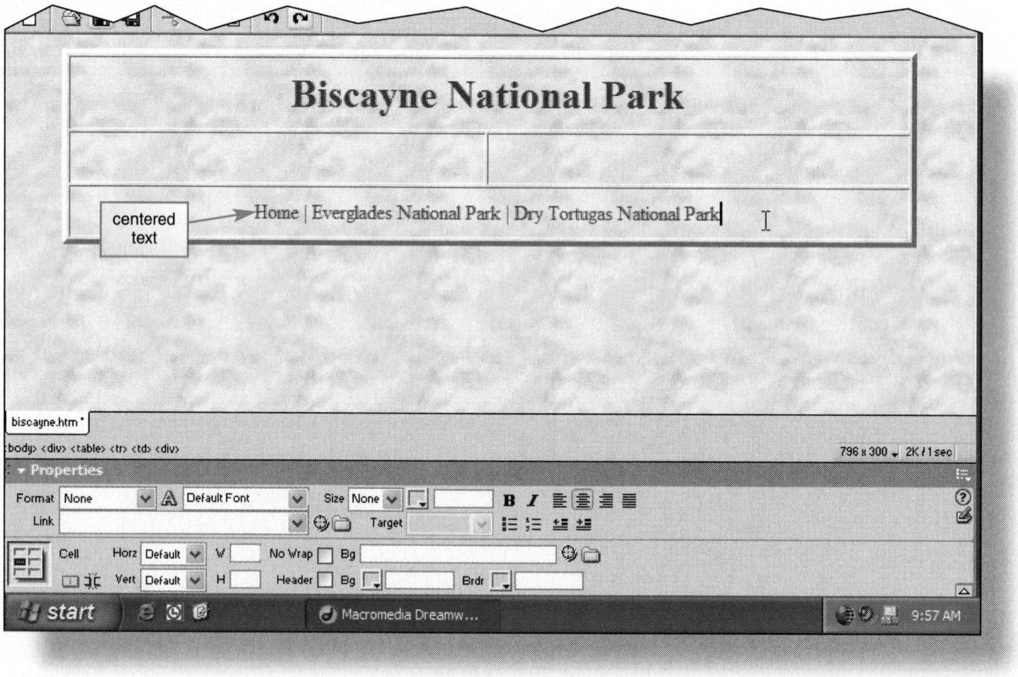

FIGURE 3-64

Splitting and Merging Cells

Tables in a traditional sense generally are thought of as having an internal **symmetry**; that is, cells of the same size form neatly arranged columns and rows. On a Web page, however, by varying the size of a cell, you can use tables to create an asymmetrical arrangement. This design option allows for more visual variation on a Web page. In a three-column table, for example, you could specify the first column as 20 percent and the second and third columns as 40 percent each. Depending on the number of columns, hundreds of variation percentages can be applied. In the Biscayne National Park page, you adjust the width for columns 1 and 2 and then change the vertical alignment to Top within both columns. Perform the following steps to adjust the width and change the vertical spacing.

 To Adjust the Column Width

1 Click row 2, column 1.

The insertion point is located in row 2, column 1 (Figure 3-65).

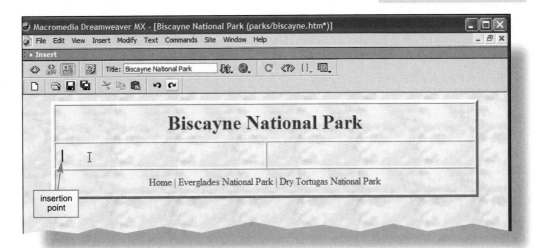

FIGURE 3-65

2 Click the W box in the Property inspector. Type 40% and then press the ENTER key. Click row 2, column 2. Click the W box in the Property inspector. Type 60% and then press the ENTER key.

Column 1 is decreased in size to reflect the new percentage and column 2 is increased in size to reflect the new percentage (Figure 3-66).

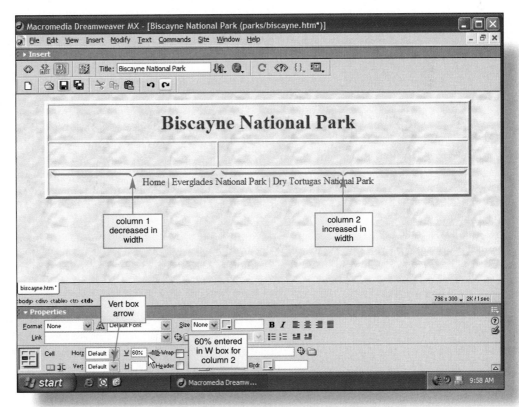

FIGURE 3-66

3 **Select row 2, columns 1 and 2. Click the Vert box arrow in the Property inspector and then select Top from the Vert pop-up menu.**

Top is selected in the Vert box (Figure 3-67).

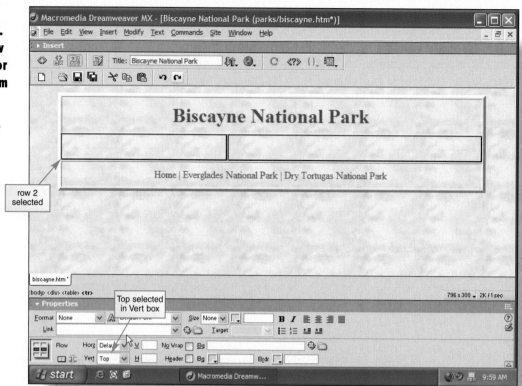

FIGURE 3-67

Now you will add the text and images to row 2, columns 1 and 2. Table 3-4 contains the text for the Biscayne National Park Web page.

Inserting Images into a Table

In Macromedia Dreamweaver MX, you can work in Design view or Code view to insert images in a document.

Table 3-4	Biscayne National Park Web Page Text
SECTION	**TEXT FOR BISCAYNE NATIONAL PARK WEB PAGE**
Part 1	Located off the eastern coast of Florida, the 180,000-acre Biscayne National Park is less than an hour's drive from Miami. The park originally was established as a national monument in 1968. It became a national park in 1980, specifically to protect the incredible diversity of mammals, birds, fish, and plants.<ENTER><ENTER>
Part 2	Park Service Information Office: Biscayne National Park P. O. Box 1369 Homestead, FL 33090<ENTER> E-mail: Biscayne National Park
Part 3	More than 95 percent of the park is underwater and includes mangrove swamps, coral reefs, and the waters of Biscayne Bay. The remaining 5 percent includes 44 islands that form an 18-nautical mile north-south chain. In this watery paradise, one can find more than 200 varieties of fish, which inhabit the coral reefs. Starfish, sponges, soft corals, and other marine plants and animals live and thrive in Biscayne Bay.<ENTER>
Part 4	Biscayne National Park is best explored with snorkels or scuba gear. For those not quite so adventurous, glass-bottom boat trips and canoe rentals are available.<ENTER>

Steps **To Add Text and Images to the Biscayne National Park Web Page**

1 **Press F8 to display the Site panel. If necessary, click the plus (+) sign to the left of Images to display the image files. Click row 2, column 1.**

The insertion point is positioned in row 2, column 1 and the Site panel is displayed (Figure 3-68). The island.gif image will be inserted at the location of the insertion point.

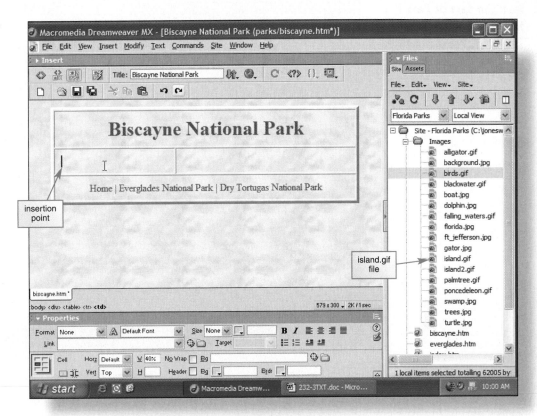

FIGURE 3-68

2 **Drag the island.gif image to the insertion point in row 2, column 1.**

The island.gif image is displayed in row 2, column 1. The insertion point is blinking to the right of the image (Figure 3-69).

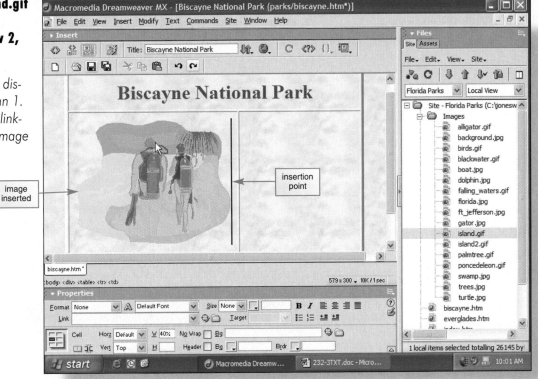

FIGURE 3-69

3 Press the ENTER key and then type the text of Part 1 in Table 3-4 on page DW 3.48. Press the ENTER key two times after you type the text.

The text is entered as shown in Figure 3-70.

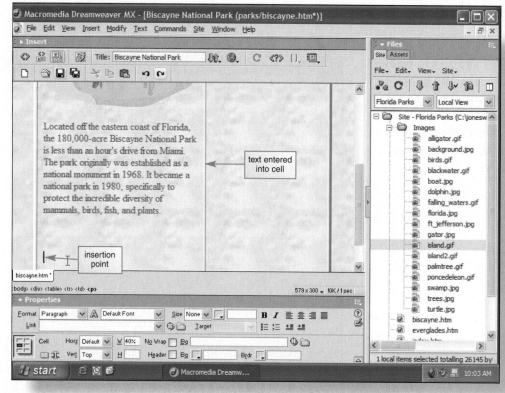

FIGURE 3-70

4 Type the text of Part 2 in Table 3-4. Insert line breaks and press the ENTER key as indicated in Table 3-4.

The text is entered as shown in Figure 3-71.

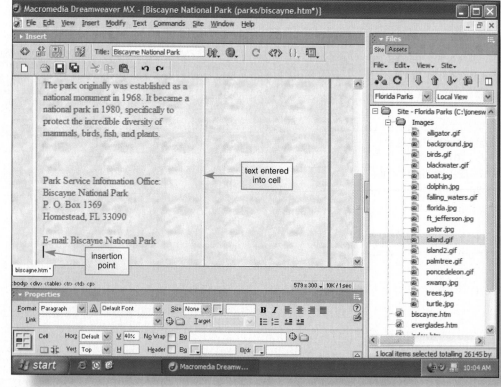

FIGURE 3-71

5 Scroll up and click row 2, column 2.

The insertion point is positioned in row 2, column 2 (Figure 3-72).

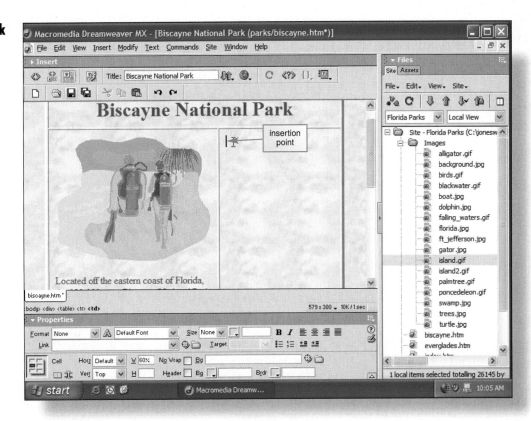

FIGURE 3-72

6 Type the text of Part 3 in Table 3-4.

The text is entered as shown in Figure 3-73. The palmtree.gif image will be inserted at the location of the insertion point.

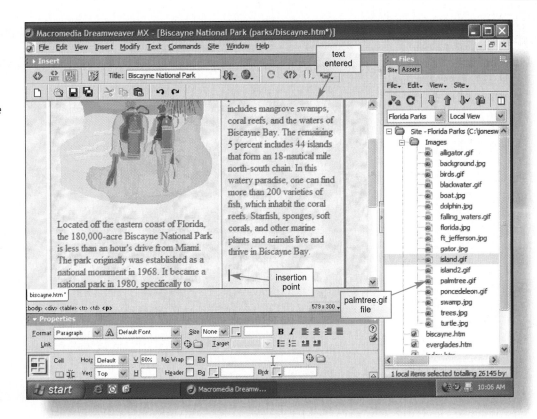

FIGURE 3-73

7 Drag the palmtree.gif image to the insertion point.

The palmtree.gif image is inserted into the cell. The insertion point is blinking to the right of the image (Figure 3-74).

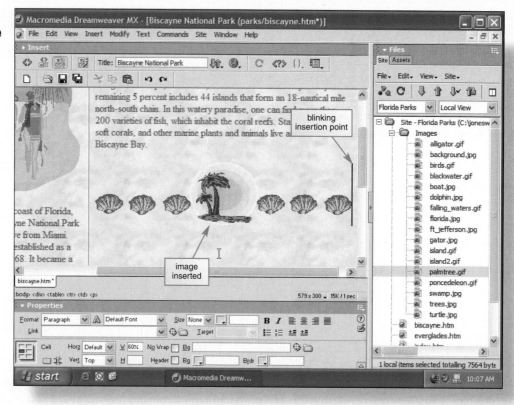

FIGURE 3-74

8 Press the ENTER key and then type the text of Part 4 in Table 3-4. Press the ENTER key after entering the text.

The text is entered as shown in Figure 3-75. The island2.gif image will be inserted at the location of the insertion point.

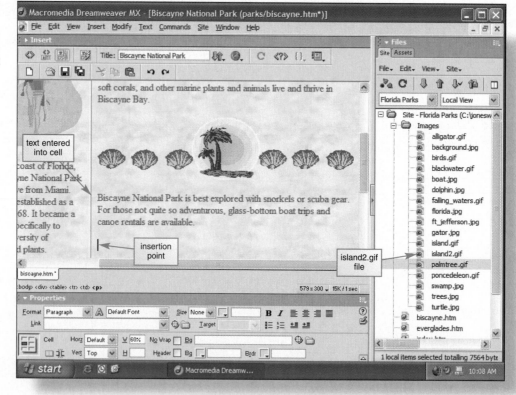

FIGURE 3-75

9 Drag the island2.gif image to the insertion point. Click the image to select it. Double-click the W box in the Property inspector. Type 375 as the new value. Double-click the H box and then type 220 as the new value. Click the Align Center button. Type island for the Alt text.

The image is inserted into the cell, resized, and centered (Figure 3-76).

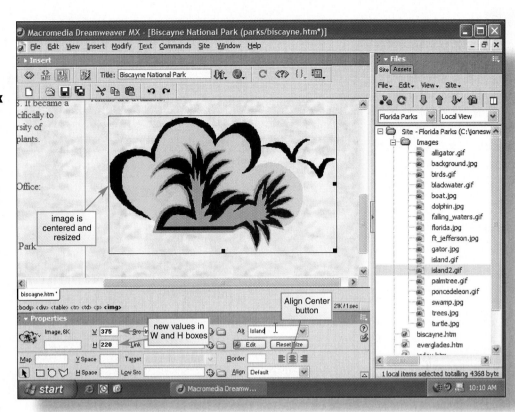

FIGURE 3-76

Adding a Border and a Border Color

A **border** is the width, in pixels, of the table border. The purpose of most tables in a Web page is to provide a structure for the positioning of text and images. When creating a table within Dreamweaver, therefore, the default border is 0 (zero) or no border. Adding a border to a Web page, however, transforms the table into a graphical element within itself. Depending on the content, a border can become a visual cue for the reader by separating content. A border is applied to the full table. You cannot apply a border to an individual cell unless the table consists of only one cell.

When you created the table for the Biscayne National Park Web page, you specified a border size of 4. By default, borders are gray, but the border color can be changed. Using the color picker, you can apply a color of your choice. Although you cannot apply a border to an individual cell, you can apply a border color to a single cell or to a range of cells.

Background images and background color work the same for a table as they do for a Web page. The image or color, however, is contained within the table and does not affect the rest of the page. Background color (unlike borders) and images can be applied to a single cell or to a range of cells. Perform the steps on the next two pages to add a border color to the table and a background color to a merged cell.

Borders

A border can help separate content within a table. Borders are especially useful if the table includes information that contains data that must be read across a row or down a column.

To Add Border Color and Cell Background Color

1 Click <table> in the tag selector and then click the Brdr Color box arrow in the Property inspector. Point to row 9, column 2.

The table is selected and the Continuous Tone color palette is displayed (Figure 3-77).

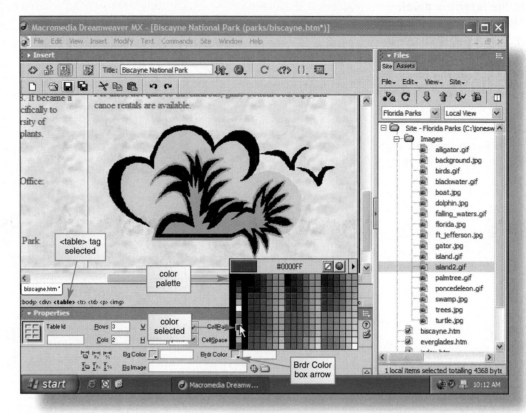

FIGURE 3-77

2 Click row 9, column 2 to select the blue color, hexadecimal #0000FF.

A shade of blue is applied to the border (Figure 3-78).

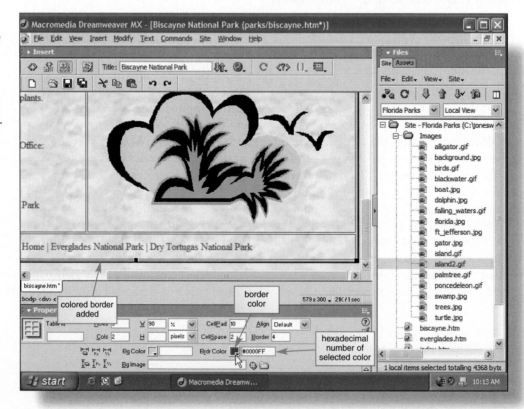

FIGURE 3-78

3 If necessary, scroll up and left. Click anywhere in row 1. Click the Bg Color box arrow. If necessary, select the Color Cubes palette and then point to the second column from the right and fourth row from the bottom — hexadecimal color #FFCC66.

The color palette displays the selected background (Figure 3-79).

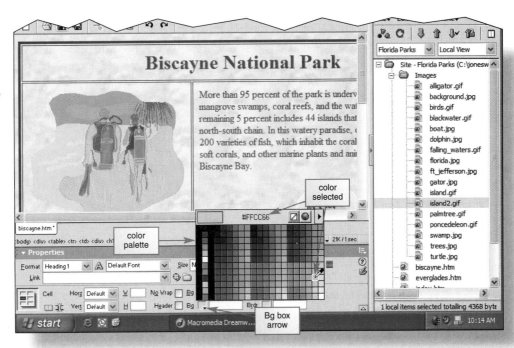

FIGURE 3-79

4 Click the mouse pointer.

The palette is closed and the background color is applied to the row (Figure 3-80).

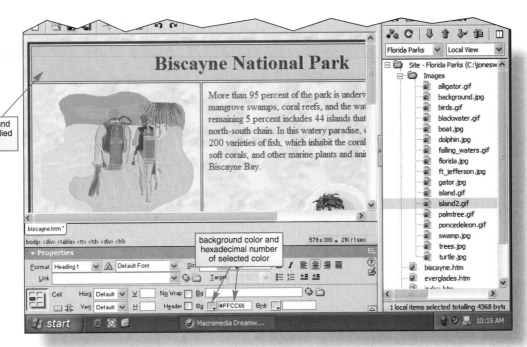

FIGURE 3-80

Your last task for the Biscayne National Park page is to spell check, add links, and save the page. Perform the steps on the next page to spell check, add the absolute, relative, and e-mail links to the Biscayne National Park page, and then save the Web page.

TO ADD LINKS TO AND SPELL CHECK THE BISCAYNE NATIONAL PARK PAGE

1 Scroll down select the first instance of Biscayne National Park in the address in row 2, column 1. Type `http://www.nps.gov/bisc/` in the Link box.

2 Select the second instance of Biscayne National Park. Click Insert on the menu bar and then click Email Link. Type `biscayne@parks.gov` in the E-Mail text box. Click the OK button in the Email Link dialog box.

3 Double-click Home in row 3 and then type `index.htm` in the Link box.

4 Select Everglades National Park and then type `everglades.htm` in the Link box.

5 Select Dry Tortugas National Park and then type `dry_tortugas.htm` in the Link box.

6 Click the Save button on the Document toolbar.

7 Check spelling.

8 Press the F12 key to view the Web page in the browser as shown in Figure 3-81. Close the browser and then close the Web page. If necessary, save any changes.

In the browser, the Biscayne National Park page is displayed as shown in Figure 3-81.

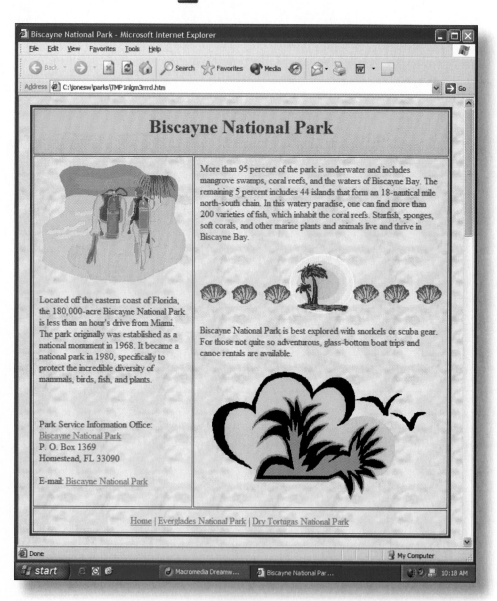

FIGURE 3-81

Layout View

Tables created in Standard view are useful for creating Web pages that are simple in format or contain tabular data. A second option for creating tables in Dreamweaver is the Layout view. Layout view provides more flexibility than Standard view. In Layout view, you draw your own table and cells. When using Layout view, you are creating the framework for the entire table. The layout can be as simple or as complex as you want.

Layout view is a tool unique to Dreamweaver. Terms such as layout view and layout cell do not exist in HTML. When you draw a **layout table**, Dreamweaver creates an HTML table. When you draw a **layout cell**, Dreamweaver creates a tag (<TD>) in the table. When a cell is drawn in a table, it stays within the row-and-column grid as it does in Standard view. Cells cannot overlap, but they can span rows and columns. When you draw cells of different widths and different heights, Dreamweaver creates additional cells in the HTML table. These cells are displayed with a gray background.

You can use Layout view to modify the structure of an existing page created in Standard view. Layout view, however, provides the greatest advantage when designing the page from the start. As you draw the table and/or cells in Layout view, Dreamweaver creates the code. If you draw a layout cell first, a layout table is inserted automatically to serve as a container for the layout cell. A layout cell cannot exist outside of a layout table. You can create your page using one layout table with several layout cells contained within the table or you can have multiple layout tables. Using multiple layout tables isolates parts of your layout so that one section is not affected by another. For example, the cell size within a table can affect the other cells in the same row and column. Using multiple tables eliminates this problem.

When you draw a table in Layout view, the table is outlined in green. A tab labeled Layout Table is displayed at the top of each table. Clicking the tab selects the table. When you complete your page design for the Dry Tortugas National Park, it will look similar to Figure 3-82 on the next page.

Perform the following steps to add a new page, add a background image, and prepare the work area of the page.

TO ADD A COLOR SCHEME AND BACKGROUND IMAGE TO THE DRY TORTUGAS NATIONAL PARK WEB PAGE

1 Open a new Document window. Apply the settings in Table 3-1 on page DW 3.10 to add the color scheme and then click the OK button in the Set Color Scheme Command dialog box.

2 Apply the settings in Table 3-1 to add the background image. Click the OK button in the Page Properties dialog box.

3 Type Dry Tortugas National Park for the title.

4 Click the Save button on the Standard toolbar and save the Web page in the parks folder. Type dry_tortugas for the file name.

Using Visual Guides

Dreamweaver provides three types of visual guides to help you design documents and project how the page will appear in a browser: ruler, tracing image, and grid.

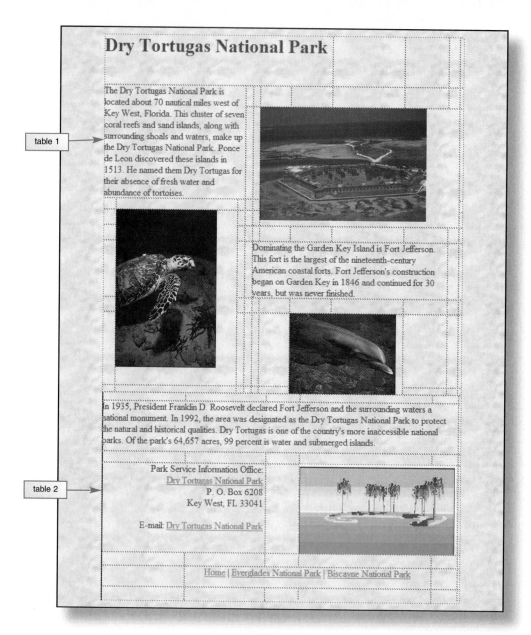

FIGURE 3-82

RULER   Provides a visual cue for positioning and resizing layers or tables.

TRACING IMAGE   Used as the page background to duplicate a design.

GRID   Provides precise positioning and resizing of layers.

You will use the ruler to help approximate cell width and height and cell location within a table. Then, you will make final adjustments to the cells and table using settings in the Property inspector. Perform the following steps to display the ruler in the Document window.

To Display the Ruler

1 **Click View on the menu bar, point to Rulers, and then point to Show on the Rulers submenu.**

Dreamweaver displays the View menu and the Rulers submenu (Figure 3-83).

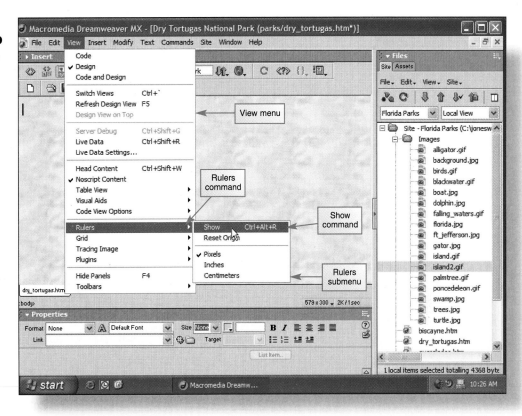

FIGURE 3-83

2 **Click Show. Expand the Insert bar. If necessary, click the Layout tab in the Insert bar.**

The ruler is displayed at the top and left margins of the Document window (Figure 3-84). Measurements are in pixels.

3 **Right-click the Files title bar and then click the Close Panel Group command. Click the Property inspector expander arrow.**

The lower pane of the Property inspector collapses.

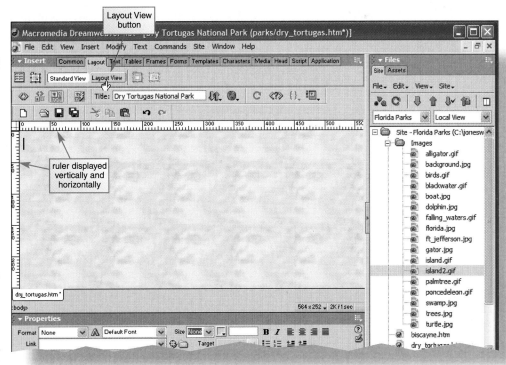

FIGURE 3-84

Creating a Layout Table for the Dry Tortugas National Park Web Page

You begin creating the Dry Tortugas National Park page by drawing a table. This is one of two tables you will create for the Dry Tortugas National Park page. In the first table, you will create six cells: one cell to hold the heading, two cells to hold text content, and three cells to hold images. The second table is below the first. This table will contain four cells: a cell to hold informational content, a cell to hold address and contact information, a cell to hold an image, and a cell to contain links to the home page and the other two national park pages.

Your next task is to draw the first layout table. This table has an approximate width of 620 pixels and an approximate height of 575–590 pixels. Perform the following steps to create the layout table.

Steps **To Create the First Layout Table**

1 **Click the Layout View button. Point to the OK button.**

The Getting Started in Layout View dialog box is displayed (Figure 3-85). The dialog box contains help information on how the layout feature works. The dialog box may not display if the Don't show me this message again box previously was checked.

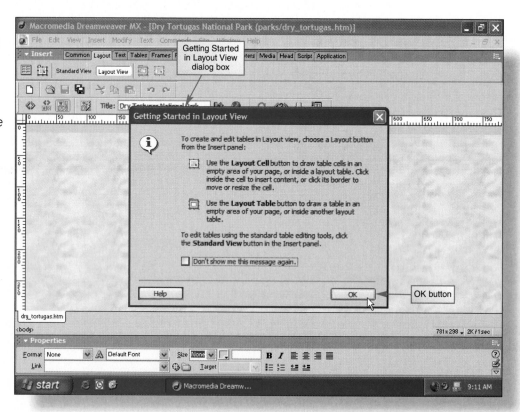

FIGURE 3-85

2 **Read the information in the Getting Started in Layout View dialog box and then click the OK button. Move the mouse pointer to the Document window.**

The mouse pointer changes to a plus sign, which indicates you can draw a table (Figure 3-86).

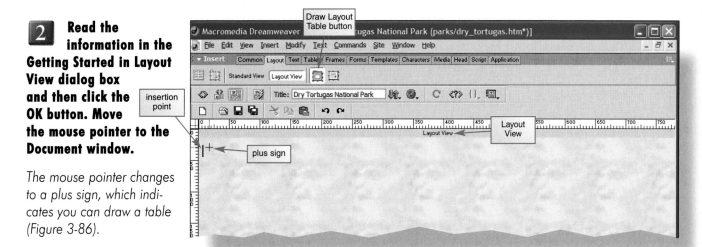

FIGURE 3-86

3 **Position the mouse pointer in the upper-left corner of the Document window. Use the ruler as a guide and drag to draw a table with a width of approximately 600 pixels and a height of approximately 575 pixels. Scroll to the top of the page.**

The table is added to the Document window and is outlined in green. The Property inspector changes to reflect the table in Layout view (Figure 3-87). The Layout Table tab is displayed at the top of the table and the table width displays in the column header area. The table displays with a gray background.

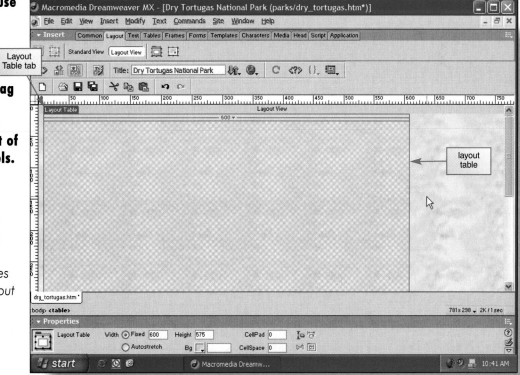

FIGURE 3-87

Layout Table and Layout Cell Properties

When a layout table is selected, the Property inspector displays properties related to the layout table. Some properties, such as width and height, background color, cell padding and cell spacing, are the same as those for a table in Standard view. The following describes the properties unique to the table in Layout view (Figure 3-88 on the next page).

FIXED   Sets the table to a fixed width.

AUTOSTRETCH   The rightmost column of the table stretches to fill the browser window width. The column header area for an autostretch column displays a wavy line instead of a number. If the layout includes an autostretch column, the layout always fills the entire width of the browser window.

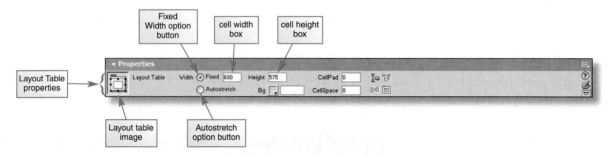

FIGURE 3-88

If the table is not the correct width or height or needs other modifications, adjustments can be made through the Width and Height properties of the Property inspector.

The next step is to add a cell that will contain the table heading and the five cells that will contain text and images. The heading is aligned left at the top of the table. Perform the following steps to add layout cells and a table heading cell to the table.

 To Add Layout Cells

1 If necessary, make any adjustments in the Property inspector Width and Height boxes. Click the Draw Layout Cell button on the Layout tab.

The status bar indicates the function of the button (Figure 3-89).

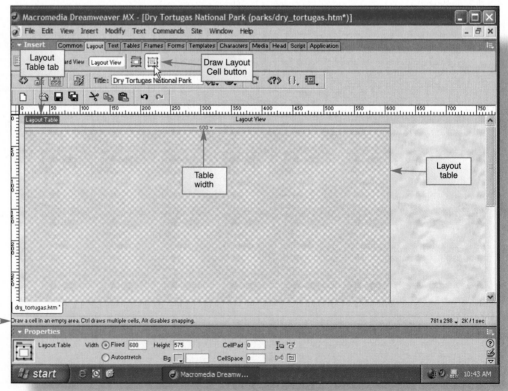

FIGURE 3-89

2 **Click the upper-left corner of the layout table and drag to draw a cell with an approximate width of 425 and an approximate height of 85. Click the blue outline of the cell to select it and make any necessary width and height adjustments in the Property inspector Width and Height boxes.**

A layout cell is created in the upper-left corner of the layout table. The cell is displayed in the table with a blue outline (Figure 3-90). The handles on the borders indicate the cell is selected.

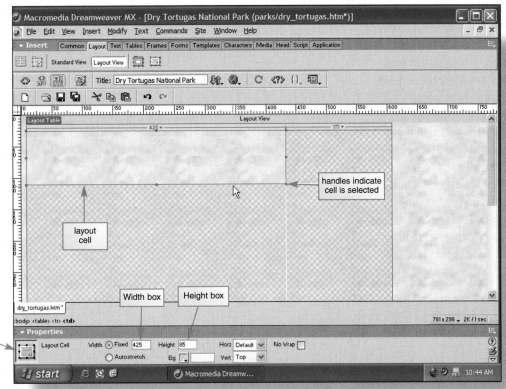

FIGURE 3-90

3 **Click the cell and type** Dry Tortugas National Park. **Apply Heading 1 to the text. Point to the Draw Layout Cell button.**

The heading is inserted into the cell and Heading 1 is applied to the text (Figure 3-91). Text properties are displayed in the Property inspector.

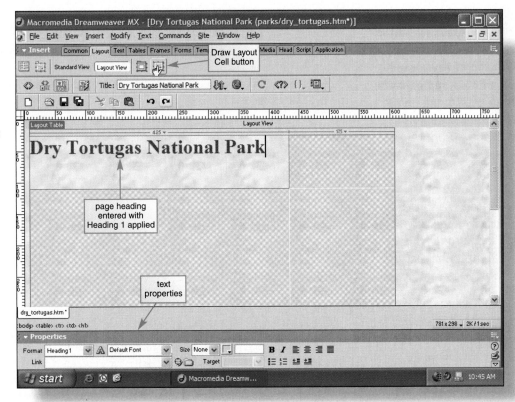

FIGURE 3-91

4 **Click the Draw Layout Cell button. Click to the left and below the first cell and then draw a cell with an approximate width of 250 and an approximate height of 190 as shown in Figure 3-92. Click the blue outline of the cell to select it and make any necessary width and height adjustments in the Property inspector Width and Height boxes.**

The second cell is added to the table and is selected (Figure 3-92). This cell will contain text.

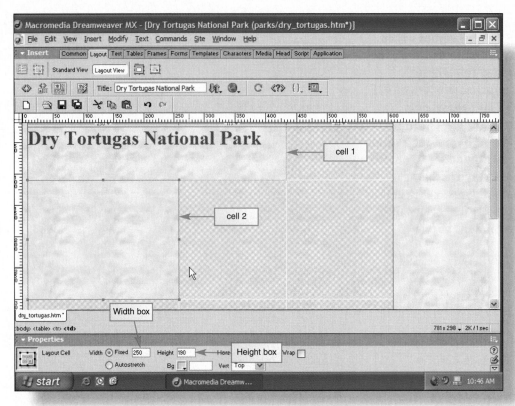

FIGURE 3-92

5 **Click the Draw Layout Cell button and then draw a cell to the right of the second cell with an approximate width of 290 and an approximate height of 200 as shown in Figure 3-93. If necessary, scroll to view the entire cell. Click the blue outline of the cell to select it and make any necessary width and height adjustments in the Property inspector Width and Height boxes.**

The third cell is added to the table and is selected (Figure 3-93). This cell will contain an image.

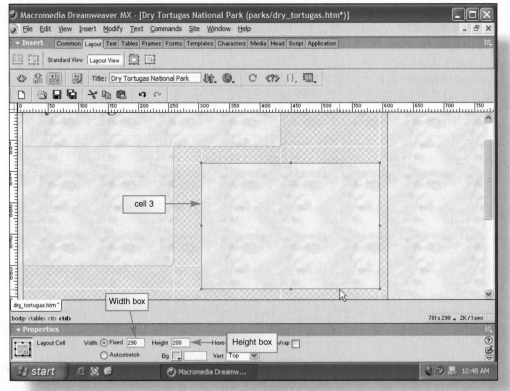

FIGURE 3-93

6 Scroll down and then click the Draw Layout Cell button. Click approximately 20 pixels below the second cell and about 20 pixels to the right of the table border. Draw a cell with a width of approximately 180 and a height of approximately 275 as shown in Figure 3-94. Click the blue outline of the cell to select it and make any necessary width and height adjustments in the Property inspector Width and Height boxes.

The fourth cell is added to the table and is selected (Figure 3-94). The cell will contain an image.

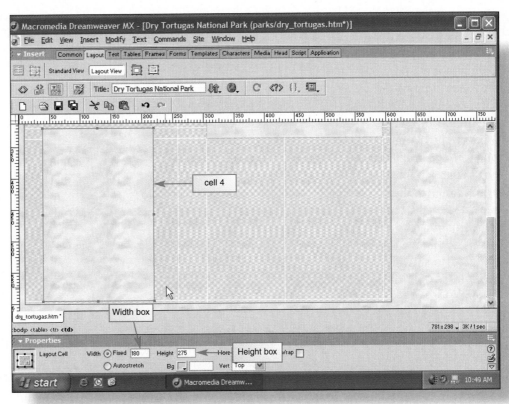

FIGURE 3-94

7 Click the Draw Layout Cell button. Click 20 pixels below and 50 pixels to the left of the third cell and draw a cell with a width of approximately 300 and a height of approximately 75 as shown in Figure 3-95. Click the blue outline of the cell to select it and make any necessary width and height adjustments in the Property inspector Width and Height boxes.

The fifth cell is added to the table and is selected (Figure 3-95). The cell will contain text.

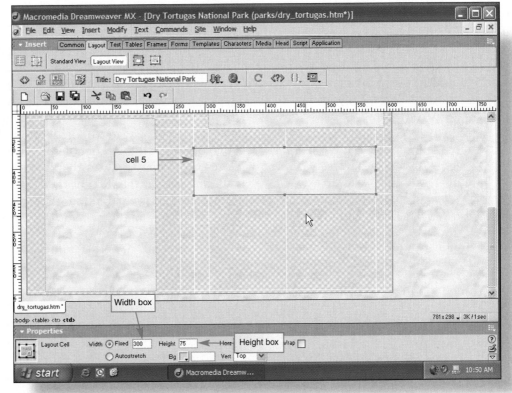

FIGURE 3-95

8 **Click the Draw Layout Cell button. Click about 20 pixels below and about 50 pixels to the right of the fifth cell and draw a cell with a width of approximately 185 and a height of approximately 135 as shown in Figure 3-96. Click the blue outline of the cell to select it and make any necessary width and height adjustments in the Property inspector Width and Height boxes.**

The sixth cell is added to the table and is selected (Figure 3-96). The cell will contain an image.

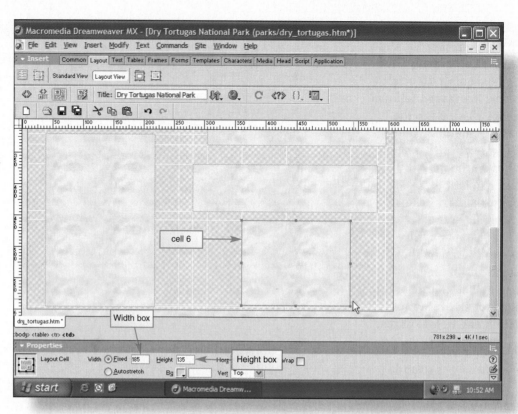

FIGURE 3-96

Adding Content and Images to the Cells

Adding text content and images to layout cells is similar to adding content and images to cells in a Standard view table. The only place content can be inserted in a layout table is in a layout cell. When Dreamweaver creates a layout cell, it automatically assigns a vertical alignment of Top. You have the same options as you did in Standard view to change the alignment to Middle, Bottom, or Baseline. When you insert an image into a layout cell, all the properties in the Property inspector that were available for images in Standard view also are available in Layout view.

Next, you will enter and format the text for the first table for the Dry Tortugas National Park Web page. The text is entered into the layout cells just as you entered it in the cells in the Standard view table. Then you will display the Site panel and drag images into the cells. Table 3-5 contains the text for the Dry Tortugas National Park Web page.

Layout Cells

To delete a layout cell, click the edge of the cell to select it, and then press the DELETE key. The space is replaced with noneditable cells.

TABLE 3-5	Dry Tortugas National Park Web Page Text
SECTION	TEXT FOR DRY TORTUGAS NATIONAL PARK WEB PAGE
Part 1	The Dry Tortugas National Park is located about 70 nautical miles west of Key West, Florida. This cluster of seven coral reefs and sand islands, along with surrounding shoals and waters, make up the Dry Tortugas National Park. Ponce de Leon discovered these islands in 1513. He named them Dry Tortugas for their absence of fresh water and abundance of tortoises.
Part 2	Dominating the Garden Key Island is Fort Jefferson. This fort is the largest of the nineteenth-century American coastal forts. Fort Jefferson's construction began on Garden Key in 1846 and continued for 30 years, but was never finished.
Part 3	In 1935, President Franklin D. Roosevelt declared Fort Jefferson and the surrounding waters a national monument. In 1992, the area was designated as the Dry Tortugas National Park to protect the natural and historical qualities. Dry Tortugas is one of the country's more inaccessible national parks. Of the park's 64,657 acres, 99 percent is water and submerged islands.
Part 4	Park Service Information Office: Dry Tortugas National Park P. O. Box 6208 Key West, FL 33041 <ENTER> E-mail: Dry Tortugas National Park <ENTER>
Part 5	Home | Everglades National Park | Biscayne National Park

More About

Positioning Images

The Property inspector contains two different sets of tools for positioning images. The top panel of the Property inspector lets you change the alignment of the image itself. The bottom panel of the Property inspector contains tools that change the cell's alignment settings.

To Add Text and Images to Table 1 of the Dry Tortugas National Park Web Page

1 **Scroll to the top of the Document window. Click the second cell and type the text of Part 1 in Table 3-5.**

The text is entered (Figure 3-97).

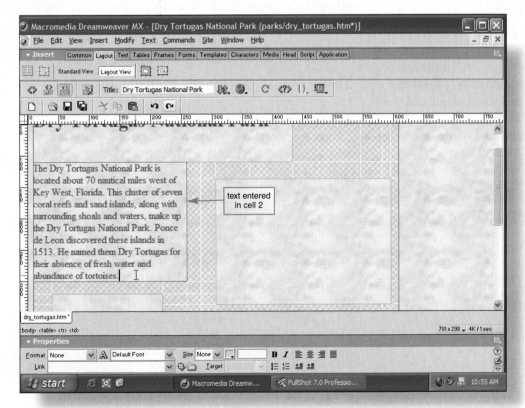

FIGURE 3-97

2 Scroll down and click the fifth cell you added. Type the text of Part 2 in Table 3-5.

The text is entered (Figure 3-98).

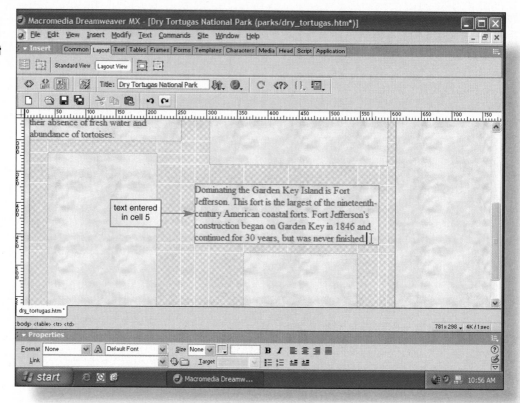

FIGURE 3-98

3 Scroll up and click the third cell. Press the F8 key to display the Site panel. If necessary, expand the Image folder. If necessary, adjust the horizontal scroll and vertical scroll bars to display the file names in the Site panel.

The insertion point is blinking in the third cell and the Site panel is displayed (Figure 3-99).

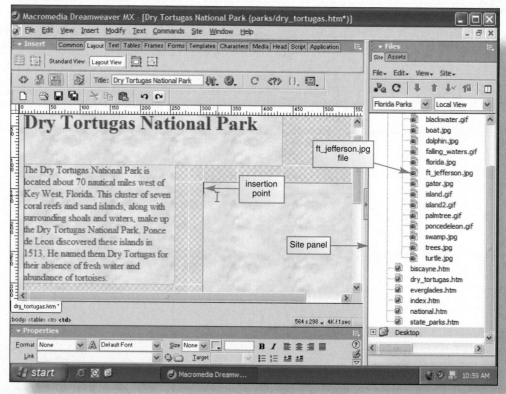

FIGURE 3-99

4 **Drag the ft_jefferson.jpg file to the insertion point.**

The image is displayed in the cell (Figure 3-100). The insertion point is blinking to the right of the image.

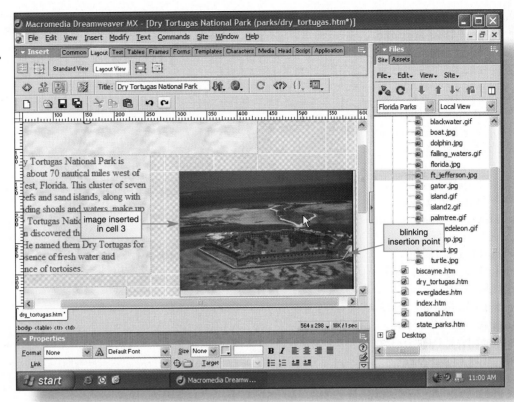

FIGURE 3-100

5 **Scroll down and click the fourth cell. Drag the turtle.jpg image to the cell.**

The turtle image is displayed in the cell (Figure 3-101). The insertion point is blinking to the right of the image.

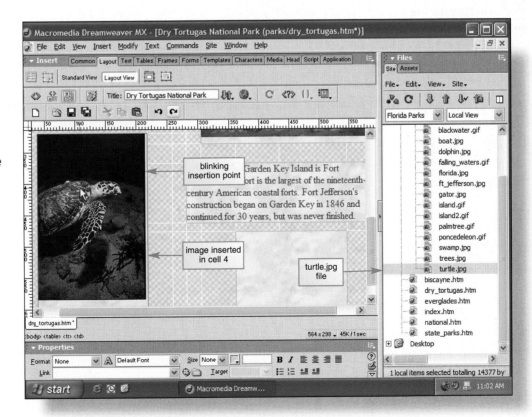

FIGURE 3-101

6 **Click the sixth cell and then drag the dolphin.jpg image to the cell.**

The dolphin image is displayed (Figure 3-102). The insertion point is blinking to the right of the image.

7 **Scroll up and then click the ft_jefferson image in cell 3. Type** Ft. Jefferson **in the Alt box in the Property inspector. Click outside the image to deselect it. Repeat these steps for the other two images: type** Turtle **for the turtle image and** Dolphin **for the dolphin image.**

8 **Click the Save button on the Standard toolbar.**

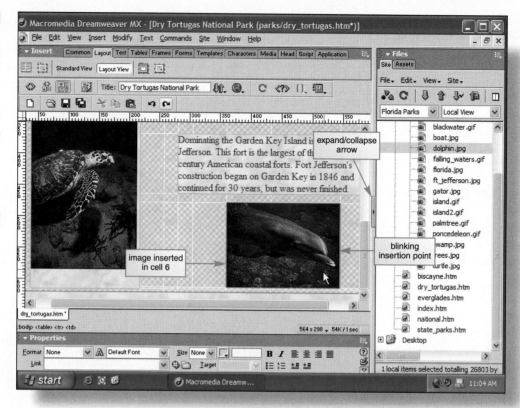

FIGURE 3-102

Layout Tables

For more information about Dreamweaver MX layout tables, visit the Dreamweaver MX More About Web page (scsite.com/ dreamweavermx/ more.htm) and then click Dreamweaver MX Layout Tables.

Adding a Second Table to the Dry Tortugas National Park Web Page

The second table in the Dry Tortugas National Park Web page will go immediately below the first table. This table will contain four cells. Three of the cells will contain text and the fourth cell will contain an image.

Steps **To Add a Second Table to the Dry Tortugas National Park Web Page**

1 **Click the Site panel expand/collapse arrow. If necessary, scroll down. Click the Draw Layout Table button on Layout tab and then position the mouse pointer outside the lower-right border of the first table.**

The mouse pointer changes to a plus sign and is positioned to the right and lower border of the first table (Figure 3-103).

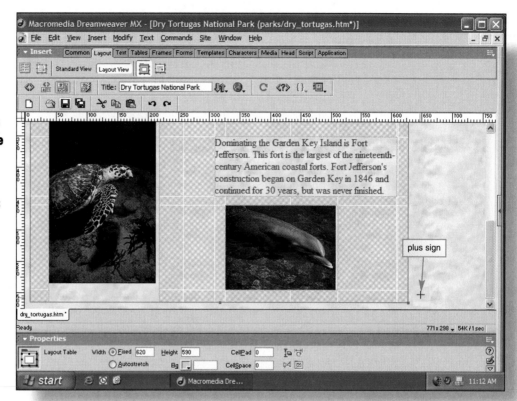

FIGURE 3-103

2 **Drag to the left to create a table with an approximate width of 620 and an approximate height of 350 as shown in Figure 3-104. Make any necessary width and height adjustments in the Property inspector.**

The new table is inserted into the Document window (Figure 3-104).

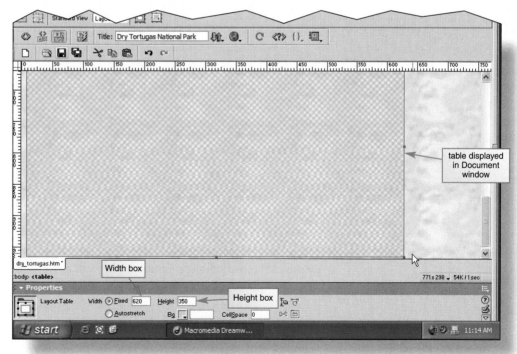

FIGURE 3-104

The next task is to add the cells to the table. Perform the following steps to add the four cells.

TO ADD THE FOUR CELLS TO THE DRY TORTUGAS NATIONAL PARK WEB PAGE

1 If necessary, scroll up. Click the Draw Cell Layout button on the Layout tab and then position the insertion point about 10 pixels below the top of the table. Draw a cell with an approximate width of 615 pixels and an approximate height of 85 pixels. Select the cell and make any necessary adjustments to the width and height in the Property inspector.

2 Click the Draw Cell Layout button and draw a second cell about 5–10 pixels below the first cell with an approximate width of 285 and an approximate height of 150. Select the cell and make any necessary adjustments to the width and height in the Property inspector.

3 Click the Draw Cell Layout button and draw a third cell to the right of the second cell and about 5–10 pixels below cell 1 with an approximate width of 275 and an approximate height of 130. Select the cell and make any necessary adjustments to the width and height in the Property inspector.

4 Click the Draw Cell Layout button and draw a fourth cell about 10 pixels below the second cell and about 100 pixels from the left border with an approximate width of 425 and an approximate height of 35. Select the cell and make any necessary adjustments to the width and height in the Property inspector.

5 Scroll the page to view the tables and cells as shown in Figure 3-105.

An overview of the tables and cells in the Dry Tortugas Document window is shown in Figure 3-105.

Next, you will add content to the cells in table 2. Three of the cells will contain text and one of the cells will contain an image. Two of the text cells will contain links. Complete the following steps to add text and the image to the cells and to create the links for table 2. Figure 3-82 on page DW 3.58 shows the completed project.

TO ADD CONTENT TO TABLE 2 OF THE DRY TORTUGAS NATIONAL PARK PAGE

1 Click cell 1 and type the text from Part 3 in Table 3-5 on page DW 3.67 into the cell.

2 Click cell 2 and type the text from Part 4 in Table 3-5 into the cell.

3 Click cell 4 and type the text from Part 5 in Table 3-5 into the cell.

4 Select the text in cell 2 and then click the Align Right button in the Property inspector.

5 Select the first instance of Dry Tortugas National Park in cell 2. Type http://www.nps.gov/dry_tort/ in the Link box to create an absolute link.

6 Select the second instance of Dry Tortugas National Park. Click Insert on the menu bar and then click Email Link. When the Email Link dialog box is displayed, type dry_tortugas@parks.gov for the e-mail address. Click the OK button.

7 Select the text in cell 4 and then click the Align Center button in the Property inspector.

8 Select Home in cell 4 in the second table (last cell in the table). Type index.htm in the Link box to create the relative link.

9 Select Everglades National Park. Type everglades.htm in the Link box to create the relative link.

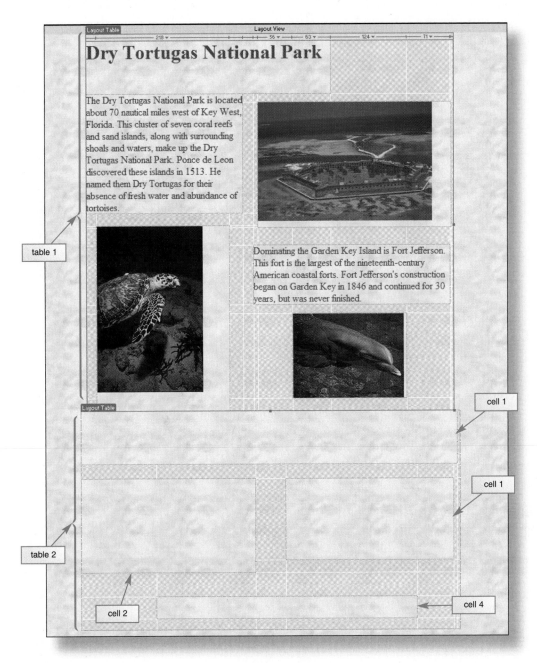

FIGURE 3-105

10 Select Biscayne National Park. Type `biscayne.htm` in the Link box to create the relative link.

11 Click the expand/collapse arrow on the Site panel. Drag the trees.jpg image to the third cell. Click the image and then drag a handle to resize the image to fit the cell. Click anywhere outside the cell to deselect it.

12 Click the Save button in the Standard toolbar.

13 Collapse the Site panel (Figure 3-106 on the next page).

The table is displayed as shown in Figure 3-106.

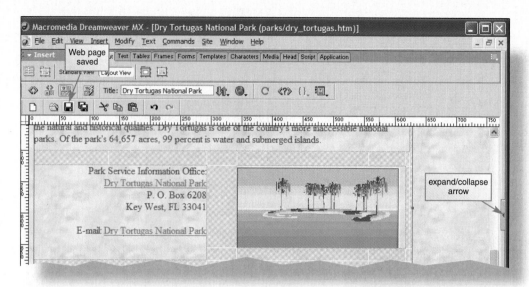

FIGURE 3-106

Centering the Table in Standard View

Layout view does not provide all the features that are provided for a table in Standard view. For example, you cannot select a number of rows or select a number of columns when creating Web pages in Layout view, and you cannot center a table when in Layout view. To access these features requires that the table be displayed in Standard view. Your next task is to center the two tables. Each table in the Document window must be centered separately. Perform the following steps to display the Web page in Standard view and to center the tables.

Steps **To Center a Table Created in Layout View**

1 **Click the Standard View button on the Layout tab. If necessary, click in a cell in the second table. Point to the <table> tag in the tag selector.**

The table is displayed in Standard view (Figure 3-107).

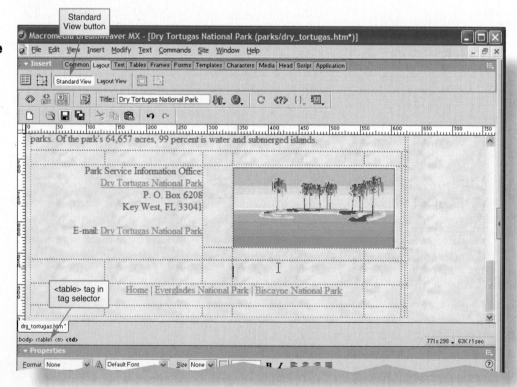

FIGURE 3-107

2 Click the <table> tag. Click the Align box arrow in the Property inspector and then click Center.

The second table is selected and centered in the Document window (Figure 3-108).

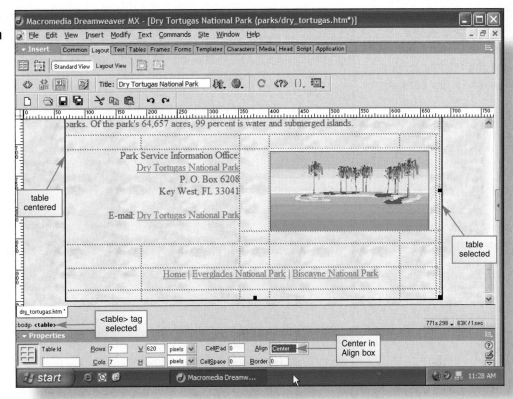

FIGURE 3-108

3 Scroll to the top and then click any cell in the first table. Click the <table> tag in the tag selector. Click the Align box arrow and select Center.

The first table is centered in the Document window (Figure 3-109).

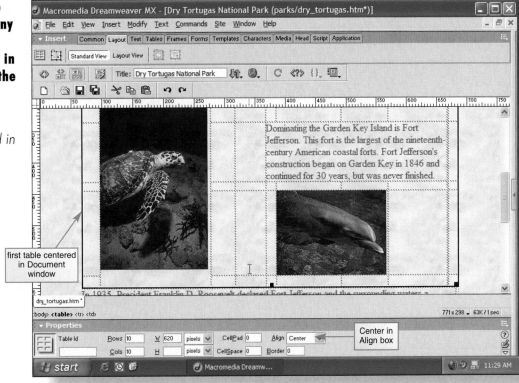

FIGURE 3-109

4 **Click the Save button in the Standard toolbar and then press the F12 key to view the page in the browser.**

The Web page displays centered in the browser (Figure 3-110)

5 **Close the browser and then close the Dry Tortugas page in Dreamweaver.**

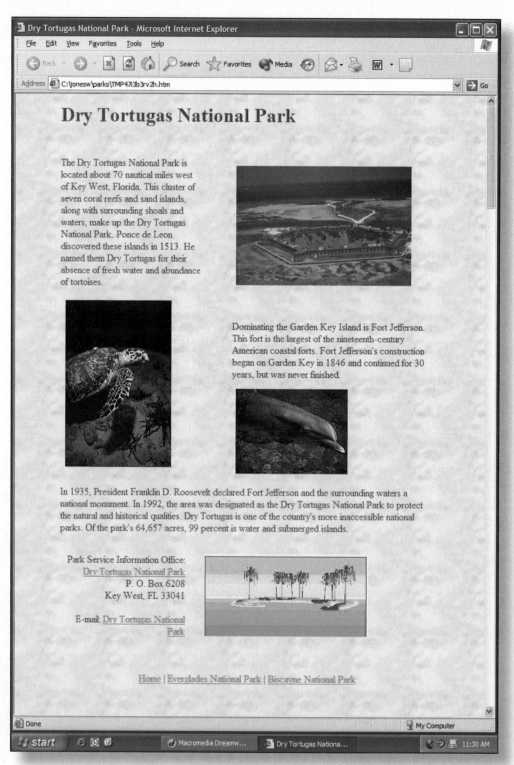

FIGURE 3-110

Head Content

HTML files consist of two main sections: the head section and the body section. The head section is one of the more important sections of a Web page. A standard HTML page contains a <head> tag and a <body> tag. Contained within the head section is site and page information. With the exception of the title, the information contained in the head does not display in the browser. Some of the information contained in the head is accessed by the browser and other information is accessed by other programs such as search engines and server software. In Figure 3-111, the head content of the Everglades page is displayed. The title and the default meta tag are the only pieces of information currently contained between the start <head> and end </head> tags.

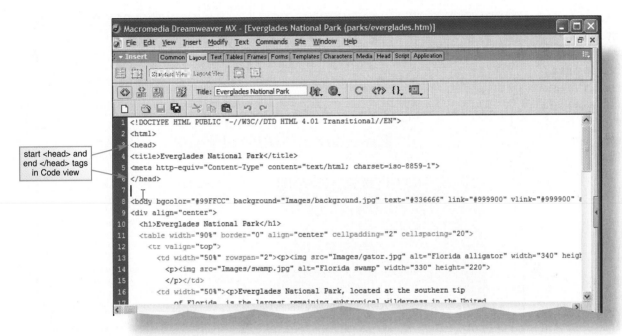

start <head> and
end </head> tags
in Code view

FIGURE 3-111

Head Content Elements

Dreamweaver makes it easy to add content to the head section by providing the Head tab in the Insert bar. The Head tab contains the following elements that can be added to your Web page.

META   A <meta> tag contains information about the current document. This information is used by servers, browsers and search engines. HTML documents can have as many <meta> tags as needed, but each item uses a different set of tags.

KEYWORDS   Keywords is a list of words that someone would type into a search engine search field.

DESCRIPTION   The description contains a sentence or two that can be used in a search engine's results page.

REFRESH   The <refresh> tag is processed by the browser to reload the page or load a new page after a specified amount of time has elapsed.

More About

Head Content

Meta tags are information inserted into the head content area of Web pages. The meta description tag allows you to influence the description of a page in the search engines that support the tag. For more information about meta tags, visit the Dreamweaver MX More About Web page (scsite.com/ dreamweavermx/ more.htm) and then click Dreamweaver MX Meta tags.

BASE The base tag sets the base URL to provide an absolute link and/or a link target that the browser can use to resolve link conflicts.

LINK The link element defines a relationship between the current document and another file. This is not the same as a link in the Document window.

Keywords, descriptions, and refresh settings are special-use cases of the meta tag. Complete the following steps to add keywords and a description to the Everglades National Park page.

Steps | To Add Keywords and a Description

1 Press the F8 key to display the Site panel and double-click everglades.htm to open the Everglades National Park page. Close the Site panel. Point to the Head tab in the insert bar (Figure 3-112).

FIGURE 3-112

2 Click the Head tab.

The buttons on the Head tab are displayed (Figure 3-113).

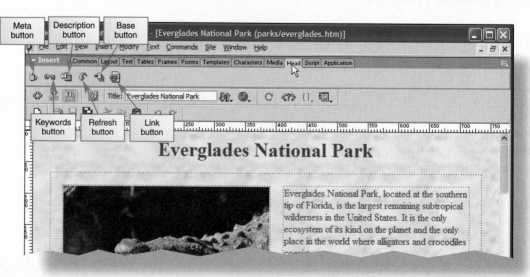

FIGURE 3-113

3 **Click the Keywords button on the Head tab. Type the following keywords in the Keywords text box. Separate each keyword with a comma:** parks, Florida, national parks, state parks **and then point to the OK button.**

Keywords are added to the Keywords dialog box (Figure 3-114). When a search is done with a search engine for any of the keywords, the Web site address will be displayed in the browser search results.

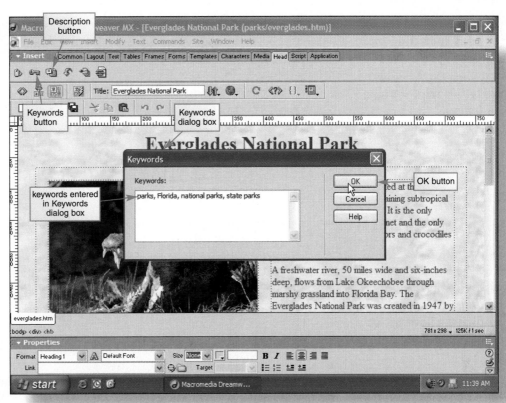

FIGURE 3-114

4 **Click the OK button and then click the Description button on the Head tab. Type** A Web site featuring Florida state and national parks **in the Description text box and then point to the OK button.**

The Description dialog box is displayed as shown in Figure 3-115.

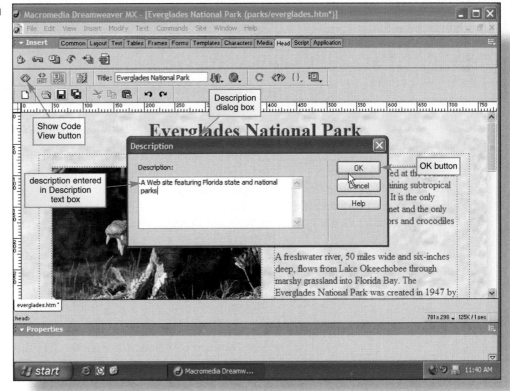

FIGURE 3-115

5 **Click the OK button and then click the Show Code View button on the Document toolbar. Point to the Show Design View button.**

The keywords and description that you entered are displayed in Code view (Figure 3-116).

6 **Click the Show Design View button on the Document toolbar and then click the Save button on the Standard toolbar.**

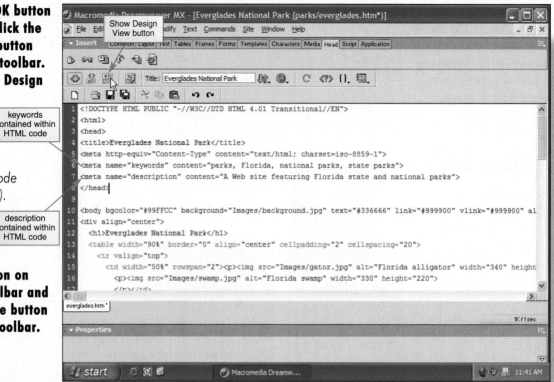

FIGURE 3-116

1. Click Show Code View button on Document toolbar, type keywords code in code window

Publishing a Web Site

In Project 1 you defined a local site, and in Projects 1, 2, and 3, you added Web pages to the local site. This local site resides on your computer's hard disk, a network drive, or possibly a Zip disk. You can view the organization of all files and folders in your site through the Site panel.

To prepare a Web site and make it available for others to view requires that you **publish** your site by putting it on a Web server for public access. A **Web server** is an Internet- or intranet-connected computer that delivers, or *serves up*, Web pages. You **upload** files to a folder on a server and **download** files to a folder in the Site panel. Generally, when Web site designers publish to a folder on a Web site, they do so by using a file transfer (FTP) program such as WS_FTP or Cute FTP. Dreamweaver, however, includes built-in support that enables you to connect and transfer your local site to a Web server without requiring an additional program. To publish to a Web server requires that you have access to a Web server.

Publishing and maintaining your site using Dreamweaver involves the following steps:

1. Use the Site Definition Wizard to enter the FTP information.
2. Specify the Web server to which you want to publish your Web site.
3. Connect to the Web server and upload the files.
4. Synchronize the local and remote sites.

Your school or company may have a server that you can use to upload your Web site. Free Web hosting services such as those provided by Angelfire, Tripod, or GeoCities are other options. These services, as well as many other hosting services, also offer low-cost Web hosting from approximately $3.95 to $9.95 a month. The FreeSite.com contains a list of free and inexpensive hosting services, and FreeWebspace.net provides a PowerSearch form for free and low-cost hosting. Table 3-6 contains a list of Web hosting services. Appendix D contains step-by-step instructions on publishing a Web site to a remote folder.

Table 3-6	Web Site Hosting Services	
NAME	*WEB SITE*	*COST*
Angelfire®	angelfire.lycos.com	Free (ad supported); starting at $4.95 monthly ad free
Yahoo! GeoCities	geocities.yahoo.com	Free (ad supported); starting at $4.95 monthly ad free
Tripod®	tripod.lycos.com/	Free (ad supported); starting at $4.95 monthly ad free
The FreeSite.com	thefreesite.com/Free_Web_Space	A list of free and inexpensive hosting sites
FreeWebspace.net	freewebspace.net	A searchable guide for free Web space

For an updated list of Web site hosting services, visit the Macromedia Dreamweaver Web page (scsite.com/dreamweavermx) and then click Web Hosting. If required by your instructor, publish the Florida Parks Web site to a remote server by following the steps in Appendix D.

With your work completed, you are ready to quit Dreamweaver.

More *About*

Publishing Your Florida Parks Web Site

Appendix D contains step-by-step instructions on publishing the Florida Parks Web site.

Quitting Dreamweaver

After you add pages to your Web site and add the head content, Project 3 is complete. To close the Web site, quit Dreamweaver MX, and return control to Windows, perform the following step.

TO CLOSE THE WEB SITE AND QUIT DREAMWEAVER

1 Click the Close button on the right corner of the Dreamweaver title bar.

The Dreamweaver window, the Document window, and Florida Parks Web site all close. If you have unsaved changes, Dreamweaver will prompt you to save the changes. Clicking the Yes button in the Dreamweaver MX dialog box saves the changes.

CASE PERSPECTIVE SUMMARY

As planned, your team finished designing the three pages for the Florida Parks Web site. Using tables to help with the layout enabled you to design the pages better. Joan obtained server space for your Web site and you used Dreamweaver to define, connect, and upload the Web site. Then, you used Dreamweaver's synchronization feature. All team members agree that this feature will become more important as you continue to expand the site. You shared with Joan and Will the importance of adding head content to all Web pages. Everyone agrees that adding the new pages made the Web site more impressive.

Project Summary

Project 3 introduced you to tables and to Web page design using tables. You created three Web pages, using the Standard view for two pages and the Layout view for the third page. You merged and split cells and learned how to add text and images to the tables. Next, you added a border color and cell background color. Finally, you added head content to one of the Web pages.

What You Should Know

Having completed this project, you now should be able to perform the tasks in Table 3-6.

Table 3-7   Project 3 What You Should Know

TASK NUMBER	TASK	PAGE NUMBER
1	Start Dreamweaver and Close Open Panels	DW 3.08
2	Copy Data Files to the Parks Web Site	DW 3.09
3	Add a Color Scheme and Background Image to the Everglades National Park Web Page	DW 3.10
4	Insert and Format the Heading	DW 3.11
5	Display the Insert Bar and Select the Layout Category	DW 3.12
6	Insert a Table Using Standard View	DW 3.13
7	Select and Center a Table	DW 3.21
8	Change Vertical Alignment from Middle to Top	DW 3.23
9	Specify Column Width	DW 3.24
10	Add Everglades National Park Text	DW 3.25
11	Add a Second Table to the Everglades National Park Web Page	DW 3.27
12	Adjust the Table Width	DW 3.30
13	Add Links to the Everglades National Park Page	DW 3.31
14	Merge Two Cells	DW 3.34
15	Add Images to a Standard View Table	DW 3.35
16	Add a Color Scheme and Background Image to the Biscayne National Park Web Page	DW 3.42
17	Insert and Center a Table	DW 3.43
18	Merge Cells in Rows 1 and 3	DW 3.44

TASK NUMBER	TASK	PAGE NUMBER
19	Add a Heading to Row 1	DW 3.45
20	Adjust the Column Width	DW 3.47
21	Add Text and Images to the Biscayne National Park Web Page	DW 3.49
22	Add Border Color and Cell Background Color	DW 3.54
23	Add Links to and Spell Check the Biscayne National Park Page	DW 3.56
24	Add a Color Scheme and Background Image to the Dry Tortugas National Park Web Page	DW 3.57
25	Display the Ruler	DW 3.59
26	Create the First Layout Table	DW 3.60
27	Add Layout Cells	DW 3.62
28	Add Text and Images to Table 1 of the Dry Tortugas National Park Web Page	DW 3.67
29	Add a Second Table to the Dry Tortugas National Park Web Page	DW 3.71
30	Add the Four Cells to the Dry Tortugas National Park Web Page	DW 3.72
31	Add Content to Table 2 of the Dry Tortugas National Park Page	DW 3.72
32	Center a Table Created in Layout View	DW 3.74
33	Add Keywords and a Description	DW 3.78
34	Close the Web Site and Quit Dreamweaver	DW 3.81

Apply Your Knowledge

1 Modifying the B & B Lawn Service Web

Instructions: Start Dreamweaver. If the panels display, press the F4 key to close all panels. See the inside back cover of this book for instructions for downloading the Data Disk or see your instructor for information on accessing the files in this book.

The B & B Lawn Service Web site currently contains four pages. You will add a fifth page with a table created using Standard View. You use the Untitled-1 window that displays when you start Dreamweaver. The new Web page will include a 7-row, 3-column centered table with a list of services, how often the services are scheduled, and the price of each service. You merge one of the rows and then add and center an image in the row. A border color is applied to the entire table and the first row has a background color applied. Keywords and a description are added. You then add a link to the home page, save the page, and upload the Web site to a Web server. The new page added to the Web site is shown in Figure 3-117. Software and hardware settings determine

how a Web page is displayed in a browser. Your Web page may display differently than the one in Figure 3-117. For a selection of images and backgrounds, visit the Dreamweaver MX Media Web page (scsite.com/ dreamweavermx/media) and then click Media below Project 3.

Appendix D contains instructions for uploading your local site to a remote site.

1. Display the Insert bar, Property inspector, Standard toolbar, and Site panel. Select Lawn Service from the Site pop-up menu in the Site panel.

2. Use Dreamweaver's integrated file browser to copy the triming.gif image from the Data Files to your /lawn/Images folder.

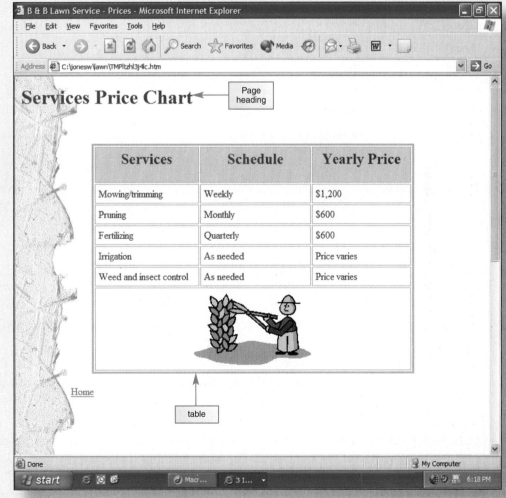

FIGURE 3-117

(continued)

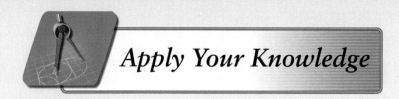

Apply Your Knowledge

Modifying the B & B Lawn Service Web *(continued)*

3. Apply the color scheme you added in Project 1 (Green background and Brown, Yellow, Red text and links). Use the Page Properties dialog box to add the background.gif image and to change the Links color to #CC3333 (Color Cubes palette, row 8 from the top and column 11 from the left).

4. Click the upper-left corner of the Document window. Type Services Price Chart and then apply Heading 1 to the text. Press the ENTER key and then click the Layout tab on the Insert bar. If necessary, click the Standard View button and then click the Insert Table button on the Layout tab. Type the following data in the Insert Table dialog box: 7 for Rows, 5 for Cell Padding, 3 for Columns, 2 for Cell Spacing, 70 for Width, and 3 for Border.

5. Type the text as shown in Table 3-8. Press the TAB key to move from cell to cell.

Table 3-8 Lawn Services Price Chart		
SERVICES	*SCHEDULE*	*YEARLY PRICE*
Mowing/trimming	Weekly	$1,200
Pruning	Monthly	$600
Fertilizing	Quarterly	$600
Irrigation	As needed	Price varies
Weed and insect control	As needed	Price varies

6. Click anywhere in row 1 and then click the <tr> tag in the tag selector to select row 1. Apply Heading 2 and center the heading. Click the Bg box in the Property inspector and apply background color #FF9900 (Color Cubes palette, row 7 from the top and column 3 from the right).

7. Click anywhere in row 7 in the table and then click the <tr> tag in the tag selector to select row 7. Click the Merge Cells button and then click the Align Center button in the Property inspector. With the insertion point in the middle of the merged row 7, drag the triming.gif image to the insertion point. Select the image and then type Tree trimming for the Alt text.

8. Click the <table> tag in the tag selector and then apply border color #FF9900 (Color Cubes palette, row 7 from the top and column 3 from the right). Center the table.

9. Position the insertion point outside the table by clicking to the right of the table. Press the ENTER key and then click the Text Indent button two times. Type Home and then create a relative link to the index.htm file.

10. Click the Head tab on the Insert bar and then click the Keyword button. When the Keyword dialog box is displayed, type lawn service, price schedule, your name in the Keywords text box and then click the OK button. Click the Description button. When the Description dialog box is displayed, type B & B Lawn Service price schedule in the Description text box, and then click the OK button.

11. Title the page B & B Lawn Service - Prices. Check spelling. Save the Web page and name it prices.

12. Print a copy of the page if required by your instructor. Close the Lawn Service Web site. Close Dreamweaver.

In the Lab

1 Adding a Page with a Table to the CandleDust Web Site

Problem: Publicity from the Web site has generated several requests for examples of Mary Stewart's candles. Mary has asked you to add a page to the site that shows some of her creations and the price of each candle. The Web page will have a link to the home page and will be named products. The new page is shown in Figure 3-118. Appendix D contains instructions for uploading your local site to a remote site. For a selection of images and backgrounds, visit the Dreamweaver MX Media Web page (scsite.com/dreamweavermx/media) and then click Media below Project 3.

Instructions: Perform the following tasks:

1. Start Dreamweaver. If necessary, press F4 to close the open panels. Display the Insert bar, Property inspector, Standard toolbar, and Site panel. Select CandleDust from the Site pop-up menu in the Site panel.

2. Use Dreamweaver's integrated file browser to copy the six images (candle3.gif through candle8.gif) from the Data Files to your /candle/Images folder.

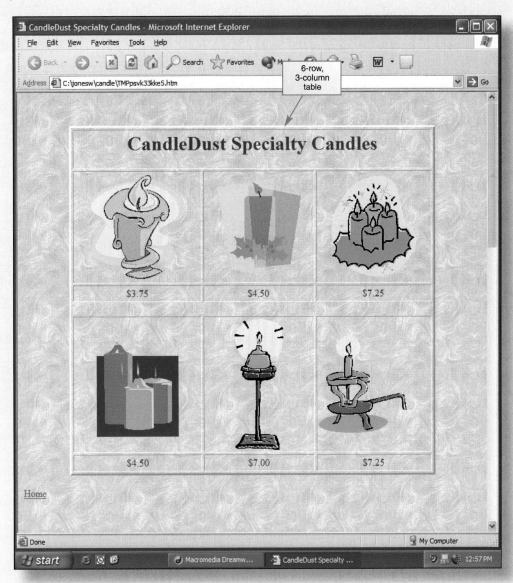

FIGURE 3-118

(continued)

In the Lab

Adding a Page with a Table to the CandleDust Web Site *(continued)*

3. Apply the color scheme you added in Project 1 (Purple background and Blue,Purple,Green text and links). Use the Page Properties dialog box to add the background.gif image. Title the page CandleDust Specialty Candles and save the page as products.

4. Click the upper left corner of the page and then press the ENTER key.

5. If necessary, click the Insert bar's Layout tab, the Standard View button, and then the Insert Table button. Enter the following data in the Insert Table dialog box: 6 for Rows, 3 for Cell Padding, 3 for Columns, 3 for Cell Spacing, 80 for Width, and 3 for Border. Center the table.

6. Merge the three cells in row 1 into one cell. Click the Align Center button in the Property inspector and then type CandleDust Specialty Candles for the heading. Apply Heading 1 to the text heading.

7. Click column 1, row 2 and then drag to select all cells in rows 2 through 6. Click the Align Center button, click the Vert box arrow, and then select Middle. Select column 1, rows 2 through 6. Click the Width box and type 33% as the new width. Repeat this step for column 2, rows 2 through 6, and column 3, rows 2 through 6.

8. Click column 1, row 2 and drag candle3.gif to the insertion point. Repeat this step dragging candle4.gif to column 2, row 2, and candle5.gif to column 3, row 2.

9. Type the following information in row 3: $3.75 in column 1, $4.50 in column 2, and $7.25 in column 3.

10. Merge the three cells in row 4.

11. Click column 1, row 5 and drag candle6.gif to the insertion point. Repeat this step dragging candle7.gif to column 2, row 5, and candle8.gif to column 3, row 5.

12. Type the following information in row 6: $4.50 in column 1, $7.00 in column 2, and $7.25 in column 3.

13. Click outside of the table to the right and then press the ENTER key. Type Home and create a link from the products page to the index.htm page.

14. Save the products page and then view your page in your browser. Verify that your link works. Save the page. Print a copy of the Web page if required and hand it in to your instructor. Close your browser. Close Dreamweaver.

In the Lab

2 Adding a Table Page to the Credit Web Site

Problem: The Credit Protection Web site has become very popular. Marcy receives numerous e-mail messages requesting that the Web site be expanded. Several messages have included a request to provide some hints and tips about how to save money. Marcy asks you to create a new page for the Web site so she can share some of this information. Figure 3-119a shows the table layout, and the Web page is shown in Figure 1-119b on the next page. Appendix D contains instructions for uploading your local site to a remote site. For a selection of images and backgrounds, visit the Dreamweaver MX Media Web page (scsite.com/dreamweavermx/media) and then click Media below Project 3.

Instructions: Perform the following tasks:

1. Start Dreamweaver. Display the Insert bar, Property inspector, Standard toolbar, and Site panel. Select Credit Protection from the Site pop-up menu in the Site panel.

2. Apply the color scheme you added in Project 1 (Yellow background and Green,Blue,Purple text and links) and then add the background image. Title the page Tips and Hints and then save the page with the file name saving.

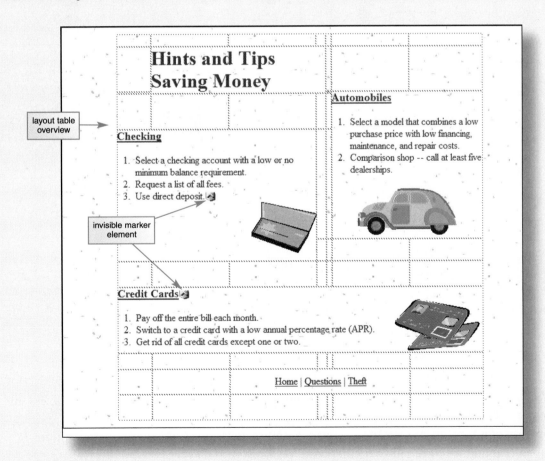

(a) Table Layout

FIGURE 3-119

(continued)

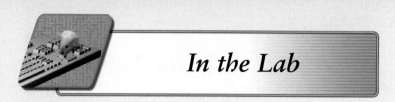

In the Lab

Adding a Table Page to the Credit Web Site *(continued)*

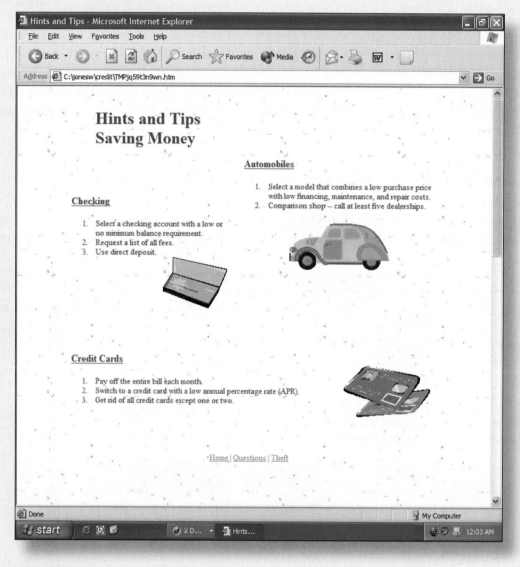

(b) Web Page

FIGURE 3-119 *(continued)*

3. Use Dreamweaver's integrated file browser to copy the three images (car.gif, check.gif, and credit_card.gif) from the Data Files to your /credit/Images folder. Display the ruler. Click the Insert bar's Layout tab and then click the Layout View button.

4. Click the Draw Layout Table button on the Layout tab and then create a table with a fixed width of approximately 600 and a height of approximately 615 pixels.

5. Use Figure 3-119a on the previous page as a guide and draw the five layout cells. Use Table 3-9 for widths and heights.

In the Lab

Table 3-9	Credit Protection Cell Layout Guide				
NUMBER	CELL NAME	W	H	IMAGE ALT TEXT	IMAGE NAME
1	Heading	285	75	None	None
2	Checking	325	210	Checking Account	check.gif
3	Automobiles	250	235	Car	car.gif
4	Credit Cards	600	105	Credit Cards	credit_card.gif
5	Links	295	40	None	None

6. Use Figure 3-119a as a reference and type the text into each of the layout cells. Apply Heading 1 to the text in the first cell. Apply Heading 3 to the headings in cells 2 through 4 and then underline the headings.

7. Insert the images into the cells. Refer to the invisible element marker in Figure 3-119a as the insertion point for the images in cells 2 and 4. For cell 3, press the ENTER key after item 2 and then click the Align Center button in the Property inspector. Drag the car.gif to the insertion point.

8. Add relative links to the three text items in cell 5.

9. Click the Standard View button on the Layout tab, select the table, and then center the table.

10. Click the Head tab in the Insert bar and then click the Description button. Click the Keyword button and then type credit, money, tips, checking, saving, your name in the Keywords dialog box. Click the Description button and then type Tips and hints on how to save money in the Description dialog box. Save the Web page as saving.

11. View the Web site in your browser and verify that your links work. Close the browser. If required, print a copy for your instructor.

3 Adding a Table Page to the Plant City Web Site

Problem: In his job as a member of the Plant City marketing group, Juan Benito has been exploring the city's history. On a recent tour, Juan discovered that the city contains many well-preserved historic homes. He would like to feature some of these homes on the Web site and has requested that you add a new page to the Plant City Web site. You elect to use a layout table to create this page. Figure 3-120a shows the layout table, and the Web page is displayed in 3-120b. Appendix D contains instructions for uploading your local site to a remote site. For a selection of images and backgrounds, visit the Dreamweaver MX Media Web page (scsite.com/dreamweavermx/media) and then click Media below Project 3.

Instructions: Perform the following tasks:

1. Start Dreamweaver. Display the Insert bar, Property inspector, Standard toolbar, and Site panel. Select Plant City from the Site pop-up menu in the Site panel.

2. Add the background image border you added in Project 2. Title the page Plant City, Florida - Historic Homes and then save the page with the file name homes.

(continued)

In the Lab

Adding a Table Page to the Plant City Web Site *(continued)*

3. Use Dreamweaver's integrated file browser to copy the four images (house01.gif through house04.gif) from the Data Files to your /city/Images folder. Display the ruler. Click the Insert bar's Layout tab and then click the Layout View button.

4. Create a layout table with a fixed width of approximately 650 and a height of approximately 675 pixels.

5. Use Figure 3-120a as a guide and draw the 10 layout cells. Use Table 3-10 on page DW 3.92 for widths, heights, and file names.

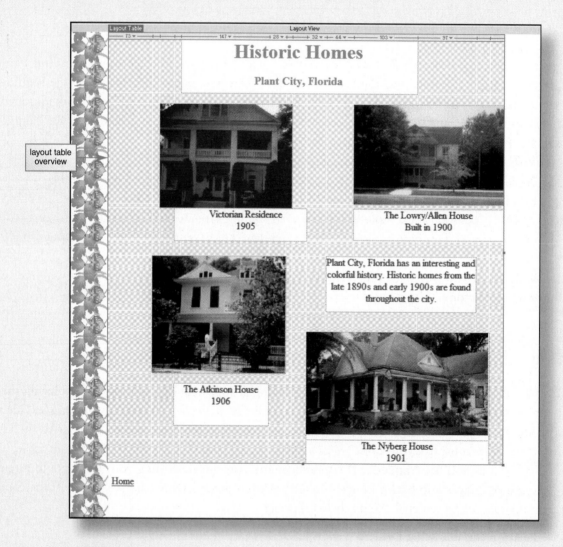

(a) Table Layout

FIGURE 3-120

In the Lab

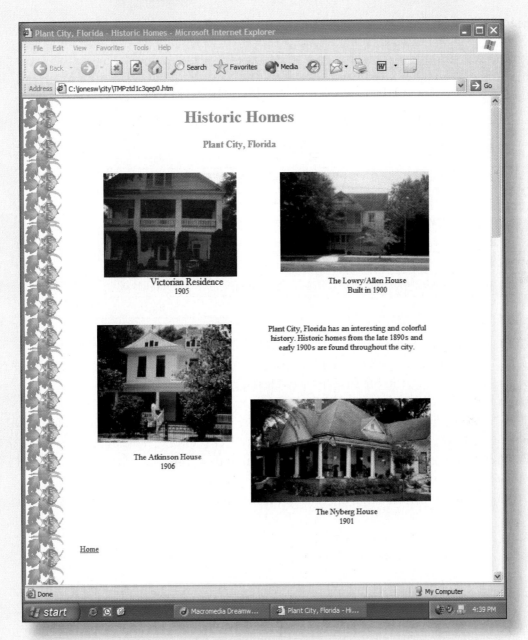

(b) Web Page

FIGURE 3-120 *(continued)*

(continued)

In the Lab

Adding a Table Page to the Plant City Web Site *(continued)*

Table 3-10	Plant City Cell Layout Guide				
NUMBER	**CELL NAME**	**W**	**H**	**IMAGE ALT TEXT**	**FILE NAME**
1	Heading	390	85	None	None
2	Victorian House	220	160	Victorian House	house01.gif
3	Text	220	50	None	None
4	Atkinson House	225	190	Atkinson House	house02.gif
5	Text	160	70	None	None
6	Lowry/Allen House	245	160	Lowry/Allen House	house03.gif
7	Text	245	50	None	None
8	Text	245	90	None	None
9	Nyberg House	300	170	Nyberg House	house04.gif
10	Text	300	40	None	None

6. Use Figure 3-120a on page DW 3.90 as a reference and type the text into each of the layout cells. Apply Heading 1 to the first line of text in the first cell and Heading 3 to the second line of text.

7. Insert the images into the cells. Refer to Table 3-10 for the image file names.

8. Click the Standard View button on the Layout tab, select the table, and then center the table.

9. Click the Keywords button, and then type `Plant City, Florida, homes, history, your name` in the Keywords dialog box. Click the Description button and then type `A tour of Plant City, Florida historic homes` in the Description dialog box.

10. View the Web site in your browser. Close the browser. If required, print a copy for your instructor.

Cases and Places

The difficulty of these case studies varies:
▌ are the least difficult; ▌▌ are more difficult; and ▌▌▌ are the most difficult.

1 ▌ The sports Web site has become very popular. Several of your friends have suggested that you add a statistics page. You agree that this is a good idea. Create the new page. Using the Internet or other resources, find statistics about your selected sport. Add a background image to the page and use Standard view to insert a table that contains your statistical information. Add an appropriate heading to the table and an appropriate title for the page. Create a link to the home page. Save the page in your sports Web site. For a selection of images and backgrounds, visit the Dreamweaver MX Media Web page (scsite.com/dreamweavermx/media) and then click Media below Project 3.

2 ▌ Modify your hobby Web site. Expand the topic and add an additional page with a table created in Standard view. The table should contain a minimum of three rows, three columns, and a 2-pixel border. Include information in the table about your hobby. Include a minimum of two images in the table. Merge one of the rows or one of the columns and add a border color. Add a background image to the page and give your page a title. Create a link to the home page. Save the page in your hobby Web site. For a selection of images and backgrounds, visit the Dreamweaver MX Media Web page (scsite.com/dreamweavermx/media) and then click Media below Project 3.

3 ▌▌ Modify your favorite type of music Web site by adding a new page. The new page should contain a table with three columns and four rows created in Standard view. Merge one of the rows and add a background color to the row. Add at least two images to your table. Center the images in the cell. View your Web pages in your browser. Give your page a title and save the page in your music subfolder. Appendix D contains instructions for uploading your local site to a remote site. For a selection of images and backgrounds, visit the Dreamweaver MX Media Web page (scsite.com/dreamweavermx/media) and then click Media below Project 3.

4 ▌▌ Your running for office campaign is going well. You want to add a new page to the Web site to include pictures and text listing some of your outstanding achievements. Apply a color scheme and a background image to the page. Draw a layout table with a minimum of four layout cells. Include your picture in one of the cells. Add an appropriate title, keywords, and a description to the page. Center the table. Save the page in the office subfolder and then view the page in your browser. Appendix D contains instructions for uploading your local site to a remote site. For a selection of images and backgrounds, visit the Dreamweaver MX Media Web page (scsite.com/dreamweavermx/media) and then click Media below Project 3.

Cases and Places

5 ▶▶▶ The students at your school are requesting more information about the student trips. Add another page to the student trips Web site. Add a heading and format it appropriately. Draw a layout table with a minimum of six layout cells. Include an image in three of the cells and text describing the three possible school trip destinations in the other three cells. Format the text and center the table. Center the images in each of three cells and add Alt text for each. Add a title, keywords, meta tags, and a description. Save the page and view it in your browser. Appendix D contains instructions for uploading your local site to a remote site.For a selection of images and backgrounds, visit the Dreamweaver MX Media Web page (scsite.com/dreamweavermx/media) and then click Media below Project 3.

APPENDIX A
Dreamweaver Help

Dreamweaver Help

This appendix shows you how to use the many components of Dreamweaver Help. At anytime while you are using Dreamweaver, you can interact with its Help system and display information on any Dreamweaver topic. It is a complete reference manual at your fingertips.

The Using Dreamweaver MX Help system is viewed through your browser. Comprehensive HTML-based information about all Dreamweaver features is included. The Using Dreamweaver MX Help system contains the following:

▶ A table of contents in which the information is organized by subject.
▶ An alphabetical index that points to important terms and links to related topics.
▶ A search tool that allows you to find any character string in all topic text.
▶ A Favorites list in which you can create a Favorites folder and store named groups of assets within a given category.

Other Help features include tutorial lessons, Guided Tour movies, context-sensitive help, Extending Dreamweaver Help, Using Cold Fusion Help, and eight online reference manuals, including an HTML reference manual.

The Dreamweaver Help Menu

You access Dreamweaver's Help features through the **Help menu** and function keys. Dreamweaver's Help menu provides an easy method to access the available Help options (Figure A-1).

FIGURE A-1

The Help menu commands access the following components:

WELCOME AND WHAT'S NEW The Welcome and What's New commands display buttons for an introduction to Design, Code, Develop, and What's New (Figure A-2). The What's New? button in the Welcome window and the What's New command both access the new features for returning Dreamweaver users.

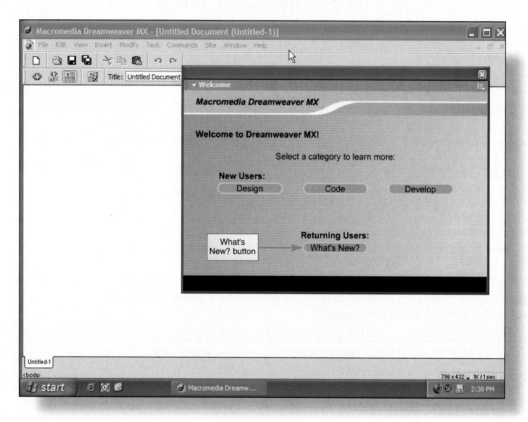

FIGURE A-2

TUTORIALS The Tutorials command accesses the Using Dreamweaver MX window. This window provides links to six tutorials. Each tutorial takes 30 to 45 minutes to complete. Tutorials include:

- Using Tables to Design a Page Layout Tutorial
- Image Alignment and Image Maps Tutorial
- Working with Dreamweaver Design Files Tutorial
- Designing with Cascading Style Sheets Tutorial
- Building a Master-Detail Page Set Tutorial
- Building an Insert Record Page Tutorial

USING DREAMWEAVER The Using Dreamweaver command displays the Using the Dreamweaver MX window. This feature is the most commonly used for locating information. Using Dreamweaver is covered in more detail later in this appendix.

EXTENDING DREAMWEAVER The Extending Dreamweaver MX Help system contains descriptions of the tools that are available for developers to extend Dreamweaver using Dreamweaver application programming interfaces.

USING COLDFUSION ColdFusion is an add-on Macromedia program used to build dynamic Web sites. ColdFusion Help in Dreamweaver MX is a subset of the documentation in ColdFusion MX. It includes all the topics that ColdFusion developers might find useful, including a full language reference.

REFERENCE When you click the Reference command, the Reference manual is displayed on the Reference tab in the Code panel in the Dreamweaver workspace. The Reference manual contains the complete text from several Web reference manuals, including references on HTML, cascading style sheets, JavaScript, and other Web-related features.

DREAMWEAVER EXCHANGE The Dreamweaver Exchange command allows access to the online Macromedia Exchange for Dreamweaver. This Web site contains resources for accessing extensions, learning about the extensions, and learning how to create extensions. Examples of extensions include a sales cart and a pop-up calendar. Some extensions are free and others are commercially developed and require payment.

MANAGE EXTENSIONS An **extension** is an add-on piece of software or plug-in that enhances Dreamweaver's capabilities. Extensions provide the Dreamweaver developer with the capability to customize how Dreamweaver looks and works. Clicking the Manage Extensions command displays the Manage Extension dialog box. Through this dialog box, the developer can install, manage, and import extensions.

CREATING AND SUBMITTING EXTENSIONS The Creating and Submitting Extensions command displays the Using the Extension Manager Help. This Help file is set up with the same configuration as Using Dreamweaver Help, which is covered in detail later in this appendix.

DREAMWEAVER SUPPORT CENTER The Dreamweaver Support Center command provides access to the online Macromedia Dreamweaver Support Center. This Web site offers technical notes, tutorials, an online forum, and other support information.

MACROMEDIA ONLINE FORUMS The Macromedia Online Forums command allows access to the Macromedia Online Forums Web page. The forums provide a place for developers of all experience levels to share ideas and techniques.

Using Dreamweaver MX Help

The Using Dreamweaver command accesses Dreamweaver's primary Help system and provides comprehensive information about all Dreamweaver features. Four options are available: Contents, Index, Search, and Favorites.

Using the Contents Sheet

The **Contents sheet** is useful for displaying Help when you know the general category of the topic in question, but not the specifics. Each topic in the Contents list is preceded by a book icon or question mark icon. A **book icon** indicates subtopics are available. Clicking the book icon (or associated link) displays the list of subtopics below that particular book. A **question mark icon** means information on the topic will display if you click the icon or the associated linked text. The steps on the next two pages show how to use the Contents sheet to obtain information on changing text color.

Steps **To Obtain Help Using the Contents Sheet**

Click Help on the menu bar and then click Using Dreamweaver. Dreamweaver displays the Using Dreamweaver MX window. If necessary, double-click the title bar to maximize the window and click the Contents tab. If necessary, adjust the width of the left pane by moving the mouse pointer over the border separating the two panes. When the mouse pointer changes to a double-headed arrow, drag to the right to expand the left pane. Point to the Adding Content book.

The Using Dreamweaver MX Help window displays (Figure A-3). Four options are available: Contents, Index, Search, and Favorites.

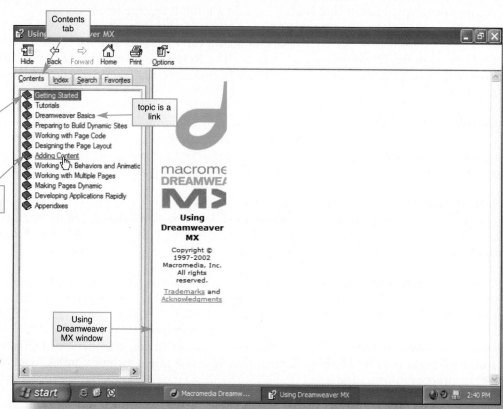

FIGURE A-3

2 **Click the Adding Content book link.**

The Adding Content book is opened, and the help information is displayed in the right pane (Figure A-4). Additional books are displayed below the topic. Links to these books also are displayed in the right pane.

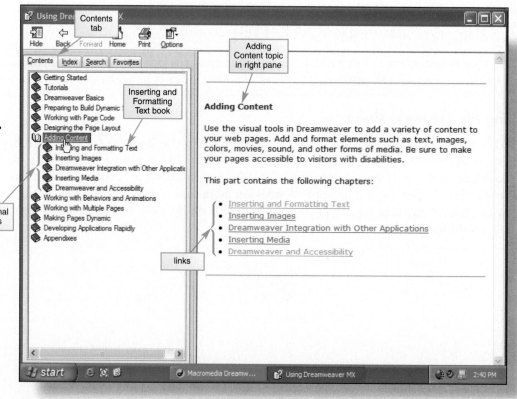

FIGURE A-4

3 **Click the Inserting and Formatting Text book, and then click the Formatting text book. Point to the Changing the text color link.**

The Formatting text book is opened and the linked topics are displayed in the left pane (Figure A-5). Related topics also are displayed in the right pane.

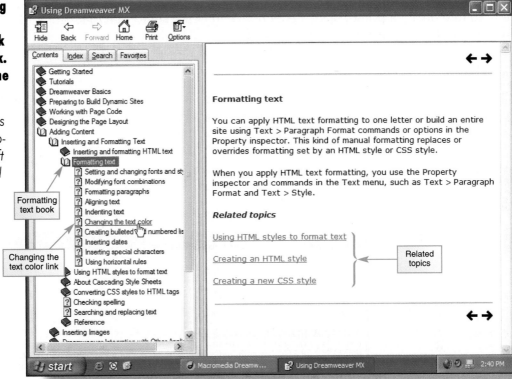

FIGURE A-5

4 **Click the Changing the text color link.**

The information on the subtopic is displayed in the right pane (Figure A-6).

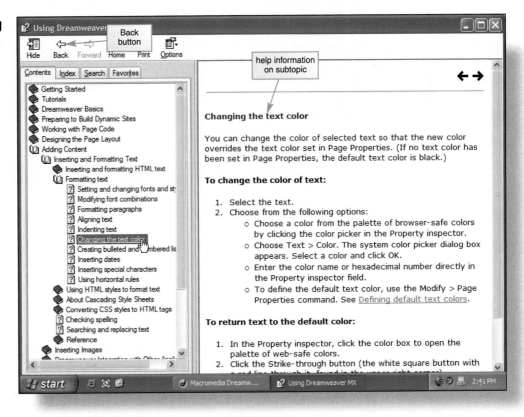

FIGURE A-6

Once the information on the subtopic is displayed, you can scroll through and read it or you can click the Print button to obtain a printed copy. If you decide to click another subtopic on the left or a link on the right, you can return to the original Help page by clicking the Back button.

Using the Index Sheet

The second sheet in the Using Dreamweaver MX window is the Index sheet. Use the **Index sheet** to display Help when you know the keyword or the first few letters of the keyword you want to look up. The following steps show how to use Index to obtain help on inserting images.

 To Use the Index Sheet

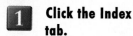 **Click the Index tab.**

The Index sheet is displayed (Figure A-7). The insertion point is blinking in the Type in the keyword to find text box.

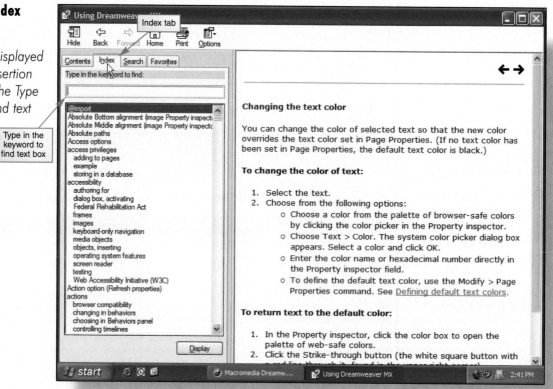

FIGURE A-7

2 Type images in the text box. Click inserting and then point to the Display button.

Dreamweaver scrolls through the list of topics. The topic, images, and subtopics below images are displayed in the left pane (Figure A-8). The subtopic, inserting, is highlighted.

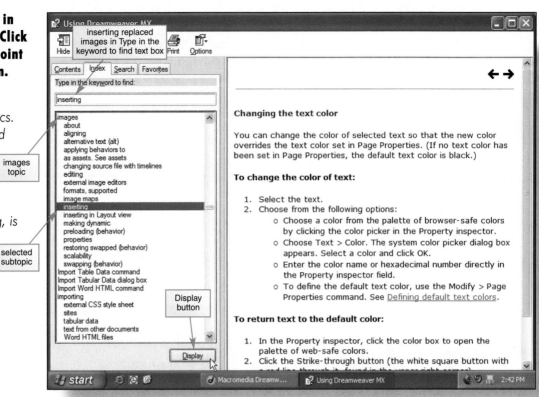

FIGURE A-8

3 Click the Display button.

Information about inserting an image is displayed in the right pane (Figure A-9).

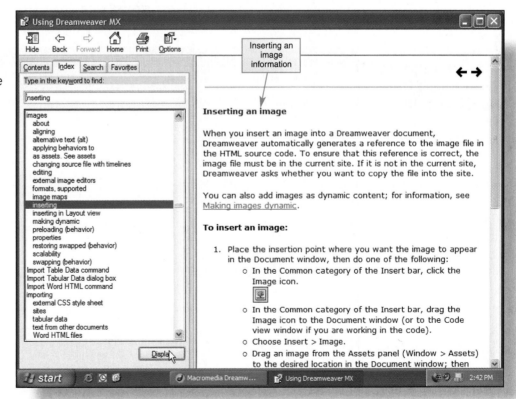

FIGURE A-9

Using the Search Sheet

Using the **Search** feature allows you to find any character string, anywhere in the text of the Help system. The following steps show how to use Search to obtain help about using bold text.

Steps **To Use the Search Sheet**

1 **Click the Search tab.**

The Search sheet is displayed (Figure A-10). The insertion point is blinking in the Type in the keyword to find text box.

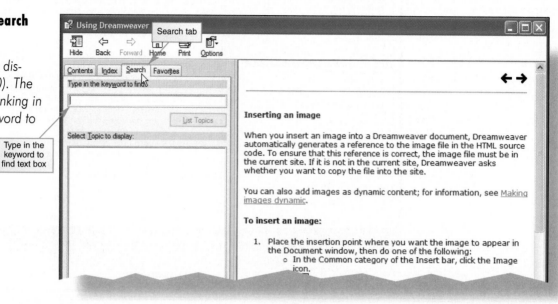

FIGURE A-10

2 **Type** Bold text **and then click the List Topics button. Click Setting Text property options and then point to the Display button.**

A list of topics containing references to bold and text is displayed in the left pane (Figure A-11). All of these topics contain the words bold and text somewhere within the document.

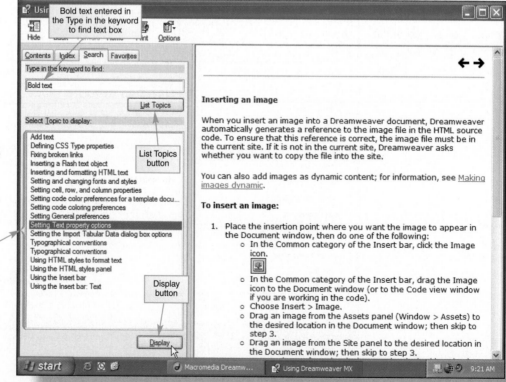

FIGURE A-11

3 Click the Display button.

The help screen for Setting Text property options is displayed in the right pane. All incidents of the words bold and text are highlighted in the document in the right pane (Figure A-12).

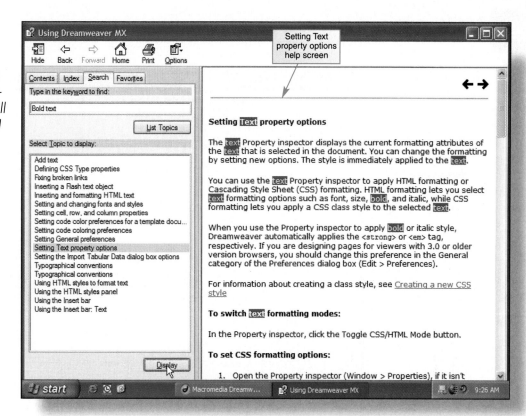

FIGURE A-12

Using the Favorites Sheet

If you find that you search or reference certain topics frequently, you can save these in the Favorites sheet. The steps on the next page show how to add the information about the bold text topic to the Favorites sheet.

Steps **To Add a Topic to the Favorites Sheet**

1 **Click the Favorites tab. Point to the Add button.**

The Favorites sheet is displayed in the left pane. The title of the information (Setting Text property options) is displayed in the Current topic text box in the left pane. The information on bold text that displayed as a result of your previous search is displayed in the right pane (Figure A-13).

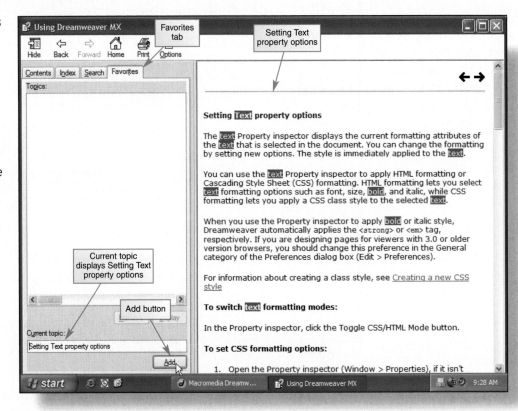

FIGURE A-13

2 **Click the Add button.**

The Setting Text property options topic is added to the Favorites sheet (Figure A-14).

3 **Close the Using Dreamweaver MX window and return to Dreamweaver.**

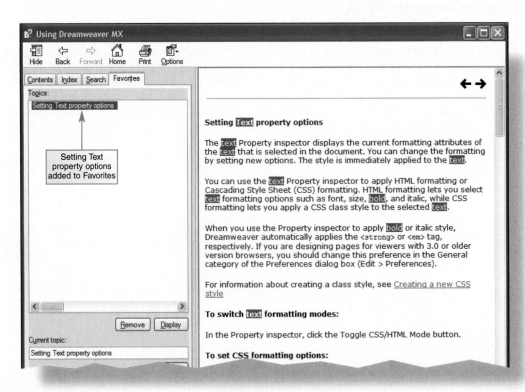

FIGURE A-14

You can add as many additional topics as you choose to the Favorites sheet. Then, when you need to reference the information, click Help on the menu bar, click Dreamweaver Help, and then click the Favorites tab. Another popular and easy-to-use Dreamweaver Help feature is context-sensitive help.

Context-Sensitive Help

Using **context-sensitive help,** you can open a relevant Help topic in each dialog box, panel, and inspector. To view these help features, click a Help button in a dialog box, choose Help on the Options pop-up menu in a panel group, or click the question mark icon in an inspector or other kind of window.

Using the Question Mark Icon to Display Help

Many of the windows and inspectors within Dreamweaver contain a question mark icon. Clicking this icon displays context-sensitive help. The following steps show how to use the question mark icon to view context-sensitive help about tables. In this example, a table is displayed and selected in the Document window and the Property inspector displays table properties.

 To Display Context-Sensitive Help on Tables

1 Point to the question mark icon in the Property inspector (Figure A-15).

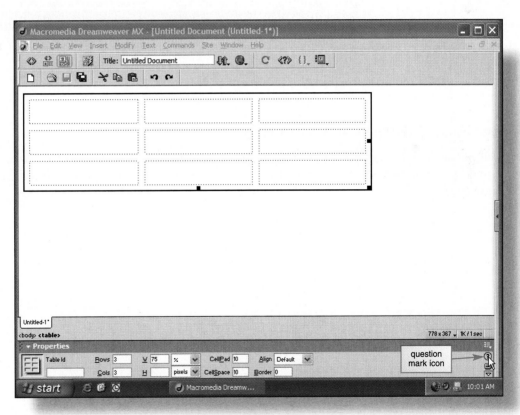

FIGURE A-15

2 Click the question mark icon.

The Using Dreamweaver MX window is displayed, and information pertaining to table properties is displayed in the right pane (Figure A-16). The Favorites tab is selected in the left pane because this was the last tab previously selected.

3 Close the Using Dreamweaver MX window and return to Dreamweaver.

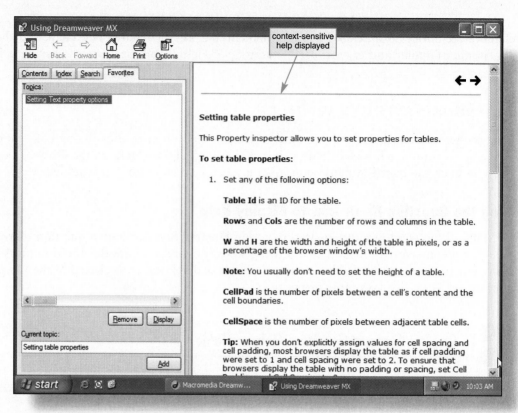

FIGURE A-16

Using the Options Menu to Display Help

All panels and dialog boxes also contain context-sensitive help. The following steps show how to display context-sensitive help for the Site panel. In this example, the Site panel is open and displayed within the Dreamweaver window.

To Use the Options Menu to Display Context-Sensitive Help for the Site Panel

Steps

1 **Click the Options button on the panel title bar and then point to Help on the Options pop-up menu.**

The Options pop-up menu is displayed (Figure A-17).

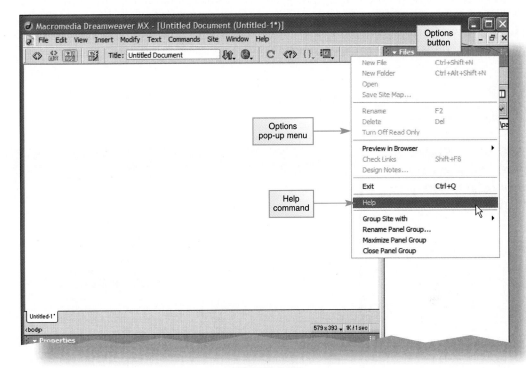

FIGURE A-17

2 **Click the Help command.**

The Using Dreamweaver MX window is displayed, and information pertaining to Using the Site panel is displayed in the right pane (Figure A-18). The Favorites tab is selected in the left pane because this was the last tab previously selected.

3 **Close the Using Dreamweaver MX window and return to Dreamweaver.**

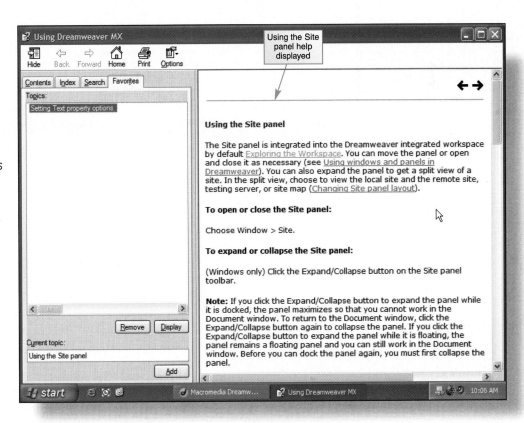

FIGURE A-18

Using the Reference Panel

The Reference panel in the Code panel group is another valuable Dreamweaver resource. The **Reference panel** provides you with a quick reference tool for HTML tags, JavaScript objects, cascading style sheets, and other Dreamweaver features. The following steps show how to access the Reference panel, review the various options, and select and display information on the <BODY> tag.

 Steps To Use the Reference Panel

1 Click Window on the menu bar and then point to Reference (Figure A-19).

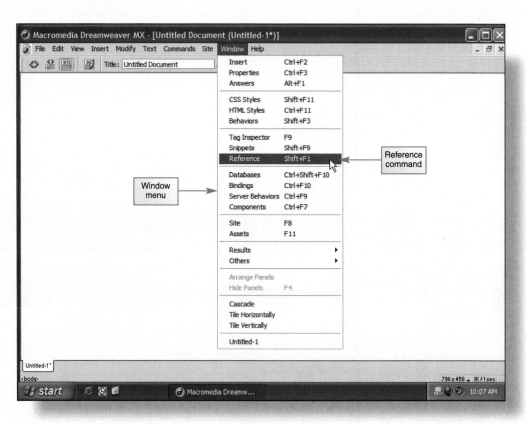

FIGURE A-19

2 **Click Reference.**

The Reference panel in the Code panel group is displayed (Figure A-20). The <A>...</A> tag is selected. Your screen may display a different tag.

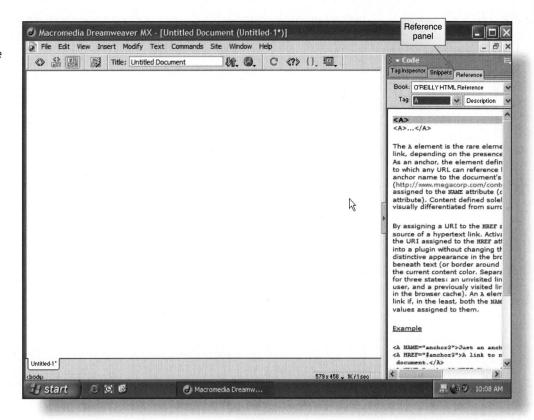

FIGURE A-20

3 **Click the Tag box arrow and then point to BODY in the tag list.**

BODY is highlighted in the tag list (Figure A-21).

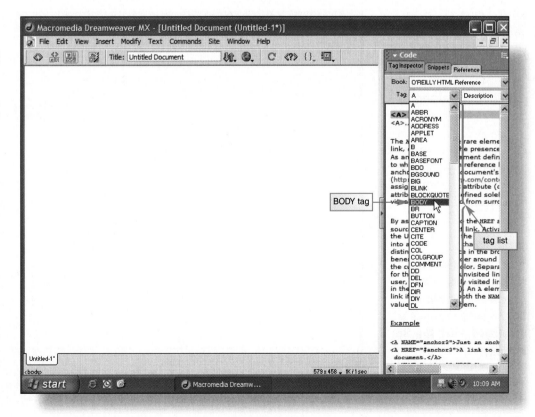

FIGURE A-21

4 **Click BODY.**

Information for the
<BODY> tag is displayed
(Figure A-22).

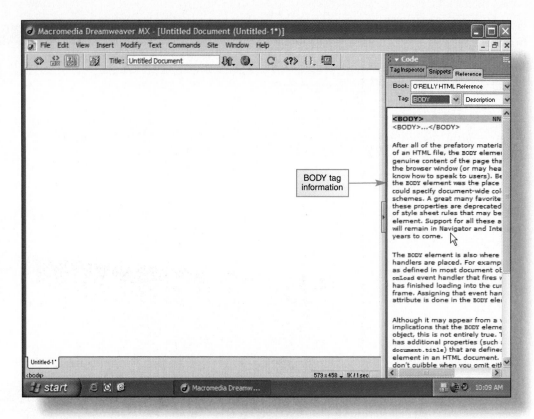

FIGURE A-22

5 **Click the Book box arrow and review the list of available reference books.**

A list of eight reference
books is displayed
(Figure A-23). These are
complete books and can be
accessed in the same way
the HTML reference book
was accessed.

6 **Close Dreamweaver. If the Macromedia Dreamweaver dialog box to save changes is displayed, click the No button.**

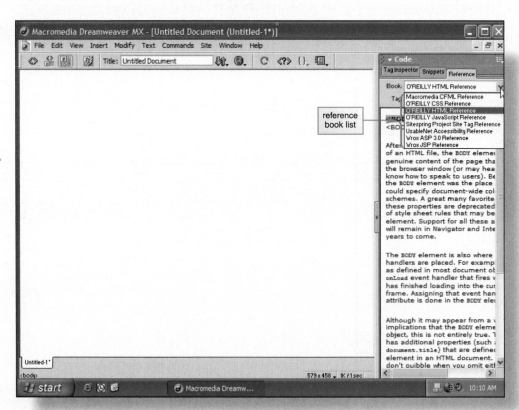

FIGURE A-23

Online Help Support

Dreamweaver provides several support Web sites, including online forums and links to third-party online forums. Examples of these online forums and discussion groups are as follows:

▶ Dreamweaver — For Dreamweaver users developing Web sites.

▶ Dreamweaver Application Development — For Dreamweaver users creating dynamic Web sites.

▶ Dreamweaver Extensibility — For Dreamweaver users interested in extending the functionality of Dreamweaver.

▶ Dynamic HTML — This group discusses questions and issues regarding Dynamic HTML.

▶ General Information — This group discusses general information regarding Macromedia products that does not pertain to the other online forums.

For a selection of Help links, visit the Dreamweaver MX Web page (scsite.com/dreamweavermx) and then click Appendix Help.

Use Help

1 Viewing the Dreamweaver What's New Features

Instructions: Start Dreamweaver. Perform the following tasks using the Dreamweaver What's New movie feature.

1. Click Help on the menu bar and then click What's New.
2. Select a movie in the What's New dialog box. The movie is a series of screens with forward and back buttons.
3. Click the buttons and view the movie by clicking the forward buttons.
4. Use a word processing program and write a short overview of what you learned.
5. Print a copy and hand in the printout to your instructor.

2 Using the Index Sheet

Instructions: Start Dreamweaver. Perform the following tasks using the Index sheet in the Using Dreamweaver MX Help system.

1. Click Help on the menu bar and then click Using Dreamweaver or press the F1 key to display the Using Dreamweaver MX window.
2. Click the Index tab and then type links in the Type in the keyword to find text box.
3. Click the subtopic, checking, and then click the Display button.
4. Read the information. Print a copy and hand in the printout to your instructor.

3 Using Context-Sensitive Help

Instructions: Start Dreamweaver. Perform the following tasks using context-sensitive help in the Assets panel.

1. Click Window on the menu bar and then click Assets to display the Assets panel.
2. Click the Assets panel Options button and then click Help on the Options pop-up menu.
3. Read each of the topics about the Assets panel.
4. Use your word processing program and prepare a report on how to set up a favorite list of assets.
5. Print a copy of your report and hand in the printout to your instructor.

APPENDIX B
Dreamweaver and Accessibility

Dreamweaver and Accessibility

Tim Berners-Lee, World Wide Web Consortium (W3C) founder, and inventor of the World Wide Web, indicates that the power of the Web is in its universality. He says that access by everyone regardless of disability is an essential aspect. In 1997, the World Wide Web Consortium launched the **Web Accessibility Initiative** and made a commitment to lead the Web to its full potential. The initiative includes promoting a high degree of usability for people with disabilities. The United States government established a second initiative addressing accessibility and the Web through Section 508 of the Federal Rehabilitation Act.

Dreamweaver includes features that assist you in creating accessible content. To design accessible content requires that you understand accessibility requirements and make subjective decisions as you create a Web site. Dreamweaver supports three accessibility options: screen readers, keyboard navigation, and operating system accessibility features.

Using Screen Readers with Dreamweaver

Screen readers assist the blind and vision impaired by reading text that is displayed on the screen through a speaker or headphones. The reader starts at the top-left corner of the page and reads the page content. If the Web site developer uses accessibility tags or attributes during the creation of the Web site, the screen reader also recites this information and reads non-textual information such as button labels and image descriptions. Dreamweaver makes it easy to add text equivalents for graphical elements and to add HTML tags to tables and forms through the accessibility dialog boxes. Dreamweaver supports two screen readers: JAWS and Window Eyes.

Activating the Accessibility Dialog Boxes

To create accessible pages in Dreamweaver, you associate information, such as labels and descriptions, with your page objects. After you have created this association, the screen reader recites the labels and descriptions information. You create the association by activating and attaching the accessibility dialog boxes to objects on your page. These dialog boxes appear when you insert an object for which you have activated the corresponding Accessibility dialog box. You activate the Accessibility dialog boxes through the Preferences dialog box. You can activate Accessibility dialog boxes for form objects, frames, images, media objects, and tables. The steps on the next two pages use the Florida Parks index page to show how to display the Preferences dialog box and activate the Image Accessibility dialog box.

Dreamweaver MX

 To Activate the Images Accessibility Dialog Box

1 **Start Dreamweaver and close all open panels. Click Edit on the menu bar and then point to Preferences (Figure B-1).**

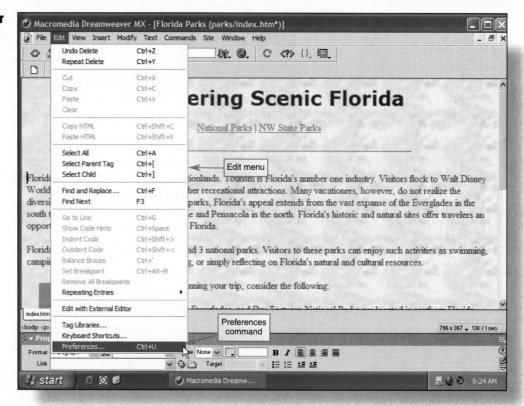

FIGURE B-1

2 **Click Preferences.**

The Preferences dialog box is displayed (Figure B-2).

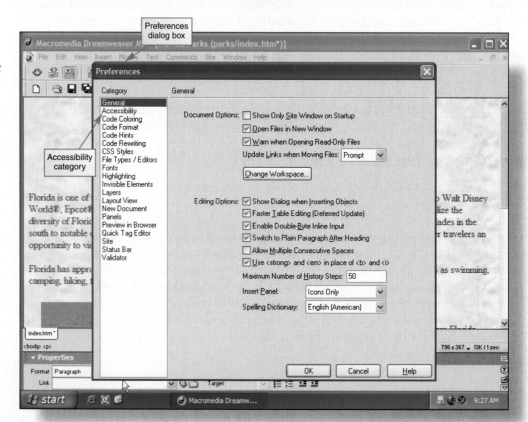

FIGURE B-2

Click Accessibility in the Category list, click Images in the Accessibility area, and then point to the OK button.

The Accessibility category is highlighted and the Images check box is selected (Figure B-3). The Accessibility area includes five different options for which you can activate Accessibility dialog boxes: Form Objects, Frames, Media, Images, and Tables.

4 **Click the OK button.**

The Preferences dialog box closes and the Dreamweaver Document window is displayed. No change is apparent in the Document window, but the Image Tag Accessibility Attributes dialog box is activated.

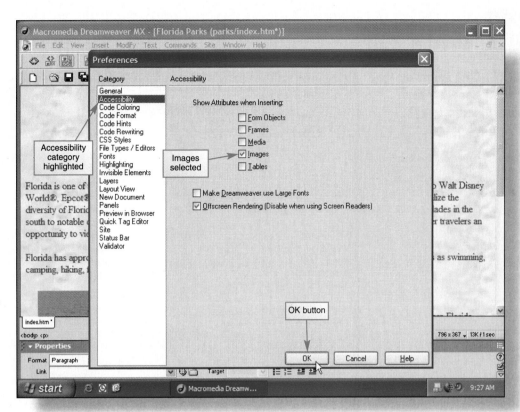

FIGURE B-3

Inserting Accessible Images

Selecting Images in the Accessibility area activates the Image Tag Accessibility Attributes dialog box. Thus, anytime you insert an image into a Web page, the dialog box will display. This dialog box contains two text boxes — Alternate Text and Long Description. The screen reader reads the information you enter in both text boxes. You should limit your Alternate Text entry to about 50 characters. For longer descriptions, provide a link in the Long Description text box to a file that gives more information about the image. It is not required that you enter data into both text boxes. The steps on the next three pages show how to use the Image Tag Accessibility Attributes dialog box when inserting an image.

To Insert Accessible Images

1 **Click Insert on the menu bar and then point to Image (Figure B-4).**

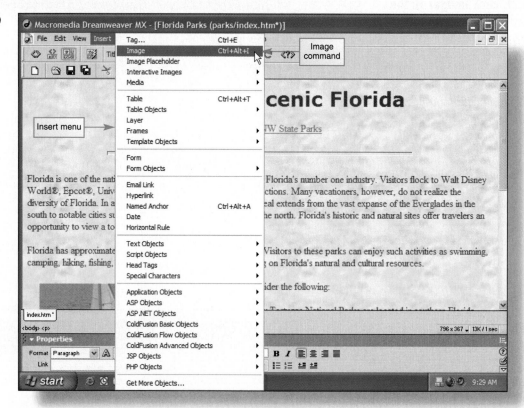

FIGURE B-4

2 **Click Image. If necessary, open the Images folder and then click a file name. Point to the OK button.**

The Select Image Source dialog box is displayed (Figure B-5).

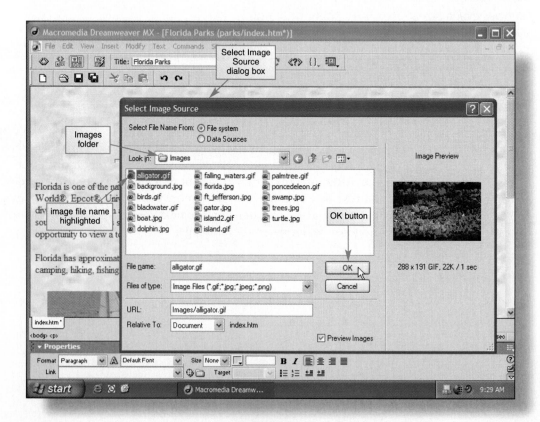

FIGURE B-5

3 Click the OK button.

The Image Tag Accessibility Attributes dialog box is displayed. The insertion point is blinking in the Alternate Text text box (Figure B-6). To display the Image Tag Accessibility Attributes dialog box requires that the image be inserted by using the Insert menu or by clicking the Image button on the Common tab of the Insert bar. Dragging an image from the Site panel to the Document window does not display the Image Tag Accessibility Attributes dialog box.

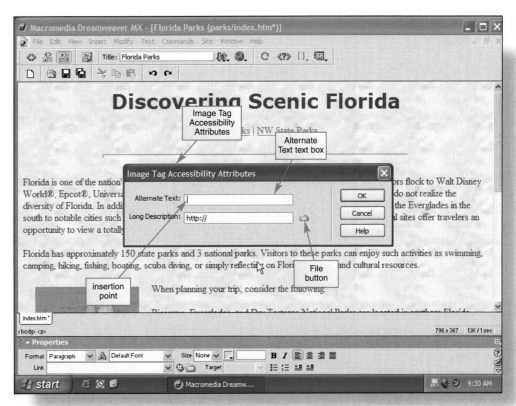

FIGURE B-6

4 Type a description of the image. Click the File button to display the Select File dialog box. If necessary, open the Images folder and then locate and click the image file. Point to the OK button.

The image description is displayed in the Alternate Text box and the long description file location is displayed in the Long Description text box (Figure B-7).

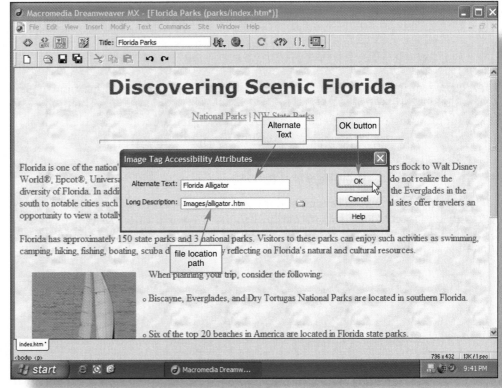

FIGURE B-7

5 **Click the OK button.**

The image is inserted into the Document window (Figure B-8). When the page is displayed in the browser, the screen reader recites the information you entered in the Image Tag Accessibility Attributes Alternate Text box. If you included a link to a file with additional information in the Long Description text box, the screen reader accesses the file and recites the text contained within the file.

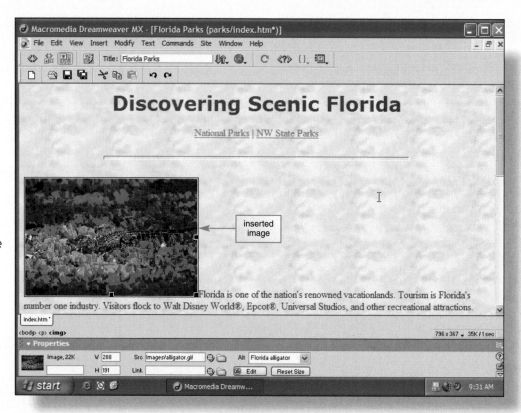

6 **Close Dreamweaver. Do not save the changes to the Web page.**

FIGURE B-8

Navigating Dreamweaver with the Keyboard

Keyboard navigation is a core aspect of accessibility. This feature also is of particular importance to users who have repetitive strain injuries (RSI) or other disabilities, or for those who would prefer to use the keyboard instead of a mouse. You can use the keyboard to navigate the following elements in Dreamweaver: floating panels, the Property inspector, dialog boxes, frames, and tables.

Using the Keyboard to Navigate Panels

When working in Dreamweaver, several panels may be open at one time. To move from panel to panel, press CTRL+ALT+TAB. A dotted white outline around the panel title bar indicates the panel is selected (Figure B-9). Press CTRL+ALT+SHIFT+TAB to move to the previous panel. If necessary, expand the selected panel by pressing the SPACEBAR. Pressing the SPACEBAR again collapses the panel.

FIGURE B-9

Using the Keyboard to Navigate the Property Inspector

The following steps use the Florida Parks index page to show how to use the keyboard to navigate the Property inspector.

 Steps **To Use the Keyboard to Navigate the Property Inspector**

1 **Start Dreamweaver and close all panels. Open a Web page. If necessary, press CTRL+F3 to display the Property inspector and then press CTRL+ALT+TAB until the Property inspector is selected.**

The dotted white outline around Properties indicates that the focus is on the Property inspector (Figure B-10).

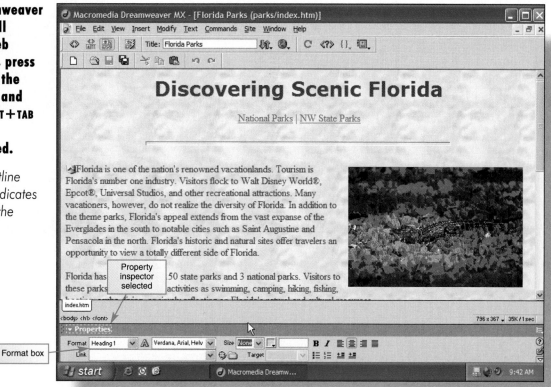

FIGURE B-10

2 **Press the TAB key to move to the Format box.**

Heading 1 is highlighted in the Format box (Figure B-11).

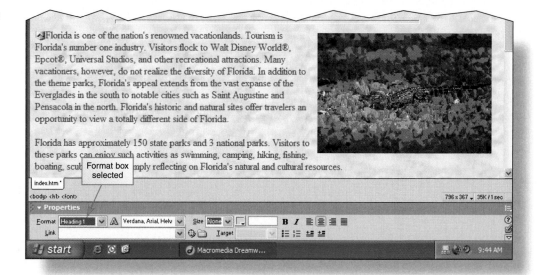

FIGURE B-11

3 Use the keyboard DOWN ARROW key to select Heading 3 and then press the ENTER key.

A dotted outline is displayed around the Heading 3 selection (Figure B-12). Heading 3 is applied to the text.

4 Close Dreamweaver. Do not save any of the changes.

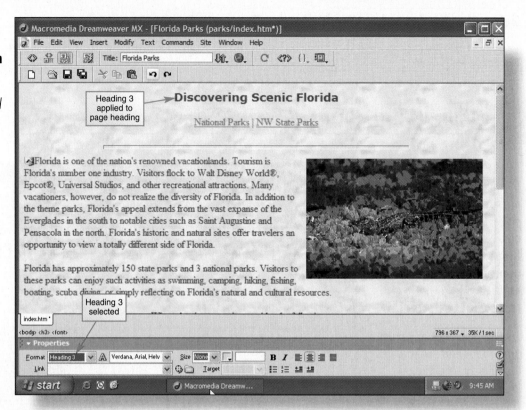

FIGURE B-12

Operating System Accessibility Features

The third method of accessibility support through Dreamweaver is through the Windows operating system high contrast setting. **High contrast** changes the desktop color themes for individuals who have vision impairment. The color schemes make the screen easier to view by heightening screen contrast with alternative color combinations. Some of the schemes also change font sizes.

You activate this option through the Windows Control Panel. The high contrast setting affects Dreamweaver in two ways:

▶ The dialog boxes and panels use system color settings.
▶ Code view syntax color is turned off.

Design view, however, continues to use the background and text colors you set in the Page Properties dialog box. The pages you design, therefore, continue to render colors as they will display in a browser. The following steps show how to turn on high contrast and how to change the current high contrast settings.

Steps **To Turn on High Contrast**

In Windows XP, click the Start button on the taskbar and then click Control Panel on the Start menu. If necessary, switch to Classic View and then double-click the Accessibility Options icon. Point to the Display tab.

The Accessibility Options dialog box is displayed (Figure B-13).

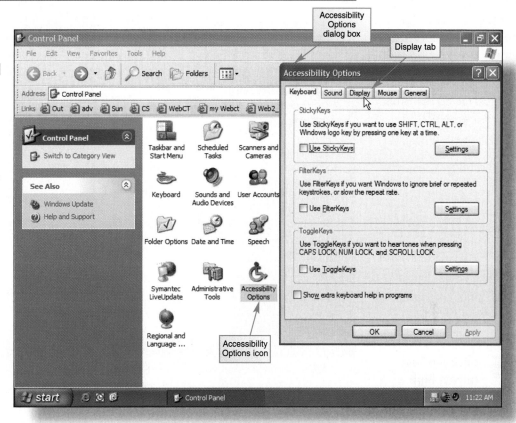

FIGURE B-13

2 **Click the Display tab and then click Use High Contrast. Point to the Settings button.**

The Display sheet is displayed. A check mark is in the Use High Contrast check box (Figure B-14).

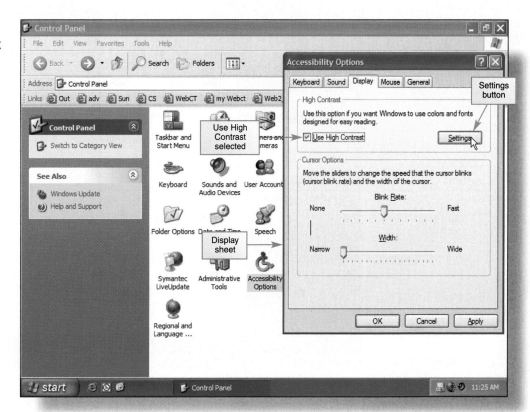

FIGURE B-14

3 **Click the Settings button. Point to the Your current high contrast scheme is box arrow.**

The Settings for High Contrast dialog box is displayed (Figure B-15).

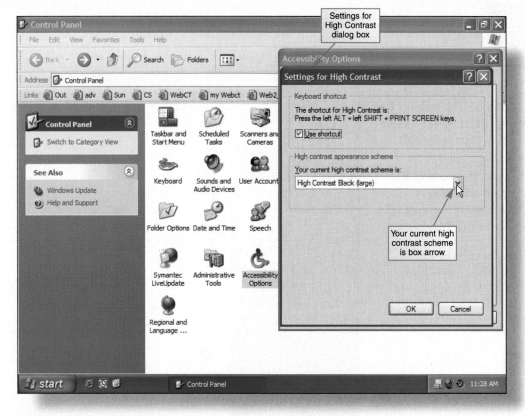

FIGURE B-15

4 **Click the Your current high contrast scheme is box arrow.**

A list of available high contrast options is displayed (Figure B-16). High Contrast Black (large) is selected. The Web designer, however, would select the option to meet the needs of the project for which he or she is designing.

5 **Click the Cancel button.**

The settings return to their original settings. To retain these settings on your computer would require that you click the OK button.

6 **Click the Control Panel Close button.**

The Control Panel closes and the Windows XP desktop displays.

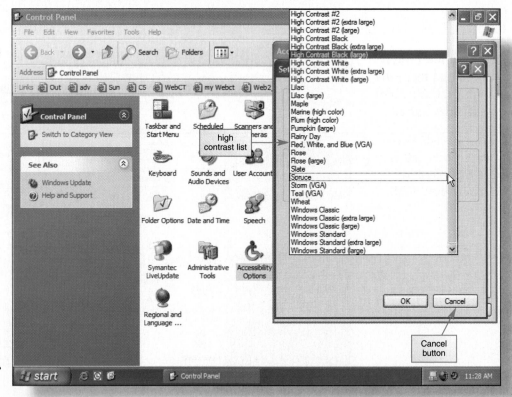

FIGURE B-16

APPENDIX C
Dreamweaver and Fireworks

Dreamweaver and Fireworks

Macromedia Fireworks MX is a graphics application and companion tool to Dreamweaver. Fireworks comes with a complete graphics toolset and includes workflow options that promote easy integration with Dreamweaver and other programs. Firework images are saved with a .png extension. The Fireworks interface is consistent with other applications in the Macromedia MX Studio suite, including Dreamweaver. Fireworks and Dreamweaver share many commonalities, including changes to links, image maps, table slices, and other elements. If set up properly, the two applications provide a streamlined workflow for editing, optimizing, and placing Web image files in HTML pages.

To create the integrated work environment, a local site must be defined in Dreamweaver and Design Notes enabled for the site. Design Notes are a default setting in Dreamweaver. The name of the original source file is saved in the Design Notes folder. Fireworks also must be set as the primary external image editor for Dreamweaver.

Setting Fireworks as the External Image Editor

One of Dreamweaver's more valuable features is the capability to open a selected image in an external image editor. You can edit the image, save the changes, and then return to Dreamweaver. Changes you make to the image are visible in the Document window. The steps on the next three pages use an image from the Florida Parks index page to show how to select Fireworks as the external image editor.

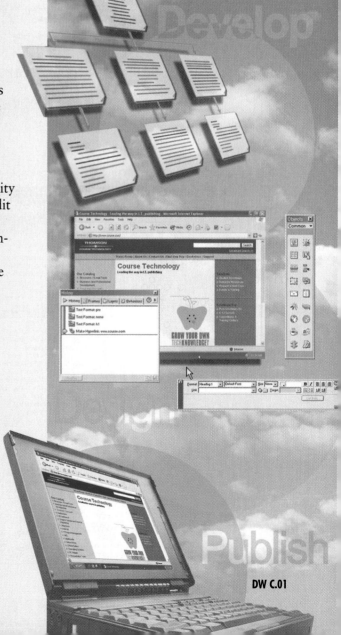

Steps To Select Fireworks as the External Image Editor

1 **Start Dreamweaver and close all open panels. If necessary, insert an image in the Document window and then click the image to select it. Click Edit on the menu bar and then point to Preferences (Figure C-1).**

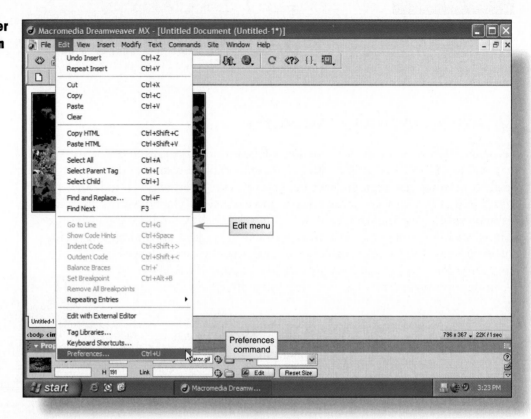

FIGURE C-1

2 **Click Preferences, click the File Types/Editors category, and then point to the plus sign (+) button (Figure C-2).**

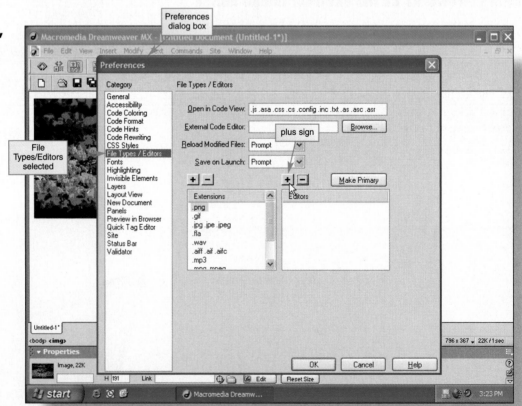

FIGURE C-2

3 **Click the Plus sign.**

The Select External Editor dialog box is displayed (Figure C-3). Most likely, the Look in text box displays Program Files and Macromedia is one of the choices in the Program Files folder. Your screen will display different files and folders.

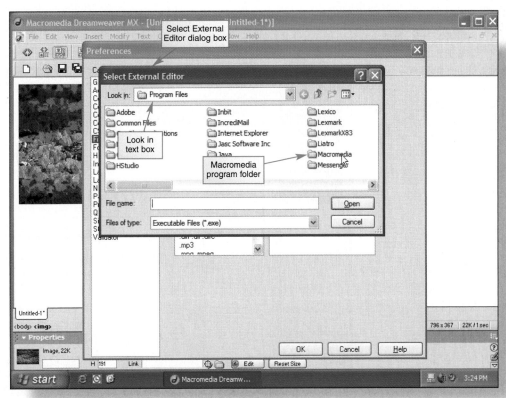

FIGURE C-3

4 **Double-click Macromedia (or navigate to the Macromedia folder) and then click Fireworks MX. Point to the Open button.**

Fireworks MX is selected in the Select External Editor dialog box (Figure C-4).

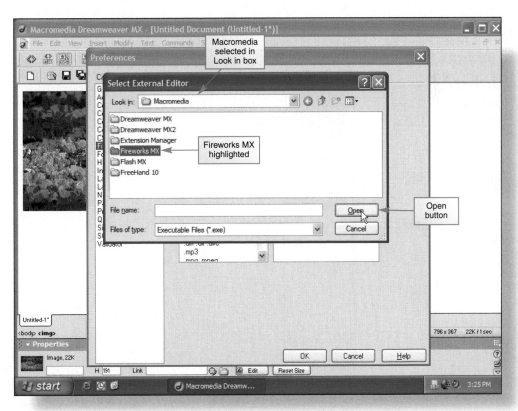

FIGURE C-4

5 **Click the Open button and then click Fireworks.exe. Point to the Open button.**

The file Fireworks.exe is selected (Figure C-5).

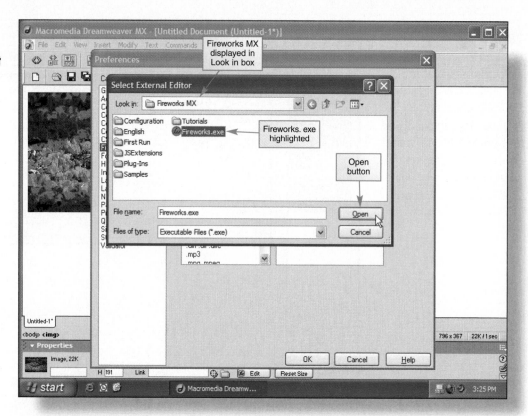

FIGURE C-5

6 **Click the Open button. Point to the OK button.**

Fireworks is selected as the primary editor for image, sound, and other file types (Figure C-6).

7 **Click the OK button.**

The Preferences dialog box closes.

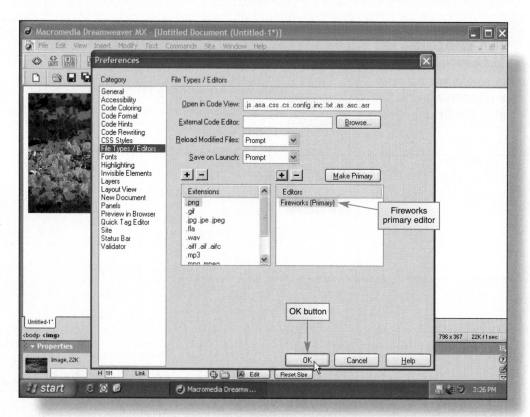

FIGURE C-6

Adding Text to an Image

You can launch Fireworks from within Dreamweaver to edit an image, add text to an image, resize an image, recolor an image, and so on. The following steps show how to launch Fireworks and add text to an image placed in a Dreamweaver document.

 To Launch Fireworks and Add Text to an Image

1 **If necessary, insert an image into a Dreamweaver Document window and then select the image. If necessary, display the Property inspector. Point to the Edit button in the Property inspector.**

The image is selected and the image properties are displayed in the Property inspector (Figure C-7). The Edit button displays the Fireworks logo.

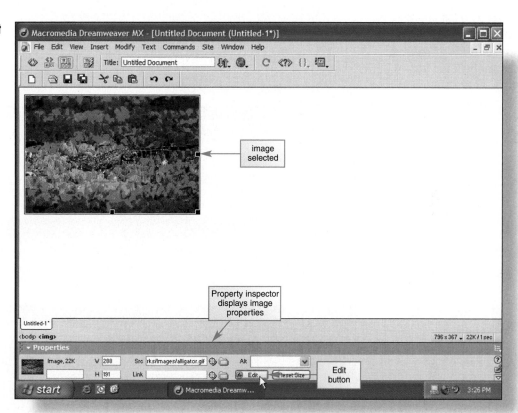

FIGURE C-7

2 Click the Edit button in the Property inspector. Point to the No button.

The Find Source dialog box is displayed (Figure C-8). The message indicates that the alligator.gif image (or the image you selected) is not an existing Fireworks document.

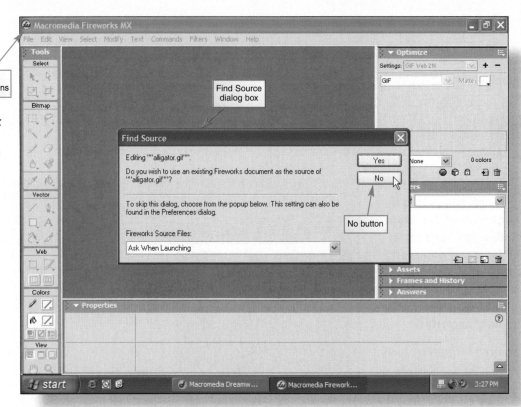

FIGURE C-8

3 Click the No button.

The image is displayed in the Fireworks window (Figure C-9).

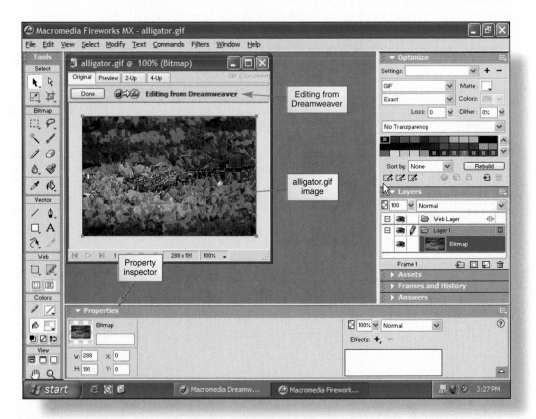

FIGURE C-9

4 **Click the Text tool and then click the image.**

The entry point for the text block displays (Figure C-10). The Property inspector changes to reflect that text is selected.

FIGURE C-10

5 **Use the Property inspector properties to change the font, font size, color, and other text features. Point to the Done button.**

In Figure C-11, the font is changed to Comic Sans MS, the font size to 26, the font color to red, and bold is applied. If you applied different properties, your screen will look different.

FIGURE C-11

6 Click the Done button.

The focus returns to Dreamweaver. The revised image is displayed in the Dreamweaver Document window (Figure C-12).

7 Save the file and close Dreamweaver. Close Fireworks.

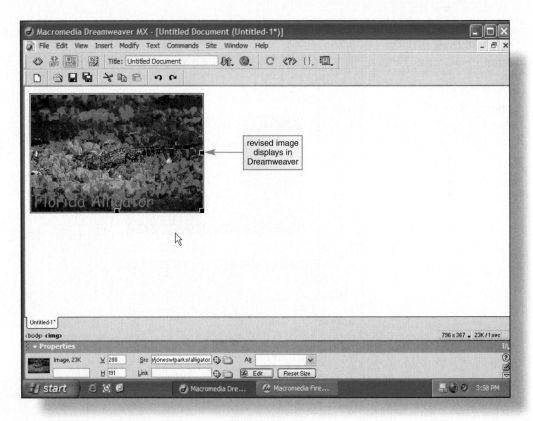

FIGURE C-12

Inserting a Fireworks Image in the Dreamweaver Document

In addition to editing a Dreamweaver image in Fireworks, several methods are available to insert Fireworks files into a Dreamweaver document. These methods are as follows:

▶ Insert Firework files the same way in which you insert other images — the Image command on the Insert menu, drag and drop from the Site panel or Library panel, and the Insert bar using the Image button on the Common tab.

▶ Copy and paste Fireworks HTML code into Dreamweaver code view.

▶ Insert Fireworks-generated HTML code, including the associated image(s), into the HTML document using the Interactive Images command on the Insert menu and then selecting the Fireworks HTML command on the Interactive Images submenu.

▶ Export a Fireworks file as a library item using the Export command on the Fireworks File menu and then selecting Save as type in the Dreamweaver Library. A library folder must exist in the Web site local root folder.

APPENDIX D
Publishing to a Web Server

Publishing to a Remote Site

With Dreamweaver, Web designers usually define a local site and then do the majority of their site designing using the local site. In Project 1 you defined a local site. In creating the projects in this book, you have added Web pages to the local site, which resides on your computer's hard disk, a network drive, or possibly a Zip disk. To prepare a Web site and make it available for others to view requires that you publish your site by putting it on a Web server for public access. A Web server is an Internet- or intranet-connected computer that delivers the Web pages to visitors online. Dreamweaver includes built-in support that enables you to connect and transfer your local site to a Web server. To complete the steps and exercises in this appendix to publish to a Web server requires that you have access to a Web server. Your instructor will provide you with the location, user name, and password information for the Web server on which you will publish your Web site.

After you establish access to a Web server, you will need a remote root folder. The remote folder is the folder that will reside on the Web server and will contain your Web site files. Generally, the remote folder is defined by the Web server administrator or your instructor. Your local root folder is your last name and first initial. Most likely, your remote folder also will be your last name and first initial. You upload your local site to the remote folder on the Web server. The remote site connection information must be defined in Dreamweaver through the Site Definition Wizard. You display the Site Definition Wizard and then enter the remote site information. Dreamweaver provides five different protocols for connecting to a remote site. These methods are as follows:

- **FTP** (File Transfer Protocol) is the protocol used on the Internet for sending and receiving files. It is the most widely used method for uploading and downloading pages to and from a Web server.
- **Local/Network** This option is used when the Web server is located on a local area network (LAN) or a company or school intranet. Files on LANs generally are available for internal viewing only.
- **SourceSafe Database, RDS (Remote Development Services), and WebDAV** These three protocols are versioning systems that permit users to edit and manage files collaboratively on remote Web servers.

Most likely, you will use the FTP option to upload your Web site to a remote server.

Defining a Remote Site

You define the remote site by changing some of the settings in the Site Definition Wizard. To create a remote site using FTP, your instructor will supply you with the following information:

- **FTP host** is the Web address for the remote host of your Web server.
- **Host directory** is the directory name and path on the server where your remote site will be located.
- **Login** is your user name.
- **Password** is the FTP password to authenticate and access your account.

Perform the following steps to define the remote site.

Steps **To Define a Remote Site**

1 **Close the Property inspector. Click Site on the menu bar and then click Edit Sites to display the Edit Sites dialog box. If necessary, click Florida Parks in the Edit Sites dialog box. Point to the Edit button.**

The Edit Sites dialog box is displayed and Florida Parks is selected (Figure D-1).

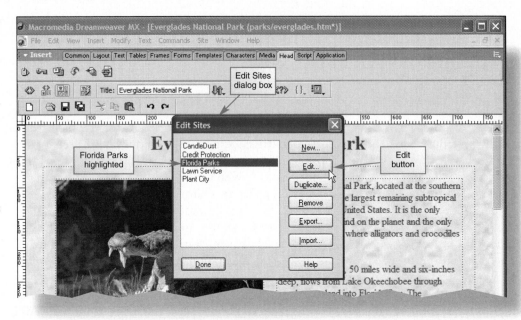

FIGURE D-1

2 **Click the Edit button. If necessary, click the Basic tab. Point to the Next button.**

The Site Definition dialog box is displayed (Figure D-2).

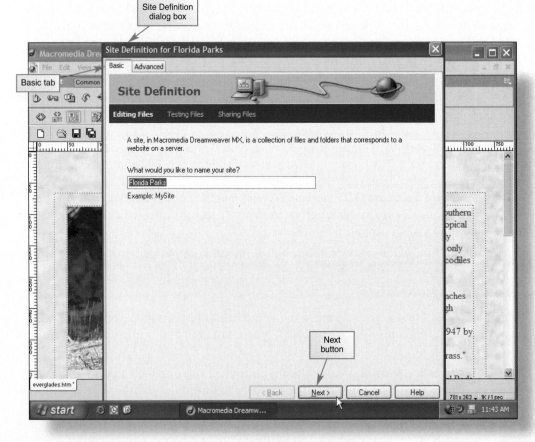

FIGURE D-2

3 **Click the Next button in the next three options of the Site Definition dialog box. Click the How do you connect to your remote server? box arrow and then click FTP.**

The Site Definition dialog box displays the Sharing Files options. FTP is selected in the How do you connect to your remote server? box (Figure D-3).

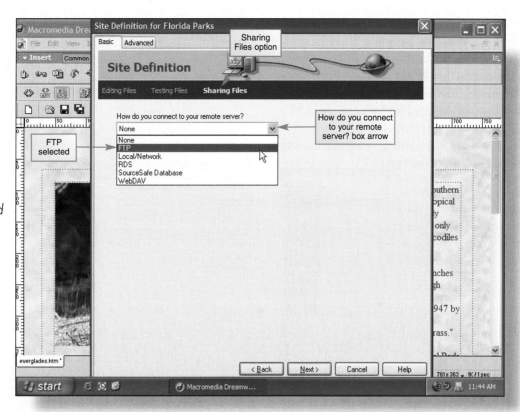

FIGURE D-3

4 **Click each of the other boxes on the page and fill in the information as provided by your instructor. Click Save. Point to the Test Connection button.**

Information for Will Jones is displayed in Figure D-4. Your screen will contain the information provided by your instructor.

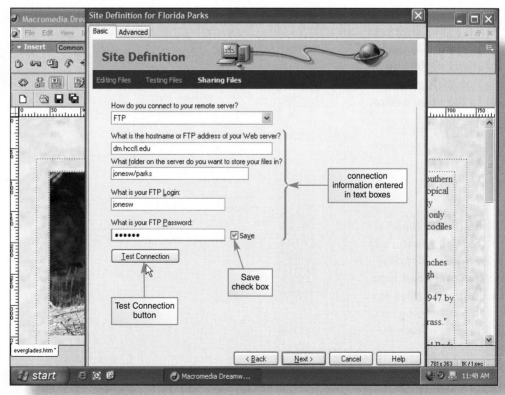

FIGURE D-4

5 **Click the Test Connection button. Point to the OK button. If your connection is not successful, review your text box entries and make any necessary corrections. If all entries are correct, check with your instructor.**

Dreamweaver tests the connection and responds with a Macromedia Dreamweaver MX dialog box (Figure D-5).

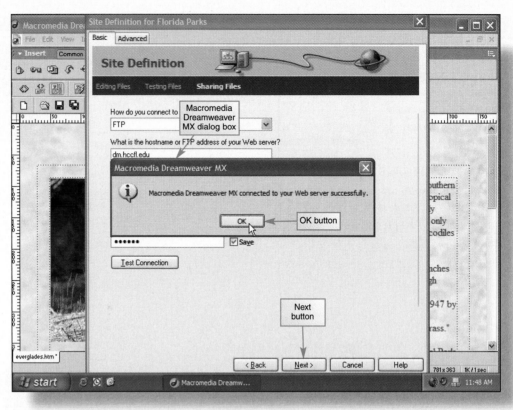

FIGURE D-5

6 **Click the OK button and then click the Next button in the next two options of the Site Definition dialog box. Point to the Done button.**

The Summary options are displayed and include both Local Info and Remote Info (Figure D-6).

7 **Click the Done button to return to the Everglades National Park Web page and then click the Done button in the Edit Sites dialog box. The Site panel displays.**

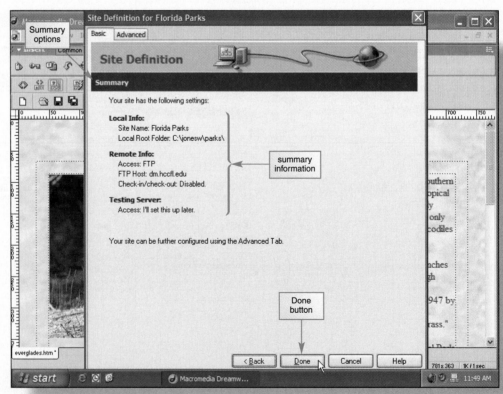

FIGURE D-6

Connecting to a Remote Site

Now that you completed the remote site information and tested your connection, you can interact with the remote server. The remote site folder on the Web server for your Web site must be established before a connection can be made. This folder, called the **remote site root**, generally is created by the Web server administrator or your instructor. This book uses the last name and the first initial (jonesw) for the remote site folder. Naming conventions other than your last name and first initial may be used on the Web server to which you are connecting. Your instructor will supply you with this information. If all information is correct, connecting to the remote site is done easily through the Site panel. Complete the following steps to connect to the remote site and your remote root folder.

Steps | **To Connect to a Remote Site**

1 **Point to the Site panel Expand/Collapse button (Figure D-7).**

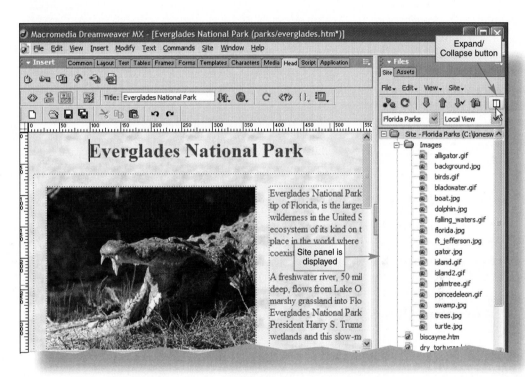

FIGURE D-7

2 **Click the Expand/Collapse button. Point to the Connects to remote host button.**

The Site panel expands to show both a right and left pane (Figure D-8). The right pane contains the local site. The left pane contains information for accessing your remote files by clicking the Connects to remote host button.

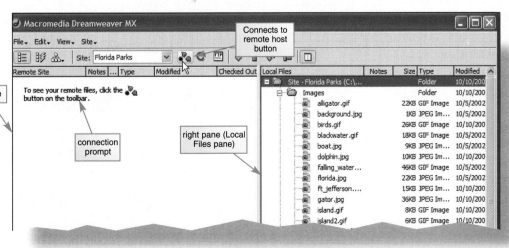

FIGURE D-8

3 **Click the Connects to remote host button. Point to the Put file(s) button.**

A brief message flashes on the screen, indicating Dreamweaver is connecting to the remote site and retrieving remote information. The jonesw/parks root folder is displayed (Figure D-9). The Connects to remote host/Disconnects from remote host button is a toggle button and changes to indicate that the connection has been made. The root folder on the remote site must be created by your instructor or Web server administrator before a connection can be made.

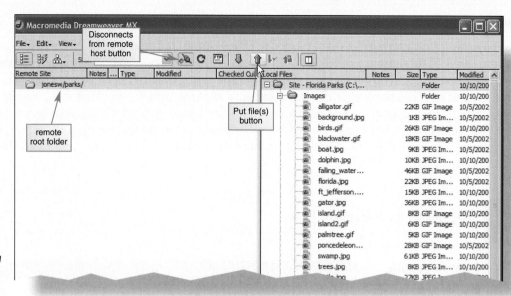

FIGURE D-9

Uploading Files to a Remote Server

Your next step will be to upload your files to the remote server. **Uploading** is the process of transferring your files from your computer to the remote server. **Downloading** is the process of transferring files from the remote server to your computer. Dreamweaver uses the term **put** for uploading and **get** for downloading.

 To Upload Files to a Remote Server

1 **Click the Put File(s) button. Point to the OK button.**

The Macromedia Dreamweaver MX dialog box is displayed to verify that you want to upload the entire site (Figure D-10).

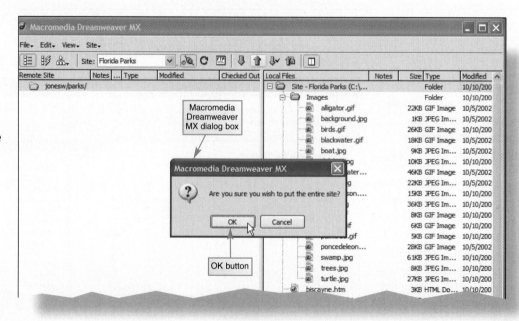

FIGURE D-10

2 | **Click the OK button.**

As the files begin to upload, a Status dialog box displays the progress information. The files are uploaded to the server (Figure D-11). The files may display in a different order from that on the local site. The display order on the server is determined by the settings on that computer.

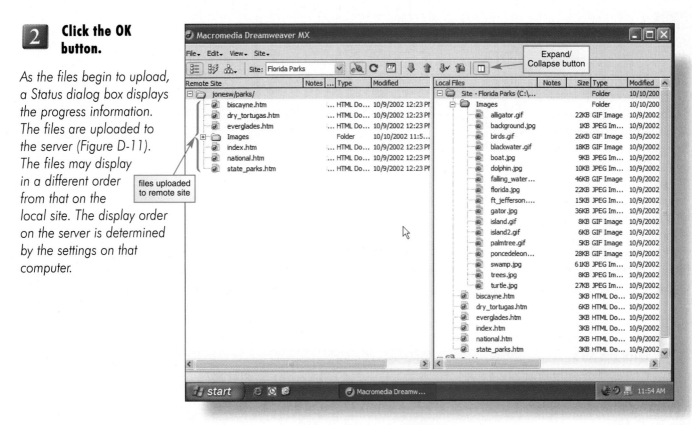

FIGURE D-11

Remote Site Maintenance and Site Synchronization

Now that your Web site is on a Web server, you will want to continue to maintain the site. When you are connected to the remote site, you can apply many of the same commands to a folder or file on the remote site as you do on the local site. You can create and delete folders; cut, copy, delete, duplicate, paste, and rename files; and so on. These commands are available through the context menu.

To mirror the local site with the remote site, Dreamweaver provides a synchronization feature. **Synchronizing** is the process of transferring files between the local and remote sites so that both sites have an identical set of the most recent files. You can select to synchronize the entire Web site or select only specific files. You also can specify Direction. Within **Direction**, you have three options: upload the newer files from the local site to the remote site (put); download newer files from the remote site to the local site (get); or, upload and download files to and from the remote and local sites. Once you specify a direction, Dreamweaver automatically synchronizes files. If the files are already in sync, Dreamweaver lets you know you that no synchronization is necessary.

To illustrate how synchronization works, a change will be made to the local site. You will make a change to the Everglades National Park Web page, and then resave the page. This will give the Everglades National Park Web page a different save date and time and will make it appear to the system as though a change was made in the page. Perform the steps on the next three pages to make the change and to synchronize your files.

Steps **To Synchronize the Local and Remote Sites**

1 **Click the Expand/Collapse button on the Site panel menu bar to display the Everglades National Park page. Click at the end of the heading and add an s to park and then backspace to delete the s. Click the Save button on the Standard toolbar and then click the Expand/ Collapse button to display the remote site pane.**

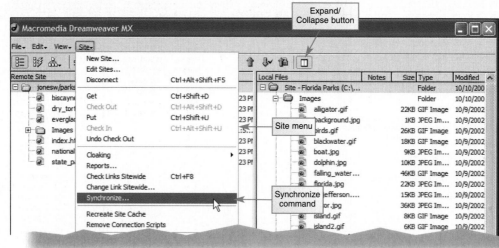

FIGURE D-12

2 **Click the Site menu on the Site panel menu bar and then point to Synchronize (Figure D-12).**

3 **Click Synchronize and then click the Synchronize box arrow.**

The Synchronize Files dialog box is displayed (Figure D-13). You can select the entire Florida Parks site or you can choose just the files you want to synchronize from the Synchronize pop-up menu.

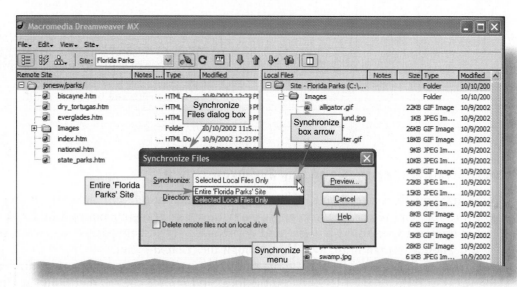

FIGURE D-13

4 **Click the Entire 'Florida Parks' Site in the Synchronize pop-up menu and then click the Direction box arrow.**

The Direction list is displayed and contains three options (Figure D-14).

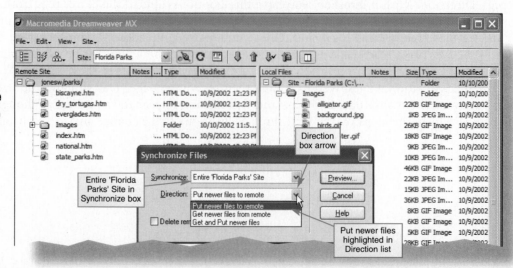

FIGURE D-14

5 **Select Get and Put newer files in the Direction list and then point to the Preview button (Figure D-15).**

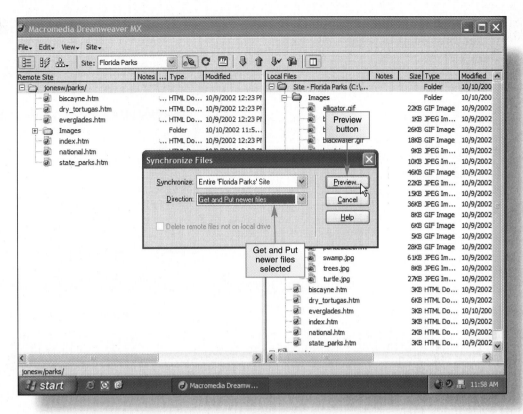

FIGURE D-15

6 **Click the Preview button. Point to the OK button.**

A list of files that need to be updated is displayed (Figure D-16). Unchecked files will not be uploaded.

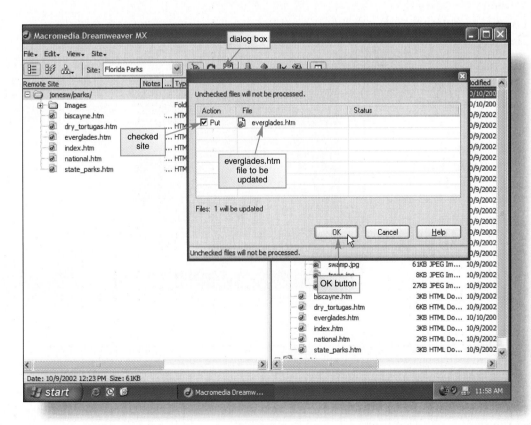

FIGURE D-16

7 Click the OK button and then point to the Close button.

The file is updated and the synchronization is complete (Figure D-17). Dreamweaver automatically transfers, and then updates the dialog box with the status.

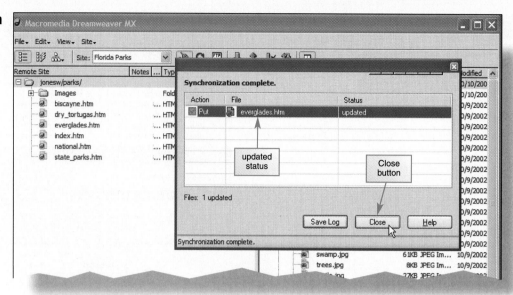

FIGURE D-17

8 Click the Close button, click the Disconnects from remote host button, and then click the Expand/Collapse button to redisplay the Everglades National Park Web page.

Dreamweaver displays the updated Everglades Web page (Figure D-18).

9 Close Dreamweaver.

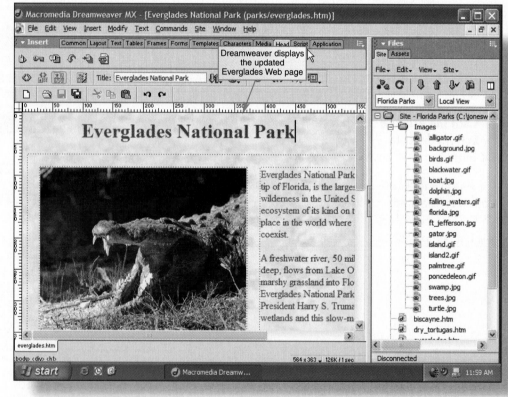

FIGURE D-18

To save the verification information to a local file, click the Save Log button at the completion of the synchronization process. Another feature within Dreamweaver is to verify which files are newer on the local site or the remote. These options are available through the Site panel Edit menu by selecting Select Newer Local or Select Newer Remote.

Apply Your Knowledge

1 Defining and Uploading the B & B Lawn Service Web to a Remote Server

Instructions: Perform the following steps to define and upload the B & B Lawn Service Web site to a remote server.

1. Click Site on the Document window menu bar and then click Edit Sites. Click Lawn Service and then click the Edit button. When the Site Definition dialog box is displayed, click the Next button in the next three options and then select FTP in the How do you connect to your remote server? list. Click each of the other boxes on the page, fill in the information as provided by your instructor, and then test the connection. Click the OK button, click the Next button in the next two options, and then click the Done button.
2. Click the Expand/Collapse button in the Site panel toolbar and then click the Connects to remote host button. Click the local file root folder and then click the Put File(s) button on the Site panel toolbar to upload your Web site. Click the OK button in response to the Are you sure you wish to put the entire site? dialog box. Review your files to verify that they were uploaded. The files on the remote server may be displayed in a different order from that on the local site.
3. Click the Disconnects from remote host button on the Site panel toolbar. Click the Expand/Collapse button on the Site panel toolbar to display the local site and the Document window.
4. Close Dreamweaver.

2 Defining and Uploading the CandleDust Web Site to a Remote Server

Instructions: Perform the following steps to define and upload the CandleDust Web site to a remote server.

1. Click Site on the Document window menu and then click Edit Sites. Click CandleDust and then click the Edit button. When the Site Definition dialog box displays, click the Next button three times and then select FTP in the How do you connect to your remote server? list. Click each of the other options boxes, fill in the information as provided by your instructor, and then test the connection. Click the OK button, click the Next button two times, and then click the Done button.
2. Click the Expand/Collapse button on the Site panel toolbar and then click the Connects to remote host button. Click the local file root folder and then click the Put File(s) button on the Site panel toolbar to upload your Web site. Click the OK button in response to the Are you sure you wish to put the entire site? box. Review your files to verify that they were uploaded. The files on the remote server may display in a different order from that on the local site.
3. Click the Disconnects from remote host button. Click the Expand/Collapse button to display the local site and the Document window. Close Dreamweaver.

Apply Your Knowledge

3 Defining and Uploading the Credit Protection Web Site to a Remote Server

Instructions: Perform the following steps to define and upload the Credit Protection Web site to a remote server.

1. Click Site on the Document window menu and then click Edit Sites. Click Credit Protection and then click the Edit button. When the Site Definition dialog box displays, select FTP from the How do you connect to your remote server? list. Click each of the other boxes in the dialog box, fill in the information as provided by your instructor and then test the connection. Click the OK button, click the Next button two times, and then click the Done button.
2. Click the Expand/Collapse button on the Site panel toolbar and then click the Connects to remote site button. Click the local file root folder and then click the Put File(s) button on the Site panel menu bar to upload your Web site. Upload your files to the remote site. Review your files to verify that they were uploaded. The files on the remote server may display in a different order from that on the local site.
3. Disconnect from the site. Click the Expand/Collapse button to display the local site and the Document window. Close Dreamweaver.

4 Defining and Uploading the Plant City Web Site to a Remote Server

Instructions: Perform the following steps to define and upload the Plant City Web site to a remote server.

1. Click Site on the Document window menu bar and then click Edit Sites. Click Plant City and then click the Edit button. When the Site Definition dialog box displays, select FTP in the How do you connect to your remove server? list. Click each of the other option boxes, fill in the information as provided by your instructor, and then test the connection. Click the OK button, click the Next button two times, and then click the Done button.
2. Connect to the remote site and then click the local file root folder. Upload your files to the remote site. Disconnect from the site. Click the Expand/Collapse button to display the local site and the Document window. Close Dreamweaver.

MANAGING FILES

Action	Shortcut
New document	Control+N
Open an HTML file	Control+O
Open in frame	Control+Shift+O
Close	Control+W
Save	Control+S
Save as	Control+Shift+S
Exit/Quit	Alt+F4 or Control+Q

GENERAL EDITING

Action	Shortcut
Undo	Control+Z
Redo	Control+Y or Control+Shift+Z
Cut	Control+X or Shift+Delete
Copy	Control+C
Paste	Control+V or Shift+Insert
Clear	Delete
Bold	Control+B
Italic	Control+I
Select All	Control+A
Move to page up	Page Up
Move to page down	Page Down
Select to page up	Shift+Page Up
Select to page down	Shift+Page Down
Select line up/down	Shift+Up/Down
Move to start of line	Home
Move to end of line	End
Select to start of line	Shift+Home
Select to end of line	Shift+End
Go to previous/next paragraph	Control+Up/Down
Go to next/previous word	Control+Right/Left
Delete word left	Control+Backspace
Delete word right	Control+Delete
Select character left/right	Shift+Left/Right
Find and Replace	Control+F
Find next/find again	F3
Replace	Control+H
Copy HTML (in Design view)	Control+Shift+C
Paste HTML (in Design view)	Control+Shift+V
Preferences	Control+U

PAGE VIEWS

To toggle the display of	Shortcut
Standard view	Control+Shift+F6
Layout view	Control+F6
Live Data mode	Control+R
Live Data	Control+Shift+R
Switch to next document	Control+Tab
Switch to previous document	Control+Shift+Tab
Switch between Design and Code views	Control+`
Server debug	Control+Shift+G
Refresh Design view	F5

VIEWING PAGE ELEMENTS

To toggle the display of	Shortcut
Visual Aids	Control+Shift+I
Show Rulers	Control+Alt+R
Show Grid	Control+Alt+G
Snap to Grid	Control+Alt+Shift+G
Head content	Control+Shift+W
Page properties	Control+J
Selection properties	Control+Shift+J

CODE EDITING

Action	Shortcut
Switch to Design view	Control+`
Print Code	Control+P
Validate markup	Shift+F6
Open Quick Tag Editor	Control+T
Open Snippets panel	Shift+F9
Show Code Hints	Control+Spacebar
Indent Code	Control+Shift+>
Outdent Code	Control+Shift+<
Insert tag	Control+E
Edit tag (in Design view)	Control+F5
Select parent tag	Control+[
Select child	Control+]
Balance Braces	Control+`
Toggle breakpoint	Control+Alt+B
Go to line	Control+G
Move to top of code	Control+Home
Move to end of code	Control+End
Select to top of code	Control+Shift+Home
Select to end of code	Control+Shift+End

TEXT EDITING

Action	Shortcut
Create a new paragraph	Enter
Insert a line break ‹BR›	Shift+Enter
Insert a nonbreaking space	Control+Shift+Spacebar
Move text or object to another place in the page	Drag selected item to new location
Copy text or object to another place in the page	Control-drag selected item to new location
Select a word	Double-click
Add selected items to library	Control+Shift+B
Open and close the Property inspector	Control+Shift+J
Check spelling	Shift+F7

FORMATTING TEXT

Action	Shortcut
Indent	Control+Alt+]
Outdent	Control+Alt+[
Format › None	Control+0 (zero)
Paragraph Format	Control+Shift+P
Apply Headings 1 through 6 to a paragraph	Control+1 through 6
Align › Left/Center/Right/Justify	Control+Alt+Shift+L/C/R/J
Edit Style Sheet	Control+Shift+E

WORKING IN TABLES

Action	Shortcut
Select table (with cursor inside the table)	Control+A
Move to the next cell	Tab
Move to the previous cell	Shift+Tab
Insert a row (before current)	Control+M
Add a row at end of table	Tab in the last cell
Delete the current row	Control+Shift+M
Insert a column	Control+Shift+A
Delete a column	Control+Shift+ - (hyphen)
Merge selected table cells	Control+Alt+M
Split table cell	Control+Alt+S
Defer table update	Control+Spacebar
Increase column span	Control+Shift+]
Decrease column span	Control+Shift+[

WORKING WITH IMAGES

Action	Shortcut
Change image source attribute	Double-click image
Edit image in external editor	Control-double-click image

WORKING IN FRAMES

Action	Shortcut
Select a frame	Alt-click in frame
Select next frame or frameset	Alt+Right Arrow
Select previous frame or frameset	Alt+Left Arrow
Select parent frameset	Alt+Up Arrow
Select first child frame or frameset	Alt+Down Arrow
Add a new frame to frameset	Select frame, then Alt-drag frame border
Add a new frame to frameset using push method	Select frame, then Alt+Control-drag frame border

WORKING WITH LAYERS

Action	Shortcut
Select a layer	Control+Shift-click
Select and move layer	Shift+Control-drag
Add or remove layer from selection	Shift-click layer
Move selected layer by pixels	Arrow keys
Move selected layer by snapping increment	Shift+arrow keys
Resize selected layer by pixels	Control+Arrow keys
Resize selected layer by snapping increment	Control+Shift+arrow keys
Toggle the display of the grid	Control+Alt+G
Snap To grid	Control+Shift+Alt+G
Align layers left	Control+Shift+1
Align layers right	Control+Shift+3
Align layers top	Control+Shift+4
Align layers bottom	Control+Shift+6
Make same width	Control+Shift+7
Make same height	Control+Shift+9

GETTING HELP

Action	Shortcut
Using Dreamweaver Help Topics	F1
Using ColdFusion Help Topics	Control+F1
Reference	Shift+F1

INSERTING OBJECTS

Action	Shortcut
Any object (image, Shockwave movie, and so on)	Drag file from the Explorer or Site panel to the Document window
Image	Control+Alt+I
Table	Control+Alt+T
Named anchor	Control+Alt+A

MANAGING HYPERLINKS

Action	Shortcut
Check links sitewide	Control+F8
Check selected links	Shift+F8
Create hyperlink (select text, image, or object)	Control+L
Remove hyperlink	Control+Shift+L
Drag and drop to create a hyperlink from a document	Select the text, image, or object, then Shift-drag the selection to a file in the Site panel
Drag and drop to create a hyperlink using the Property inspector	Select the text, image, or object, then drag the point-to-file icon in Property inspector to a file in the Site panel
Open the linked-to document in Dreamweaver	Control–double-click link

PREVIEWING AND DEBUGGING IN BROWSERS

Action	Shortcut
Preview in primary browser	F12
Preview in secondary browser	Shift+F12
Debug in primary browser	Alt+F12
Debug in secondary browser	Control+Alt+F12

SITE MANAGEMENT AND FTP

Action	Shortcut
Connect/Disconnect	Control+Alt+Shift+F5
Refresh	F5
Create new file	Control+Shift+N
Create new folder	Control+Alt+Shift+N
Open selection	Control+Shift+Alt+O
Delete file	Control+X
Copy file	Control+C
Paste file	Control+V
Duplicate file	Control+D
Rename file	F2
Get selected files or folders from remote site	Control+Shift+D
Put selected files or folders to remote site	Control+Shift+U
Check out	Control+Alt+Shift+D
Check in	Control+Alt+Shift+U
View site map	Alt+F8
Refresh Local pane	Shift+F5
Refresh Remote pane	Alt+F5

SITE MAP

Action	Shortcut
View site files	F8
Refresh Local pane	Shift+F5
View as root	Control+Shift+R
Link to new file	Control+Shift+N
Link to existing file	Control+Shift+K
Change link	Control+L
Remove link	Control+Shift+L
Show/Hide link	Control+Shift+Y
Show page titles	Control+Shift+T
Zoom in site map	Control+ + (plus)
Zoom out site map	Control+ - (hyphen)

OPENING AND CLOSING PANELS

Action	Shortcut
Insert bar	Control+F2
Properties	Control+F3
Answers	Alt+F1
CSS Styles	Shift+F11
HTML Styles	Control+F11
Behaviors	Shift+F3
Tag Inspector	F9
Snippets	Shift+F9
Reference	Shift+F1
Databases	Control+Shift+F10
Bindings	Control+F10
Server Behaviors	Control+F9
Components	Control+F7
Site	F8
Assets	F11
Results > Search	Control+Shift+F
Results > Validation	Control+Shift+F7
Results > Target Browser Check	Control+Shift+F8
Results > Link Checker	Control+Shift+F9
Results > Site Reports	Control+Shift+F11
Results > FTP Log	Control+Shift+F12
Results > Server Debug	Control+Shift+F5
Others > Code inspector	F10
Others > Frames	Shift+F2
Others > History	Shift+F10
Others > Layers	F2
Others > Sitespring	F7
Others > Timelines	Alt+F9
Show/Hide panels	F4

Index